Birds *of* Northern California

David Fix
Andy Bezener

Range Maps by Don Roberson and David Fix

The Publisher: Lone Pine Publishing

1808 B Street NW, Suite 140
Auburn, WA 98001
U.S.A.

10145-81 Ave.
Edmonton, AB T6E 1W9
Canada

Website: http://www.lonepinepublishing.com

Canadian Cataloguing in Publication Data

Fix, David, 1957-
  Birds of Northern California

  Includes bibliographical references and index.
  ISBN 1-55105-227-X

  1. Birds—California, Northern—Identification. 2. Bird
watching—California, Northern. I. Bezener, Andy. II. Title.
QL684.C2F59 2000   598'.09794   C99-911289-9

Editorial Director: Nancy Foulds
Project Editor: Eloise Pulos
Editorial: Eloise Pulos, Roland Lines
Production Manager: Jody Reekie
Layout & Production: Michelle Bynoe
Book Design: Michelle Bynoe
Cover Design: Rob Weidemann
Cover Illustration: Great Horned Owl by Gary Ross
Illustrations: Gary Ross, Ted Nordhagen, Ewa Pluciennik
Cartography: Michelle Bynoe, Rob Weidemann
Scanning: Elite Lithographers Co., Edmonton, Alberta
Separations & Film: Elite Lithographers Co., Edmonton, Alberta

We acknowledge the financial support of the Government of Canada through the Book Publishing Industry Development Program (BPIDP) for our publishing activities.

PC: P3

Canadä

CONTENTS

ACKNOWLEDGMENTS

Many thanks go to Don Roberson and Joe Morlan, who were of great help during the writing of this book. Don contributed much time and expertise to the project, and in doing so, he has elevated the quality of this book. His contributions have been invaluable, and his effort is greatly appreciated. The book owes its final form to discussions with Shane Kennedy, Nancy Foulds, Jody Reekie, Eloise Pulos, Roland Lines, Michelle Bynoe and Rob Weidemann at Lone Pine Publishing. Many thanks go to Gary Ross and Ted Nordhagen, for their wonderful artwork, and to Chris Fisher whose contributions are also appreciated and recognized. Finally, a special thanks goes to Jude Claire Power for her continual support and encouragement.

Red-throated Loon
size 25 in • p. 38

Pacific Loon
size 26 in • p. 39

Common Loon
size 32 in • p. 40

Pied-billed Grebe
size 13 in • p. 41

Horned Grebe
size 13 in • p. 42

Red-necked Grebe
size 20 in • p. 43

Eared Grebe
size 13 in • p. 44

Western Grebe
size 22 in • p. 45

Clark's Grebe
size 21 in • p. 46

Black-footed Albatross
size 28 in • p. 47

Northern Fulmar
size 18 in • p. 48

Pink-footed Shearwater
size 19 in • p. 49

Sooty Shearwater
size 17 in • p. 50

Black-vented Shearwater
size 13 in • p. 51

Fork-tailed Storm-Petrel
size 8 in • p. 52

Ashy Storm-Petrel
size 8 in • p. 53

Black Storm-Petrel
size 9 in • p. 54

American White Pelican
size 62 in • p. 55

Brown Pelican
size 48 in • p. 56

Brandt's Cormorant
size 33 in • p. 57

Double-crested
Cormorant
size 29 in • p. 58

Pelagic Cormorant
size 26 in • p. 59

American Bittern
size 25 in • p. 60

Great Blue Heron
size 52 in • p. 61

Great Egret
size 39 in • p. 62

Snowy Egret
size 24 in • p. 63

Cattle Egret
size 20 in • p. 64

Green Heron
size 18 in • p. 65

Black-crowned
Night-Heron
size 25 in • p. 66

White-faced Ibis
size 23 in • p. 67

Turkey Vulture
size 29 in • p. 68

California Condor
size 48 in • p. 69

Greater White-fronted
Goose
size 30 in • p. 70

Snow Goose
size 31 in • p. 71

Ross's Goose
size 24 in • p. 72

Canada Goose
size 36 in • p. 73

Brant
size 25 in • p. 74

Tundra Swan
size 54 in • p. 75

Wood Duck
size 18 in • p. 76

Gadwall
size 20 in • p. 77

Eurasian Wigeon
size 18 in • p. 78

American Wigeon
size 20 in • p. 79

Mallard
size 25 in • p. 80

Blue-winged Teal
size 15 in • p. 81

Cinnamon Teal
size 16 in • p. 82

Northern Shoveler
size 19 in • p. 83

Northern Pintail
size 28 in • p. 84

Green-winged Teal
size 14 in • p. 85

Canvasback
size 20 in • p. 86

Redhead
size 20 in • p. 87

Ring-necked Duck
size 16 in • p. 88

Greater Scaup
size 18 in • p. 89

Lesser Scaup
size 16 in • p. 90

Harlequin Duck
size 16 in • p. 91

Surf Scoter
size 19 in • p. 92

White-winged Scoter
size 22 in • p. 93

Black Scoter
size 19 in • p. 94

Oldsquaw
size 18 in • p. 95

Bufflehead
size 14 in • p. 96

Common Goldeneye
size 18 in • p. 97

Barrow's Goldeneye
size 18 in • p. 98

Hooded Merganser
size 18 in • p. 99

Common Merganser
size 24 in • p. 100

Red-breasted Merganser
size 23 in • p. 101

Ruddy Duck
size 15 in • p. 102

Osprey
size 23 in • p. 103

White-tailed Kite
size 16 in • p. 104

Bald Eagle
size 38 in • p. 105

Northern Harrier
size 21 in • p. 106

Sharp-shinned Hawk
size 13 in • p. 107

Cooper's Hawk
size 17 in • p. 108

Northern Goshawk
size 23 in • p. 109

Red-shouldered Hawk
size 19 in • p. 110

Swainson's Hawk
size 19 in • p. 111

Red-tailed Hawk
size 23 in • p. 112

Ferruginous Hawk
size 24 in • p. 113

Rough-legged Hawk
size 22 in • p. 114

Golden Eagle
size 35 in • p. 115

American Kestrel
size 8 in • p. 116

Merlin
size 11 in • p. 117

Peregrine Falcon
size 17 in • p. 118

Prairie Falcon
size 16 in • p. 119

Chukar
size 13 in • p. 120

Ring-necked Pheasant
size 30 in • p. 121

Ruffed Grouse
size 17 in • p. 122

Sage Grouse
size 30 in • p. 123

Blue Grouse
size 18 in • p. 124

Wild Turkey
size 43 in • p. 125

Mountain Quail
size 11 in • p. 126

California Quail
size 10 in • p. 127

Black Rail
size 6 in • p. 128

Clapper Rail
size 14 in • p. 129

Virginia Rail
size 10 in • p. 130

Sora
size 9 in • p. 131

Common Moorhen
size 13 in • p. 132

American Coot
size 14 in • p. 133

Sandhill Crane
size 45 in • p. 134

Black-bellied Plover
size 12 in • p. 135

Pacific Golden-Plover
size 10 in • p. 136

Snowy Plover
size 6 in • p. 137

Semipalmated Plover
size 7 in • p. 138

Killdeer
size 10 in • p. 139

Black Oystercatcher
size 17 in • p. 140

Black-necked Stilt
size 14 in • p. 141

American Avocet
size 17 in • p. 142

Greater Yellowlegs
size 14 in • p. 143

Lesser Yellowlegs
size 10 in • p. 144

Solitary Sandpiper
size 8 in • p. 145

Willet
size 15 in • p. 146

Wandering Tattler
size 10 in • p. 147

Spotted Sandpiper
size 7 in • p. 148

Whimbrel
size 17 in • p. 149

Long-billed Curlew
size 23 in • p. 150

Marbled Godwit
size 18 in • p. 151

Ruddy Turnstone
size 9 in • p. 152

Black Turnstone
size 9 in • p. 153

Surfbird
size 9 in • p. 154

Red Knot
size 10 in • p. 155

Sanderling
size 8 in • p. 156

Western Sandpiper
size 6 in • p. 157

Least Sandpiper
size 6 in • p. 158

Baird's Sandpiper
size 7 in • p. 159

Pectoral Sandpiper
size 9 in • p. 160

Rock Sandpiper
size 8 in • p. 161

Dunlin
size 8 in • p. 162

Short-billed Dowitcher
size 10 in • p. 163

Long-billed Dowitcher
size 12 in • p. 164

Common Snipe
size 11 in • p. 165

Wilson's Phalarope
size 9 in • p. 166

Red-necked Phalarope
size 7 in • p. 167

Red Phalarope
size 8 in • p. 168

Pomarine Jaeger
size 22 in • p. 169

Parasitic Jaeger
size 18 in • p. 170

Bonaparte's Gull
size 13 in • p. 171

Heermann's Gull
size 17 in • p. 172

Mew Gull
size 15 in • p. 173

Ring-billed Gull
size 19 in • p. 174

California Gull
size 19 in • p. 175

Herring Gull
size 24 in • p. 176

Thayer's Gull
size 23 in • p. 177

9

GULLS, TERNS & ALCIDS

Western Gull
size 25 in • p. 178

Glaucous-winged Gull
size 26 in • p. 179

Glaucous Gull
size 27 in • p. 180

Sabine's Gull
size 13 in • p. 181

Black-legged Kittiwake
size 17 in • p. 182

Caspian Tern
size 21 in • p. 183

Elegant Tern
size 16 in • p. 184

Common Tern
size 15 in • p. 185

Arctic Tern
size 15 in • p. 186

Forster's Tern
size 15 in • p. 187

Least Tern
size 9 in • p. 188

Black Tern
size 9 in • p. 189

Common Murre
size 16 in • p. 190

Pigeon Guillemot
size 13 in • p. 191

Marbled Murrelet
size 9 in • p. 192

Xantus's Murrelet
size 10 in • p. 193

Ancient Murrelet
size 10 in • p. 194

Cassin's Auklet
size 8 in • p. 195

Rhinoceros Auklet
size 14 in • p. 196

Tufted Puffin
size 15 in • p. 197

DOVES & CUCKOOS

Rock Dove
size 12 in • p. 198

Band-tailed Pigeon
size 14 in • p. 199

Mourning Dove
size 12 in • p. 200

Yellow-billed Cuckoo
size 12 in • p. 201

Greater Roadrunner
size 23 in • p. 202

Barn Owl
size 15 in • p. 203

Flammulated Owl
size 6 in • p. 204

Western Screech-Owl
size 9 in • p. 205

Great Horned Owl
size 21 in • p. 206

Northern Pygmy-Owl
size 7 in • p. 207

Burrowing Owl
size 8 in • p. 208

Spotted Owl
size 18 in • p. 209

Great Gray Owl
size 29 in • p. 210

Long-eared Owl
size 14 in • p. 211

Short-eared Owl
size 15 in • p. 212

Northern Saw-whet Owl
size 8 in • p. 213

Lesser Nighthawk
size 8 in • p. 214

Common Nighthawk
size 9 in • p. 215

Common Poorwill
size 8 in • p. 216

Black Swift
size 7 in • p. 217

Vaux's Swift
size 5 in • p. 218

White-throated Swift
size 6 in • p. 219

Black-chinned Hummingbird
size 3 in • p. 220

Anna's Hummingbird
size 4 in • p. 221

Costa's Hummingbird
size 3 in • p. 222

Calliope Hummingbird
size 3 in • p. 223

Rufous Hummingbird
size 3 in • p. 224

Allen's Hummingbird
size 3 in • p. 225

Belted Kingfisher
size 12 in • p. 226

Lewis's Woodpecker
size 11 in • p. 227

Acorn Woodpecker
size 9 in • p. 228

Williamson's Sapsucker
size 9 in • p. 229

Red-naped Sapsucker
size 8 in • p. 230

Red-breasted Sapsucker
size 8 in • p. 231

Nuttall's Woodpecker
size 7 in • p. 232

Downy Woodpecker
size 6 in • p. 233

Hairy Woodpecker
size 8 in • p. 234

White-headed Woodpecker
size 9 in • p. 235

Black-backed Woodpecker
size 9 in • p. 236

Northern Flicker
size 13 in • p. 237

Pileated Woodpecker
size 17 in • p. 238

Olive-sided Flycatcher
size 7 in • p. 240

Western Wood-Pewee
size 5 in • p. 241

Willow Flycatcher
size 5 in • p. 242

Hammond's Flycatcher
size 5 in • p. 243

Gray Flycatcher
size 6 in • p. 244

Dusky Flycatcher
size 5 in • p. 245

Pacific-slope Flycatcher
size 5 in • p. 246

Cordilleran Flycatcher
size 5 in • p. 247

Black Phoebe
size 6 in • p. 248

Say's Phoebe
size 7 in • p. 249

Ash-throated Flycatcher
size 7 in • p. 250

Cassin's Kingbird
size 8 in • p. 251

Western Kingbird
size 8 in • p. 252

Eastern Kingbird
size 8 in • p. 253

Loggerhead Shrike
size 9 in • p. 254

Northern Shrike
size 10 in • p. 255

Cassin's Vireo
size 5 in • p. 256

Hutton's Vireo
size 5 in • p. 257

Warbling Vireo
size 5 in • p. 258

Gray Jay
size 11 in • p. 259

Stellar's Jay
size 11 in • p. 260

Western Scrub-Jay
size 11 in • p. 261

Pinyon Jay
size 10 in • p. 262

Clark's Nutcracker
size 12 in • p. 263

Black-billed Magpie
size 20 in • p. 264

Yellow-billed Magpie
size 17 in • p. 265

American Crow
size 19 in • p. 266

Common Raven
size 24 in • p. 267

Horned Lark
size 7 in • p. 268

Purple Martin
size 7 in • p. 269

Tree Swallow
size 5 in • p. 270

Violet-green Swallow
size 5 in • p. 271

Northern Rough-winged Swallow
size 5 in • p. 272

Bank Swallow
size 5 in • p. 273

Cliff Swallow
size 5 in • p. 274

Barn Swallow
size 7 in • p. 275

Black-capped Chickadee
size 5 in • p. 276

Mountain Chickadee
size 5 in • p. 277

Chestnut-backed Chickadee
size 4 in • p. 278

Oak Titmouse
size 5 in • p. 279

Juniper Titmouse
size 5 in • p. 280

Bushtit
size 4 in • p. 281

Red-breasted Nuthatch
size 4 in • p. 282

White-breasted Nuthatch
size 5 in • p. 283

Pygmy Nuthatch
size 4 in • p. 284

Brown Creeper
size 5 in • p. 285

Rock Wren
size 6 in • p. 286

Canyon Wren
size 5 in • p. 287

Bewick's Wren
size 5 in • p. 288

House Wren
size 4 in • p. 289

Winter Wren
size 4 in • p. 290

Marsh Wren
size 5 in • p. 291

American Dipper
size 7 in • p. 292

Golden-crowned Kinglet
size 4 in • p. 293

Ruby-crowned Kinglet
size 4 in • p. 294

Blue-gray Gnatcatcher
size 4 in • p. 295

Western Bluebird
size 7 in • p. 296

Mountain Bluebird
size 7 in • p. 297

Townsend's Solitaire
size 8 in • p. 298

Swainson's Thrush
size 7 in • p. 299

Hermit Thrush
size 7 in • p. 300

American Robin
size 10 in • p. 301

Varied Thrush
size 9 in • p. 302

Wrentit
size 6 in • p. 303

Northern Mockingbird
size 10 in • p. 304

Sage Thrasher
size 8 in • p. 305

California Thrasher
size 12 in • p. 306

European Starling
size 8 in • p. 307

American Pipit
size 6 in • p. 308

Cedar Waxwing
size 7 in • p. 309

Phainopepla
size 7 in • p. 310

Orange-crowned Warbler
size 5 in • p. 311

Nashville Warbler
size 4 in • p. 312

Yellow Warbler
size 5 in • p. 313

Yellow-rumped Warbler
size 5 in • p. 314

Black-throated
Gray Warbler
size 5 in • p. 315

Townsend's Warbler
size 5 in • p. 316

Hermit Warbler
size 5 in • p. 317

MacGillivray's Warbler
size 5 in • p. 318

Common Yellowthroat
size 5 in • p. 319

Wilson's Warbler
size 5 in • p. 320

Yellow-breasted Chat
size 7 in • p. 321

Western Tanager
size 7 in • p. 322

Green-tailed Towhee
size 7 in • p. 323

Spotted Towhee
size 8 in • p. 324

California Towhee
size 9 in • p. 325

Rufous-crowned Sparrow
size 6 in • p. 326

Chipping Sparrow
size 6 in • p. 327

Brewer's Sparrow
size 5 in • p. 328

Black-chinned Sparrow
size 5 in • p. 329

Vesper Sparrow
size 6 in • p. 330

Lark Sparrow
size 6 in • p. 331

Black-throated Sparrow
size 5 in • p. 332

Sage Sparrow
size 5 in • p. 333

Savannah Sparrow
size 6 in • p. 334

Grasshopper Sparrow
size 5 in • p. 335

Fox Sparrow
size 7 in • p. 336

Song Sparrow
size 6 in • p. 337

Lincoln's Sparrow
size 5 in • p. 338

White-throated Sparrow
size 7 in • p. 339

White-crowned Sparrow
size 6 in • p. 340

Golden-crowned Sparrow
size 6 in • p. 341

Dark-eyed Junco
size 6 in • p. 342

Lapland Longspur
size 6 in • p. 343

Black-headed Grosbeak
size 8 in • p. 344

Blue Grosbeak
size 7 in • p. 345

Lazuli Bunting
size 6 in • p. 346

Red-winged Blackbird
size 8 in • p. 347

Tricolored Blackbird
size 8 in • p. 348

Western Meadowlark
size 9 in • p. 349

Yellow-headed Blackbird
size 10 in • p. 350

Brewer's Blackbird
size 9 in • p. 351

Brown-headed Cowbird
size 7 in • p. 352

Hooded Oriole
size 7 in • p. 353

Bullock's Oriole
size 8 in • p. 354

Gray-crowned Rosy-Finch
size 6 in • p. 355

Pine Grosbeak
size 9 in • p. 356

Purple Finch
size 6 in • p. 357

Cassin's Finch
size 6 in • p. 358

House Finch
size 6 in • p. 359

Red Crossbill
size 6 in • p. 360

Pine Siskin
size 5 in • p. 361

Lesser Goldfinch
size 4 in • p. 362

Lawrence's Goldfinch
size 4 in • p. 363

American Goldfinch
size 5 in • p. 364

Evening Grosbeak
size 8 in • p. 365

House Sparrow
size 6 in • p. 366

BIRDWATCHING IN NORTHERN CALIFORNIA

By David Fix

I n a past era, birdwatching was a pursuit followed by far fewer persons. It was something done largely by two distinct groups of people: those for whom the observation of birds was rewarded with moments of esthetic delight, and those for whom the shooting, classification, and trading of scientific specimens represented the advance of knowledge and, perhaps, a living wage. During the 20th century, we find that the understanding and awareness spawned through the marriage of these interests has enabled thousands of people to more readily and, more thoroughly, enjoy the spectacle and the miracle of birds.

Now most familiarly referred to as birding, the recognition and study of these creatures was made accessible to everyone with the advent of modern field guides. Today, there are scores of excellent guidebooks available, as well as a burgeoning body of literature and portraiture available on-line. Once a hobby lacking organization, public standing and economic clout, birding has become among the most respected and diverse pursuits, claiming participants in nearly every nation and in nearly every walk of life.

Blue-gray Gnatcatcher

An appreciation of birds offers the potential for moments of beauty, thought, inspiration and sheer refreshment throughout one's life. Practiced with patience and reserve, it is a minimally consumptive devotion that respects, rather than degrades, the environment. Watching birds is, plainly put, good medicine. It is a ready source of mental and physical exercise, one well worth 'self-prescribing' in an age of increasing awareness of the benefits of everyday stress reduction.

Birding is, in its essence, the mere act of watching birds. Beyond this, any variety or degree of study can be imagined: watching sparrows at a window feeder, traveling short distances to well-birded parks or shores, engaging in academic behavioral or distribution studies, or jet-setting to and from exotic locales in dogged, cheerful (and expensive!) pursuit of the world's rare or little-known species. Many persons are initially drawn to birding through the discovery of the far-flung social network represented by those who look at birds just for sporting fun. Travel at home and abroad is given a special tang indeed when one is attuned to the changing bird world! Tours guided by professional birders in search of regional or specialty birds have emerged as a well-established facet of the ecotourism industry. The schism of disrespect and misunderstanding that once served to divide academic ornithologists and the untutored public has narrowed dramatically in recent decades. A strong corps of birders adept at both identifying birds and observing in a scientific manner has emerged. Their well-presented input now allows a greater body of

Lincoln's Sparrow

evidence to be weighed in the course of making resource-management decisions. Such 'birder-scientists' have received growing recognition and acclaim for their continuing contributions to our knowledge of avian distribution, behavior, life history and impacts on economic and land-use concerns. The northern California birding fraternity is a group of well-intentioned, friendly people who are committed to sharing their varying expertise in a forum of mentoring, education and involvement.

Chestnut-backed Chickadee

The birdlife of northern California is complex. The topography of the region varies greatly, as does the effect of ever-increasing 'humanization.' Rainfall and land use are important factors dictating what birds are found, when and where. The list of species occurring at a given site routinely differs from that of another site perhaps but a dozen miles away. Although the effect of human land use and water management can be deleterious to habitat integrity, protected parcels of California's original plant cover and bird communities—often preserved within magnificent settings—attract birders from across North America. Taking into consideration even the rarest avian visitors, altogether about 560 of the more than 600 species known to have occurred in the state have been spotted here. With perhaps 450 species either resident, dropping in during migration or otherwise of regular occurrence, northern California offers endless exploration and satisfaction for birders.

The diverse habitats found in northern California support a wide array of breeding birds and year-round residents. Species typically thought of as northern birds reach the southern limits of their nesting ranges in the forests of the coastal strip and the Coast Range, in the Klamath and Warner mountains, and in the Cascades and Sierra Nevada. Birds characteristic of the southwestern desert-and-canyon bioregions extend northward into the Great Basin or along the arid foothills of the San Joaquin Valley and the inner Coast Range. The islands and headlands of the coast afford critical breeding sites for highly specialized seabirds. Swarms of tubenosed swimming birds hatched on oceanic islands thousands of miles removed from California annually visit offshore waters during their non-breeding season. Additionally, the region hosts a great number and variety of spring and fall migrants moving between northern breeding grounds and more southern wintering grounds. The temperate influence of the north Pacific Ocean and the generally mid-to-southerly latitude of the region also attracts millions of overwintering waterbirds, birds of prey and songbirds.

Widely dispersed 'oases' of vegetation throughout the arid sections and along the outer coast offer 'any port in a storm' for misoriented or disadvantaged migrants. Birders have long recognized the isolating and concentrating effects of these areas—'migrant traps' are prone to hosting occasional spectacular rarities from distant points. Such sites are intensively scoured by birders, and the weekend hunt for the 'big shocker' has long been a staple of birding 'list-builders.' Through Information Age communications technology, word of a great rarity now spreads promptly from the point of discovery to the most remote message machine or e-mail inbox. The effect generated secondarily by the search for unusual

Vesper Sparrow

birds at 'hotspots' and elsewhere has been a fine-tuned perception of the nature of migration in common bird species. When do Hutton's Vireos stray outside their breeding habitat? How late do northbound Townsend's Warblers linger in spring? To what extent are Spotted Towhees migratory? Answers, explanations and the inevitable further questions concerning these topics have been posed as a result of birding activities throughout the region.

Aside from the excitement of sharing achievements and special moments with friends and acquaintances, birding is an intensely personal activity. Its challenges and rewards are different for everyone. The degree to which one wishes to get into birding can only be determined by the individual. Some people are happy to feed wintering seed-eaters in the backyard each year, or to show their children the drama of routine events at a songbird nest. Others broaden the scope of their interest to assume contributing or leadership roles in local, regional or even international bird censuses and conservation programs. Regardless of your own level of curiosity, it is hoped that this introduction to the 328 species most commonly encountered in northern California will prove appealing, enlightening and enjoyable to browse.

Anna's Hummingbird

BEGINNING TO LEARN THE BIRDS

Birdwatching, or 'birding' as most people now call it, is a hobby that is simple to begin. Getting started and becoming oriented to resources and possibilities is a pleasant task. The key to learning the names of birds is an easy-to-use reference book. Many fine field guides can be found, all of which are helpful and few of which will lead one astray. Any field guide to North American or 'western' birds will set you off on the right foot. By focusing specifically on northern California in this book, we hope to ease the challenge ahead of you by describing the region's birds and attempting to offer additional insight into the world of birds.

Learning birds well is a lifelong process. Achieving familiarity with even the commonest of species is actually an endless endeavor. Birds are among the most highly mobile animals; they may be seen clearly and closely one moment and then become little more than a backlit, rapidly vanishing speck in the next! Because of their powers of flight, their guarded behavior and their frequent posture changes, all species offer glimpses of their flighty selves in a huge spectrum of poses. Artwork in a book such as this cannot provide more than a stylized snapshot of a living bird. Birders hoping to experience a precise replica of what meets their eye in leafing through a book will be disappointed, for the sheer plasticity of life on the move is well exemplified by birds. An inexperienced observer soon understands that the ability to recognize a bird at a glance is earned through building a set of useful 'search images' of that species: mental file-cards representing that species in any one of a great number of poses and under different circumstances.

To make this clearer, consider an American Robin running about on a lawn. It may best be known by its brick red breast in conjunction with a grayish back, broken white lines around the eyes and a black-and-white-streaked throat. The same bird flying high overhead, however, can be more easily recognized by its dark breast contrasting with white undertail coverts, combined with a habit of folding the wings tightly shut for an instant between wingbeats. Again, the same bird detected at a distance, harshly back-lit in a treetop, might be distinguished by its squarish head, alert posture, full chest and frequent, repeated tail-flicking. Over time, one perceives 'robin' almost peripherally without even bothering to look directly at the bird. A beginner may be astounded by such offhand insight, but the Wise Birder might reply, "How did you know that was your friend crossing the street a block away?" The answer may be that no one particular feature was seen—rather, an intangible collection of subtle features served to identity both bird and friend.

Birders who are skilled at recognizing rare birds are able to do so precisely because they have worked hard at learning the routine species; they know in an instant which individual seems 'different.' This expertise lends much enjoyment and much possibility to one's birding, but it requires exhaustive repetition and practice. Do not expect to become an expert in the course of a season or a year. It is a conundrum of sorts that the 'experts' often are those who are most keenly aware that they remain inexpert: they know best what they don't know, or don't yet understand.

In biology, the species is the fundamental unit of classification. The concept of species has been defined in many ways, but, essentially, a species is a group of freely inter-breeding individuals that share similar characteristics and are reproductively isolated from members of all other species. Each species is described with a scientific name (a Latin 'genus' name and 'species' name that are always underlined or *italicized*), and a single, accredited common name (even though local vernacular may suggest or assign other names). Most birders will agree that a bird has not been identified unless it has been distinguished to species level. For example, the Steller's Jay (*Cyanocitta stelleri*) is a separate species from the Gray Jay (*Perisoreus griseus*). 'Gray Jay' is the official common name of the latter species, even though people in various areas may refer to it as the 'Canada Jay,' 'Camp Robber' or even 'Whiskey-Jack.'

To help make sense of the hundreds of bird species in northern California, biologists and birders alike group similar species together into recognizable assemblages. The most commonly used groupings, in order of increasing scope, are genus, family and order. The Blue Grouse and Sage Grouse are considerably different from each other, and happen not to share a genus grouping, yet they are both clearly members of the family Phasianidae (the grouse and ptarmigan family). In turn, the Phasianidae is one family within the order Galliformes, the chicken-like birds. Families of birds in an order are assigned in a 'standard' arrangement that begins with those families and member species that are, in a general sense, most like the evolutionary ancestors of modern birds. It ends with those species thought to have been most strongly modified by evolutionary change and most departed from the 'ancestral norm.' Forever subject to disagreement and debate, the scientific classification of birds is in an unusually vigorous state of change owing to revelations

Purple Martin

made possible by the expanding application of DNA analysis.

To beginners, this evolutionary order might not initially make much sense, but birders soon come to know that all books of this sort begin with what could informally be called diving birds, wading birds, waterfowl, shorebirds, birds of prey and, chicken-like birds, followed by other birds that look more and more like songbirds (everything from hummingbirds and doves to woodpeckers); the last half of the book is thus devoted to the songbirds (the 'passerines').

Ruby-crowned Kinglet

There is no simple way to arrange the diversity of birdlife, in part because a patchy fossil record makes untangling ancestral relationships difficult, and also because various classification schemes are aimed at achieving differing intents. In practice, the customary 'tried and true' order, to which this guide conforms, provides the easiest format for learning. It presents birds in a traditional progression that has long been adhered to by many field guides. To help with the learning process, this book features color-coded keys to help you find bird groupings or specific birds easily and efficiently.

THE TOOLS AND TECHNIQUES OF BIRDING
Binoculars

The small size, fine details and wariness of birds make binoculars an indispensable piece of equipment for birdwatching. They can cost anywhere from $50 to $1500, and at times it may seem there are as many choices as there are species of birds. You get what you pay for. Properly cared for, precision optics are a real joy. They last for years. They offer great looks at plumage features at a distance or in poor light. Improperly cared for—dropped in a parking lot, forgotten in a cafe booth, idly hung from an untightened tripod arm, or left atop the roof of a vehicle—they are a huge regret waiting to happen.

Novice birders who are just taking up the pastime are encouraged to pay as much as they can possibly afford, but they are advised to keep in mind that what is less precious is less difficult to replace. Sturdy, 'ding-forgiving' binoculars may be purchased for upward of $200. It is a definite fact that most birders upgrade their optics within the first few years of getting into birding. Wear-and-tear on frequently used but unfamiliar equipment is a grim matter to bear in mind when selecting your first binoculars. If you're uncertain what to obtain, remember that it's the application of the tool that ultimately counts. A skilled golfer playing with old mismatched clubs shoots a better round than a duffer using the latest glitzy high-tech offering. In a broad sense, the same holds true with respect to birding and to one's choice of binoculars. Many experienced birders use 20- or even 30-year-old binoculars … and they wouldn't dream of switching.

Cedar Waxwing

Binoculars come in two basic types: porro-prism (in which there is a distinct, angular bend in the body of the binoculars) and roof-prism (in which the body is straight). Generally, porro-prism binoculars are less expensive than roof-prism binoculars. A first-rate pair of porros will cost about $300 to $400; roof-prism binoculars can cost up to $800 or more. Binoculars are optionally rubber-armored and covered by a long-term warranty. Ordering by mail saves money, but having a chance to handle the pair you want will guard against disappointment. Slight misalignment is a hazard to watch for. 'Insta-focus,' 'click-stop' focus and zoom-power mechanisms are cheap gimmicks and hallmarks of inferior binoculars. Don't stick with a product that doesn't feel right in your hands.

The magnification of binoculars is specified by the first numeral in a two-numeral code. Their light-gathering ability, determined by the millimeter width of the front lenses, is known by the second numeral. For example, a compact binocular might be a '7 x 21,' while a larger pair might have '8 x 50' stamped on it. Seven-power binoculars are the easiest to hand-hold and to find birds with; 10-power binoculars give a shakier but more distinctly detailed view. Larger lenses gather more light, so a 40-mm or 50-mm lens will perform better at dusk than a 20-mm or 30-mm lens of the same magnification. For the beginner, an eight-power porro-prism binocular with front lenses at least 35 mm in diameter (thus an 8 x 35 or 8 x 40) is a good place to start.

Pink-footed Shearwater

Spotting Scopes

A spotting scope and a tripod can be helpful, especially for viewing distant waterfowl and shorebirds. One might bird enthusiastically for years without owning a scope—at the same time, one might bird enthusiastically for years without enjoying great views of any number of distant birds! Spotting scopes capable of at least 20-power magnification are useful for birds out of binocular range. A wide range of spotting scopes is now available. None worth owning is inexpensive, yet it should be borne in mind that a good scope may last a lifetime. Become familiar with the spectrum of possibilities by asking to look through the scope of any birder you encounter and chat with. Before making a purchase, be sure to inquire among your birding community: there may be a perfectly serviceable, pre-owned scope just a phone call away. People do upgrade their optics. After all, who really needs two or three spotting scopes? Glare filters, rugged cloth sleeves and persistent use of dust caps help preserve the glass. Tripods or window mounts with 'fluid heads' allowing smooth movement are strongly advised. Attached to a quality tripod, the better scopes on the market may seem at first to be fearsomely heavy, but durability and breathtaking performance more than make up for their heft.

Hermit Thrush

American White Pelican

Birding by Ear

Seeing birds is only half the experience—or less. Recognizing even a handful of species by their songs and call-notes will enrich anyone's sensory involvement with birds. Within a short time, any attentive beginning birder with normal hearing will come to believe the claim that 90 percent of forest birds are heard rather than seen. Detecting birds by ear demands that what is heard must be listened to—an act of attention rather than effort. Perceiving the presence, or the absence, of birds through listening for their distinctive voices is important in birding efficiently. It is a delight and a source of pride to become familiar with the utterances of most of the common birds. Each spring, birders scan the valleys and hillsides with their ears, straining to hear that first Warbling Vireo or Lazuli Bunting of the season. One's first Common Snipe of fall may be known only as a sneezy rasp, its source racing away unseen against the sky. And who could begin to grasp the abundance and distribution of night birds without knowing their various hoots and tremolos?

Learning 'ear-birding,' as it is often called, initially takes bird identification one step beyond the process used in visual observation. Unless one wishes to take the identification of an unseen bird on the word of another, ear-birding requires that the identity of an unfamiliar bird must be corroborated through sight. Because it often requires a tedious 'effort of patience' to locate and identify an unseen singer, any birder doing so will try to remember the voice. The ability to remember, recall and promptly assign a correct identity to a bird voice can be enhanced through the use of tapes, mnemonic devices and written phrasing. Some of the most talented ear-birders in northern California attempt to perceive bird sounds in a physical sense, as if the utterance itself is liquid or scratchy, a thick or thin shape or a deep or shallow waveform. The best way to learn bird songs and calls is through the mentoring of a good ear-birder, reinforced by repetition of the lessons one learns.

Although crude, the use of language in describing songs and calls is unavoidable. We have freely offered alliterative or 'catchy' phrases to describe those songs and calls most frequently heard. It should be noted that many of the word renditions and mnemonic aids in this book are original and are presented here for the first time. The wretched limitation of our alphabet causes much phraseology to fall well short, but the point is to provide you with at least a starting point from which to expand your awareness of the truly vast spectrum of bird sounds.

Oldsquaw

Watching Bird Behavior

Once you can confidently identify a given bird, you have 'attached a name to a face.' Just as in matters of human acquaintance, nearly all meaningful knowledge of any bird springs from this simplest familiarity. The looks, behavior and voice of a few birds, once learned even in passing, can never be thoroughly forgotten. Encountered frequently and in many places, they become well known, providing a vague sense of reassurance and a humble comfort in a world adrift in change. The particulars of a bird's life are often attractive and alluring: most people interested in birds find themselves curious about where the birds may be expected, whether they are abundant or endangered, what they eat, how they form pair-bonds, and with which species they consort—in short, how they live their lives.

Throughout most of their typically very brief lives, birds balance precariously between burning too many calories and consuming too few. Energy is the currency of existence, so unnecessary behaviors are avoided and meaningless behaviors are rare. The birder whose interest extends anywhere beyond mere recognition of species will inevitably discover that the need to conserve energy tends to marshal and condense avian movements into discrete patterns. Indeed, it might be said that recreational birding at its best is all about anticipating, discerning and thinking about patterns. If you pay attention to the arrival, increase, decrease and departure of migrants passing through the shrubbery of a local park or woodlot, the differences in timing among various songbirds will gradually become apparent. Sit at a dripping faucet in a desert campground in the heat of early afternoon, and you will understand a bit more about birds and water. Spend an hour squinting at the sea through a scope every so often, and you will suspect correctly that the volume and variety of coastwise migration varies at least a little from day to day.

Observing wild birds is an investment guaranteeing a twofold payoff. While patiently awaiting whatever reward it is we seek, we are witness to the display of natural phenomena that many people have no idea even take place: the routine of parental attention; extraordinary or heroic acts of predation or survival; moments of stirring and transcendent beauty.

Red-tailed Hawk

Birding by Habitat

Simply put, a bird's habitat is the place in which it normally lives. Some species prefer dense conifer forest, while others favor widely spaced oaks; some are hardly ever found outside marshes, while many live nearly all their lives on the open ocean and return to land only to breed. Birds are able to co-exist in great diversity owing to their ability to inhabit unique 'niches.' For example, there are various species of treetop warblers that all occupy separate niches in parts of the same kind of tree. They sort themselves out according to their own distinctive needs: each species has its own unique combination of requirements, including where it places its nest and where and how it gathers food. Each species feeds on insects that are gathered in different parts of the tree, and each nest sits at various heights above the ground. Specifically, Hermit Warblers prefer stands of tall conifers whose crowns nearly touch one another; 'Audubon's' Yellow-rumped Warblers go for full-crowned conifers that are somewhat more widely spaced; Black-throated Gray Warblers prefer an abundance of oaks with a few conifers sticking up here and there. Some overlap regularly occurs, but, on the whole, members of each species stick to their own niche, so that one basic patch of ground may provide the needs of many.

Chukar

It is impossible to see, or even just hear, birds without beginning to recognize this separation in habitats. In finding birds, it is a great aid to learn what birds we can expect to find in a given place at a given season, and which birds would be distinctly out of place. We come to anticipate hearing Western Meadowlarks in grassy expanses with minimal trees, and we would scarcely think to listen for one in a high Sierran fir forest. While studying birds of the ocean, we expect any number of shearwaters to fly into sight, but vireos and finches could hardly be imagined (although it does happen at times—any landbird well out to sea is drama on the wing!). Traveling through a canyon dotted with oaks and chaparral, we recall the times we have encountered Ash-throated Flycatchers. While visiting the shady and humid redwood parks, we forget the Ash-throat; our mind naturally turns to the Pacific-slope Flycatcher.

This concept of species separation is so important that, with experience, any birder begins to recognize how infrequently some birds ever appear outside their habitat. While some, like the Great Horned Owl, are indeed generalists and may be found nearly anywhere, many of northern California's birds are specialized. Some inhabit remnant patches of prisitine habitats that were formerly more widespread and are now diminished or degraded. As the 'malignant hominoma' of poorly checked human development gobbles and transforms these special places, such regional habitat specialists as the Least Tern, Marbled Murrelet, Greater Roadrunner and Black-chinned Sparrow become scarcer. The old saying 'divide and conquer' begins to apply as habitat is broken and fragmented, with groups of individuals increasingly unable to cross habitat barriers to continue vital genetic mixing with neighboring members. The introduction of aggressive exotic species, such as the European Starling and House Sparrow, has added another volatile factor to the array of threats facing many of our birds.

Owing to the alteration of lowlands for agriculture and settlement, the suppression of wildfire, the stubborn drenching of the landscape with persistent chemicals and such natural events as fires, floods and long-term climate change, the already complex mosaic of habitats in northern California changes ceaselessly. Bird populations, always dynamic in nature, change hand in hand with the varying intensity of these phenomena. Beyond doubt, many local changes will have taken place between the time this text is written and the hour the printer's ink has dried.

*Northern
Saw-whet Owl*

Calling Birds Closer

Birds of brush and treetops are often very difficult to see. 'Pishing,' 'squeaking,' and 'pygmy-owling' are three strategies commonly employed by birders to call birds in closer. Pishing (or spishing) simply involves making busy, repeated *psh-psh-psh* sounds through pursed lips. Squeaking is done by kissing the back of the hand. Pygmy-owling is the imitation of the common series-call of the Northern Pygmy-Owl, which is accomplished by uttering a mellow, low-pitched whistle at the same pitch about once every two seconds. An alternation of these noises amplifies the effect. Ever-vigilant and keenly attuned to possible threats, small birds of many species will stop foraging and pop briefly into view when distracted in this fashion. Take care not to bother the birds any more than is necessary, as incubating adults may be pulled off eggs or nestlings, and any bird made more conspicuous to predators is at increased risk.

Bird Listing and Record-keeping

Many birders keep lists of the species they see and hear. Listing is a highly personal matter. Some people maintain county, state, provincial or national lists, yard lists or year lists of birds they have identified. Friendly competition arises when numerous observers attempt to build the biggest list. While this sort of competition has little basis in science, that fact does not minimize its importance. County listing, for example, is a widespread and eagerly pursued sideline across the United States. County-listers make it a point to explore each corner of their chosen realm, and they will visit uncommon habitats and discover new 'hotspots' in the process. Lists from unusual locations can become cherished souvenirs of special times spent chasing birds in the company of special friends. The well-established American Birding Association serves to regulate and standardize lists from practically every political and geographical entity in North America.

Keeping track of your observations through the use of a field journal or notebook is a practice to be encouraged. In northern California, the time-honored 'Grinnell method' employs a small side- or top-bound field notebook, into which observations and sketches are made; later, these notes are transcribed into a durable loose-leaf binder. Birders who encounter rare birds will want to document their sightings through carefully written details, photographs or tape recordings. The subject of note-taking and documentation of rarities is, in itself, a topic of broad interest and appeal. Find out how the leading observers in your area take notes, and have fun working out your own system.

Xantus's Murrelet

BIRDING ACTIVITIES
Birdwatching Groups

Birding alone is a lot of fun. Birding with others is even more fun as it is an activity offering the less-experienced birder the expertise, experience, thoughts and insights of others who have been in the field for years. We recommend that you join in on such activities as Christmas Bird Counts, local and regional 'bird festivals,' workshops and regular meetings of your local birding or natural history club. If you are interested in bird conservation and environmental issues, there are natural history groups and a growing number of birder-conscious retail stores that can keep you informed about ongoing issues in your area. Bird 'hotlines' can provide up-to-date information on sightings of birds unusual at the local, northern California or even North American level. Many rarities are stragglers well off the 'beaten path,' and remain at or near the point of discovery for days or even weeks. These waifs are in themselves marvelous creatures that inspire wonder, and joining a group of excited birders assembled from distant cities for the same purpose has served to foster innumerable friendships—even marriages!

Bird Conservation

Northern California is a great place to watch birds. Fine habitat persists in the region, but a great deal has been lost. The rate of change itself is steadily increasing. California's throng of humanity demands single-family housing, so hillsides clothed in native chaparral are paved. Waterways prone to natural flooding are riprapped and straightened. Thousands of acres of maturing forest are set back to clearcuts each year. The replacement of the family farm with the corporate mega-farm minimizes shrubby fencerows, eliminates valuable windbreaks and douses ancient and vulnerable aquifers with toxins. In the long term, development for housing, agriculture and forestry are threatening to destroy bird habitat throughout the region.

Birds can neither speak nor vote. They know nothing of the precarious situation now facing life on Earth. They cry for a voice. With the increasing separation of Urban Man from the tableau

Vaux's Swift

27

*Yellow-billed
Cuckoo*

of nature in which we are entwined, we have lost the capacity to feel we are one with the Earth. No matter their political affiliation or economic standing, birders everywhere agree that it is urgently important to continually fight for the marvels of the natural world. As our children must some day become our leaders, it is vital that awareness, knowledge and love for what was here before is taught and instilled. If we elect not to speak out for the considerate use and renewal of fragile resources, we are abandoning our privilege to maintain biodiversity and habitat integrity.

Bird Feeding

Many people set up a backyard birdfeeder to attract birds to their yard, especially during the colder months. By choosing the appropriate seed or other food, it is possible to attract specific birds. If you have a feeder, keep it stocked through late spring. The weather might seem balmy, but before flowers bloom, seeds develop and insects hatch, birds can find the cusp of early springtime tough to survive. When migratory birds return in early spring, resident birds must compete with them, and after a long winter the pickings are slim. Extra food supplies at this time of year can be especially helpful.

Hummingbird feeders are great fun, but they carry with them the responsibility to maintain clean artificial nectar. If your feeder develops mildew, you must strive to clean and change it more often. Take care that the mixture does not contain artificial coloring, and that it does not ferment. Three or four parts water to one part white sugar works. Sip the mix before putting it out. If it tastes sweeter than anything you'd care to drink much of, then dilute it.

In general, feeding birds is a good thing, especially if you provide food in the form of native shrubbery, annuals or other seed-producing plants. Birdbaths, particularly those with a running-water inlet or outlet, are also an effective way to bring birds to your yard.

Nest Boxes

Another popular way to attract birds is to set out nest boxes, especially for wrens, chickadees, bluebirds and swallows. Not all birds will use nest boxes—only species that naturally use tree-hole cavities are comfortable in such confined spaces. Larger, specially designed nest boxes can also attract kestrels, owls and cavity-nesting ducks. Baffles, oval entrances and other tricks described in books and pamphlets offer advice on discouraging European Starlings and House Sparrows from using nest boxes.

BIOREGIONS OF NORTHERN CALIFORNIA

It has rightfully been said by biologists and sociologists alike that California comprises many 'states' encompassing one political entity. Northern California is characterized by habitat diversity that is rivaled by few other areas of comparable size in the western United States. The presence, absence and seasonal abundance of water plays the most critical role in determining vegetation cover type. Average annual precipitation is directly affected by landform, with coastal or windward slopes receiving the greatest share. Landforms within this region are complex. Accordingly, rain- and snowfall may vary dramatically across the span of only a few miles. Also, various habitats have been enhanced or, more routinely, degraded by a burgeoning human population. The result of this interplay of variables is an intricate mosaic of habitats—a puzzle so involved that it becomes the pleasant labor of a lifetime to attempt to become familiar with each particular habitat. Nevertheless, the following brief descriptions summarize northern California's important bioregions.

Ocean

The Pacific Ocean offers open-sea habitat for tubenoses, alcids, phalaropes, jaegers and some gulls and terns. The deep blue 'tuna water' of the North Pacific Gyre beyond the continental slope is generally fairly warm throughout the year. Near-shore cold and warm currents, varying somewhat in temperature each year, bathe the continental shelf, influencing prey availability for coastal-breeding cormorants, Western Gulls and alcids. Incursions of post-breeding subtropical seabirds are more intense during El Niño–Southern Oscillation events and less so during cooler-water years. The abundance and species diversity of seabirds in the vicinity of the Farallon Islands, above the Monterey Submarine Canyon and around the Cordell Banks off Point Reyes indicate the importance of cold-water upwelling on avian distribution and abundance. Seabirds are generally widely scattered but numerous over seafloor with subdued physical variation. Opportunities to closely observe shearwaters and storm-petrels from well-run chartered 'birding boats' has given the region a profile unique in West Coast seabirding.

Ashy Storm-Petrel

Coast

Northern California's coastline is characterized by irregularity. Sandy or rocky beaches are closely backed by steep foothills and headland ridges of the western slope of the Coast Range. This rugged scenery reaches its greatest expression in the Big Sur of southern Monterey County and along the Lost Coast of northern Mendocino and southern

Horned Grebe

Humboldt counties. Outside these areas, sand beaches of variable length are distributed spottily along the entire coast. Stretches of shoreline, particularly north of San Francisco, have numerous small offshore islands or 'sea stacks' that provide nesting habitat for most of the region's breeding seabirds. There are few significant estuaries, and by far the most important is the San Francisco Bay system. This includes the San Francisco, San Pablo and Suisun bays and adjacent managed tidal land and remnant tidal marshes. The many low islands and hundreds of miles of channelized waterways and sloughs of the adjacent Sacramento–San Joaquin River delta provide tidal gradation and habitat links between the open estuary and the wetlands of the Central Valley. Bird use of the combined San Francisco Bay, Delta and Central Valley ecosystems is very high despite growing development pressure, pollution threats and reduced fisheries. Humboldt Bay, near the northern end of the California coast, comprises two interconnected ancient tidal lagoons that are fronted by low, open country. Monterey Bay, in the south of the region, occupies a great semicircular arc and is notable for its deep nearshore water. Coastal bottomland occurs locally throughout this subregion, providing habitat for migrant and wintering waterfowl, raptors and songbirds. Many sites are intensively explored by birders all year.

Coast Range

With the exception of interior valleys and basins and major river corridors, much of northern California is quite mountainous. The Coast Range is actually a series of ranges differing in origin and in biogeography. Many of the ridgelines and stream canyons trend northwest and southeast, creating an interesting array of closely set sunny and shady microsites. The seaward slopes of the Coast Range are more well watered. In the northern portion of the region, they support moist conifer forests dominated by Coast Redwood or Douglas-fir. Toward the south, a hodgepodge of mixed-species oak and conifer stands interspersed with grassy hillsides and stretches of 'soft chaparral' brushfields defines much of the area. The eastern slopes of the Coast Range receive less precipitation and enjoy less ameliorating overcast; hence, they become much warmer in summer. Great expanses of semiarid oak-dotted grassland, grading upward through interior hard chaparral and then into pine and mixed-conifer forest, characterize this region. Brushfields featuring heat-tolerant 'hard chaparral' shrubs and evergreen oaks sprawl across unmanaged ridgelines and higher slopes. Similar habitat stretches around the northern edge of the Sacramento Valley, offering a habitat connection with the drier, lower west slopes of the southern Cascades and the Sierra Nevada. Curious and relict plant species of limited range occur within higher forest and brushfield communities in the Klamath Mountain ecoregion of the far northwest. Heat- and dry-adapted plants that are characteristic of the Mojave Desert or of southern California foothills reach northward locally into the southern fringes of the region, providing some desert birds with their northernmost habitats.

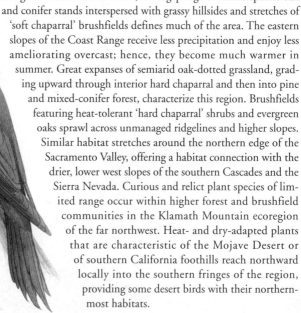

Lewis's Woodpecker

Topography of Northern California

Habitats of
Northern California

OREGON

Klamath
Mountains

CASCADE RANGE

MODOC
PLATEAU

GREAT
BASIN

Warner Mts.

NEVADA

COAST RANGES

Sacramento Valley

Lake
Tahoe

Sacramento

SIERRA NEVADA

BASIN AND RANGE

San
Francisco
Bay

Monterey
Bay

San Joaquin Valley

COAST RANGES

Inyo Mountains

Death Valley

Mojave
Desert

Los Angeles

Channel
Islands

Salton
Sea

Colorado River

ARIZONA

San
Diego

Colorado Desert

MEXICO

- Mountains
- Deserts
- Grasslands / Agricultural
- Foothills
- Coastal Shrub / Chaparral
- Coastal Areas

The region covered by
the book is highlighted.
The distribution maps
for each species show
only this area.

Central Valley

The San Joaquin Valley and the Sacramento Valley together comprise California's Central Valley. The valley is enclosed by the foothills of the southern Cascades and the Sierra Nevada on the east, and by the interior Coast Range slopes on the west. Its only outlet is to the San Francisco Bay system via an extensive delta. It is semiarid to arid country and receives precipitation only during winter storms and occasional summer showers. Water in the Central Valley has long been strictly managed for agriculture. The valley is exceptionally flat, with gradients frequently amounting to but inches per mile. In pristine times, the Central Valley supported fabulous riparian forests. Pronghorn, 'tule' elk and the extirpated California grizzly bear once grazed the open country and wetland fringes. During the colder months, it was a vast wetland hosting enormous numbers of waterfowl. In the era since Gold Rush settlement and the emergence of the valley as an agricultural center, the two master streams have been tamed and the riparia reduced to sorry remnants. Today, important parcels of managed wetland are administered as National Wildlife Refuges and as state and private waterfowl areas. Nearly none of the original grassland and marsh cover persists. The valley floor has been thoroughly altered, and the result is a consistent patchwork of crop fields, orchards, fallow ground, towns, cities and other human constructions and developments. Despite these changes, sanctuaries, parks and reserves offer tantalizing suggestions of past glories.

Burrowing Owl

Klamath Basin

The Klamath Basin, straddling the Oregon-California state line, is not actually an enclosed basin, because its waters ultimately find the sea through the well-defined canyon of the Klamath River. However, in its geography and birdlife, the Klamath Basin reflects an interior flavor. It incorporates vitally strategic Pacific Flyway waterfowl staging sites, shrub-dotted 'cold desert' uplands, pine forests, aspen-lined lakes and a hint of the Great Basin playa landscape that is more common to the east. The allocation of limited water to agricultural lands at the expense of wildlife has sparked discussion about the comparative values of each, underscoring a controversy hardly limited to this region.

Modoc Plateau/Great Basin

The sagebrush sea of the western Great Basin laps irregularly across the northeastern portion of California. The Modoc Plateau and associated landforms comprise a sere and rugged country borne of extensive fluid lava flows that covered an enormous reach of land in prehistory. It is characterized by cinder cones, lava caves, alkali flats and saline lakes, pine-dotted ridges, narrow riparian strips, small areas of cultivated land and extensive cattle range. The 'basin-and-range' topography so associated with the Great Basin experience is easily perceived

Sage Thrasher

here. The dramatic and seldom-explored uplift of the isolated Warner Mountains provides an island of mountain forest habitat for a collection of bird species that are otherwise scarce in this district. Surface water is at a premium—where lakes occur, significant nesting colonies of waterbirds and wetlands supporting migrating waterfowl and waders are also found. Mono Lake, at the base of the Sierra Nevada 'East Slope,' is set within harsh but beautiful surroundings. It is a threatened jewel, the subject of heroic grass-roots efforts—spearheaded by the late birder-activist David Gaines—to renew its former extent and importance to birds. To the north, Honey Lake lies below the east slope of the southern Cascade Range; it is the only large Great Basin lake-and-wetland system so situated. Goose Lake, among the larger Great Basin lakes, straddles the California-Oregon line. This region is mostly semi-arid, with stands of trees of any extent restricted chiefly to the foothills and mountain slopes. Juniper and pinyon pine woodlands of considerable extent occur along the western fringe of the basin. Thousands of square miles are carpeted with 'shrub-steppe' plant communities typical of the intermountain West. Rolling uplands are dominated by tall sagebrush, low sagebrush, rabbitbrush, remnant native bunchgrasses, native and exotic annual grasses and many colorful wild-flowers and forbs. Alkaline basins are grown to greasewood, saltbush, hopsage and Great Basin giant wild rye. Birdlife in this region is varied and abundant. With no large population centers, birding coverage is modest—much remains to be learned about birds of the more remote sites and specialized habitats.

Cascade Range

The Cascade Range is generally envisioned as a string of snow-capped volcanic peaks stretching through Washington and Oregon, but in truth this postcard image falls short of reality. Although the spectacular peaks are eye-catching, they are actually isolated exceptions to the general lay of the land. The Cascades comprise a series of medium- to high-elevation ridges, with the rather uniform skyline broken here and there by high points and by deeply incised canyons. The range is situated beneath the Pacific storm track, and the western slopes are well watered. Vigorous forests, perhaps more characteristic of the Pacific Northwest, originally covered much of the region; they have been intensively 'managed,' yet regrowth is rapid. Plant diversity here is great, especially in the higher valleys and meadows of the southern fringe of the range, where the Cascades grade into the northern Sierra Nevada. The Klamath River is the only stream to completely bisect the range in California. The Cascades' eastern slopes are more arid, with Douglas-fir forest giving way to picturesque

Western Tanager

ponderosa pine, white fir and incense-cedar stands that are under-grown with bitterbrush, ceanothus, currant and manzanita. Lightning from summer thunderstorms has written a history in weathered charcoal on the trunks of innumer-able ancient trees throughout the range. The parched and sprawling brushfields in the vicinity of Mt. Shasta amaze one with their array of colors and plant textures and the play of harsh light and shadow. Birds abound in the Cascades, especially in summer, and particularly about wet meadow-edges where stands of trees containing numerous snags front the openings.

Sierra Nevada

Standing as a mighty wall firmly astride east-central California, the Sierra Nevada has been the subject of artistic and poetic tributes for as long as people have lived in the region. The Sierra is a long and remarkably tall uplift that vividly separates two entirely distinct climatic regimes. The power of continuous high mountains to dictate weather patterns—and indeed, the course of settlement—is nowhere better illustrated in the United States. Moist marine airmasses arriving from the north Pacific rise, expand, cool and drop their moisture across the western slopes of the range. The clouds

Calliope Hummingbird

having been wrung dry, little precipitation falls east of the general Sierran summit. During periods of glacial advance in the Ice Age, alpine and valley glaciers carved gorges of such dimension that visitors from throughout the world have flocked to experience their grandeur. In the warm interglacial period in which we now live, the Ice Age is (happily) 'off duty,' leaving us time and opportunity to enjoy these profound and scenic results. Owing to its great range of elevation, its north-to-south extent and the meeting of 'west-side' and 'east-side' fauna and flora, the Sierra Nevada presents biological complexity that requires more than a mere lifetime to comprehend fully. In a broad sense, the oak and grassland habitats of the lower western slopes finger upward into blue oak and gray pine woodlands across a broken but broad front. These semi-arid plant communities give way to typical Sierran conifer forests of various pines, red fir, white fir, sugar pine and scattered black oak where the zone of persistent winter snowpack is reached. In turn, semi-open and clumped stands of subalpine trees reach their limit about the edges of the abundant glacial basins and snow-fed tarns below the crest of the range. The lower eastern slopes support plants and birds that are characteristic of the fringes of the Great Basin (in the north) and the northern Mojave Desert (in the south). Pinyon and juniper woodlands, white fir and aspen stands and tortuous canyons characterize the arid and winter-chilled higher elevations of the eastern front. The highest ridgelines and peaks of the range stand boulder-strewn, windswept and nearly barren. The numerous national parks and national forests of the region offer any number of interesting birding venues, which are at their best from late spring into early fall.

The Urban Environment

No brief outline of northern California's important habitats would be complete without a mention of towns and cities. Familiar to nearly everyone living in the region, the urban and urban/rural edge environment offers a distinct set of living situations for birds. The pattern of settlement in

House Sparrow

northern California is irregular. Population centers are most densely clustered around the San Francisco Bay region. Smaller cities are scattered throughout the Central Valley, along the coast and much more sparingly east of the mountains. Bird communities vary in species composition and in abundance. As a rule, diversity is greatest around the edges of cities, where the suburban California 'botanical hodgepodge' of remnant native plants and a host of exotics forms a frontier with the original outlying vegetation types. Urban environments are important to birders as well as to birds. Most observers initially gain experience with birds in their backyards or at nearby parks, woodlots and shores. Because even the best insulation works only so well, the aura of warmth generated by clustered buildings may assist lingering, 'semi-hardy' songbirds during the worst chill of winter. Suburban bird-feeders help support wintering seed-eaters ... and the Sharp-shinned and Cooper's hawks that prey upon them.

ABOUT THE SPECIES ACCOUNTS

RANGE MAP SYMBOLS

- year-round
- winter
- summer

This book gives detailed accounts of the 328 bird species that either occur regularly in northern California or are of special interest. The sequence of the birds and their common and scientific names follow the the American Ornithologists' Union's *Check-list of North American Birds* (7th edition).

The most important identifying characteristics for each species have been presented in a concise and cap-sule format. Owing to limitations of space, it has been impossible to discuss identi-fication in extreme detail, and many plumages, such as females, immatures, subadults and eclipse, are not illustrated.

Each species account also attempts to paint a word portrait of the bird as an animal, honoring its uniqueness and emphasizing its various character traits. Our limited understanding of non-human creatures causes our descriptions to deal largely with traits and habits most easily discerned by members of another nation, peering in through a window forever open but a crack. Interpretations presented here assume that no one fully perceives or understands the hidden complexities of bird behavior. Nevertheless, it is hoped that you will attain some greater degree of familiarity with each species through the concepts we have chosen to address.

ID: It is difficult to describe the features of a bird without being able to visualize it, so this section should be used in combination with the illustrations. Where appropriate, the description is subdivided to highlight the differences between male and female birds, breeding and non-breeding birds and adults and immatures. The descriptions strive to use minimal technical words in favor of easily understood terms. Bird's don't really have 'jaw lines,' 'ear patches' or 'chins,' but these and other terms are easily understood by all readers, in spite of their scientific inaccuracy. Some of the most common features of birds are pointed out in a glossary illustration.

Size: The size measurement, an average length of the bird's body from bill to tail, is an approximate measurement of the bird as it is seen in nature. The size is generally given as a range for larger birds, because there is variation between individuals and subspecies. In addition, wingspans are given for some of the larger birds that are often seen in flight. Please note that birds with long tails will have large measurements that do not neces-sarily reflect 'body' size.

Status: A general comment, such as common, uncommon or rare, is usually sufficient to describe the regional context. Specific situations are bound to differ somewhat, as migratory pulses, seasonal changes and centers of activity tend to concentrate or disperse birds in some situations. Residents are those birds that are found year-round and, generally, they do not travel far during their lifetimes. It should be noted, however, that while some species are found year-round in northern California, individuals of that species may at one time or another move in and out of the state. Finally, it is assumed that the reader recognizes that birds are generally scarce or infrequent away from preferred habitats.

Habitat: The habitats we have described suggest where each species can most commonly be found. In most cases, it is a fairly generalized description, but if a bird is primarily restricted to a specific habitat, it is described more precisely. Because of the freedom flight gives them, birds can turn up in just about any type of habitat, but in most encounters they will occur in appropriate environments.

Nesting: The reproductive strategies employed by birds vary tremendously. Nest location and structure, clutch size, incubation period and parental duties are among the reproductive aspects that are discussed. Please remember that proper birdwatching ethics discourage the study of active bird nests in an invasive manner. Nest disturbance interferes with the reproductive cycle in any of several ways. Humans are clumsy creatures; predators watch our noisy intrusions and will promptly investigate opportunities to secure a meal.

Feeding: Birds are frequently encountered while they are foraging, so a description of their feeding styles and diets can provide valuable identifying characteristics, as well as intriguing dietary facts.

Voice: You will hear many birds, particularly songbirds and species of open country, before you find them in your binoculars. A novel or memorable paraphrase of the species' most distinctive sounds can often aid in your identification. Given the restrictions of language, these paraphrases only loosely resemble sounds produced by the bird. Should one of our paraphrases not work for you, feel free to make up your own. This rewarding personal exercise can reinforce the sound in your memory.

Similar Species: Easily confused species are discussed in a brief and concise manner in this section. By concentrating on the most relevant field marks, the subtle differences between species can be reduced to easily identifiable traits. You might find it useful to consult this section when finalizing your identification between a few species—knowing the most relevant field marks will shortcut the identification process. Even experienced birders can mistake one species for another.

NON-PASSERINES

Non-passerine birds represent 17 of the 18 orders of birds found in northern California, but only about 60% of the species. They are grouped together and called 'non-passerines' because, with few exceptions, they are easily distinguished from the passerines, which make up the 18th order and account for approximately 40% of northern California's bird species. Being from 17 different orders, however, non-passerines vary considerably in their appearance and habits—they include everything from the 50-inch-tall Great Blue Heron to the 3¹/₄ inch-long Calliope Hummingbird.

Many non-passerines are large, so they are among our most notable birds. Waterfowl, raptors, gulls, shorebirds and woodpeckers are easily identified by most people. Some of the smaller non-passerines, such as doves, swifts and hummingbirds, are frequently thought of as passerines by novice birdwatchers, and they can cause those beginners some identification problems. With a little practice, however, they will become recognizable as non-passerines. By learning to separate the non-passerines from the passerines at a glance, birdwatchers effectively reduce by half the number possible species for an unidentified bird.

Red-breasted Merganser

American Avocet

Western Screech-Owl

Herring Gull

RED-THROATED LOON
Gavia stellata

In northern California, Red-throats are routine winter birds of expansive coastal waters, infrequently occurring inland. A few may linger in summer far south of their usual breeding range, but most Red-throats begin to appear in numbers in October: some migrate through the region to winter southward; others settle into winter quarters they will occupy until March or April. Individuals and straggling lines are readily detected flying up or down the open coastline in spring and fall. Though many dot the water, these loons seldom flock; instead they disperse at some distance from one another, mixed among other waterfowl.

non-breeding

ID: small, slim bill is held upward. *Breeding:* deep reddish throat; gray head; plain dark back. *Non-breeding:* light underparts; dark gray upperparts; small white spots on the upper back; eye is surrounded narrowly by white.

Size: L 24–27 in; W 42–45 in.

Status: fairly common to very common coastal migrant and visitor from September through April, with the push of migrants north over the ocean decreasing through May; scarce but annual inland, mostly in late fall and early winter.

Habitat: primarily coastal waters, including river mouths, bays, estuaries and the open ocean from surfline to just offshore.

Nesting: in northern Canada and Alaska.

Feeding: dives for small fish, crustaceans,

mollusks, insects and other invertebrates; prefers sandy or muddy bottoms in shallow water.

Voice: flight call is a guttural *gwowk*; hysterical rhythmic wails are given on breeding waters; seldom heard in northern California.

Similar Species: *Common Loon* (p. 40): much heavier, straighter bill; non-breeding plumage lacks the fine white spotting on the back; back of immature may be finely barred. *Pacific Loon* (p. 39): bill is held level; eye is indistinct against the all-dark face; non-breeding plumage lacks the fine white spotting on the back.

PACIFIC LOON
Gavia pacifica

The onrush of spring assumes a most kinetic incarnation in the immense northward passage of Pacific Loons. From mid-April through May, hundreds of thousands of these arctic breeders sprint the length of the northern California shore in large, open flocks that sometimes stretch for a mile or more. Sporting twin white racing stripes across the shoulders, a black throat and a lustrous, gray head and nape, this loon is a sight to see in breeding plumage. Birds returning southbound in fall are somberly attired and thus much less easily detected. • From October to March, flocks of Pacific Loons can be observed from select shore points; others retire to the Sea of Cortez for winter. Pacific Loons generally avoid upper-estuarine waters, preferring to raft on the open ocean beyond the surfline, often in the immediate lee of a headland or jetty.

non-breeding

ID: slender; thin, straight bill is held level; high, smoothly rounded crown. *Breeding:* gleaming silver crown and nape; finely white-streaked, black throat; dense white spangling on the shoulders. *Non-breeding:* dark gray above; white below; eye is set against a dark face; thin, black trim at the side of the neck; crown and nape are paler than the back; often has a very thin, dark 'chinstrap.'
Size: *L* 23–29 in; *W* 41–49 in.
Status: abundant migrant in April and May, with stragglers continuing north into mid-June; abundant but less obvious migrant from September into November; very rare late fall migrant at larger lakes and reservoirs inland; uncommon in winter all along coast, most sparingly northward; a few birds regularly summer on the ocean.
Habitat: coastal ocean waters, including harbors, bays and waters well away from shore.

Nesting: in northwestern Canada and Alaska.
Feeding: dives deeply for small fish; summer diet includes aquatic insects, crustaceans, mollusks and some plant material.
Voice: at breeding sites it issues a sharp *kwao* and a rising wail; seldom heard in northern California.
Similar Species: *Common Loon* (p. 40): larger; heavier bill; regular rows of white spots on the underparts in breeding plumage; dim white eye-arcs in non-breeding plumage. *Red-throated Loon* (p. 38): slimmer bill is tilted upward; plain upperparts and a reddish throat in breeding plumage; fine, white spotting on the back and the eye is surrounded by white in non-breeding plumage.

39

COMMON LOON

Gavia immer

Resting at attention or slipping phantom-like beneath the water, scattered Common Loons are a constant sight around estuaries, on larger waterways and along the open coast during all but the warmest months. These birds once summered on lakes in northeast California, but today they occur only as migrant and wintering nonbreeders. Most Common Loons favor salt water, ranging from nearshore open ocean to freshwater influences in estuaries. • Loons are well adapted to their aquatic lifestyle: these divers have nearly solid bones that make them less buoyant (most birds have hollow bones), and their feet are placed well back on their bodies for underwater propulsion. • An extinct loon precursor, the flightless, five-foot *Hesperornis*, caught prey in its heavily toothed bill during the Cretaceous period. • The word 'loon' is derived from the Scandinavian *lom*, meaning 'clumsy'—perhaps referring to this bird's awkwardness ashore.

non-breeding

ID: dagger-like bill; relatively short neck. *Breeding:* black, green-glossed head; stout, black bill; lacy, white 'necklace'; white underparts; white-on-black spotting on the upperparts; red eyes. *Non-breeding:* much duller plumage; dark, flat gray above; white below; dark eye is framed dimly by pale eye-arcs. *Juvenile:* back is fringed with white. *In flight:* long wings beat constantly; hunch-backed appearance; legs and feet trail behind the tail.

Size: L 28–35 in; W 47–57 in.

Status: uncommon to locally very common migrant and winter visitor; most numerous in March and April and from September to November; scattered birds in non-breeding plumage linger through summer; small numbers are expected inland on larger bodies of water in spring and fall (very local in winter).

Habitat: open water; nearshore ocean, estuaries, lakes, reservoirs and large rivers.

Nesting: in Canada and Alaska and spottily in the northern tier of the U.S.

Feeding: pursues fish underwater to depths of 180 ft; occasionally feeds on aquatic invertebrates and amphibians.

Voice: a brief tremolo; contact call is a long, simple wail; breeding notes are soft, short hoots; male utters an undulating, complex 'yodel.'

Similar Species: *Red-throated Loon* (p. 38): smaller; thinner bill is held upward; white extends from the throat to the chin and ear region in non-breeding plumage. *Pacific Loon* (p. 39): more smoothly rounded crown; slimmer bill; gleaming silver crown in breeding plumage; eye is indistinct against the dark face; usually shows a faint 'chinstrap' in non-breeding plumage.

PIED-BILLED GREBE
Podilymbus podiceps

Pied-billed Grebes are common and widespread in North America, but they are not always easy to find. Pied-bills are generally secretive and inconspicuous, and they most often hide behind the shady, overgrown, protective cover of their marshland habitat. This grebe's boisterous call is an integral part of any wetland ensemble, and hearing it may be your only clue that a Pied-bill is nearby. When frightened by an intruder, this bird will often use stealthy submarine tactics by slowly submerging, so that only its bill and eyes remain abovewater. • Only locally numerous in summer, a fall influx brings many of these night-migratory birds to northern California's ponds, lakes and estuarine waters. Pied-billed Grebes assemble in loose concentrations at preferred feeding sites along lakeshores or in the sheltered sections of bays. • Grebes' individually lobed toes, extreme hindward placement of the legs and aquatic nesting behavior suggests that these birds descend from ancestors that pursued similar life-histories in habitats much like today's.

breeding

ID: small and squat; drab brown; short tail; outsized head and pale, laterally compressed 'chicken bill.' *Breeding:* black throat; black ring neatly divides the bill; narrow white eye ring; dark eyes. *Juvenile:* boldly striped.
Size: *L* 12–15 in.
Status: uncommon to locally common migrant and visitor from August to April; local, rare to locally uncommon breeder; occurs routinely at isolated bodies of water.
Habitat: *Breeding:* deep freshwater lakes, secluded pondshores, golf course reservoirs and overgrown mill ponds from sea level into lower mountains. *Non-breeding:* varied open and semi-open fresh and estuarine waters; kelp patches and eelgrass beds.
Nesting: in or at the margin of thick vegetation in lakes marshes; shallow saucer of wet and decaying plants is anchored to emergent vegetation; pair incubates 4–5 eggs and raises the striped young together; occasionally nests outside spring and summer.
Feeding: dives and submerges in pursuit of fish, amphibians, invertebrates and water plants; gleans seeds and insects from the water's surface.
Voice: seldom heard away from breeding sites; loud series of whoops: *kuk-kuk-kuk cow cow cow cowp cowp cowp.*
Similar Species: *Other grebes:* slender, stiletto-like bills; very dark underparts. *American Coot* (p. 133): larger; all-black body; chalky white bill and bill 'shield'; often grazes on land.

HORNED GREBE
Podiceps auritus

Beginner birders who scan expansive, open waters during fall, winter and early spring are sure to make acquaintance with Horned Grebes. These grebes are most numerous on estuaries and large reservoirs, but in migration they are indiscriminate, visiting nearly any sizable pond. • During most of their stay in northern California, they are nondescript, but as March turns to April, they assume a striking breeding plumage featuring deep colors and golden head ornaments. • Horned Grebes are common waterbirds of harbors, industrial waterfronts and shipping channels. Spending 90 percent of their lives on the water's surface, Horned Grebes are at risk from oil spills. • Grebes appear hunchbacked in flight: their wings beat hastily, their head is held low and their feet trail behind the tail. Because Horned Grebes migrate at night, however, they are infrequently seen in flight. • The Horned Grebe's scientific name, *auritus*, refers to the golden feather tufts, or 'horns,' that these grebes acquire in breeding plumage.

breeding

ID: small; straight, stubby bill; red eyes; flat crown. *Breeding:* rufous neck and flanks; black cheek and forehead; golden ear tufts ('horns'); black back; white underparts. *Non-breeding:* well-defined dark crown, hindneck and upperparts; white underparts.
Size: L 12–15 in.
Status: uncommon to locally very common from mid-October to early May; more numerous coastally, but small numbers appear widely inland.
Habitat: unspecialized in northern California; lakes, reservoirs, estuaries, sloughs and fast-flowing rivers; some may appear on nearshore open ocean.
Nesting: in western Canada and Alaska and spottily in north-central U.S.; also in the Old World.

Feeding: dives for small fish, crustaceans, insects and other aquatic or marine animals.
Voice: croaking and shrieking notes while breeding; rarely heard in northern California.
Similar Species: *Eared Grebe* (p. 44): slimmer neck; smaller head; slightly upturned lower mandible; black neck and breast in breeding plumage; dingier neck and mottled dark on the face in nonbreeding plumage. *Pied-billed Grebe* (p. 41): thicker bill usually has a black ring; drab brown body; bulbous head; thick, pale 'chicken bill.' *Other grebes:* larger; longer-necked; longer, dagger-like bills.

RED-NECKED GREBE
Podiceps grisegena

Scattered sparsely among various sharply patterned diving birds at harbor entrances are occasional Red-necked Grebes. Their middling size and obscure, dingy markings generally makes them a species well known only to birders. Occasional post-breeders returning in late summer are in largely showy condition. Western populations are both northerly breeders and winterers, and from early September to late April, only modest numbers of Red-necked Grebes ride the waves along the coastline of northern California. They favor lee waters around rocky coves, breakwaters and jetties, and the more exposed estuarine environments. Very few are encountered anywhere away from tidal waters or adjacent lagoons.

• The scientific name *grisegena* means 'gray cheek'—a distinctive field mark of this bird's winter plumage.

non-breeding

ID: large; thick, yellowish bill; long neck; heavy bill. *Breeding:* red neck; white cheek; black crown; yellow bill; dark eyes. *Non-breeding:* dingy neck; dusky cheek; pale crescent behind the ear; duller bill. *Immature:* lacks the crescent behind the ear.

Size: L 17–22 in.

Status: rare to locally uncommon migrant and visitor from late September to late April; a few appear by late July or linger into May; reasonably numerous in Humboldt and Del Norte counties, decreasing southward; rare elsewhere.

Habitat: inshore coastal waters, including bays, estuaries and harbors.

Nesting: in western Canada and Alaska and spottily in the northern U.S.

Feeding: dives for small fish, crustaceans and invertebrates; also eats amphibians; gleans the water's surface in summer.

Voice: breeders give excited, braying calls; rarely heard in northern California.

Similar Species: the only grebe with a thick, yellowish bill. *Western Grebe* (p. 45) and *Clark's Grebe* (p. 46): lack any brown; slender, stiletto bills. *Horned Grebe* (p. 42): smaller; shorter bill; golden 'horns' in breeding plumage; white foreneck; all-white lower face in non-breeding plumage. *Eared Grebe* (p. 44): smaller; shorter bill; round head; black, thinner neck; golden 'ears' in breeding plumage. *Red-throated Loon* (p. 38): shorter neck; smaller head; slimmer bill is held upward.

EARED GREBE
Podiceps nigricollis

Inconspicuous, nearly tail-less waterbirds with thin, dark necks and tiny, thorn-like bills may just prove to be Eared Grebes. These birds carry their small, high-rounded heads craned slightly forward, suggesting an 'eager' look not commonly observed in grebes. In northern California, they are most often seen in their dingy, non-breeding plumage. In spring and summer, however, their heads are adorned with bright golden 'ears,' so they are easily spotted among the cattails and bulrush-lined coves of the large marshes they prefer during these seasons. • As do all grebes, Eared Grebes consume feathers—either old discarded feathers or ones plucked from their own bodies. The feathers pack the digestive tract, and it is thought that they may protect the stomach lining and intestines from sharp fish bones, or they might slow the passage of food, allowing more time for essential nutrients to be absorbed. • As many as 1 million Eared Grebes have gathered in fall on Mono Lake to fatten on brine shrimp.

breeding

ID: thin, all-dark bill with a slightly uptilted lower mandible. *Breeding:* thin, black neck, cheek, forehead and back; reddish flanks; gold ear tufts; slightly raised, black crown; red eyes. *Non-breeding:* dark back, head and neck, with some white on the foreneck, chin and behind the ear; fluffy white hind end.
Size: *L* 12–14 in.
Status: locally uncommon to abundant year-round; much less numerous in far northwestern California.
Habitat: *Breeding:* freshwater or slightly alkaline shallow lakes and wetlands with floating or emergent vegetation. *Non-breeding:* coastal waters, lagoons, open estuaries and interior lakes, reservoirs, sluggish rivers and sewage ponds.
Nesting: usually colonial; in thick vegetation in lake edges, ponds and marshes;

shallow, flimsy platform of floating wet and decaying plants is anchored to, or placed among, emergent vegetation; pair incubates the eggs and raises the young.
Feeding: makes shallow dives and gleans the surface for aquatic insects, crustaceans, mollusks, small fish and amphibians.
Voice: seldom heard away from breeding waters; mellow *poo-eee-chk* during courtship.
Similar Species: *Horned Grebe* (p. 42): straighter, evenly tapered bill with a small white tip; rufous neck in breeding plumage; white cheek and foreneck in winter plumage. *Pied-billed Grebe* (p. 41): thicker bill; mostly brown throughout. *Red-necked Grebe* (p. 43): longer, thicker, yellowish bill; drab brown throughout. *Other grebes:* distinctly larger, with larger bills.

WESTERN GREBE
Aechmophorus occidentalis

A medium-sized, black-and-white diving waterbird with a long, swan-like neck and 'letter-opener' bill seen anywhere on open water in northern California is likely to be either a Western Grebe or its look-alike 'sibling species,' the Clark's Grebe. • Western Grebes exhibit a spectacular courtship display in which pair members posture with bits of water plants in their bills, then arise from the surface and patter along frantically on parallel courses, heads held high, ultimately dropping back into the water. • Familiar on estuaries and lagoons during much of the year, most Western Grebes retreat to larger lakes and deepwater marshes of the interior for breeding. • *Aechmophorus* is derived from the Greek words *aichme* and *phoreus,* meaning 'spear bearer.'

ID: long, slender, yellowish-green bill (slightly longer in the male); dark crown obscures the eye at all seasons; red eyes; long, slender neck; black upperparts; white underparts. *Juvenile:* downy young are dark.
Size: L 20–24 in.
Status: common to abundant migrant and visitor from September to late April; locally common breeder from April to September; non-breeding individuals are variable in summer along the outer coast.
Habitat: *Breeding:* large lakes with dense areas of emergent vegetation or thick mats of floating aquatic plants. *Non-breeding:* almost any sizable, open or semi-open body of water; lakes, reservoirs, estuaries, sluggish rivers, lagoons and open seacoast up to several miles offshore; rafts of dozens or hundreds commonly assemble at favored sites.
Nesting: colonial; pair builds a floating nest of wet or decaying vegetation anchored to submerged plants; pair incubates 2–4 pale bluish-white eggs for about 24 days; young climb onto adult's back within minutes of hatching.
Feeding: dives for small fish, invertebrates and other aquatic or marine creatures.
Voice: shrill, brief, 2-noted *kreee-krreeet!*; frequently heard away from breeding grounds.
Similar Species: *Clark's Grebe* (p. 46): white around the eyes in breeding plumage; orange-yellow bill; short, thin, white line from the eye to the base of the bill. *Double-crested Cormorant* (p. 58): underparts are not clean white. *Other grebes:* smaller; shorter bills. *Loons* (pp. 38–40): bulkier; shorter necks; lack the greenish bill.

CLARK'S GREBE
Aechmophorus clarkii

Just when you think you are looking at a pair of Western Grebes, a second glance leaves you questioning your eyesight. Ornithologists have long recognized that Western Grebes come in two varieties: those whose eyes in summer are set against a low black crown, and those whose eyes are distinctly set against an encompassing white face. Birds of each form mate assortively, like with like, with occasional mixed-pair exceptions, so that, by and large, each variety behaves as a separate species, remaining reproductively isolated.
• Clark's Grebes look and act like Western Grebes and are most often found among them, both in summer and winter. Overlapping ranges and similar habitat preferences also add to the challenge of distinguishing between Clark's and Westerns. • Clark's Grebe was named in honor of John Henry Clark, a mathematician, surveyor and successful bird collector who procured the first scientific specimen for science in 1858.

ID: long, slender, yellow-orange bill (slightly longer in the male); long, slender neck; white on the face extends up to surround the red eyes; black upperparts; white underparts. *Juvenile:* downy young are whitish.
Size: L 20–23 in.
Status: rare to locally common migrant and visitor from September to late April; uncommon to fairly common local breeder from April to September.
Habitat: *Breeding:* large lakes with dense areas of emergent vegetation or thick mats of floating aquatic plants. *Non-breeding:* any sizable, open or semi-open body of water; sluggish rivers, lagoons and open seacoast up to several miles offshore; rafts of dozens or hundreds commonly assemble at favored sites.

Nesting: colonial; pair builds a floating nest of wet or decaying vegetation that is anchored to submerged plants; pair incubates 2–4 pale bluish-white eggs for about 24 days; young climb onto adult's back within minutes of hatching.
Feeding: dives for small fish, invertebrates and other aquatic or marine creatures.
Voice: ascending, shrill single note: *kreek!*; frequently heard away from breeding waters.
Similar Species: *Western Grebe* (p. 45): black on the face extends down to surround the red eyes; greenish-yellow bill; short, thin, line from the eye to the base of the bill is never white. *Double-crested Cormorant* (p. 58): underparts are not clean white. *Other grebes:* smaller; shorter bills. *Loons* (pp. 38–40): bulkier; shorter necks.

BLACK-FOOTED ALBATROSS
Phoebastria nigripes

Albatrosses are the greatest winged creatures of Earth's greatest wilderness. Ranging over hundreds of miles of open ocean on foraging trips between visits to the nest—and surely tens of thousands of miles prior to even reaching breeding age—they endure the toughest storms, putting to shame the rigors of the human commute. • Black-footed Albatrosses visit northern California waters throughout the year in varying numbers. They are most common over the mid-continental shelf and seaward and are spotted from the mainland regularly only around Monterey Bay. Occasional birds may be seen from shore elsewhere with perserverance and luck. • Like other albatrosses, Black-footeds have a well-developed sense of smell, so they are able to locate food over great distances. They often follow fishing vessels, consuming the remains of discarded fish and other ocean creatures caught in fishing nets. • Their extremely long, slender wings are not built for flapping: these birds glide in strong ocean wind currents, flying for long periods without more than an infrequent deep dip of the wings. • Members of this species routinely live for decades if they are able to avoid potentially life-threatening drift nets and longlines. International high-seas fisheries are a great threat to many North Pacific seabirds, and many albatrosses are killed each year.

ID: ashy brown overall; long, narrow wings; black feet; massive, dark bill; white on the face at the base of the bill and under the eye; white crescent at the base of the tail; undertail coverts may be white; older birds develop greater amounts of white, occasionally extending to the underparts.
Size: L 27–29 in; W 80 in.
Status: rare to locally common year-round; most numerous from May to August.
Habitat: open ocean, except during breeding.
Nesting: on Hawaiian Islands and on islands off Japan.

Feeding: snatches fish, squid and carrion from the water's surface; plunges to just beneath the surface; young are fed by regurgitation.
Voice: generally silent, but may groan, shriek or squawk.
Similar Species: *Laysan Albatross*: dark back; white underparts. *Immature Short-tailed Albatross*: larger; much heavier bubble-gum pink bill. *Dark shearwaters* and *dark-morph Northern Fulmar* (p. 48): smaller; smaller bills; frequent, rapid wingbeats.

NORTHERN FULMAR
Fulmarus glacialis

I f it's the size of a shearwater, flies like a shearwater and is built like a shearwater, then it may just be a fulmar—other than a stubby, greenish-yellow bill, the Northern Fulmar shares many physical attributes with the closely related shearwaters. • Slim-winged but thick-necked and bull-headed, the Northern Fulmar ranges into cooler North Pacific waters during much of the year, returning to arctic and subarctic nesting cliffs in summer. Next to the Sooty Shearwater, it is the 'tubenose' most frequently and widely seen from land, most often in fall and early winter. This scavenger can often be found following fishing vessels, but it only occasionally enters harbors and coastal piers in search of food scraps and refuse. Specialized for cutting through the wild winds of open ocean expanses, fulmars are fast, swift flyers, and a telescope may be needed to scan for them well beyond the surfline.

• Fulmars occur in a spectrum of 'color morphs,' from all-dark to generally all-pale. The dark morph predominates in northern California. • 'Fulmar' is derived from Old Norse words meaning 'foul gull'—when disturbed, fulmars have a nasty habit of spewing foul-smelling fish oil.

light morph

dark morph

ID: short, pale yellow, tubed bill; thick neck; stubby tail; long, tapered wings; pale flash at the base of the primaries. *Dark morph:* deep bluish-gray throughout, except for paler flight feathers. *Light morph:* whitish head and underparts; bluish-gray upperparts (many birds are intermediate). *In flight:* alternates rapid, stiff-winged flapping with graceful glides low over waves.
Size: *L* 17–20 in; *W* 42 in.
Status: uncommon to locally abundant winter visitor; irregular and rare in spring and summer.
Habitat: favors open ocean waters over upwellings and along outer continental shelf; rarely approaches coastline, entering harbors and bays; nests on sea cliffs.
Nesting: on arctic and subarctic islands.

Feeding: seizes almost any edible item while swimming; makes shallow plunges beneath the water's surface; diet includes fish, squid, invertebrates, carrion and marine fishery by-catch.
Voice: generally silent; low quacking call may be given when competing for food.
Similar Species: *Shearwaters* (pp. 49–51): more slender bills; less heavy heads and necks. *Albatrosses* (p. 47): much larger; longer, heavier bills; do not flap wings rapidly. *Gulls* (pp. 171–81): slimmer neck and body; slower, more consistent and less stiff wingbeats.

PINK-FOOTED SHEARWATER

Puffinus creatopus

Shearwaters are long-winged seabirds that fly with shallow, rapid wingbeats and stiff-winged glides. Outside the breeding season, Pink-footed Shearwaters are birds of the open ocean and are generally seen from land only infrequently. Among the swarms of other shearwaters encountered at sea from April to November, small numbers of Pink-footed Shearwaters may be seen—they are best spotted from strategic coastal points with the aid of a telescope. • Once their nesting duties are complete, Pink-foots migrate north along the continental shelf in search of large schools of fish and squid. As is true with other members of the shearwater family, Pink-foots assemble with astonishing quickness at any food source. They will closely approach a boat if food of any description is tossed overboard.

ID: slender, pinkish bill with a black, hooked tip; pink legs; dark brown above; whitish below; white underparts with dark mottling on the sides, wing linings and the tip of the undertail coverts.
Size: L 19–20 in; W 43 in.
Status: uncommon to common non-breeding visitor from March to November; very rare from December to March.
Habitat: open ocean, usually well out over the continental shelf; uncommon within several miles of shore.
Nesting: on offshore islands of Chile.
Feeding: plunges into the water or dives shallowly; swims underwater over short distances; gleans from the surface; fish, squid and crustaceans probably form the bulk of the diet.

Voice: generally silent; birds competing for food may make quarrelsome noises.
Similar Species: *Light-morph Northern Fulmar* (p. 48): stout, greenish bill; stouter body; unmarked white undersides and head. *Buller's Shearwater:* all-black bill; gray-and-black upperwing pattern; more gleaming, thoroughly white underparts, especially the narrow-bordered underwing. *Black-vented Shearwater* (p. 51): smaller; all-dark bill is smaller; dark undertail coverts; more rapid wing-beats. *Flesh-footed Shearwater* and *Sooty Shearwater* (p. 50): entirely dark bodies.

SOOTY SHEARWATER

Puffinus griseus

Each summer, Sooty Shearwaters arrive from breeding islands in the Southern Hemisphere in numbers beyond estimation. During spring and fall, scattered individuals are almost constantly in sight on the open ocean, and concentrations may include tens of thousands. • Various seabird families, including albatrosses, shearwaters and storm-petrels, are categorized broadly as 'tubenoses': they all have external tubular nostrils, hooked bills and only come ashore to breed. The Sooty Shearwater is the 'tubenose' most frequently seen from land, and it is most abundant along the northern California coast from May through September, although a telescope may be needed to scan well beyond the surfline. Large concentrations of fish often draw these birds closer to land—the presence of schooling fish often results in a multi-species feeding frenzy that includes Sooties and other seabirds. Sooties dominate most mixed-seabird foraging flocks over the continental shelf, with scarcer species occurring in their midst. To recognize the uncommon shearwaters at a distance with assurance, one must first get to the know the Sooty.

ID: all-dark brown body; slender, black bill; silvery flash in the underwing linings.
Size: L 16–18 in; W 40 in.
Status: uncommon to abundant post-breeding visitor from April to November; very rare to rare from December to March.
Habitat: open ocean; concentrates at upwellings and current edges along the continental shelf.
Nesting: on islands off New Zealand, Australia and southern South America.
Feeding: gleans the water's surface or snatches items from below; often enters the water in a shallow dive; eats mostly fish, squid and crustaceans; inspects passing vessels, quickly forming concentrations if food is available.

Voice: generally silent; occasionally utters quarrelsome calls when competing for food.
Similar Species: *Short-tailed Shearwater:* slightly smaller; shorter bill; higher forehead; touch of pale on the throat; more uniformly colored underwings. *Flesh-footed Shearwater:* larger; black-tipped, pinkish bill; pale pinkish legs and feet; slower wing-beats; uniformly dark under-wings. *Dark-morph Northern Fulmar (p. 48):* thick, greenish-yellow bill; dark wing linings. *Other shearwaters:* variably pale underparts.

BLACK-VENTED SHEARWATER
Puffinus opisthomelas

The graceful Black-vented Shearwaters that appear in varying numbers along the California coast each fall and winter originate in Mexico. Following nesting, a portion of the population disperses northward within the warm Davidson Current, sometimes crowding shallows shortly beyond the surf zone by the hundreds or, in southern California, by the thousands. Although most tubenoses forage well out at sea, these pint-sized shearwaters are seldom encountered over truly deep water, remaining within several miles of land. Because of this, they may readily be observed from shore points. They are distinctly most numerous during El Niño events, when they follow warmer-than-average ocean water well northward. El Niño years of 1891 and 1895 took Black-vented Shearwaters as far north as British Columbia. During years when near-shore ocean water is cooler than average, this species may be found only in small numbers on Monterey Bay, or it may even remain absent. • The comparatively small size of this petite shearwater is suggested at a distance by its noticeably rapid wingbeats. Given the general similarity in size, shape and speed of wingbeats, an over-eager or inexperienced birder may misidentify a distant flying Common Murre as a Black-vented Shearwater. Shearwaters cruise the waves dreamily in slow-moving, open flocks, appearing forever married to the ocean surface. Murres spotted in prolonged flight are generally headed somewhere in a big hurry, flying flat-out and paying no attention to the waves.

ID: dark brown upperparts, including most of the head; slim, dark bill; pale breast with variably mottled sides; pale belly; blackish undertail coverts.
Size: *L* 13–14 in; *W* 34 in.
Status: absent to abundant, irregular post-breeding visitor along outer coast from September to December.
Habitat: open ocean over the continental shelf; often detected in flocks from shore points or from boats within several miles of land.
Nesting: on islands off the west coast of Mexico.
Feeding: takes prey by plunging to just beneath the surface or while swimming; small fish, crustaceans and squid probably form the bulk of the diet.

Voice: generally silent at sea, although argumentative calls may be heard from foraging flocks.
Similar Species: *Pink-footed Shearwater* (p.49): larger; black-tipped, pink bill; slower, less-hectic wingbeats. *Light-morph Northern Fulmar* (p. 48): larger; stouter body; white flash at the base of the primaries; thick, yellowish bill. *Buller's Shearwater:* silvery-white underparts; dark primaries and coverts above; underwings have a neat, thin, black margin. *Flesh-footed, Short-tailed* and *Sooty* (p. 50) *shearwaters:* all-dark bodies.

FORK-TAILED STORM-PETREL

Oceanodroma furcata

Fork-tailed Storm-Petrels typify the smaller species of tubenoses in their secretive nesting strategy. To minimize predation, pairs place their single egg at the end of a burrow that is excavated either by the storm-petrel pair or by a previous occupant. The adults maintain a strictly nocturnal schedule of incubation shift changes and make nightly visits with food for the growing nestling. • Dispersing miles out to sea while foraging, Fork-tails are encountered from boats only occasionally. In some years, small numbers appear near shore in April and May regardless of the severity of weather, closely approaching beaches, jetties and harbor piers. They appear to be irregularly distributed at sea and prefer colder water over seamounts and banks. • Fork-tails are northern-nesting birds whose southernmost colonies are on sea islands and 'bird rocks' along the coast of Del Norte and Humboldt counties. A few may breed on the Farallon Islands or elsewhere among dense colonies of Leach's and Ashy storm-petrels.

ID: only pale-bodied storm-petrel in the region; dark eye patch; bluish-gray upperparts; gray underparts, with darker wing linings; forked tail. *In flight:* flutters low across the ocean surface with rapid, comparatively shallow wingbeats interspersed with brief glides.
Size: L 8–9 in.
Status: rare to uncommon year-round resident; rarer southward; detected more frequently, and in larger numbers, in some years than in others.
Habitat: prefers cold regions of open ocean, occuring from nearshore waters to beyond the continental shelf; nests on off-shore islands with sufficient soil, grass or shrub cover.
Nesting: colonial; may use a rock crevice or an old burrow created by other species;

burrow may have many side tunnels with additional nest chambers; pair incubates 1 white egg with dark terminal dots for 37–68 days; colonies are active exclusively at night.
Feeding: skims or snatches items from the surface while hovering; may drop briefly onto the water or glean and pick while swimming; diet consists of small fish, crustaceans and floating natural oils.
Voice: generally silent.
Similar Species: *Other storm-petrels*: much darker. *Phalaropes* (pp. 166–68): flashing, white wing stripes; needle-like bills.

ASHY STORM-PETREL

Oceanodroma homochroa

One can imagine that if the Earth had far fewer oceanic islands, there would surely be far fewer species of seabirds. In particular, the great clan of the 'tubenosed swimmers' has diverged and speciated largely through the dramatic isolation enforced by nesting on islands. • Nearly all of the fewer than 10,000 Ashy Storm-Petrels in the world nest on islands off the coast of California, except a few on Los Coronados Islands along the extreme northern coast of western Mexico. During September and October, a larger percentage of the world population of Ashy Storm-Petrels concentrates on Monterey Bay than that of any other bird species. On boats chartered especially for the purpose, birders from across North America and elsewhere crowd the rails to revel in the annual fall spectacle of thousands of storm-petrels gathered above the rims of the Monterey Submarine Canyon.

ID: dark gray-brown overall; dark rump; forked tail. *In flight:* direct flight with shallow wingstrokes.

Size: *L* 8 in.

Status: locally abundant summer breeder and fall visitor from late April through October; most birds concentrate on Monterey Bay in late summer and fall; seldom detected in winter, possibly dispersing offshore.

Habitat: open ocean; in summer, prefers the cooler waters of the California Current just beyond the edge of the continental shelf.

Nesting: colonial; in an unlined natural cavity, crevice or disused burrow excavated by other species; pair incubates 1 white egg with faint reddish-brown dots for about 45 days; single nestling is fed by regurgitation.

Feeding: hovers over or skims along the water's surface to snatch food; may glean while swimming; diet is probably composed of aquatic crustaceans and small fish.

Voice: generally silent when at sea; at night, issues twittering, trilling calls at the nest.

Similar Species: *Black Storm-Petrel* (p. 54): slightly larger and blacker; longer, more pointed wings; darker wing linings. *Leach's Storm-Petrel*: whitish rump patch; erratic flight. *Fork-tailed Storm-Petrel* (p. 52): paler gray, with contrasting, dark wing linings. *Least Storm-Petrel*: smaller; blacker; wedge-shaped tail; deeper wingstrokes.

BLACK STORM-PETREL

Oceanodroma melania

Black Storm-Petrels are the largest of the dark storm-petrels found in ocean waters along the northern California coast. They nest on islands off the coast of Baja California and disperse to outlying waters following the breeding season. During years of warmer weather, they range farther north, but they are still essentially unknown from Mendocino County northward. Most birders in the northern half of California will encounter Black Storm-Petrels only during the course of birding trips on Monterey Bay. • Black Storm-Petrels occur either mixed among other species of storm-petrels or in groups of their own kind. They may be distinguished from the other storm-petrels found in the region by their black coloration, their size and their slow, graceful flight style.

ID: black overall; long, forked tail; tan carpal bars. *In flight:* direct flight with deep wingstrokes that carry the wings above the horizontal.

Size: L 9 in.

Status: rare to locally abundant post-breeding visitor from August to October; a few may remain into early winter; most frequently seen on Monterey Bay; rare northward; accidental inland.

Habitat: open ocean; prefers warm waters over the continental shelf; exceptional in harbors.

Nesting: on rocky islands off both sides of Baja California and at one site off southern California.

Feeding: snatches food from the water's surface while hovering or fluttering; diet is poorly known; may rely on pelagic crustaceans and small fish.

Voice: generally silent at sea; issues staccato calls when flying over the colony; trilling call is given from within the nest cavity.

Similar Species: *Ashy Storm-Petrel* (p. 53): slightly smaller; browner; flies with shallow, fluttery wingbeats. *Leach's Storm-Petrel:* northern California form has a smudgily divided white rump; distinctive, erratic flight. *Fork-tailed Storm-Petrel* (p. 52): smaller; paler; dark wing linings contrast with a much paler body and wings. *Least Storm-Petrel:* much smaller; shorter tail.

AMERICAN WHITE PELICAN
Pelecanus erythrorhynchos

The two species of pelicans that occur in North America are massive waterbirds that are dramatically adapted for specialized feeding. American White Pelicans swim through schools of small fish, plunging their bills beneath the surface and scooping out one or several fish. The pelicans lift their bills from the water, keeping the fish within the flexible pouch as water is drained out before they swallow their prey. Members of flocks often work together to herd schools of fish into the shallows, where each bird then earns the reward of teamwork. • White Pelicans are distributed much differently than are Brown Pelicans: they breed in highly disjunct colonies on undisturbed sandy islands in expansive lakes and deep-water marshes. In northern California, the two species are regularly seen together only around San Francisco Bay. • White Pelicans may appear ungainly, but on the wing they glide and soar efficiently. Flocks may rise to several thousand feet on thermals, remaining undetected until their massed shadows are seen sweeping across the ground below.

non-breeding

ID: huge, white waterbird; massive, yellow-orange bill; orange throat patch; extensive black in the wings; short, white tail; naked, orange skin patch around the eyes. *Breeding:* small, keeled, upright plate develops on the upper mandible; pale yellow crest on the back of the head. *Immature:* grayish bill, hindcrown and throat patch; brown instead of black on the wings.
Size: L 54–70 in; W 8–9 1/2 ft.
Status: locally fairly common to abundant migrant and visitor from late August to April; very local breeder from April to September.
Habitat: *Breeding:* large interior lakes, including Clear Lake. *Winter:* Central Valley lakes, large coastal bays and lagoons. *In migration:* lakes, rivers and large ponds.

Nesting: colonial; on bare, low-lying islands; nest scrape is either lined with pebbles and debris or is completely unlined; 2 eggs hatch asynchronously, after approximately 33 days; young are born naked and helpless.
Feeding: dips along the water's surface for small fish and amphibians; small groups of pelicans often feed cooperatively by herding fish into schools.
Voice: generally quiet.

Similar Species: *Snow Goose* (p. 71): much smaller; smaller bill; does not flap-and-glide. *Tundra Swan* (p. 75) and *Trumpeter Swan:* lack the white wing tips; longer, thinner necks.

BROWN PELICAN
Pelecanus occidentalis

Just about everyone sees Brown Pelicans where they are numerous. They are among the most conspicuous waterbirds, perching on rocks and pilings or coursing the troughs in single file. Much unlike American White Pelicans, they are a strictly coastal species. Despite their abundance and their ease of flight, they are seldom encountered away from marine or intertidal habitats in northern California. • Prior to a big decline in the 1950s and 1960s caused by DDT-related reproductive failure, they nested north to Point Lobos, Monterey County. Populations recovered strongly after a domestic ban on most persistent pesticides was enacted in 1972, but nearly all of the Brown Pelicans visiting northern California still originate in Mexico. • After breeding each year, as many as 20,000 Brown Pelicans move northward, ultimately spending summer and early fall in estuaries, at river mouths and along the open seacoast. Because they traverse the surf zone for the entire length of the state, a great many people are able to savor the sheer spectacle of pelicans. When summer has become just a memory, the northward flow of pelicans begins to reverse itself—the frequent lines of subtropical wanderers then move mostly back toward Mexico.

breeding

ID: grayish-brown body; very large bill. *Non-breeding:* white neck; head is washed with yellow; pale yellowish pouch. *Breeding:* yellow head; white foreneck; dark brown hindneck; red pouch. *1st-year immature:* uniformly dusky; buff-tipped head and neck contrast with the pale underparts; lacks the upperwing contrast of the adult; requires several years to reach maturity.
Size: *L* 48 in; *W* 84 in.
Status: common to locally abundant non-breeding visitor year-round; rarest from mid-December to early June, with numbers depending on food and water temperatures.
Habitat: coastal and estuarine waters; ranges over the continental shelf in some areas; visits offshore islands; roosts on protected islets, sea stacks, sandbars and piers.
Nesting: in southern California, Mexico, southeastern U.S. and northern South America.
Feeding: forages almost exclusively for fish, which are caught by diving headfirst into the water from heights of up to 60 ft; fish are held in the flexible pouch until the water is drained; concentrations feeding over extensive schools of fish commonly number in the hundreds.
Voice: generally silent.
Similar Species: *American White Pelican* (p. 55): all-white body; extensive black in the wings.

BRANDT'S CORMORANT

Phalacrocorax penicillatus

Three species of cormorants occur throughout the year along the northern California coast. The two most common species, the Brandt's and the Pelagic, often nest and forage in proximity to each other at 'bird rocks,' around mainland promontories and on the open ocean nearshore. A division of breeding habitat is obvious: Brandt's Cormorants nest in expansive colonies on flat or sloping ground; Pelagic Cormorants scatter in pairs among the ledges and shallow nooks found here and there on the cliffs and pinnacles. • Although colonies of Brandt's Cormorants may be separated by miles of coastline, breeding adults scatter widely to the north and south while feeding, so they dot the ocean at low densities far from the nearest nest site. They feed from within the surf zone to several miles offshore, regularly assembling in flocks in and around harbor entrances and in the lee waters of jetties and headlands.

breeding

ID: dark throughout; pale brown feathers on the throat below the dull blue pouch; heavy bill; green eyes. *Breeding:* brighter blue throat pouch; remarkably long, fine, white plumes extending from the neck and upper back (visible only at close range). *Immature:* dark, deep brown overall; slightly paler upper breast. *In flight:* 'long and lean,' with an outstretched neck; seldom glides or flies high in the sky.

Size: *L* 30–35 in; *W* 48 in.

Status: locally uncommon to abundant year-round resident; numbers withdraw from the northern coast in winter; forages to several miles offshore, occasionally over the continental shelf; almost unknown inland.

Habitat: flat or sloping, barren areas on offshore islands, islets, sea stacks and protected promontories are preferred for nesting; roosts on offshore rocks, reefs and breakwaters.

Nesting: colonial; pair builds a nest of eelgrass or seaweed, cemented by droppings; pair incubates 4 blue to whitish eggs; eggs are often nest-stained.

Feeding: forages underwater; may dive more than 150 ft below the surface; eats mostly fish; also takes some crabs and shrimp.

Voice: generally silent; may give deep, low grunts and croaks at the nesting colony.

Similar Species: *Double-crested Cormorant* (p. 58): proportionally larger head; conspicuous yellowish or yellow-orange throat pouch; flies with a kinked neck, often high in the sky; regularly found inland. *Pelagic Cormorant* (p. 59): smaller; proportionally smaller head; thinner neck and bill; white patches on the flanks in breeding season. *Loons* (pp. 38–40): generally have pale underparts and shorter, thicker necks; lack the hooked bill.

DOUBLE-CRESTED CORMORANT

Phalacrocorax auritus

Double-crested Cormorants are a familiar sight at most bodies of water in northern California. Whether swimming or diving, loafing and drying their wings atop pilings or in trees, or flying past, this is a bird known to boaters, beachcombers and birders alike. • In response to cleaner water, diverse inland fisheries, reduced use of persistent pesticides and diminished persecution, Double-crested Cormorants have rebounded dramatically in North America within the past two decades. • Unlike most water birds, cormorants lack the ability to waterproof their feathers, and they are often observed with their wings partially spread in an attempt to dry their flight feathers. Although they may seem to be at a disadvantage, water-logged feathers actually help their diving ability by decreasing their buoyancy. The cormorant's long, rudder-like tail, sealed nostrils and excellent underwater vision also contribute to the success of its aquatic lifestyle.

breeding

ID: black overall; pale yellowish to yellow-orange throat pouch; thin bill is hooked at the tip; long tail and neck; green eyes. *Breeding:* throat pouch becomes intense orange-yellow; fine, white plumes trail from the eyebrows. *Immature:* brownish-tinged upperparts; dingy whitish throat and breast. *In flight:* kinked neck; choppy wing-beats, broken by brief glides; flies alone or in ragged lines, often high in the sky.
Size: L 26–32 in; W 52 in.
Status: fairly common year-round resident; fall and winter visitors increase coastal populations; uncommon to locally abundant breeder from April to September; regularly appears on lakes and rivers well removed from nest sites; immatures may over-summer on nearly any larger body of water.
Habitat: *Summer:* interior wetlands, lakes, rivers and reservoirs; offshore islands and various coastal habitats. *Winter:* retreats from colder areas, concentrates on lowland and near-coastal waters; uncommon along most of open coast.

Nesting: colonial; nest is built on a low-lying island, on a sea stack, in an extensive marsh or high in a tree; nest platform is made of sticks, any available vegetation and guano; may nest in loose association with other waterbirds.
Feeding: long underwater dives of up to 30 ft; feeds on fish or, less often, amphibians and invertebrates; young are fed by regurgitation.
Voice: generally quiet; occasionally grunts or croaks.
Similar Species: *Brandt's Cormorant* (p. 57): all-black bill; lacks the conspicuous yellow throat patch; holds bill nearly level while swimming; flies with its neck out-stretched. *Pelagic Cormorant* (p. 59): smaller; slimmer; much thinner, all-black bill; flies with a straight neck; white flank patches and small red throat patch in breeding plumage. *Common Loon* (p. 40): paler beneath; shorter neck; dagger bill lacks the hooked tip.

PELAGIC CORMORANT

Phalacrocorax pelagicus

Despite its name, the Pelagic Cormorant leaves the open ocean beyond the turbulent nearshore zone to its larger neighbor, the Brandt's Cormorant. The Pelagic is the smallest West Coast cormorant, a sleek black waterbird shimmering with a subtle iridescent gloss at close range. • These birds lay their eggs on narrow cliff ledges in precarious nests of seaweed and guano. Because cliffs with nest ledges occur widely along the mainland shore as well as around the edges of 'bird rocks,' nesting Pelagic Cormorants are a bit more thoroughly distributed along the immediate coast than are Brandt's. • Like their close relatives, the pelicans, cormorants have a naked, extensible throat pouch and fully webbed feet. During midday heat, cormorants may regulate their body temperature by passing cooling air across the blood vessels of the throat in a 'panting' behavior called gular fluttering. • Much unlike the more sociable Double-crested and Brandt's cormorants, Pelagics are almost never seen flying in lines or flocks.

breeding

ID: sleek body; dark plumage; small head; long tail. *Breeding:* white flank patches; inconspicuous red throat pouch. *In flight:* straight neck.
Size: L 25–28 in; W 39 in.
Status: fairly common year-round resident.
Habitat: forages on the ocean within a mile of shore, visiting the lower reaches of estuaries and harbors; nests on narrow cliff ledges along the coast and offshore islands; roosts on rocks, reefs, breakwaters, piers, cliffs and islets.
Nesting: colonial; on a narrow cliff ledge or flat rock; pair builds a nest of grass, seaweed and moss, often including sticks; nests are usually reused in subsequent years; pair incubates 3–5 bluish-white eggs for 26–37 days.
Feeding: forages while swimming underwater; fish form the bulk of the diet; also takes shrimp, crabs, amphipods, marine worms and some algae; known to reach food 120 ft below the water's surface.
Voice: generally silent; may give groans at the nesting colony.

Similar Species:
Double-crested Cormorant (p. 58): larger; heavier bill; conspicuous, pale yellowish to yellow-orange throat pouch; neck is kinked in flight. *Brandt's Cormorant* (p. 57): larger; heavier bill; relatively short tail. *Loons* (pp. 38–40): shorter necks; pale underparts; bills lack the hooked tip.

AMERICAN BITTERN

Botaurus lentiginosus

The American Bittern's deep, booming call is as characteristic of a spring marsh as the sounds of croaking frogs. • When approached by an intruder, this bird's first reaction is to freeze. Facing danger, its bill points skyward and its longitudinal brown streaking blends well with its vegetated surroundings. An American Bittern will always face an intruder, and it moves imperceptibly to keep its streaked breast toward the danger. Some intruders simply pass by without noticing the cryptic bird. An American Bittern will adopt this frozen stance even if it is encountered in an open area—it is apparently unaware that a lack of cover betrays its presence!

ID: large, stocky heron; brown upperparts; brown streaking from the chin down through the breast; straight, stout bill; noticeable black 'whisker'; yellow legs and feet; dark brown outer wings. *Immature*: lacks the longitudinal streaking through the breast.
Size: *L* 23–27 in; *W* 42 in.
Status: rare to uncommon year-round resident; many interior breeders move southward or to coastal locations for winter; absent or only occasional across large areas of inadequate habitat.
Habitat: quality freshwater and brackish saltwater marshes with tall, dense, emergent grasses, sedges, bulrushes, cattails and tules; migrants may visit isolated or marginal habitats, such as vernal pools, flooded ditches, wet fields, saltmarshes, dune hollows and sewage ponds.
Nesting: singly; above waterline in dense cattail and bulrush marshes; nest platform is made of grass, sedges and dead reeds; nest often has separate entrance and exit paths; female incubates 4–5 eggs over about 28 days.
Feeding: patient stand-and-wait predator; stabs for small fish, amphibians and aquatic invertebrates; active in deep twilight as well as during the day.
Voice: slow, resonant, repetitive *coom-pa-loonk* or *plum pudding*, given in steady series followed by long pauses; often heard at night.
Similar Species: *Least Bittern*: very much smaller; black crown; pale brown inner wing linings. *Black-crowned Night-Heron* (p. 66) and *Green Heron* (p. 65): immatures lack the black streak from the bill to the shoulder.

GREAT BLUE HERON

Ardea herodias

Great Blue Herons have been described, more poetically than accurately, as 'solitary sentinels' or as 'sentries.' In truth, such anthropomorphic license misrepresents them. Even a passing observation of herons will reveal that each bird appears to go about life on its own, concerned with the welfare of none but itself. • Great Blue Herons are found across most of temperate North America. They are widespread, given to visiting even the smallest and most isolated patches of habitat in a territory. Because they are commonly seen along rivers, lakeshores, piers and other watery edge habitats visited by people, they are seen more closely and more frequently by more people than any other species of heron. • Great Blues are persistently misnamed 'cranes' by the untutored, but their slow-motion movements, preference for feeding individually and lack of fluffy, bunched tertials hanging over the tail mark them as something other than cranes. These large wetland birds appear inexpert when lurching heavily into the air, but once aloft they may travel long distances with seeming ease.

breeding

ID: large, rangy, blue-gray bird; tallest bird widely seen in northern California; long, flexible neck; long, dark legs; long, straight, dagger-like, yellow bill; blue-gray wing coverts and back; chestnut thighs. *Breeding*: colors are more intense; thin, pointed plumes extend from the crown and throat. *In flight*: head and upper neck fold back over the shoulders; legs and big, bunched feet extend beyond the tail; deep, lazy-looking wingstrokes.
Size: *L* 50–54 in; *W* 72 in.
Status: uncommon to fairly common resident; retreats from districts where open water is lacking in winter.
Habitat: occurs widely in freshwater and calm-water intertidal habitats of nearly every description.
Nesting: colonial; flimsy to elaborate stick and twig platform is built in a tree, snag, tall bush or marsh vegetation and can be up to 4 ft in diameter; pair incubates 3–5 eggs for 28 days.

Feeding: waits for prey to move within striking range or slowly stalks; impales items with its bill; takes fish, amphibians, reptiles, small mammals, small birds and invertebrates; occasionally scavenges carrion, such as fish remains discarded on docks.
Voice: generally silent; when disturbed it utters a deep, harsh, measured *fraank, fraank, fraank* when taking flight; nestlings enliven larger colonies with constant rhythmic notes.
Similar Species: *Adult Black-crowned Night-Heron* (p. 66): much smaller and stockier; short neck; black crown and back. *Sandhill Crane* (p. 134): tall and gray, but with a red cap and a fluff of bunched tertials hanging over the tail; almost always seen in pairs or social flocks.

GREAT EGRET

Ardea alba

Egrets are a group of herons that are generally white, or nearly so, and are of small to medium-large size. During the breeding season, they develop characteristic ornamental plumes, and the color of the face and leg skin intensifies. • Shores and shallows nearly throughout the tropical and temperate regions of the world are graced by the Great Egret's gleaming whiteness. These fish-eaters forage by day, and where they are numerous, they gather in large flocks at sunset to return to communal, nighttime roosting sites in undisturbed stands of trees. Individuals may commute many miles each day in provisioning their chicks with regurgitated meals. • Over a century ago, Great Egrets and a host of other showy, colonial-nesting waterbirds were nearly decimated in North America because their plumes were widely used to decorate women's hats. Outrage over the destruction of adults—and the consequent starvation of dependent nestlings—helped initiate a change in public opinion and conservation legislation. Although once essentially extirpated as a breeding bird in California, Great Egrets rebounded under protection.

breeding

ID: slender, long-necked, white heron; yellow-orange, dagger-like bill; long, all-black legs; long neck; short tail. *Breeding:* elegant, white plumes trail from the throat and rump; small green patch develops between the base of the bill and the eyes. *In flight:* head is held back over the folded neck.
Size: L 37–41 in; W 51 in.

Status: generally uncommon to locally abundant year-round resident; fairly common coastal winter visitor; retreats from higher elevations and much of the interior from late fall to early spring.

Habitat: open or semi-open, fish-bearing habitats of nearly any description; favors expansive shallows, marshes and rushy lakeshores; roosts in undisturbed trees. *Breeding:* nests chiefly in dense stands of trees or snags.

Nesting: colonial; in a tree, shrub or thicket; pair builds a stick platform and incubates 3–4 pale blue-green eggs for 23–26 days; both adults feed the young by regurgitation.

Feeding: forages in shallow water over semifluid mud or in grassy areas or stands motionless and waits for prey to appear within striking range; eats mostly fish, but also takes aquatic and intertidal invertebrates, amphibians, reptiles, rodents and small birds.

Voice: utters an abrupt, deep *cuk cuk* or a grating *kraahnk*.

Similar Species: *Cattle Egret* (p. 64): much smaller and stockier; shorter bill with more conspicuous feathering along the lower mandible. *Snowy Egret* (p. 63): half the size; thin, spike-like, black bill; black legs with 'golden slippers'; immature has pale greenish legs and feet.

SNOWY EGRET
Egretta thula

The subject of much evocative photo portraiture, the Snowy Egret in breeding plumage is the glamour heron. Loose flocks and scattered individuals occur locally but widely across lowland northern California, where they hunt shallow marshes, bayshores and ponds in open country. Along with other showy, colonially nesting waterbirds, Snowies were shot whole-sale for the millinery trade around the end of the 19th century. After the plumes of countless egrets had come to ornament the hats of fashionable women, a dwindling supply of 'aigrettes' and protective legislation put an end to the slaughter. They have subsequently more than made up for the punishment of the innocent received during the era of gunning: Snowy Egrets have recolonized extirpated sites and have moved generally northward during the 1900s.

• Instead of patiently waiting for prey, Snowy Egrets prefer to shuffle and stalk about in more active pursuit of prey items.

breeding

ID: small, slender; all-white plumage; straight, slender, black bill; yellow feet; dark legs. *Breeding:* elegant plumes originating at the head, neck and back; erect crown; orange-red loral skin; orange feet. *Immature:* lacks the plumes; pale green legs, becoming darker on the front with age; bill is paler-based. *In flight:* feet extend beyond the tail; head is folded back over the shoulders.

Size: L 22–26 in; W 41 in.

Status: uncommon to locally common year-round resident or migrant and summer breeder; rare or seldom-detected migrant across much of mountainous northern California.

Habitat: shallow, standing or slow-moving water of marshes, lakes, floodplain streamsides and tidal wetland environments. *In migration:* may appear at reservoirs or along confined river corridors far from the nearest population.

Nesting: colonial; nests in undisturbed stands of trees, shrubs and marshes; flimsy platform of twigs is lined with finer plant materials; pair incubates 3–5 eggs over 20–24 days; both adults raise the young.

Feeding: hunts small animals, such as aquatic invertebrates, fish, amphibians and reptiles, walking and running to stab prey; engages in a 'shake and stir' technique, in which one foot is raised and shuffled quickly beneath the water's surface.

Voice: low, rhythmic noise is given at colonies; mostly silent away from the nest, but utters an unflattering, harsh croak when alarmed .

Similar Species: *Great Egret* (p. 62): much larger; yellow-orange bill; black feet. *Cattle Egret* (p. 64): chunkier; yellow to yellow-orange bill; yellowish feet on yellow, reddish or dark green legs; breeding adult has large rusty patches on the crown, back and foreneck.

63

CATTLE EGRET
Bubulcus ibis

Through the ages, herons have evolved to exploit foraging niches ranging from dense marshes to open mudflats, and riverside tangles to kelp beds. • Cattle Egrets were originally an Old World species, at home on the semi-arid savannahs where herds of large herbivores constantly stirred up insects as they foraged through the grasses. Cattle Egrets appeared in South America in the first half of the 20th century, either through natural dispersal or, possibly, by the hand of man. By the 1940s, Cattle Egrets had popped up in Florida—the floodgates had opened. With large herds of wild ungulates no longer roaming temperate North America, Cattle Egrets readily took to consorting with domestic cattle. Having entrenched their numbers in the southeastern U.S., they spread westward across the southern tier of states, reaching the Golden State in 1964. By 1970, this species was nesting among other herons and egrets in the Imperial Valley, which remains their stronghold in California. In the years since, they have nested irregularly in association with other herons north into the Central Valley and even to Humboldt Bay.

non-breeding

ID: small, chunky egret. *Breeding:* rich, orange-buff crown, back and foreneck; long plumes on the throat and rump; orange-red legs and bill; lores may become purple. *Non-breeding:* all-white; yellowish legs and feet; short, stout, yellow-orange bill with extension of feathers along the lower mandible. *Immature:* dark green feet. *In flight:* head folds back over the shoulders.
Size: *L* 19–21 in; *W* 36 in.
Status: uncommon visitor from October to April; locally fairly common from May to October.
Habitat: forages among grazing cattle in lowland pastures rich in invertebrates; some birds hunt in freshwater or brackish marshes, pond margins or croplands; roosts in trees and shrubs; occasionally seen in comical situations, such as backyards, landfills, varied urban settings and even aboard ship.

Nesting: colonial; female builds a stick platform in a tree or shrub using materials gathered by the male; pair incubates 3–4 pale blue eggs for 21–26 days; both parents feed the young by regurgitation.
Feeding: captures insects flushed by the movements of grazing animals; also takes snakes, frogs, nestling birds, eggs, earthworms, crayfish and rarely fish; routinely scavenges at garbage dumps in some areas.
Voice: generally silent; *kok* alarm call; *rick-rack* call given at colonies.
Similar Species: *Snowy Egret* (p. 63): slender, black bill; black (adult) or pale green (immature) legs. *Great Egret* (p. 62): twice the size; more slender; longer neck and bill.

GREEN HERON
Butorides virescens

A birder's first encounter with a Green Heron often comes as a surprise to each party involved. When alarmed, these small dark herons stretch in alertness, flick their short tails, and then take flight. • Green Herons are birds of shrubby stream meanders, the backwaters of sluggish rivers, undisturbed pond margins and protected estuarine shallows. While foraging, they move slowly, preferring to remain within easy flight distance of sheltering vegetation. However, they will venture into semi-open situations, such as exposed stream outflows, rushy tidal channels, breakwaters, disused piers and sheltered mudflats. At some locations they are quite tolerant of background human activity: they often hunt the shores of golf course water hazards and walk along floating booms in small craft basins. • Green Herons are widely known for their use of floating lures. Hunting birds may drop feathers, leaves and other small objects onto the surface of the water in an attempt to attract small fish within striking distance. Because of their typically closed-in habitat, slow movements, cryptic plumage and wide dispersal as singles or pairs, Green Herons are surely under-detected relative to their actual numbers.

ID: small, stocky heron; green-black crown; chestnut face and neck; white streaks on the throat and underparts; blue-gray of the back and wings is mixed with iridescent green; comparatively short, orange legs; dark bill; short tail. *Breeding male:* bright orange legs. *Immature:* heavy streaks on the underparts; dull brown upperparts. *In flight:* flies with pumping strokes of arched wings.
Size: L 15–22 in; W 26 in.
Status: uncommon to fairly common year-round resident.
Habitat: freshwater and tidal shores, ponds, lagoons, willow-grown streamsides, mudflat edges and similar sheltered or semi-wooded situations.
Nesting: singly or in small, loose groups; male constructs a stick platform in a tree or shrub, usually very close to water; pair incubates 3–5 pale blue-green to green

eggs for 19–21 days; pair feeds the young by regurgitation.
Feeding: stabs prey with its bill after slowly stalking or while standing-and-waiting; sometimes walks quickly toward intended prey; eats mostly small fish, frogs, tadpoles, crustaceans, aquatic insects and other small animals.
Voice: generally silent; alarm call is a loud *kyow, skyowp!* or *skow!*
Similar Species: *American Bittern* (p. 60): larger; rich brown body is streaked nearly throughout; noticeable black 'whisker.' *Black-crowned Night-Heron* (p. 66): black and white; red eyes; 2 long, white plumes; 1st-year immature is drabber gray-brown and is densely stippled with white on the upperparts. *Least Bittern:* tiny, with bold, buffy upperwing patches; much less often detected.

BLACK-CROWNED NIGHT-HERON
Nycticorax nycticorax

The natural realm offers innumerable variations on successful themes, as though the maxim 'if it works, diversify it' were the operating concept. We can perceive that the early advent of birds that speared prey must have been the ecological equivalent of a smash hit, for today's world supports herons that are big or tiny, brilliantly colored or drab, reclusive or highly social, and diurnal or nocturnal. • Black-crowned Night-Herons hunt in a great variety of settings. Having to endure no competition from day-feeding herons and egrets, they disperse widely at night into practically any habitat within reasonable flight distance which offers aquatic or estuarine creatures vulnerable to capture. Surely, there can be no sweet dreams for frogs and little fishes wherever Black-crowned Night-Herons police the wetland night beat. Adults are boldly patterned, yet their dark-above, pale-below countershading and extended inactivity causes them to remain inconspicuous in the dappled shadows of their daytime hangouts. • Night-herons comprise a group of six species whose respective members are distributed widely throughout the tropical and temperate regions.

breeding

ID: chunky; stout, black bill; black cap and back; large, red eyes; white cheek and underparts; gray wings; dull yellow legs. *Breeding:* 2 long, white plumes trail from the crown. *1st-year immature:* dingy brownish; blurry, dark streakings on the upperparts; fine, elongate, creamy spots across the upperparts. *2nd-year immature:* reduced breast-streaking and back spotting; blackish crown. *In flight:* wingstrokes lack 'snap.'
Size: L 23–26 in; W 42 in.
Status: uncommon to fairly common year-round resident; rare to uncommon breeder and transient from April to August.
Habitat: *Foraging:* freshwater and salt marshes, pond edges, mudflats, cropland and along slow-moving streams. *Roosting and Nesting:* in dense stands of trees and brush, often in seclusion, but sometimes remarkably near human activity.
Nesting: colonial; loose stick nest with fine lining is constructed by the female as

the male gathers the nesting material; pair incubates 3–5 eggs for about 25 days; both adults raise the young.
Feeding: chiefly at night, but often by day; stalks or waits motionlessly for fish, amphibians, reptiles, invertebrates, small birds and mammals; known to be a significant predator on ducklings and rails at some sites.
Voice: flying or disturbed birds utter a distinctive, surprised-sounding *quok!*
Similar Species: *American Bittern* (p. 60): larger; richer brown; lacks the whitish back spotting and seldom sits hunched in pondside shrubbery. *Great Blue Heron* (p. 61): much larger; longer legs. *Green Heron* (p. 65): smaller; darker flanks; pale eyes; not found in flocks.

WHITE-FACED IBIS
Plegadis chihi

Ibises are slender, long-legged wading birds of social habits. The White-faced Ibis is a bird of the remnant large wetlands of western North America. It is perhaps most at home in the expansive reedbeds and muddy shallows of state and federal wildlife refuges and in flooded croplands. With its long legs, slender toes and remarkable downcurved bill, this bird is well adapted to life in the marsh. Wet or pooled meadows and reed-fringed, muddy shorelines are preferred foraging sites, offering soft or semi-fluid soil from which the birds can extract food items. • This species is probably less abundant today than during pristine times, when permanent or seasonal wetlands sprawled across much of the Central Valley and water in the alkaline bottoms of the Great Basin was less restricted. Ibises require high-quality marshes for nesting and, like most other colonial birds of similar habitat, they are known to abandon and relocate breeding sites in accordance with changing habitat suitability. They fly rapidly, readily traversing the miles that may separate secluded nesting colonies and outlying feeding locations. Although White-faced Ibises are migratory, they tend to be restricted to traditional flyways, so they may be a familiar sight in some regions while scarcely known a few miles away. • Seen at any distance in flight or on the ground, White-faced Ibises look entirely dark brown.

breeding

ID: slender; elegant; dark chestnut overall; long, downcurved bill; dark red eyes; long, dark legs; narrow strip of white feathers bordering a naked facial patch; iridescent greenish lower back and wing coverts. *Breeding:* rich red legs and facial patch. *In flight:* gangly-looking but graceful, with outstretched neck and long, downcurved bill visible at long range; intersperses rapid wingbeats with brief periods of gliding on stiffly bowed wings.
Size: *L* 19–26 in; *W* 36 in.
Status: rare to uncommon spring and fall migrant; locally rare to common visitor from October to April; rare to fairly common local breeder from late April to September.
Habitat: marshes, lake edges, mudflats, ricefields, wet pastures and irrigation ditches.

Nesting: colonial; in bulrushes or other emergent vegetation; deep cup nest of coarse materials is lined with fine plant matter; pair incubates 3–4 bluish-green eggs for about 22 days.
Feeding: probes and gleans soil and shallow water for aquatic invertebrates, amphibians and other small vertebrates.
Voice: generally quiet; occasionally gives a series of low, duck-like quacks.

Similar Species: *Herons and egrets* (pp. 60–66): all lack the thick-based, downcurved bill. *Long-billed Curlew* (p. 150): rich buffy-brown; cinnamon underwing linings; uniformly thin bill.

TURKEY VULTURE
Cathartes aura

Some types of birds, such as marsh dwellers, are numerous yet seldom seen. Other birds are uncommon but can readily be observed. Turkey Vultures combine 'abundance and advertisement' in singular fashion—across the miles and the months, no other winged creature of northern California skies is as conspicuous. • A high sail area to weight ratio, coupled with a strict dependence on its sense of smell, has enabled the Turkey Vulture to become a 'floating nose.' These birds patrol broad stretches of countryside for dead animals by moving from one bubble of warm, rising air to another, spreading their wings and tails to the fullest extent as they tease the greatest performance possible from the lowest expenditure of precious energy. • Scavengers are commonly maligned by the public, but Turkey Vultures perform a valuable service in promptly disposing of carcasses a humble role for which we can be grateful. These vultures eat carrion almost exclusively, and their bills and feet are not designed to crush or kill living animals. The naked head of the Turkey Vulture is an adaptation denying bacteria and parasites sufficient foothold to cause disease.

ID: very large, all-black bird; small, featherless, red head. *Immature:* gray head. *In flight:* silver-gray flight feathers; black wing linings; wings are held in a shallow V; head seems 'hunched' between the shoulders; tilts when it soars.

Size: L 26–32 in; W 68–72 in.

Status: common resident nearly throughout lowlands and foothills; retreats from colder regions in winter.

Habitat: aerial cruises take in nearly all terrestrial and shoreline habitats at one time or another; in many areas, forages most regularly over valley edge and foothill topography.

Nesting: on bare ground, among boulders, in hollow trees or on the forest floor; no nest material is used; pair incubates 2 dull white eggs for up to 41 days; nestlings are fed through regurgitation.

Feeding: feeds entirely on available carrion in nearly any form; scavenges vehicle- and harvester-struck animals as well as ungulates, reptiles, beached fish and many other animals.

Voice: almost never heard.

Similar Species: *Golden Eagle* (p. 115) wings are held flat or very slightly uptilted in profile; does not rock in flight. *Bald Eagle* (p. 105): holds wings flat when soaring; white head and tail. *California Condor* (p. 69): extremely rare and local; much larger; bold, elongate, white underwing lining panel.

CALIFORNIA CONDOR
Gymnogyps californianus

The shadows cast by great birds across the upturned eyes of aboriginal peoples have left more than a passing imprint upon mythology. The recesses of canyon walls over which huge vultures once wheeled still bear stylized images of the 'Thunderbird.' • Having witnessed the extinction of the Pleistocene megafauna whose carcasses once sustained it, the California Condor has become an emblem of the complex issues of wildlife conservation. It once occupied a range extending far beyond the state's borders: bones of *Gymnogyps* have been unearthed in Florida, and the Lewis and Clark expedition recorded the species near the mouth of the Columbia River. Its decline since European settlement is the result of a combination of shooting, poisoning, egg collection, harrassment at nest sites and food scarcity. The modern story of the condor involves the passage into captivity of the last wild individual, the bitterness that divided pro- and anti- 'captive propagation' groups and the release of captive-raised birds into an uncertain future. Adapted to scavenging large carcasses in vast unmanaged landscapes, the modern California Condor has been described as 'a senile species far past its prime.' Captive-bred, individually marked, and radio-tagged, and released to media fanfare, it now persists only as an intensively managed remnant—a creature unable to fulfill any meaningful environmental role.

ID: very large, black bird; conspicuous, white underwing linings; naked, orange head; outer primaries are 'slotted' and finger-like; white trim to the inner secondaries and coverts. *Immature:* mottled underwings; brownish head. *In flight:* stately soaring with wings in a shallow V; flaps only occasionally; has been spotted from aircraft at 15,500 ft.
Size: *L* 43–55 in; *W* 8.3–9.6 ft.
Status: formerly a widespread resident across much of northern California; last remaining wild bird captured on April 19, 1987; captive-bred birds have been released into Sespe Condor Sanctuary and Big Sur coast.
Habitat: formerly foraged over terrestrial habitats that supported large ungulates; released birds now forage over arid foothills, mountains and canyons.

Nesting: captive-bred; nested originally in caves, cliff crevices or large tree cavities; pair incubates 1 whitish egg for about 56 days; lengthy parenting phase results in breeding every other year; breeds at 7 years of age.
Feeding: consumes carrion located during extended aerial cruises; depends heavily on thermal uplift for takeoff and efficient foraging.
Voice: generally silent.
Similar Species: *Turkey Vulture* (p. 68): much smaller; rocks and tilts constantly in flight. *Golden Eagle* (p. 115): smaller; browner; feathered head.

69

GREATER WHITE-FRONTED GOOSE
Anser albifrons

Across the ages, wild geese have come to mean many things to many people. We flatter the goose with the attributes of pair devotion, family tenacity and vigor: traits prized and praised by humans. White-bodied or somber, imposing or diminutive, all geese are tough, vigilant and resilient birds, adapted for enduring the tests of the natural realm. White-fronted Geese know many rigors in their annual cycle. These difficulties range from the threat of late spring ice at their arctic breeding grounds to the perils presented by the shotguns of waterfowl hunters. The loss of wetlands more abundant before the era of settlement and development has been partly offset by the establishment of refuges along the Pacific Flyway. The great majority of northern California's White-fronted Geese assemble during the colder months in and around these complexes of impoundments and cropland. Straggling individuals—perhaps diseased, shot-pricked or otherwise unfit—make appearances among flocks of domestic or semi-wild ducks and geese at park ponds, dairies and farms. Although remaining wild, they may become sufficiently habituated to humans to take handouts at the 'bread line' with feral waterfowl.

ID: medium-sized goose; dark brown overall; variably dense blackish speckling or barring across the lower breast and belly; orange-pink bill and feet; white patch around the base of the bill extends onto the forehead; white hindquarters. *Immature:* pale belly lacks the dark specking; no white on the face.

Size: L 27–33 in; W 57 in.

Status: locally common to very common migrant and visitor from late September to early May.

Habitat: extensive marsh-dotted lakes and reservoirs and crop stubble; individuals and small groups may occur nearly anywhere in migration.

Nesting: in the Arctic.

Feeding: forages on land and in water by submerging its head or by tipping-up; consumes a wide variety of plant material, including grasses, sedges, seeds and waste grain.

Voice: flight call, given in flocks, creates a chorus of far-carrying, falsetto *k'LAUW lee-YOK* notes; not often heard while on the ground.

Similar Species: other species of wild geese are entirely distinctive.

SNOW GOOSE

Chen caerulescens

Where they are a common sight, Snow Geese are impossible to overlook. Their comings and goings and wintertime assemblages have long been celebrated in art, prose and legend. They are clannish birds, moving north and south across the continent in broad, wavering lines and assembling in highly localized hordes at their wintering grounds. • Along the Pacific Flyway, Snow Geese are seen chiefly in the managed wetland ecosystems of the national and state waterfowl refuges and in outlying agricultural lands. The diminution and isolation of parcels of quality wetland habitat in northern California over the past 150 years have served to concentrate them, which can create the happy illusion that their numbers are limitless. The truth is more sobering, as a significant percentage of the entire West Coast population might use a fairly discrete area, while much of the remainder of the flyway is vacated. Snow Geese have responded strongly to management in recent decades, maintaining or increasing their numbers and consequently putting a burden on the capacity for fragile tundra nesting habitat to support them. • Many of the Snow Geese that winter in California originate in northeastern Siberia and cross the Bering Strait twice each year in migration.

ID: white overall; black wing tips; dark pink feet and bill. *White-morph adult:* all white, except for black primaries and an occasional light rusty staining on the head; deep red bill; thin, black 'grin patch' along the mandible edges; base of the bill is slightly rounded. *Immature white morph:* dusky, with a dark bill. *Dark morph (Blue Goose):* rare; blue-gray body; white head and upper neck. *Immature dark morph:* dark slaty, with paler wing coverts; dark bill and legs.
Size: L 28–33 in; W 59 in.
Status: fairly common to abundant migrant and local visitor from October to mid-April.
Habitat: shallow freshwater lakes and wetlands, grain fields and croplands; a few

birds occur in coastal lowlands, at parks, reservoirs and golf courses.
Nesting: in Siberia and the North American Arctic.
Feeding: gleans from the soil or marsh; swims or wades in shallows; takes mostly plant material, including aquatic growth, waste crops, grasses, sedges, roots and seeds.
Voice: loud, nasal *houk-houk*.
Similar Species: *Ross's Goose (p. 72):* smaller; more triangular bill; slightly shorter neck; more smoothly rounded head; lacks the black 'grin.' Individuals possessing intermediate characteristics indicate that some hybridization occurs.

71

ROSS'S GOOSE
Chen rossii

The spectacle of thousands, or tens of thousands, of closely crowded white geese suddenly all in the air in a clamorous uproar astonishes everyone who experiences it. Witnessing this spectacle is possible from late fall into early spring at important Pacific Flyway concentration sites in the Klamath Basin and in the Sacramento and San Joaquin valleys. • While the Snow Goose may be more widely known to the public, the less heralded Ross's Goose contributes mightily to the swarms of white geese in northern California. Waterfowl magnets, such as Tule Lake and Merced national wildlife refuges and Gray Lodge Wildlife Management Area, may support up to 90 percent of the total world population of this species. Generations of sportsmen and bird enthusiasts perceived Ross's Goose as a bird of mystery: its migration corridor was historically quite narrow, and its northern Canadian breeding grounds were not pinpointed until 1938. Greater numbers now visit mid-continent and Gulf Coast sites. • The rare 'Blue' Ross's is a handsome plumage morph exhibited by a tiny minority of the population. It has been hypothesized that occasional hybridization between Ross's Geese and Snow Geese has introduced the Snow's dark 'Blue Goose' genes into the general Ross's Goose gene pool, where they seem to be only rarely expressed.

white morph

ID: white overall; black wing tips; dark pink feet and bill; small bill. *White-morph adult:* entirely white except for black primaries and a short, deep red bill with greenish 'warts' at the base. *Dark-morph adult:* white head; blue-gray nape and body. *Immature:* washed with pale gray.
Size: L 21–26 in; W 51 in.
Status: locally common to abundant visitor from late September to early April; a few stragglers appear outside areas of concentration during migration and winter.
Habitat: shallow freshwater wetlands, lakes and agricultural fields; rarely in tidal marshes, estuaries and lakes in urban parks.

Nesting: in the Canadian Arctic.
Feeding: gleans from the soil or marsh; swims or wades in shallows; takes mostly plant material, including aquatic growth, waste crops, grasses, sedges, roots and seeds.
Voice: flight call is a high-pitched, unmusical *kug*, *kek* or *ke-gak*.
Similar Species: *Snow Goose* (p. 71): larger; prominent dark 'grin patch' on the sides of its longer, more angular, rounded-based bill; slightly longer neck. Apparent hybrids and intergrades with Snow Goose are occasionally reported.

CANADA GOOSE
Branta canadensis

The name 'Canada Goose' is applied to not one but many distinct populations of characteristic North American geese, each known generally as a Canada by its black neck 'stocking' and white 'chinstrap.' With the white-tailed deer, the Bald Eagle and the rattlesnake, these geese are creatures long held emblematic of our continent. Yet they have been translocated, and are thriving, at some very far-flung points in both the Northern and Southern Hemispheres. Any description of Canada Geese must narrow the scope of discussion to one or another of various forms. Each exhibits not only physical differences, but also a high degree of distinctness in nuances of group behavior, such as habitat selection, winter mixing and roosting. Together with separation along lines of 'tradition,' geographic separation has caused many ornithologists to suggest that some subspecies may more properly be considered species. Canada Geese of many forms occur in northern California. By number, the great majority are winter visitors. The familiar, large, pale-breasted 'Western' Canada, *B. c. moffitti*, is the breeding bird in northern California. Its success as an introduction has created local management problems.

ID: long, black neck; rounded, white 'chinstrap' encircling the throat; light brown underparts; white rump; dark brown upperparts; short, black tail.

Size: *L* 25–48 in; *W* 70 in.

Status: common to abundant resident and migrant; uncommon to abundant winter visitor; migrant flocks may use the same flight lines each year.

Habitat: lakeshores, riverbanks, parks, waterfronts, marshes, grain fields and other cropland.

Nesting: on islets, shoreline points and cliffs, and in old eagle or Osprey nests in proximity to water; usually on the ground, but occasionally on cliffs, on large stick nests in trees or on nest platforms; female builds a nest of grass and other vegetation lined with feather down; female incubates 4–7 white eggs for 25–30 days; both adults raise the young.

Feeding: tips-up, gleans and grazes a great variety of vegetable matter from roots and tubers to submergent leaf matter, seeds, agricultural produce and sprouting grass.

Voice: familiar to nearly everyone, a loud and familiar *ha-RONK*, audible at a half mile; Canada Geese are frequently heard but not seen.

Similar Species: no other bird has the distinctive dark head and neck and contrasting 'chinstrap.'

73

BRANT
Branta bernicla

Study of the migration of waterbirds visible from shore along the northern California coast offers clues to the comparative seasonal abundance of the many species visiting the region. Each species displays different timing: some pass northward or southward well before or after another. Brant are among the later-arriving fall migrants. They begin moving north in numbers in late winter and linger well into spring before their numbers dwindle sharply. • Brant are conspicuous and recognizable at a great distance as they migrate through or shortly beyond the surf zone. Their roughly bunched, blackish forms flow in undulating masses low across the swells and troughs, each individual maintaining unbroken flight. • These geese are very strongly coastal; generally, only a token few are detected annually among the mixed-species throngs of waterfowl concentrating in the Central Valley and the Klamath Basin. • Populations of Brant on both the Pacific and Atlantic coasts rely to a great extent on eelgrass, a submergent plant intolerant of human abuse of estuaries. Consequently, they are abundant only locally, 'staging' for weeks at preferred sites as they lay on fat for migration. As many as 30,000 gather in March on Humboldt Bay. Very small numbers of Brant may linger throughout the spring, summer and early fall near harbor entrances anywhere along the coast.

ID: deep brown overall; black head, neck and breast; dark wings and bill; broken white collar is variable; barred gray-and-white sides; extensive white uppertail coverts.

Size: L 25 in; W 45 in.

Status: common migrant from October to early January and from mid-February through April; uncommon to locally abundant in winter in larger estuaries; a few linger into summer; rare visitor inland.

Habitat: tidal estuaries, river mouths and large shallow coastal lagoons dominated by eelgrass; occasionally found in plowed or sprouting fields with other grazing and gleaning waterfowl.

Nesting: in the Arctic; several subspecies breed across high latitudes of the Northern Hemisphere.

Feeding: tips-up and gleans for submergent vegetation over tidal shallows; eats mostly aquatic plants, especially eelgrass.

Voice: often silent; low, distinctly guttural *gronk* is given by birds feeding or flying in flocks.

Similar Species: *Canada Goose* (p. 73): unmistakable white 'chinstrap'; whitish breast.

TUNDRA SWAN
Cygnus columbianus

The long neck and powerful bill of the Tundra Swan reflect the rule that 'form follows function.' Swans are adapted to life in and about extensive shallows, where they may graze grass, glean from the surface of land or water or tip-up like a dabbling duck. Their exceptional underwater reach, together with an ability to root out bottom-growing tubers and shoots, allows swans to exploit wetland food resources that may be unavailable to geese and ducks. Such separation or specialization in foraging produces 'niches' occupied by one or several species, permitting the coexistence of many. • Tundra Swans are great white birds favoring unpeopled open spaces and minimal disturbance. Like most of the other large waterfowl in northern California, the bulk of their population tends to concentrate in and about the important, managed wetlands strategically located along the interior Pacific Flyway. However, smaller assemblages traditionally spend winter at a number of widely scattered sites both in the interior valleys and in the coastal lowlands. • Swans are conspicuous and stirring creatures demanding long moments of quiet admiration. Whether seen feeding at a great distance or viewed from beneath as they move ponderously overhead, few people forget their first encounter with wild swans.

ID: long neck; heavy, black bill; whitish overall; big, black feet; entirely white wings; yellow 'teardrop' in front of the eye; neck is held straight from its base. *Immature:* washed throughout with pale grayish; much pink on the bill (variable).
Size: L 47–58 in; W 80 in.
Status: locally common to abundant from October to March.
Habitat: permanent or seasonal wetlands of undisturbed open country; large shallow lakes, marshes and nearby expanses of sprouting grass or waste crops; prefers a clear line-of-sight in all directions.
Nesting: in arctic regions of both New and Old worlds.

Feeding: tips-up, dabbles and surface-gleans for aquatic vegetation and aquatic invertebrates; grazes for tubers, roots, grasses and waste grain.
Voice: muffled, hollow honking or hooting call is given frequently in flight and by nervous flocks on the ground or water: *WHOO!...HOO-wu-WHOO!*; wings make a windy rustling sound at close range.
Similar Species: *Trumpeter Swan:* larger; heavier bill; loud, bugle-like voice; lacks the yellow 'teardrop' on the bill; rare in northern California.

WOOD DUCK

Aix sponsa

The image of the gaudy male Wood Duck has adorned innumerable calendar leaves, postcards, bird-book jackets … and wooded ponds. The plumage worn by the drake through much of the year suggests that he bathed in the palette left over after all other North American birds were painted. The multicolored pattern is so well known to most of us that a first encounter with the bird in life may be at the same time thrilling, yet somewhat of a letdown: in a natural setting, Wood Ducks may flush and fly off down the creek shortly after they are spotted. However, they become remarkably 'tame' wherever handouts of bread are offered at park ponds, allowing close-range admiration. • Females are much less dramatic than males, but they are lovely in their own right, clothed in a delicate mouse-gray plumage, their large, liquid eyes given added expression by elongated white patches. • Wood ducks retreat from colder interior and foothill areas in winter, assembling in small flocks on sheltered lakes at that season. • They perch in trees and low overhanging riverine tangles more than nearly any other duck.

ID: *Male:* dark and colorful; glossy green head with slicked-back crest; contrasting white chin and throat; chestnut breast is spangled with white spots; golden-brown sides; dark back and hindquarters. *Female:* white 'teardrop' around the eye; brownish-gray upperparts; mottled brown breast is streaked with white; pale belly.

Size: *L* 15–21 in.

Status: very uncommon to fairly common migrant in spring and fall; rare to fairly common summer breeder; locally uncommon to fairly common winter visitor; much less numerous in higher mountains and east of the Cascade-Sierra.

Habitat: freshwater ponds, marshes, lakes and, rivers, usually bordered by dense stands of trees.

Nesting: in a natural hollow, tree cavity or nest box, often 30 ft above the ground and usually near water; nest is lined with down; female incubates 9–14 eggs for 25–35 days.

Feeding: gleans the water's surface and tips-up for aquatic vegetation; eats more fruits and nuts than other ducks.

Voice: male utters a soft, gurgling *jeee*; female's distressed, rising *woo-EEK!* call is most commonly heard and is frequently the first sign of presence.

Similar Species: *Hooded Merganser* (p. 99): slim bill; white patch on the crest. *Harlequin Duck* (p. 91): no crest; male is blue-gray overall; female has 3 small white spots on the side of the head; found in and along turbulent water.

GADWALL
Anas strepera

When we refer to someone as an 'odd duck,' the image of a motionless Gadwall sitting stolidly on a reedy pool certainly doesn't leap to mind—but the term might well describe this bird. In size and in general life history, Gadwalls are as typical as the next dabbling duck. However, they display nuances of habitat selection and behavior that are a bit different from the Mallards, Northern Pintails and American Wigeons with which they are often found. This subtle overall distinction is learned only through some experience with the species. • Gadwalls favor undisturbed ponds and sloughs with muddy bottoms, abundant aquatic plants and the adjacent hiding cover afforded by marsh vegetation or overhanging sprays of willows or other woody material. In such seclusion, they glean from the surface, dabble in shallows and even dive to reach submerged food items. Gadwalls are given to spending much time moving only slowly about a feeding site. Away from the principal refuges of the interior Pacific Flyway, migrants and winterers generally occur in modest numbers in the loose company of other surface-feeding ducks or in discrete flocks of their own kind.

ID: stout; grayish; small white speculum patch. *Male:* mostly subdued gray; dark bill; black hindquarters. *Female:* mottled brown; hint of white in the wing patch.
In flight: drab, except for the distinctive, small white speculum patch bordered above by a black bar (bordered by a deep, burnt-orange trim in the male).
Size: *L* 18–22 in.
Status: uncommon to abundant spring and fall migrant; uncommon to very common visitor from late August to late April; rare to very common summer breeder.
Habitat: freshwater, alkaline and brackish marshes, ponds, lagoons, tidal channels and mudflats; may concentrate in flooded crop stubble.

Nesting: well-concealed nest is a grassy, down-lined hollow placed in tall vegetation, sometimes far from water; female incubates 8–11 eggs for 24–27 days.
Feeding: dabbles, tips-up and dives for various parts of aquatic and estuarine plants; takes some waste grain, aquatic invertebrates, tadpoles and small fish.
Voice: male utters an occasional, matter-of-fact *bek*, notable for the short-e vowel tone; female gives a high *kaak kaaak kak-kak-kak* quack-series.
Similar Species: no other pond or marsh duck has a simple, small, white inner hindwing patch.

EURASIAN WIGEON
Anas penelope

The larger flocks of American Wigeons scattered throughout the wetlands of northern California in winter typically support one or a few Eurasian Wigeons. As is the rule with ducks, the males are more easily distinguished. Female Eurasian Wigeons occur in approximately equivalent numbers but are less readily noticed. They are patterned in the manner of female American Wigeons and closely resemble them: they differ only in showing no discernible contrast between throat and breast. • This species occurs each year in migration and in winter in northern California and widely elsewhere in North America, chiefly at principal waterfowl concentration sites along the Pacific and Atlantic flyways. Following an avian rule that echoes the saying, 'when in Rome, do as the Romans do,' Eurasian Wigeons consort almost exclusively with American Wigeons. Their behavior when in our region appears to be precisely the same as that of other wigeons. They are seldom found alone or in groups by themselves. Dozens may occur in dense concentrations on and about the national wildlife refuges of the Central Valley. Experienced birders should expect to see a handful of these appealing ducks each season while watching waterfowl. Scanning among throngs of American Wigeons in search of Eurasians offers observers of all abilities valuable practice in picking out the odd bird from among the host of the mundane—one of the keys to discovering true rarities.

ID: *Male:* rich orange-brown head; creamy forehead stripe; chestnut breast; steely-gray sides; dark feet; black-tipped, grayish-blue bill. *Female:* brown head and breast with rufous hints; black-tipped, grayish-blue bill; darkish eye patch. *Immature male:* brownish feathers within the gray flank panel; dull or incomplete greenish smear behind the eye. *In flight:* white 'wing pits'; large white shoulder patch; pointed tail.
Size: *L* 16½–21 in.
Status: rare to locally uncommon winter visitor, with main influx in October and remaining into April.
Habitat: shallow lakes with abundant submergent vegetation, open expanses of sprouting grass in proximity to water and intertidal eelgrass beds.

Nesting: in Europe and Asia.
Feeding: dabbles, dives or tips-up for the stems, leaves and seeds of submergent vegetation; grazes lawns and pastures.
Voice: male's call is often overlooked but is easily learned: a good-humored, mellow whistle that descends evenly throughout.
Similar Species: *American Wigeon* (p. 79): white axillars; male has a clear white forecrown, a broad iridescent green smear through the face and rusty sides; female has a grayish head and neck contrasting with a browner breast.

AMERICAN WIGEON
Anas americana

Expanses of short, lush grass near water in open country attract flocks of American Wigeons in fall, winter and spring. These ducks prefer to graze on young shoots while walking steadily along in dense, formless flocks, each individual no more than a few feet from its nearest neighbor. • Over much of lowland northern California, they are familiar visitors at city parks with reservoirs. Golf courses provide much the same opportunity for grazing—fairways adjoining water features may become fouled with droppings. American Wigeon are conspicuous in such settings, but they occur in greatest abundance in the managed wetlands and croplands of the Klamath Basin and the Central Valley. Tens of thousands annually concentrate in and around the state and federal wildlife refuges, massing by day in reed-fringed impoundments and flying forth at dusk to glean waste grain and sprouting grasses from outlying agricultural parcels. Dairies in the coastal lowlands support their share of American Wigeons as do estuarine shallows grown to eelgrass.

ID: large, white wing patch; cinnamon breast and flanks; white belly; black-tipped, blue-gray bill. *Male:* white forecrown; broad, iridescent green smear through and behind the eye; cinnamon breast and flanks; white shoulder patch; green speculum. *Female:* grayish head; slight contrast between the throat and breast; brown underparts. *In flight:* white shoulder patches flash conspicuously; wings are vaguely triangular; short, yet pointed tail.
Size: *L* 18–23 in.
Status: uncommon to abundant migrant and visitor from mid-August (a few) to early May; scarce breeder.
Habitat: shallow lakes with submergent vegetation; open expanses of sprouting grass in proximity to water and intertidal eelgrass beds; flocks raft on protected fresh or upper-estuarine waters of nearly any description. *Breeding:* near marshes and lakes.

Nesting: always on dry ground, often far from water; nest is built with grass, leaves and down and is well concealed; female incubates 7–10 white eggs for 23–25 days.
Feeding: dabbles, dives or tips-up for stems, leaves and seeds of submergent vegetation; grazes lawns, golf courses and city parks; visits coastal eelgrass beds.
Voice: male utters a descending series of 2 or 3 wheezy, giggling notes, *wheeWEE-whew.*
Similar Species: *Eurasian Wigeon* (p. 78): male has a rich orange-brown head, cream rather than white forecrown, gray sides, dusky axillars and a different voice. Female lacks the subtle contrast between the throat and breast. *Gadwall* (p. 77): female has a noticeably squarish rather than rounded forehead angle; white on the upper wing is confined to the speculum.

79

MALLARD
Anas platyrhynchos

Mallards are among the most abundant, distinctive and familiar of all waterfowl. They are highly successful, notable for their ability to do well in an array of settings ranging from tiny ponds to extensive wetlands. They are often the last duck to be pushed out of wetlands under human pressure or alteration, and, if conditions improve, the first to recolonize. Their capacity to disperse great distances has served them well: several related species or subspecies of duck found locally in North America and elsewhere clearly arose from Mallards or Mallard-like ancestors. • Wild Mallards sometimes interbreed with domestic ducks to produce the goofy-looking offspring seen at park ponds. Though they may become readily habituated to the 'bread line,' truly wild Mallards are typically quite wary and, given a choice, would prefer to tough it out in large marshes and harvested crop stubble in open country.

ID: stout; long-billed, vocal dabbling duck; dark blue speculum is bordered by white; orange feet. *Male:* highly iridescent green head; bright yellow bill; unmarked chestnut breast; white neck ring; upcurled, black central tail feathers. *Female:* finely patterned brown overall, with a thin dark line from the eye to base of the bill; dark-mottled, dull orange bill. *In flight:* flashes white wing linings; flies heavily for a duck, with little wavering or veering; bold, even wingstrokes.
Size: *L* 20–28 in.
Status: common to abundant migrant and visitor from September to April; most commonly seen flying about in pairs from midwinter to late spring.
Habitat: clean freshwater and brackish wetland habitats of nearly every description; partial to grainfields, row crop stubble, 'sheet water' and sprouting pasturage; flightless adults in early summer resort to tall, undisturbed emergent vegetation near open water.

Nesting: in tall vegetation or under a bush, often near water; nest of grass and other plant material is lined with down; female incubates 7–10 white to olive buff eggs for 26–30 days.
Feeding: tips-up, gleans and dabbles in shallows for the seeds of sedges, willows; pondweeds and other aquatic plants; takes some mollusks and other invertebrates, larval amphibians, fish eggs and waste crops.
Voice: female utters a raucous series of descending quacks; male, heard less often, gives a low *jeeeb* upon approach.
Similar Species: *Northern Shoveler* (p. 83): male has a white breast, with chestnut restricted to the sides; spatulate bill. *Gadwall* (p. 77): white speculum; lacks the dark line between the eye and bill and the abrupt forehead/ crown angle.

BLUE-WINGED TEAL
Anas discors

Birders beginning to look closely at waterfowl in northern California will likely make acquaintance of most of the routine duck species before they encounter their first small flock of Blue-winged Teals. These small ducks are found in abundance chiefly in mid-continent, concentrating along the Central and Mississippi flyways. However, they nest widely across North America and are fairly long-distance migrants, so that their appearance nearly anywhere during spring and fall can be expected. Modest numbers occur during the warmer months in the Pacific States, most merely passing through but some remaining to breed. While some northbound migrants appear in April, Blue-winged Teals are notable for continuing their passage through May and even into June—sometimes raising false hopes that they may be nesting locally. Individuals, pairs and small groups frequent marshes, reed-bordered ponds, mudflats and seasonal wetlands in both spring and fall. A few linger through winter in favored areas, often in association with Cinnamon Teals. Females and males in eclipse plumage closely resemble Cinnamon Teals and require much practice to consistently distinguish. Some birds are best left unidentified.

ID: *Male:* smoky, blue-gray head; white crescent on the face; rich brown breast and sides are evenly spotted with black. *Female:* mottled brownish-gray overall; fairly obvious, dark eye line; pale supercilium; smaller, neater, white spot on the chin. *In flight:* pale blue forewing patch; green speculum.
Size: *L* 14–16 in.
Status: very uncommon to fairly common migrant from late March to early June and from early August to November; rare to locally uncommon winter visitor; breeds in small numbers.
Habitat: freshwater wetlands, lakes, ponds and marshes; dairy and ranch ponds; migrants may use estuarine-edge habitats, such as mudflats, secluded tidal channels and saltmarsh pools.
Nesting: in grass along shorelines and in wet meadows, usually very near water; nest is built with grass and considerable amounts

of down; female incubates 8–11 eggs for 24 days.
Feeding: gleans the water's surface for sedge and grass seeds, pondweeds, duckweeds and aquatic invertebrates.
Voice: seldom heard in northern California; male utters a soft *keck-keck-keck;* female utters soft quacks.
Similar Species: *Cinnamon Teal* (p. 82): broader-ended, spatulate bill; males may have reddish eyes and lack the white facial crescent; female is virtually identical, except for the less-distinct face pattern and no well-defined white chin spot. *Green-winged Teal* (p. 85): smaller bill; lacks the blue forewing patch; male lacks the white facial crescent. *Northern Shoveler* (p. 83): distinctly larger billed.

CINNAMON TEAL
Anas cyanoptera

If the Stetson is 'the hat of the West,' then so too is the Cinnamon Teal 'the duck of the West.' The principal distribution of both the headwear and the bird define in a broad sense that great reach of arid country where the presence of water is dramatic and important. Cinnamon Teals push northward each spring from Southwestern and Middle American wintering grounds to dot the reed-fringed pools of intermountain basins. They nest in valleys on both sides of the Cascade-Sierra divide, breeding locally west to the coastal and near-coastal lowlands. They are most common in the alkaline bulrush marshes of the Great Basin and in managed Klamath Basin wetlands, where they are routinely among the most abundant summering waterfowl. • The intense reddish-brown plumage of the male Cinnamon Teal, accented by his ruby-red eyes, is worth an admiring gaze at any time of day. During the low, slanting light of early morning and near sunset, however, this bird can be a true showstopper. • Female ducks of most species are abandoned by their mates during nesting, but female Cinnamon Teals may be accompanied by their partners throughout the nesting cycle.

ID: small duck; big-billed. *Male:* intense cinnamon red head, neck and underparts; red eyes. *Female:* mottled warm brown overall; dark eyes. *In flight:* conspicuous pale blue forewing patch; green speculum.
Size: *L* 15–17 in.
Status: fairly common to common migrant from February to early May and from August to mid-November; locally rare to fairly common winter visitor; rare to locally common breeder from mid-April to August.
Habitat: freshwater ponds, marshes, sloughs and flooded swales with surface-growing or submergent aquatic vegetation; somewhat partial to sites providing nearby marsh cover; less apt than other dabbling ducks to feed in large flocks far out in open stubble fields or pastures.

Nesting: in tall vegetation, occasionally far from water; nest of grass and down is placed in a concealed hollow; female incubates 7–12 eggs for 21–25 days; ducklings fly after 7 weeks.
Feeding: gleans the water's surface for grass and sedge seeds, pondweeds, duckweeds and aquatic invertebrates.
Voice: not often heard; male utters a whistled *peep*; female gives a rough *karr, karr, karr*.
Similar Species: *Ruddy Duck* (p. 102): male has a white cheek, blue bill and stiff, upward-angled tail. *Green-winged Teal* (p. 85): small bill; no forewing patch. *Blue-winged Teal* (p. 81): male has a white crescent in front of the eye.

NORTHERN SHOVELER

Anas clypeata

No one seeing a Northern Shoveler for the first time can fail to be impressed by its remarkable bill. The broad, spatulate shape, together with the highly developed fringing lamellae, are adaptations allowing this duck to sift fine organic material from the surface of still or stagnant water. Shovelers are partial to freshwater shallows supporting abundant water plants and tiny invertebrates. • Shovelers are among the earlier-arriving fall migrant waterfowl, appearing in small numbers outside their breeding areas by late July, becoming routine by September and remaining common thereafter wherever they choose to winter. Pure flocks of migrant shovelers may be encountered about rain pools and in managed wetlands during April and early May. Although they tend to move in groups of their own kind, shovelers often concentrate in greatest numbers in loose company of Green-winged Teals, Cinnamon Teals, Ruddy Ducks and American Coots at such venues as marsh-lined lagoons and sewage ponds. Their clumsy appearance on the water is forgotten entirely when they are in flight—shovelers are speedy and skilled on the wing.

ID: large, spatulate bill. *Male:* green head; white breast; chestnut sides. *Female:* mottled brown overall; large, orange-tinged bill. *In flight:* flashes the pale blue forewing patch and green speculum; large bill gives the bird a front-heavy look.

Size: L 18–20 in.

Status: common to abundant migrant and visitor from mid-August to early May; locally rare to fairly common summer breeder.

Habitat: shallow freshwater lakes, ponds, flooded cropland, marshes and sloughs with muddy bottoms and emergent vegetation; concentrates at favored sites rich in water plants, such as sewage ponds, lagoons and semifluid mudflats with algal growth; regularly visits upper reaches of estuaries.

Nesting: in a shallow hollow on dry ground, usually within 150 ft of water; female builds a nest of dry grass and down and incubates 10–12 eggs for 25 days; ducklings show the distinctive, spoon-like bill after 2 weeks.

Feeding: dabbles and gleans water and mud; strains plant and animal matter, especially aquatic crustaceans, insect larvae and seeds; seldom tips-up.

Voice: generally quiet; birds in flocks approached closely utter a gasping *kup…hup-kup.*

Similar Species: *Mallard* (p. 80): smaller bill; male has a chestnut breast, white flanks and yellow bill; female has a blue speculum and lacks the pale blue forewing patch. *Cinnamon Teal* (p. 82): female is smaller and has a much slimmer, all-dark bill.

NORTHERN PINTAIL
Anas acuta

O f the several million waterfowl hosted annually by the marshes, lakes and grainfields of the interior Pacific Flyway, a good percentage is represented by just a handful of species. The Northern Pintail is among those species that are especially abundant in the right place at the right time. Hordes of pintails funnel through the Klamath Basin and on into the Central Valley each fall, with many spending the winter before returning northward. • While in northern California, Northern Pintails are particularly attracted to grain fields planted both as waterfowl food and as a means of relieving foraging pressure on nearby farms. Although they nest locally in some numbers in our region, most breed chiefly to the north of California. • Pintails are one of the earliest fall migrant waterfowl to appear well outside nesting areas. A few regularly show up along the coast by mid-July. However, it is not until well into fall that tens of thousands of them crowd roosting sites at reservoirs and marshes, flying miles to outlying feeding areas only at dusk. With the continued diminishment of pristine wetlands throughout the West, managed lands obtained or leased by waterfowl conservation organizations have proven of critical importance in sustaining healthy migration and wintering habitat for Pintails and many other ducks.

ID: *Male:* long, white neck; chocolate-brown head; long, tapering tail feathers; grayish body; white breast. *Female:* built much like the male, but is mottled warm-brown overall; slightly pointed tail; dark bill.
Size: *Male: L* 25–30 in. *Female: L* 20–22 in.
Status: common to abundant migrant and visitor from mid-July to late April; locally fairly common summer breeder.
Habitat: shallow freshwater or estuarine marsh; sprouting pastures, reed-bordered impoundments and 'sheet water' situations, such as flooded crop stubble.
Nesting: in a small depression in vegetation, usually near water; nest of grass, leaves and moss is lined with the female's down; female incubates 6–9 eggs for up to 24 days.

Feeding: tips-up and dabbles in shallows for the seeds of sedges, willows and pond-weeds; takes aquatic invertebrates and larval amphibians; consumes much waste grain by grazing on land in agricultural and waterfowl management areas during migration.
Voice: male gives a soft whistling call that is distinctive, but is easily lost among the hubbub of other waterfowl voices; female utters a rough quack.

Similar Species: *Mallard* (p. 80) and *Gadwall* (p. 77): females are chunkier and lack the tapering tail. *Blue-winged Teal* (p. 81): female is smaller and has a large, pale blue forewing patch.

GREEN-WINGED TEAL

Anas crecca

The name 'teal' is applied to 16 of the world's smaller waterfowl, including such far-flung subjects as the Puna Teal of the Andean plateau and the Hottentot Teal of much of Africa. However, ask any person attuned to the natural scene anywhere across the Northern Hemisphere to quickly envision a 'teal,' and what comes to mind is familiar to many: the widespread Green-winged Teal exemplifies the diminutive build, speediness and habitat of many of its relatives. • This dabbling duck favors the frontier between the cover of marsh vegetation and the enticing expanses of open country beyond. Green-wings visit even the smallest marshes offering some semi-open water and a muddy border. On the wing, their small size, darkness and habit of 'turning the corner' tightly in wheeling flocks suggests the flight of shorebirds. They are among the most widely hunted ducks and, despite their size, are esteemed as a table bird.

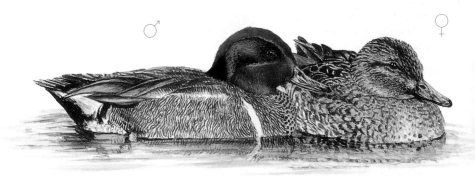

ID: petite; small, 'scoop' bill. *Male:* chestnut head with a glossy green swipe extending back from the eye; vertical, white shoulder slash; creamy breast is spotted with black; pale gray sides; noticeable yellow spot near the rear end. *Female:* mottled brown overall, with a pale belly; variable dark eye line.
Size: *L* 12–16 in.
Status: common to locally abundant migrant from early August to April; retreats from interior and mountain regions where water bodies freeze in winter; locally rare to fairly common summer breeder.
Habitat: great variety of freshwater and estuarine situations, favoring shallow marshes with semifluid mud and bulrush tussocks or other scattered, low cover; assembles along lakeshore shallows, on protected tidal flats and channels, at sewage ponds and in great numbers within the larger waterfowl refuges and management areas.

Nesting: well concealed in tall vegetation; nest of grass and leaves is lined with down; female incubates 6–11 creamy-white eggs for about 21 days.
Feeding: dabbles in shallow water and walks about in wet mud searching for sedge seeds, pondweeds, aquatic and estuarine invertebrates and larval amphibians.
Voice: male is quite vocal, uttering crisp, piping whistles; female quacks softly.
Similar Species: *American Wigeon* (p. 79): lacks the white shoulder slash and the chestnut head. *Blue-winged Teal* (p. 81) and *Cinnamon Teal* (p. 82): males are distinctively patterned; females suggest Green-winged, but have larger bills and pale blue forewing patches.

CANVASBACK
Aythya valisineria

Canvasbacks are elegant diving ducks with a uniquely sloping profile. Their long bills meet the forecrown with no apparent break in angle, allowing birds of either sex to be distinguished at long range. • Canvasbacks are members of a sizable genus of diving ducks of deep marshes, larger freshwater bodies and estuaries. The various *Aythya* ducks tend to be 'dark at both ends and pale in the middle.' They are clumsy on land, owing to their rearward-set legs, and they all require a brief running start in order to become airborne. They fly with rapid, flickering wingbeats, each species offering repeated glimpses of characteristic wing patterns. • In the U.S., Canvasbacks breed chiefly in Great Basin and Great Plains marshes, wintering southward and coastally. The cultivation of the prairies has diminished their pothole-and-marsh nesting habitat across much of the southern portion of their range, but large flocks still occur locally at traditional wintering sites and migratory staging areas.

ID: hefty, medium-large diving duck; long bill; evenly sloped forecrown. *Male:* white back; deep reddish-chestnut head; black breast and hindquarters; red eyes. *Female:* grayish body; pale brown head, neck and breast; profile is similar to the male's.
Size: L 19–22 in.
Status: very uncommon to common migrant and visitor from late October to late March; rare summer breeder.
Habitat: occurs widely on larger lakes, reservoirs, lagoons and estuaries; small numbers resort to such sites as park ponds and sewage ponds, but large concentrations prefer undisturbed expanses of open water. *Breeding:* in extensive marshes with pools of open water.
Nesting: deep, concealed nest is built upon emergent vegetation over water in marshes; female incubates 7–9 eggs for 24–29 days.
Feeding: dives to or near the bottom in water up to 30 ft deep in search of the roots, tubers, basal stems and seeds of aquatic or estuarine plants; prefers wild celery and eelgrass; takes some invertebrates.
Voice: almost never heard away from breeding sites in northern California; male utters coos and 'growls' during courtship; female gives a low, purring quack or *kuck*, and also 'growls.'
Similar Species: *Redhead* (p. 87): male has a gray back, a shorter, black-tipped, bluish bill and a more squared-off forecrown profile. *Ring-necked Duck* (p. 88): female has a sharp profile break at the hindcrown, a blurry pale area on front of the face and a shorter bill. *Common Merganser* (p. 100): male is largely white at a distance, but has a deep green head and a differently shaped, bright red bill.

REDHEAD
Aythya americana

Redheads are diving ducks with distinctly different summer and winter habitats. During the breeding season, pairs scatter across the marshes, lake edges and wetlands of central and western North America. Clean water with plenty of skirting emergent vegetation, lush bottom growth and depth sufficient to accommodate their foraging dives is required. In northern California, these needs are met wherever larger marshes occur within the intermountain Great Basin country and in the Central Valley. • During the balance of the year, flocks of varying size migrate through the region or spend the winter at widely scattered open-water sites. Redheads are quite traditional in their choice of wintering locations and often reappear in about the same numbers year after year. Hundreds, and rarely thousands, concentrate in mid-winter on large, shallow reservoirs and in the upper reaches of estuaries. Despite their local abundance, they are generally uncommon or even rare away from favored sites, dropping in to smaller lakes, reservoirs and minor estuaries in only token numbers.

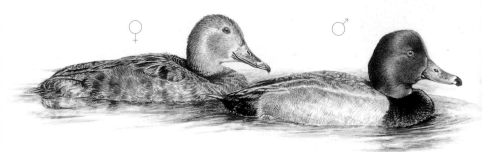

ID: stocky diving duck. *Male:* red head; black breast and hindquarters; gray back and sides; black-tipped, blue-gray bill. *Female:* dusky brown overall; face is paler toward the front; pale area between gray and black on the bill. *In flight:* flashes a broad, pale gray wing stripe.
Size: L 18–22 in.
Status: rare to locally fairly common year-round; moves toward the coast or to lower elevations in winter; almost never detected in active migration along the outer coast.
Habitat: freshwater marshes, lakes and reservoirs with bottom plants; wintering birds also use estuarine shallows, tidal channels and eelgrass beds.
Nesting: deep basket nest is well concealed at the base of emergent vegetation, suspended over water; nest is built with reeds and grass and lined with fine, white

down; female incubates 9–13 eggs for 24–28 days; noted for their frequent habit of laying eggs in other species' nests.
Feeding: dives for aquatic vegetation, especially pondweeds and duckweeds; occasionally eats aquatic invertebrates.
Voice: seldom heard away from nesting sites; in courtship, male utters a cat-like *meow* call; female gives a rolling *kurr-kurr-kurr*, and a *squak* when alarmed.
Similar Species: *Canvasback* (p. 86): male has a clean white back; both sexes have a strikingly elongated bill-and-crown profile. *Greater Scaup* (p. 89): male's head is green-glossed; female has a white patch immediately behind base of the bill; in flight, both sexes flash a broad, white wing stripe.

RING-NECKED DUCK
Aythya collaris

Birders whose ramblings during the colder months include visits to undisturbed ponds will soon discover Ring-necked Ducks. These scaup-like waterfowl typically assemble in small flocks on wooded reservoirs, along the marsh-skirted coves of lakes and in the still water of shaded river eddies. At times, however, they venture well out into the open, concentrating by the scores or even hundreds in flooded fields, on favored sewage ponds and on exposed impoundments at waterfowl refuges. • The dark brown neck ring worn by the male, and for which the species is named, is not often visible—a more fitting name would be 'Ring-billed Duck.' The archaic gunner's nickname of 'Blackjack' also retains a curious appeal and is somehow well suited to the dark, rakish good looks of the drake. • Ring-necked Ducks nest mostly to the north of our region, spanning the broad ecotone between pothole marshes and forested seclusion.

ID: smallish to mid-sized diving duck; elevated hind crown. *Male:* dark, angular head with hints of purple gloss; bright yellow eyes; black breast, back and hindquarters; vertical, white shoulder slash; gray sides; diffuse, pale patch on the front of the face; blue-gray bill with black-and-white banding. *Female:* dark brown body; light brown head; faint, white eye ring; dark eyes. *In flight:* flashes a pale gray wing stripe.
Size: L 14–18 in.
Status: fairly common migrant and visitor from mid-September to early May; uncommon local breeder; very rare in summer away from nesting areas.
Habitat: occurs widely on a variety of freshwater bodies, but prefers wooded lakes, overgrown lagoons, reed-dotted ponds, old millponds, sewage ponds with bottom growth, openings within extensive water-lily beds, forested margins of reservoirs and shady river backwaters; almost never seen on estuaries or other tidally influenced waters.

Nesting: frequently over water on a hummock or shoreline; bulky nest of grass and moss is lined with down; female incubates 8–10 olive-tan eggs for 25–29 days.
Feeding: dives underwater for aquatic vegetation, including seeds, tubers and pondweed leaves; also eats aquatic invertebrates.
Voice: alarmed birds stretch their necks, raise their fluffy crowns and utter coughing *kup-kup* notes.
Similar Species: *Lesser Scaup* (p. 90): crown is less exaggerated; male lacks the white shoulder slash and black back; female has a black-tipped, blue-gray bill. *Redhead* (p. 87): male has a red head and gray back; female lacks the obvious, suffused, pale area on the front of the face and the prominent white ring behind the black bill tip; both sexes have an abrupt forehead/crown angle rather than an elevated hindcrown.

GREATER SCAUP
Aythya marila

Greater Scaups are small to medium-sized diving ducks that are partial to open waters with submerged aquatic or estuarine plants. Greater and Lesser scaups are known to birders chiefly for their remarkable similarity. Distinguishing the two species of scaups offers a chronic challenge to many who watch waterfowl. For the inexperienced, they will seem easily separable much of the time and less so at other times. Some field guides have stressed points of difference that are inconsistent or have given emphasis to some strong points that are difficult to see clearly. Greater Scaups are larger birds with a preference for larger, deeper and more exposed settings. Contrasting with the more widespread interior distribution of Lesser Scaups, the vast majority of Greaters occur on estuaries, lagoons and reservoirs in the coastal lowlands. They often disperse thoroughly among large, mixed-species feeding flocks in open bays or along tidal channels but are known to assemble in nearly pure flocks involving hundreds or even thousands of birds. Migrants appear irregularly in very small numbers at inland lakes, wetlands and river backwaters. Flocks return each winter to a few select reservoirs in the lowlands west of the Cascade-Sierra divide.

ID: high forehead and flattish crown; heavy-based bill with a noticeable black tip; yellow eyes; gray-blue bill with a black tip; white wing strip. *Male:* iridescent dark head appears greenish; dark breast; pale gray back; white sides; dark hindquarters. *Female:* brown throughout; bold white area encircling the base of the bill. *In flight:* bright white stripe through the secondaries and inner primaries.
Size: *L* 16–20 in.
Status: uncommon to locally abundant migrant and winter visitor; a few may remain over summer; sparse migrant and local winter visitor inland.
Habitat: protected waters of estuaries, harbors, lagoons, large lakes, reservoirs and rivers; more apt than Lesser Scaup to be detected flying along outer coast in migration.

Nesting: primarily in northern Canada and Alaska; breeds across the Northern Hemisphere.
Feeding: dives for mollusks, other aquatic and estuarine creatures and some vegetation.
Voice: loud *scaup* note and other calls are seldom heard in northern California.
Similar Species: *Lesser Scaup* (p. 90): smaller bill; slightly smaller; highest point of the head is above and behind the eye; male is not as strikingly white on the sides; female is often slightly darker brown and seldom shows the large white patch on the rear of the face; white wing stripe is confined almost entirely to the secondaries.

LESSER SCAUP
Aythya affinis

Lesser Scaups are rather small diving ducks commonly encountered during the cooler months in northern California. In a sense, this species and its close relative, the Greater Scaup, are the 'dowitchers of the duck world.' These birds are similar in many respects: they are nearly identical at first glance, and, compared to some other waterfowl, they have what may politely be called a low glamour quotient. They are the source of no wondrous bird lore nor memorable works of art. • Lesser Scaups become familiar to birders early in one's experience, because they are widespread and quite abundant. They show no marked preference for habitat but occur on freshwater lakes, in open marshes and along slow-moving rivers much more commonly than do Greater Scaups. Both species mingle in an unpredictable manner, with a few Greaters appearing among large flocks of Lessers, or vice versa. It should be noted that the color of the males' head iridescence is an unreliable field mark. While Greater Scaups seldom show a purplish sheen, Lessers often flash the trademark green gloss of the opposite species. The toughest scaups to identify at close range are male Lessers that are actively diving: in the moment prior to submerging, they compress their plumage to squeeze out air, lowering the fluffy crown so that the head angle looks remarkably like that of Greater Scaup. Should such birds also show green head iridescence, the result can be confusion!

ID: small to medium-sized diving duck; gray-blue bill with a black 'nail'; white wing stripe; highest point of the head is above and behind the eye. *Male:* 'black at both ends and white in the middle'; white feathers of the sides are tipped with dark; grayish back; yellow eyes. *Female:* dark brown; white area encircling the base of the bill. *In flight:* white wing stripe.
Size: L 15–18 in.
Status: fairly common to abundant migrant and visitor from late September to late April; locally uncommon summer breeder.
Habitat: *Breeding:* large, shallow lakes of the Klamath Basin. *Winter* and *migration:* shallow, fresh and estuarine waters of nearly every description.

Nesting: in tall, concealing vegetation, generally close to water, occasionally on an island; nest hollow is built of grass and lined with down; female incubates 8–10 eggs for about 25 days.
Feeding: dives for aquatic and estuarine invertebrates and submergent vegetation.
Voice: not often heard in northern California; alarm call is a deep *scaup*.
Similar Species: *Greater Scaup* (p. 89): male has a very dark green head (often looks black); more rounded head lacks the slight peak.

HARLEQUIN DUCK
Histrionicus histrionicus

Ocean waters surging around rocky headlands or among seastacks and clusters of intertidal boulders attract Harlequin Ducks. Throughout their lives these small ducks inhabit a turbulent and spray-misted realm, at home in the roar-and-tumble of the roughest whitewater. Modest numbers of Harlequin Ducks appear in fall, remaining through winter and then returning to northern breeding areas in spring. Though they occur annually in northern California, they are never common, and are regularly encountered at only a handful of favored sites along the immediate seacoast. They are reasonably numerous only along the northernmost coast, becoming increasingly scarce and spotty farther south. Experienced birders look for them at locations in which Black Oystercatchers reach their greatest abundance: stretches of rocky shoreline that support a healthy intertidal invertebrate fauna and plenty of kelp or other marine algae. Like oystercatchers, Harlequin Ducks hauled out on rocks are easily overlooked. During their spring and fall migration to and from inland rivers, they are almost never detected. • Harlequin Ducks formerly nested at least sparingly in the Sierra Nevada and may still do so. A very few sometimes linger at wintering sites throughout the year.

ID: small, dark, rounded duck; small bill; high forehead; raises and lowers its tail while swimming. *Male:* deep gray-blue body; chestnut sides; white spots and stripes on the head, neck and flanks. *Female:* very dark brown, except for the pale belly; 3 small white spots on the side of the head.
Size: *L* 14–19 in.
Status: rare to locally uncommon visitor along the coast from October to early May; some non-breeders regularly remain along the coast in summer; formerly bred in the Sierra Nevada.
Habitat: *Breeding:* shallow, fast-flowing mountain streams. *Winter:* rocky inshore coastal waters with nearby kelp beds; may also use estuaries; rarely observed on freshwater lakes during migration.
Nesting: under bushes and shrubs or among rocks near streams or rushing rivers; shallow nest is lined with grass, plant materials and down; female incubates 5–7 cream to pale buff eggs for 27–30 days; female rears the young alone.
Feeding: dabbles, gleans from rocks and dives to inspect bottom for crustaceans, mollusks, other invertebrates and small fish.
Voice: virtually never heard while in northern California; male and female call in courtship.

Similar Species: should not be confused with other ducks; Harlequins fly more speedily and more skillfully than any of the scoters; the snub-billed silhouette is a strong clue at a distance.

SURF SCOTER
Melanitta perspicillata

Anyone becoming acquainted with the birds of open coastal waters readily learns the looks and habits of Surf Scoters. These are sturdy, heavily built ducks, at home during much of the year within the zone of steepening swells and breaking surf along the exposed ocean coast. Rafts of Surf Scoters involving hundreds or even thousands of birds assemble at frequent intervals off beaches and headlands and around harbor entrances. They are less numerous but widely seen well inside estuaries and on coastal lakes and lagoons. Although Surf Scoters are very common in winter, it is their migratory spectacle that has served most to stamp them in the minds of northern California birders who enjoy scanning the sea. • From mid-March into early May and again in October and November, immense numbers pass steadily just offshore. Flock after flock may race past a given point over the course of several hours. A thorough scope of the ocean reveals that the slowly wavering clots of dark forms extend as far as one might wish to look.

ID: large, blackish duck; large bill; no white wing patches; whitish eyes. *Male:* black overall; white patches on the forehead and on the back of the neck; clownish black, white and orange bill. *Female:* deep sooty-brown; large, black bill; 2 whitish patches on the side of the head.
Size: L 17–21 in.
Status: common to abundant migrant and visitor from October to May; varying numbers linger throughout summer; singles or very small flocks are occasional inland on lakes and reservoirs in migration, chiefly in late fall.
Habitat: varied nearshore oceanic and estuarine situations; most remain within 1 mi of shore; visits freshwater bodies inland in tiny numbers.

Nesting: in northern Canada and Alaska.
Feeding: dives in shallow to moderately deep water for mollusks, crustaceans and other marine invertebrates; takes some plant material.
Voice: generally quiet; wings whistle in flight.
Similar Species: *White-winged Scoter* (p. 93): white wing patches; male lacks the bold head patches; female is quite similar but has a less pronounced forehead/crown angle. *Black Scoter* (p. 94): more high-domed, smoothly rounded head; more snubbed bill; male has a bright orange-yellow knob on the bill; female has highly contrasting pale cheeks and a dark crown.

WHITE-WINGED SCOTER
Melanitta fusca

Scoters are big, blackish ducks commonly seen bobbing in dispersed flocks on expansive bodies of salt water. Each of the three North American species is similar in general coloration, build and habits. White-winged Scoters are the largest of the trio. On the water among Surf Scoters, their slightly greater size may be difficult to discern, but White-wings take a moment longer to become airborne, thrashing across the surface with deep wingbeats. Their bulk, combined with a habit of projecting the alula forward before submerging, causes their splash to rise 3 ft, a telltale sign of their presence when panicked birds are approached by boat. White-wings are typically somewhat warier than Surf Scoters, often seeming not to tolerate the close proximity of human activity. • These ducks are found along the entire outer coast and may become locally abundant in open harbors and over sandy bottoms offshore. Much of the time they seem markedly less common than Surf Scoters and are routinely outnumbered by them among flocks of that species. Pairs, brief lines and bunched strings of White-winged Scoters may be readily detected passing north or south from nearly any ocean viewpoint during their extended spring and fall migrations.

ID: big, black duck; conspicuous white wing patches; bulbous bill with much basal feathering. *Male*: black overall; tapering, recurved, white arc below and behind the eye; orange bill tip; pale eyes. *Female*: somber brownish-gray; 2 large whitish patches on the sides of the head. *In flight*: white wing patches; flies directly, with even, lumbering wingbeats.
Size: L 19–24 in.
Status: erratic, uncommon to common winter visitor from October to May; a few birds occasionally appear on inland lakes in spring, fall and winter; small numbers of non-breeding birds regularly remain along the coast over summer.

Habitat: varied nearshore oceanic and estuarine habitats; ranges a few miles offshore; a few appear in large lakes well inland during migration or, less frequently, in winter.
Nesting: in western and northern Canada and Alaska.
Feeding: dives in shallow to deep water in pursuit of bivalve mollusks and some crustaceans.
Voice: not heard in northern California.
Similar Species: *Surf Scoter* (p. 92): lacks the white wing patches; male has a white forehead and nape.

93

BLACK SCOTER
Melanitta nigra

Birders on the lookout for Black Scoters in northern California quickly learn that these birds are greatly outnumbered by each of the other two scoter species. As a rule, only an occasional individual or pair may be found among the big flocks of Surf and White-winged scoters rafting and diving in estuaries. Black Scoters strongly prefer outer-coastal waters, especially in the surge zone around headlands, sea stacks, reefs and rockworks, such as jetties and breakwaters. They feed singly or in very small groups of their own kind in loose association with other scoters, Pelagic Cormorants, alcids, grebes and similar inshore diving birds. The presence of Black Scoters is a clue that one or two Harlequin Ducks may also be present, because the two species often forage in the same vicinity. • Unlike Surf and White-winged scoters, these ducks typically remain landward of the outermost breakers. Although adult males are distinctive, immature or eclipse-plumaged male Surf Scoters are routinely mistaken for this species. Because of their scarcity here, Black Scoters are seen only infrequently in actual north- or southbound migration along the open coast. Thousands of Surf Scoters and hundreds of White-wingeds may pass during a 'seawatch' before a pair of Black Scoters eventually sprints by.

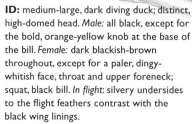

ID: medium-large, dark diving duck; distinct, high-domed head. *Male:* all black, except for the bold, orange-yellow knob at the base of the bill. *Female:* dark blackish-brown throughout, except for a paler, dingy-whitish face, throat and upper foreneck; squat, black bill. *In flight:* silvery undersides to the flight feathers contrast with the black wing linings.
Size: *L* 19 in.
Status: rare to uncommon migrant and visitor from mid-October to late April; few birds linger at favored wintering sites into or throughout summer; a great rarity inland.
Habitat: outer coast, most often in the surf zone near rocky shores and islands, edges of kelp beds or about jetties; sometimes assembles in small flocks in the lee waters of headlands; very small numbers visit the lower reaches of estuaries and, occasionally, freshwater lagoons and reservoirs along the coast.
Nesting: across the Northern Hemisphere at higher latitudes.
Feeding: dives for mollusks and other invertebrates, small fish and some plant material.
Voice: virtually never heard in northern California.
Similar Species: *White-winged Scoter* (p. 93): large, white wing patches. *Surf Scoter* (p. 92): larger, heavier bill; male usually shows at least a hint of white on the nape or forehead; female has 2 white patches on the side of the head.

OLDSQUAW
Clangula hyemalis

Oldsquaws are northern waterfowl, at home in summer on the arctic tundra and appearing in winter only sparingly along the temperate West Coast. A very thin but remarkably regular smattering of Oldsquaws occurs in northern California during the colder months, with nearly all showing up along or near the coast. • Because they are both scarce and odd-looking, a birder's first reaction to the vision in the binoculars may be momentary puzzlement. Oldsquaws are never really expected on a day's outing along the coast, so they may escape the notice of birders who do not examine large concentrations of common birds for their occasional outriders and rarities. Add to all this their lengthy dives and the cryptic markings of obscurely plumaged wintering birds, and the sum clearly is a species seen most often only by those who have gradually gained experience with them. • While in our region from October through April, Oldsquaws prefer nearshore ocean shallows over shoals or in the lee of headlands or rockwork. One or two—rarely a very small flock—establish winter quarters near harbor entrances, about piers and waterfronts, and on lagoons, seemingly at intervals of many miles along the length of the coast. • Recently, this bird's name was changed from Oldsquaw to Long-tailed Duck.

♂

♀

winter

ID: small, compact diving duck; small, rounded head; rounded-oval eyes. *1st-winter male:* long tail feathers; dark upperparts; dusky breast; whitish neck. *Winter female:* suggests male, but has a shorter tail; dark crown, cheek and upperparts.
Size: *L* 17–20 in.
Status: rare visitor from late October to late April; a few non-breeders may remain along the coast over summer.
Habitat: inshore coastal waters, including bays, harbors, lagoons and estuaries; rarely seen on inland freshwater lakes; may appear some miles out at sea.
Nesting: arctic and subarctic regions throughout the Northern Hemisphere.

Feeding: dives in water of varying depth (from intertidal shallows up to 180 ft) to pursue crustaceans, mollusks and some small fish; may take plant material.
Voice: seldom heard in northern California; loud, distinctive *ow-OWDLE-ow*; lone birds appear to remain silent.
Similar Species: *Northern Pintail* (p. 84): much longer neck and bill; most common on fresh water.

BUFFLEHEAD
Bucephala albeola

Buffleheads are frequently among the first diving ducks identified by people with a growing awareness of wild waterfowl. They are simply and boldly patterned and resemble few other species; their abundance on park ponds, urban reservoirs and similar expanses of open water causes them to be widely noticed. • Males are strikingly dressed in black and white. Their most characteristic feature is a great white patch on the rear of the head. Females are somber but appealing—their sooty heads are ornamented with a pretty white cheek spot. • Buffleheads are actually small goldeneyes. They have long been classified in the same genus, and they employ the same breeding strategy—all three species nest in tree cavities or nest boxes. • By percentage, nearly all of the Buffleheads in northern California are migrants or winter visitors. A small and scattered population nests on mountain lakes and reservoirs in the northeastern portion of the state.

ID: very small, big-headed duck. *Male:* mostly white; white wedge on the back of the head; black forecrown, back and lower face; black portion of the head is iridescent; dark eyes are surrounded by dark feathers. *Female:* charcoal gray head and upperparts; dusky sides; oblong, white patch behind and below the eye. *In flight:* small and speedy, with hectic, flickering wingbeats and white inner-wing patches above.

Size: *L* 13–15 in.

Status: fairly common migrant and visitor from mid-October to mid-April; small numbers of non-breeding birds may remain over summer; local breeder.

Habitat: prefers larger lakes, reservoirs and estuaries, but occurs widely on small lakes and ponds, river backwaters, urban impoundments and in marsh pools; breeding birds retire to the margins of wooded lakes.

Nesting: usually in an abandoned woodpecker cavity, natural tree cavity or nest box near water; nest chamber may be unlined or filled with down; 8–10 pale yellowish to buff eggs are incubated for 28–33 days; ducklings may remain in the nest for up to 3 days.

Feeding: dives for aquatic or estuarine invertebrates, such as large insects and larvae; also takes snails, crustaceans, small fish and submergent vegetation.

Voice: seldom heard in migration or winter; male utters a growling call; female gives a harsh quack.

Similar Species: *Hooded Merganser* (p. 99): darker; slim bill; male's white crest is outlined in black. *Harlequin Duck* (p. 91) found in turbulent water; female has several small white spots on the head. *Common Goldeneye* (p. 97) and *Barrow's Goldeneye* (p. 98): males are larger and have a vivid white patch between the eye and bill; females lack the white head patch.

COMMON GOLDENEYE
Bucephala clangula

Goldeneyes are characteristic nesting ducks of forested northern lakes, bog pools and beaver ponds. The bold plumage patterns and rather jutting head of the male produces a posturing appearance. The females are of a similar build but wear subdued plumages typical of female ducks as a group. • Common Goldeneyes are routine in migration and in winter in northern California, but for the most part they are truly common only on larger reservoirs and in the San Francisco Bay and other larger estuaries. While in our region, single birds, pairs and small flocks occur widely on small or secluded bodies of water, but large flocks are less apt than many other species to resort to such situations. They are only infrequently detected flying along the outer coast in migration. Common Goldeneyes are regularly among the very last migrant waterfowl to retreat from mountain lakes at the onset of ice-up. At wintering sites, they tend to scatter at some distance from one another if possible, becoming thoroughly mixed within crowded assemblages of other ducks, loons, cormorants, grebes and gulls.

ID: medium-sized diving duck; bright inner wing patches; ivory-colored eyes; wings whistle in flight. *Male:* glossy, dark green head; round white cheek patch; dark bill and back; white sides and belly. *Female:* chocolate brown head; gray-brown body; paler breast and belly; dark bill, tipped with dull yellow.

Size: *L* 16–20 in.

Status: uncommon to locally very common migrant and visitor from mid-October to April; very rare from late spring through early fall.

Habitat: lakes, reservoirs, estuaries and wide rivers; a few use ponds, channelized waterways, flooded roadside ditches and rainwater pools in pastures and fields.

Nesting: in Canada, Alaska and spottily in the northern tier of the U.S.

Feeding: dives for a great variety of aquatic or estuarine food items, such as crustaceans, mollusks, amphibians, small fish, tubers and other plant material.

Voice: male gives a shrill, abrupt *peent* note in courtship; female utters a harsh croak when agitated.

Similar Species: *Barrow's Goldeneye* (p. 98): purple-glossed head with a vivid white crescent on the front of the face; more condensed scapular spot pattern; female has a shorter, variably yellow-orange bill, a slightly smaller, deeper-brown head, fuller feathering down the nape, a more abrupt bill/forecrown angle and less white in the upperwing coverts.

BARROW'S GOLDENEYE
Bucephala islandica

The roving eyes of beginning birders poring through field guides inevitably settle on a few species they have yet to encounter. Mysterious and evocative birds, such as the Wandering Tattler, Townsend's Warbler and Barrow's Goldeneye, have often earned a spot near the top of many 'wish to see' lists. The goldeneye is certainly worthy of the honor, as both the male and female are attractive waterfowl with a subtle charm. • Adding to the moments of esthetic appreciation they invite, Barrow's Goldeneyes spur thought with their odd distribution. A great majority of these birds breed in western North America, but smaller, highly isolated populations occur in eastern Canada, Greenland and Iceland. Though their nesting range in the West is quite extensive, wintering sites are restricted, with favored locations used by about the same number of individuals year after year. Barrow's Goldeneyes once may have nested on Cascade lakes, but today in northern California they are known chiefly as a wintering species. Reservoirs in the San Francisco Bay region host most concentrations. Away from the Bay Area and the Klamath Basin they are scarce, remaining nearly unknown in many counties.

ID: medium-sized diving duck; yellow eyes. *Male:* dark purple–glossed, black head; white crescent between the eye and the bill; extensively patterned with black and white on the back and shoulders. *Female:* chocolate brown head, with an abrupt forecrown and a slightly crested hindcrown; gray-brown body; short, thick bill is variably orange-yellow.
Size: *L* 16–20 in.
Status: very rare to locally fairly common migrant and visitor from mid-October to late March.
Habitat: lakes, reservoirs, estuaries, lagoons and rivers.

Nesting: in the northwestern portion of North America, eastern Canada, Greenland and Iceland.
Feeding: dives for aquatic insects and larvae, mollusks, crustaceans and some plant material.
Voice: male's 'mewing' display note and female's croak are not often heard in northern California.
Similar Species: *Common Goldeneye* (p. 97): male has a green-glossed head with a round face spot; scapular spot pattern is less eye catching; female is slightly larger and has a longer bill, which is usually entirely dark or dark with a discrete yellow tip.

HOODED MERGANSER

Lophodytes cucullatus

Whether male or female, Hooded Mergansers are dark and dramatic, often unexpected and always a treat to see. These small mergansers are distinctive not only for their loveliness but for the characteristics of the places they live. They shun large open bodies of water, instead favoring secluded, sheltered or overgrown situations. Given a choice between the sunny and shady shorelines of a tree-fringed lake, they opt for the shady side; along streams, they retire to the edges of the bank that lies in shadow. • The spectacular plumage of the adult male blends well with the dappled and irregular fall of sunlight cast upon the water or through overarching vegetation. The female is more thoroughly dusky, in accordance with a general rule among sexes of small waterfowl. • Hooded Mergansers are very rare in northern California in late spring and summer, nesting almost entirely north of the region. Although a few are seen each year in September, they are among the latest waterbirds to arrive in fall, showing up in most areas only in October or November. Compared to most other migrant and wintering ducks, Hooded Mergansers are not especially numerous, usually appearing in pairs or in small flocks.

ID: slim body; thin, pointed bill; crested head. *Male:* black head and back; bold white crest is outlined in black; white breast; 2 white shoulder slashes; deep rusty sides. *Female:* gray-tinged, dusky-brown body; reddish-brown crest. *In flight:* small and speedy; crest is flattened, drawing attention to the long, thin bill; shows very small white wing patches.

Size: L 16–19 in.

Status: very uncommon to locally fairly common visitor from late October to April; spring and fall migrants occur widely; very rare summer breeder.

Habitat: freshwater lakes, ponds, lagoons, rivers and the upper reaches of estuarine tidal channels.

Nesting: in forested regions of north-western and eastern U.S. and Canada.

Feeding: prey is captured by diving; eats small fish, aquatic insects and larvae, snails, amphibians, crayfish and other crustaceans.

Voice: male's crooning display call is almost never heard in northern California; soft guttural croaks are heard from birds in larger flocks.

Similar Species: *Bufflehead* (p. 96): male is much whiter and lacks the black outline to the crest and the white shoulder slashes; female is quite sooty overall, with a neat white oval centered over the cheek. *Red-breasted Merganser* (p. 101): longer-bodied; smaller head; wispy, disheveled crest; reddish bill; most occur on saltwater.

COMMON MERGANSER

Mergus merganser

Rafts of big, white ducks massed on fish-bearing lakes and reservoirs in winter often prove to be Common Mergansers. These heavy-bodied, low-slung diving ducks require a running start for takeoff. Like other mergansers, they have slender bills with numerous tooth-like protrusions for grasping slippery prey. • In spring, Common Mergansers disperse thinly, but widely, throughout much of forested northern California to nest. Pairs may be seen swimming or resting every few miles along foothill rivers, within coastal creek entrances and locally high into drainage headwaters during early spring. Pair bonds dissolve with the onset of incubation, and the hen assumes full responsibility for the brood of ducklings. As the ducklings mature, families descend from creek canyons to gather in larger groups at river bars, pools and minor estuaries. Common Mergansers strictly avoid salt water, preferring expanses of clear, fresh water with a dependable fishery.

ID: large, elongated body; long, red bill.
Male: glossy green, uncrested head; brilliant orange to blood red bill and feet; white body plumage; black spinal stripe; large white patch on the upper forewing. *Female:* rusty head; clean white neck and throat; gray body. *In flight:* shallow wingbeats; body is compressed and arrow-like; white speculum.

Size: L 22–27 in.

Status: uncommon to locally common migrant and visitor from October to April; rare to uncommon, local summer breeder.

Habitat: cleaner rivers, lakes, reservoirs and the reach of estuaries above strong tidal influence.

Nesting: often in a tree cavity 15–20 ft. high; occasionally on the ground, under a bush or log, on a cliff ledge or in a large nest box; usually not far from water; female incubates 8–11 eggs for up to 35 days.

Feeding: dives underwater (up to 30 ft) for small fish, usually trout, carp, suckers, perch and catfish; may also eat shrimp, salamanders and mussels; young eat aquatic invertebrates.

Voice: *Male:* utters a harsh *uig-a*, like a guitar twang. *Female:* harsh *karr karr*.

Similar Species: *Red-breasted Merganser* (p. 101): shaggy crest; male has a spotted, red breast; female lacks the cleanly defined white throat. *Mallard* (p. 80): male has a chestnut breast. *Common Goldeneye* (p. 97) and *Barrow's Goldeneye* (p. 98): males have a white cheek patch. *Common Loon* (p. 40): white spotting on the back; bill is not orange.

RED-BREASTED MERGANSER

Mergus serrator

Many species of birds are familiar to us—hummingbirds at a feeder, the towhees in the yard and swallows nesting on a nearby building. We see details of their life history close up, without having to imagine what their more intimate existence may be like. Then there are those birds visiting northern California that most people will always know simply by their presence or absence—birds whose lives remain largely unknown. Migrant and wintering birds fit this description, because their breeding behavior and summering habitats can be known only by going where the birds go. Red-breasted Mergansers are such a species. Although they are common ducks, occurring widely throughout coastal waters, few people know them well. In the North American portion of their range, they nest in boreal forests and above treeline in Canada and Alaska. They are among the routine wintering diving ducks of estuarine shallows, shipping channels and the more protected open ocean along the entire stretch of outer coast. A very few appear well inland during migration periods, typically in late fall and early winter, favoring larger reservoirs. They associate only loosely with other waterfowl, but are commonly found sprinkled individually among grebes, loons and scoters, or in loose flocks of their own kind.

ID: large, elongated duck; thin, red, serrated bill; shaggy, slicked-back crest. *Male:* green head; light rusty breast is spotted with black; white collar; gray sides; black-and-white wing coverts; red eyes. *Female:* gray-brown overall; reddish head. *In flight:* male has 2 dark bars separating the white upperwing; female has 1 dark bar separating the white speculum from the white upperwing patch.

Size: *L* 19–26 in.

Status: fairly common visitor from mid-October to May on saltwater; a few non-breeders remain through summer; very rare inland.

Habitat: inshore coastal waters, including saltwater bays, harbors, lagoons and estuaries; may also use freshwater lakes and large rivers.

Nesting: mostly in Alaska and northern and eastern Canada; also in the northern Midwest and northeastern U.S.

Feeding: dives underwater for small fish; also takes aquatic insects, fish eggs, crustaceans and tadpoles.

Voice: generally quiet. *Male:* cat-like *yeow* during courtship and feeding. *Female:* harsh *kho-kha.*

Similar Species: *Common Merganser* (p. 100): male lacks the spotted red breast; border between the head and breast is more clearly defined; female has a cleanly defined white throat. *Hooded Merganser* (p. 99): female has a dark foreneck and smaller white speculum.

RUDDY DUCK
Oxyura jamaicensis

Give a kid a box of crayons, ask for a duck to be drawn, and the portrayal of a creature much resembling a Ruddy Duck may result. With their big heads, outsized bills, pointy tails and bold coloration, male Ruddy Ducks in their spring finery look indeed like a cartoon come alive. The male's intent is nothing but serious, however, as he advertises for prospective mates with a vigorous bill-pumping display accompanied by staccato grunting notes. • Female Ruddies are appealing as well, dressed in brown and with an odd dark stripe across the lower face. Relative to their body size, they lay extraordinarily large eggs. • Ruddy Ducks are routine breeding birds in the larger deep-water marshes and about the margins of reed-skirted ponds. Although scattered singles and pairs occur widely, they are given to assembling in large flocks. Ruddies are commonly encountered coastally and at open reservoirs throughout most of temperate northern California in winter.

breeding

ID: small and chubby; large bill and head; unique tail of 20 stiff, pointed feathers carried at an upward angle. *Breeding male:* bold white cheeks; chestnut red body; intensely blue bill; black tail and crown. *Female:* brown overall; distinct, dark cheek stripe; darker crown and back. *Winter male:* drab like the female, but with white cheeks.
Size: *L* 15–16 in.
Status: variably uncommon to abundant year-round resident; common to abundant visitor from mid-September to mid-April; most numerous in breeding season.
Habitat: *Breeding:* around openings in deeper marshes or on marsh-skirted ponds and lakes. *Winter:* birds assemble in large flocks on still or protected tidal waters of nearly every description. *In migration:* may use small impoundments, such as sewage ponds, ranch ponds, golf course water features and similar sites.

Nesting: in cattails, bulrushes or other emergent vegetation; occasionally on a muskrat lodge or a log; basket-like nest is always suspended over water; occasionally uses the abandoned nest of another duck or coot; female incubates 5–10 whitish eggs for 23–26 days.
Feeding: dives to the bottom for the seeds of pondweeds, sedges and bulrushes and for the leafy portions of aquatic or estuarine plants; also takes a few aquatic invertebrates.
Voice: male in courtship display utters a brief, chuttering series of low grunts, accelerating toward the end; otherwise appears to be among the least vocal species occurring in northern California.
Similar Species: should be confused with no other waterfowl if the tail is clearly observed.

OSPREY
Pandion haliaetus

Ospreys are often seen soaring high above expansive waterways or perched atop impressive stick nests. • This majestic raptor is specially designed for the task of catching live fish. Its primarily white undersides disappear against the sky as it flies high above lakes, rivers and bays in search of prey dwelling just below the surface. The Osprey's broad wings help it glide on rising thermals, while its dark mask reduces the blinding glare of sunshine skipping off the water. • Osprey feathers are more water resistant than those of other raptors because of frequent preening. • An Osprey's feet are specialized to ensnare its catch: two toes extend forward, two backward and the soles are heavily scaled to help it clamp tightly onto slippery fish. • Sometimes an Osprey will disappear beneath the water's surface before emerging with its catch. Rising back into the air, the Osprey, if necessary, re-positions its catch to face forward for optimum aerodynamics.

ID: large raptor; dark brown upperparts; white underparts; dark eye line; light crown. *Male:* all-white throat; lacks the visible 'brow' of many large raptors. *Female:* fine, dark 'necklace.' *In flight:* long wings are held in a distinctive M; dark 'wrist' patches; rather small tail is finely banded with black and white.
Size: L 22–25 in; W 54–72 in.
Status: rare to uncommon year-round; withdraws from the north and mountains in winter; formerly widespread throughout the state.
Habitat: lakes, reservoirs, rivers, estuaries and open seacoast.
Nesting: on exposed treetops, utility poles, transmission towers, beacons or pilings, 10–250 ft high; large stick nest; male feeds the female while she incubates 2–4 (usually 3) eggs.
Feeding: dramatic, feet-first dives into the water; fish, averaging 2 lb, make up 98% of its diet.
Voice: series of piercing, whistled notes: *chewk!-chewk!-chewk!*; also an often-heard *kip-kip-kip*; pairs may be vocal at the nest site.

Similar Species: *Bald Eagle* (p. 105): larger, with much larger bill; wings held flat when soaring; adult has a clean white head and tail, all-dark underparts and no 'wrist' patches; mottled subadult lacks the clean, well-defined, dark-and-white patterning.

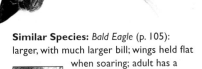

WHITE-TAILED KITE

Elanus leucurus

The White-tailed Kite, which flies with grace and buoyancy uncommon among raptors, routinely hunts from dawn until deep evening twilight. When it spots a vole scurrying through the grass, it parachutes down on the rodent with wings held high. • White-tailed Kites nest in trees and tall bushes in semi-open areas. The nests are often built near the treetop, away from the main trunk and larger horizontal limbs. Males hunt for both themselves and the incubating female and nestlings. • Kite populations exhibit swings in abundance. Now numerous, persecution early in the 20th century brought them to the brink of extripation in California. • This bird was formerly known as the Black-shouldered Kite.

ID: strikingly whitish, falcon-shaped raptor; long, white tail; pointed wings; black shoulders; gray back. *In flight:* small black patch on the outer underwing; buoyant flapping; hovers with its body held at a steep angle.
Size: L 15–17 in; W 40 in.
Status: uncommon to locally common year-round resident; numbers cyclical with prey populations.
Habitat: tree-dotted lowland or hillside fields, ungrazed or fallow grasslands, marshes, croplands and savannah; evening roosts in winter sometimes involve over 100 birds.
Nesting: in a tree, often an oak, well above the ground; pair builds a bulky stick platform lined with grass and other soft vegetation; female incubates 4 brown-blotched, creamy white eggs for 26–32 days.

Feeding: forages while flying over open ground; hovers over, then dives after prey; largely avoids man-made perches; eats mostly small rodents, such as voles; rarely takes small birds, snakes, frogs, lizards and large insects.
Voice: largely silent; call is a short, repeated *keep keep keep*; alarm call is a longer *kree-eek*.
Similar Species: *Falcons* (pp. 116–19) and *Hawks* (pp. 107–14): lack the pure white tail and the black shoulders. *Northern Harrier* (p. 106): lacks the black shoulders; has a conspicuous white rump; hovers infrequently.

BALD EAGLE
Haliaeetus leucocephalus

The Bald Eagle is a source of inspiration and wonder: time ceases for a moment in its presence. This bird is symbolically represented in both aboriginal myth and modern Native American ritual. • Fortunately, the U.S. national symbol continues to hold its place upon the landscape of northern California. Habitat protection, restoration of native salmon stocks and respectful behavior at eagle nesting and feeding sites will help Bald Eagles return to their rightful place throughout northern California. • The decision to select the Bald Eagle as the United States' national bird was not without controversy. Benjamin Franklin, a respected naturalist of his day, opposed the decision because of this bird's 'dishonorable' habit of scavenging and stealing fish from Ospreys.

immature

ID: very large raptor; unfeathered lower legs; white head and tail; dark brown body; yellow beak and feet; yellow eyes. *1st-year:* brown overall; dark eyes; dark bill; some white in the underwings. *2nd-year:* wide, white band at the base of the tail; light belly and underwings. *3rd- and 4th-year:* light head; dark eye line; yellow at the base of the bill; variable white body plumage; paler eyes. *In flight:* prolonged soaring on flat wings.
Size: *L* 30–43 in; *W* 5¹/₂–8 ft.
Status: rare to locally fairly common migrant and visitor from October to early April; local summer breeder and possible year-round resident.
Habitat: *Breeding:* lakeshores, river corridors, estuaries and seacoast. *Winter and In migration:* coastal and inland waterways, river shores, wildlife refuges.
Nesting: usually in trees bordering lakes or large rivers; huge stick nest up to 15 ft across; pair incubates 2 white eggs for 34–36 days; both adults feed the young.

Feeding: opportunistic; fish are caught by swoops to the water's surface or are pirated from Ospreys; scavenges dead fish, waterfowl and livestock carcasses.
Voice: agitated, thin, weak squeal or cackle: *kleek-kik-kik-kik!* or *kah-kah-kah*; argumentative in group foraging.
Similar Species: adult is unmistakable. *Golden Eagle* (p. 115): similar to immature Bald Eagle, but with a golden nape, smaller bill and fully feathered legs; base of the tail feathers and base of the underwing flight feathers are white, strikingly so in young birds.

NORTHERN HARRIER
Circus cyaneus

The Northern Harrier may be the easiest hawk to identify on the wing, because no other hawk routinely flies so close to the ground. This common hawk cruises low across fields, meadows and marshes, seeming to graze the tops of long grass and cattails with its belly. Although it has excellent vision, its owl-like, parabolic facial disc allows it to hunt efficiently by sound. • Determining the sex of a Northern Harrier is nearly as easy as identifying it: males are gray; females are brown. • Harriers are most common in northern California from September to April. • The genus name *Circus* is an apt tribute to this hawk's typically erratic flight pattern. • This bird was once known as the Marsh Hawk in North America and is still called the Hen Harrier in Europe. Britain's Royal Air Force has named their hovering Harrier fighter aircraft after this maneuverable winged predator.

ID: long wings and tail; white rump; facial disk. *Male:* gray upperparts; white underparts; black wing tips; indistinct tail bands. *Female:* reddish brown overall. *Immature:* dark tail bands; heavily streaked breast, sides and flanks.

Size: *L* 16–24 in; *W* 44–47 in.

Status: uncommon to locally common migrant and visitor from September to April; rare to uncommon breeder and year-round resident (formerly more widespread and numerous in summer).

Habitat: almost any type of open country, including open fields, wet meadows, fresh- and saltwater marshes, agricultural fields, hedgerows, savannah and alpine meadows; some migrate at higher elevations in fall; absent from extensively forested areas.

Nesting: on the ground, often on a mound, usually in shrubs, cattails or tall vegetation; flat platform nest is built of grass, sticks and cattails; female incubates 4–6 bluish eggs for 30–32 days.

Feeding: hunts by sight and sound in low, coursing flights, 5–30 ft above the ground; eats small mammals, birds, amphibians and reptiles.

Voice: vocal during courtship, near nest site and when repelling other harriers; peevish, complaining series of whistles.

Similar Species: *Red-tailed Hawk* (p. 112) and *Red-shouldered Hawk* (p. 110): chunkier; lack the white rump and the long, narrow tail. *Rough-legged Hawk* (p. 114): broader wings; black 'wrist' patches; fan-like tail with 1 or more whitish bands.

SHARP-SHINNED HAWK

Accipiter striatus

When delivering food to his nestlings, a male Sharp-shinned Hawk is quite cautious around his mate—she is typically one-third larger than he is. The two sexes often prey on different-sized animals, helping to reduce competition and conflict over food supplies and maximize the total available food base. • Accipiters are woodland hawks. Their short, rounded wings, long, rudder-like tails and flap-and-glide flight pattern give these birds the maneuverability to negotiate a maze of tree-trunks and foliage at high speeds. • Rural feeders will often attract 'Sharpies'—not for the seeds, but for the small birds the food attracts. • The 'sharp shins' of this hawk serve no purpose in field identification.

ID: small, slender hawk; short, rounded wings; long, straight tail; blue-gray back; fine, red, horizontal bars on the underparts; red eyes. *Immature:* brown overall; brown eyes; lengthwise, rusty-brown streaking on the breast and belly. *In flight:* flap-and-glide flyer; tail is heavily barred and is squared or notched at the tip, with a narrow white terminal band.
Size: *Male: L* 10–12 in; *W* 20–24 in. *Female: L* 12–14 in; *W* 24–28 in.
Status: fairly common to common migrant and visitor from mid-September to mid-April; fall migration extends from mid-September to late October; rare to uncommon summer breeder and year-round resident in wooded areas.
Habitat: dense to semi-open coniferous, deciduous or mixed forests; occasionally along riparian edges. *In migration:* usually seen soaring on thermals or hunting in alpine areas.
Nesting: stick or twig nest is usually built each year, normally about 2 ft across; may remodel an abandoned crow nest; female incubates 4–5 eggs for up to 35 days; male feeds the female during incubation.
Feeding: pursues small birds in quick, high-speed chases; takes more birds than other accipiters; rarely takes small mammals, amphibians and insects; hunts mostly from a perch.
Voice: silent, except during the breeding season, when an intense and often repeated *kik-kik-kik-kik* greets intruders at nest sites.
Similar Species: *Cooper's Hawk* (p. 108): larger; rounded 'spoony' tail with a noticeable white terminal band. *American Kestrel* (p. 116): long, pointed wings; vividly patterned; 2 dark 'side-burns'; usually seen perched or flying in open country. *Merlin* (p. 117): pointed wings; rapid wing-beats; lacks the red breast streaks.

COOPER'S HAWK
Accipiter cooperii

Were songbirds to dream, Cooper's Hawks would certainly populate their nightmares. This forest hawk hunts silently, using surprise and speed to ambush its wary prey. Bursting from an overhead perch, a Cooper's Hawk will pursue a songbird, using long legs equipped with sharp talons to grab its quarry in mid-air. • Since the use of DDT was banned in the U.S. and Canada, this forest hawk has slowly recolonized many of its former habitats and expanded into new ones. • This hawk bears the name of William Cooper, one of the many collectors who supplied English and American ornithologists with bird specimens for museum collections during the early 19th century.

ID: short, round wings; long, rounded tail; squarish head; blue-gray back; fine, red, horizontal barring on the underparts; red eyes; white, terminal tail band. *Immature:* brown overall; brown eyes; crisp, blackish-brown streaks on the breast. *In flight:* flap-and-glide flier; heavily barred, 'spoony,' rounded tail, with a light band at the tip.
Size: *Male: L* 15–17 in; W 27–32 in. *Female: L* 17–19 in; W 32–37 in.
Status: rare to uncommon year-round resident; uncommon to locally common migrant and visitor from mid-September to early April; fall migration extends from mid-September to mid-October.
Habitat: open woodlands and brushland. *Nesting:* broken woodlands, especially in riparian areas, canyons and floodplains. *In migration:* usually seen soaring on thermals in open areas or passing along ridgelines.
Nesting: in the fork of a tree, often in the outer branches; nest is made of sticks and twigs; may reuse an abandoned crow's nest; female incubates 4–5 bluish eggs for 30–36 days.

Feeding: pursues prey in flight through the forest or at the edges of open country; eats thrushes, sparrows, squirrels, woodpeckers, chipmunks and starlings; often takes prey to a plucking post prior to eating.
Voice: largely silent; fast, woodpecker-like *cac-cac-cac-cac* is given when agitated near the nest.
Similar Species: *Sharp-shinned Hawk* (p. 107): smaller; tail is not rounded. *Red-shouldered Hawk* (p. 110): shares the vigorous, rapid flap-and-glide flight with Cooper's, but is chunkier and larger; reddish-brown shoulder patches; longer, broader wings; wider, fan-shaped tail. *Prairie Falcon* (p. 119): long, pointed wings; 2 dark 'sideburns'; lacks the red breast streaks; dark 'wing pits.'

NORTHERN GOSHAWK

Accipiter gentilis

The disposition of our largest forest hawk is legendary, and goshawks have been observed preying on any reasonably sized animal. After chasing and catching their prey in a high-speed aerial sprint, these raptors stab repeatedly at the victims' internal organs with their long talons. When elusive prey disappears under the cover of dense thickets, goshawks have been known to chase down their quarry on foot. Human intruders at nest sites are often the subject of swooping attacks. • Because the Northern Goshawk requires extensive areas of forest in which to hunt and nest, its population has diminished in areas throughout Northern Europe, Asia and North America. Timber harvest has generally caused a decline in northern California.

ID: robust, large hawk; rounded wings; dark cap and cheek; white eyebrow; blue-gray back; gray, finely barred underparts; long, broad-banded tail; red eyes. *Immature:* brown overall; light underparts; pale eyebrow.
Size: *Male: L* 21–23 in; *W* 40–43 in. *Female: L* 23–25 in; *W* 43–47 in.
Status: rare year-round resident; rare to very uncommon migrant and visitor from October to early April.
Habitat: *Breeding:* mature montane coniferous forests in the mountains; also found in lower-elevation coastal coniferous forests. *Non-breeding:* riparian and open woodlands, canyons, forest edges and dense tree groves in more open country. *Winter* and *In migration:* visits other habitats.
Nesting: in deep woods; in a fork usually 20–60 ft up a deciduous tree; bulky nest is built with sticks and twigs; nest is often reused; female incubates 3 eggs for 28–32 days.
Feeding: very opportunistic feeder; low foraging flights through the forest; feeds primarily on ground-dwelling birds, rabbits, ground squirrels and tree squirrels.

Voice: silent except during the breeding season, when adults utter a loud, harsh and fast *kak-kak-kak-kak.*
Similar Species: Accipiter identification can be complex. *Cooper's Hawk* (p. 108) and *Sharp-shinned Hawk* (p. 107): much smaller; narrower tails; adults have fine red breast bars. *Other large hawks:* lack the bold, light eyebrow.

RED-SHOULDERED HAWK
Buteo lineatus

Red-shouldered Hawks in northern California represent a distinctive subspecies, *B. l. elegans*, that differs somewhat in habits and appearance from birds of eastern populations. Adults of the race *elegans* are more richly colored beneath than eastern Red-shouldered Hawks. • Although our Red-shoulders nest in forest-edge and woodlands, they forage a great deal from exposed perches well removed from cover. Some individuals may hunt as far as $1/2$ mi from the nearest stand of trees. Roadside wires are commonly used—a large, chunky hawk on a powerline is possibly a Red-tailed Hawk, but, especially in summer, it is much more likely a Red-shouldered. • The range of this handsome raptor has extended northward along the coast within the past half-century, probably because of the general clearing of heavy forest cover. • Red-shouldered Hawks within California are thought to be comparatively sedentary. Little movement is evident, and migrants in the classic sense are seldom encountered.

ID: medium-large, chunky hawk; finely barred, intensely reddish underparts; multi-banded tail; boldly dark-and-light-checkered upperparts. *Immature:* darkly streaked and cross-barred below; only a suggestion of the rufous coloring of adults. *In flight:* noticeable squarish or crescent-shaped whitish patch in the outer wing.
Size: L 19 in; W 40 in.
Status: locally uncommon to quite common year-round resident.
Habitat: varied, semi-open, woodland and forest-edge situations: coastal bottomlands, agricultural lands, suburbs and city parks, lightly wooded foothills and unmanaged riversides.
Nesting: within the canopy of live trees well above the ground; pair assembles a platform of sticks lined with bark and vegetation; nest is often reused; female incubates the eggs while the male hunts; both adults raise the young.

Feeding: small mammals, birds, reptiles (especially snakes) and amphibians are usually caught by plunging or swooping.
Voice: distinctive; deliberate, descending *keea!* note is almost always delivered in a slow series.
Similar Species: *Red-tailed Hawk* (p. 112): contrasting dark bar on the leading edge of the underwing; dark belly band; lacks the bright, finely barred, reddish underparts, the banded tail and the bold whitish patch in the outer wing. *Swainson's Hawk* (p. 111): dark bib; pale underwing lining contrasts with the darker trailing portion of the wings; more pointed wings are uptilted while soaring. *Cooper's Hawk* (p. 108): smaller; slimmer; blackish cap contrasts with the lighter back.

SWAINSON'S HAWK

Buteo swainsoni

While the Red-tailed Hawk can dominate the skies over much of northern California, the Swainson's Hawk takes center stage where open country far exceeds forests, especially in grassy expanses where ground squirrels are abundant. Originally more abundant in northern California, Swainson's Hawk numbers have diminished with the conversion of native grassland. • The Swainson's Hawk undertakes the longest migration of any northern California raptor: in winter, it travels as far south as the southern tip of South America. Pesticide use on South American wintering grounds has dealt the population a blow as well, reminding us that the conservation of migratory species urgently requires international cooperation.

light morph

dark morph

ID: mid-sized soaring hawk; long, narrow wings; very small bill; fan-shaped tail. *Light morph:* dark bib; white wing linings contrast with the dark flight feathers; white belly; finely barred tail. *Dark morph:* dark wing linings blend with the brown flight feathers; brown overall. *In flight:* conspicuous wing linings and bib; wings are held in a conspicuous V.
Size: *Male:* L 19–20 in; W 52 in.
Female: L 20–22 in; W 52 in.
Status: rare to uncommon migrant in March and April and from early August to October; rare to locally fairly common summer breeder; locally rare but regular winter visitor.
Habitat: grasslands, open fields, oak savannah, croplands, pastures and scattered tree groves in open country. *In migration:* may use mountain ridges or appear at coastal hawkwatch sites.
Nesting: often in solitary trees in open fields; builds a large stick nest; often uses the abandoned nests of other raptors, crows, ravens or magpies; uses the same nest repeatedly; female incubates 2–3 eggs for about 28–35 days.

Feeding: dives to the ground for voles, mice and occasionally ground squirrels; also eats snakes, small birds and large insects, such as grasshoppers and crickets; concentrations may attend outbreaks in crop fields.
Voice: generally silent; high, weak *keeeaar*.
Similar Species: *Red-tailed Hawk* (p. 112): wings are held nearly flat while soaring; bulkier overall; larger bill; adult has a red tail; lacks the light wing linings and the dark flight feathers. *Red-shouldered Hawk* (p. 110): shoulder patches; underwing linings and barred underparts are reddish; light undersides to the flight feathers; bold, whitish patch in the outer wing. *Ferruginous Hawk* (p. 113): mostly white underparts, except for the dark reddish legs. *Falcons* (pp. 116–19): pointed wings; long, narrow tails.

RED-TAILED HAWK
Buteo jamaicensis

The Red-tailed Hawk is one of the best known, most widely distributed hawks in North America. Numerous throughout northern California, the Red-tail is often perched on a snag, exposed tree limb or fencepost overlooking open fields. • The Red-tail's distinctive, shrill 'scream' is most often heard during courtship flights or when a bird is defending its nest. This screaming, squealing call, however, is also employed enthusiastically by the motion picture industry to lend wildness to any outdoor scene. • These raptors do not obtain the brick-red coloration in their tails until they mature into adults. Plumages exhibited by members of various subspecies are confounded further by individual variation and by the existence of 'light' and 'dark' morphs.

immature

ID: red tail; dark upperparts; tawny brown underside of the body, tail and underwing linings; light underwing flight feathers; dark brown 'belt' and head. *Immature:* lacks the red tail; generally darker. *In flight:* fan-shaped tail; dark leading edge on the underside of the wing; dark 'belt'; soars with the wings held flat, or nearly so.

Size: *Male: L* 18–23 in; *W* 46–58 in. *Female: L* 20–25 in; *W* 46–58 in.

Status: common year-round resident; uncommon to common migrant from early September to early December; common visitor from December to April.

Habitat: almost any terrestrial habitat, but especially open country, fields, plains, canyons and open woodlands.

Nesting: usually in woodlands adjacent to open fields or shrublands; in a fork at the crown of a deciduous tree, or occasionally a coniferous tree or cliff; bulky stick nest is usually added to each year; pair incubates 2–3 whitish eggs with brown blotches; female raises the young, which fly at about 6 weeks.

Feeding: sit-and-wait hunting strategy from a perch; dives after prey while soaring; occasionally forages by stalking on the ground; eats small mammals, mid-sized birds, amphibians, reptiles and rarely carrion.

Voice: exuberant scream: *keee-rrrr*, down-slurred and given singly; yelps given by birds near the nest.

Similar Species: *Swainson's Hawk* (p. 111): dark bib; light underwing linings (or lighter leading edge in dark morph); lacks the red tail. *Ferruginous Hawk* (p. 113): longer-winged; whitish crescent in the outer upperwing; pale underparts except for the dark legs. *Rough-legged Hawk* (p. 114): dark; white tail base; elbow patches on the underwings. *Red-shouldered Hawk* (p. 110): finely barred, reddish breast and belly; reddish shoulder patches; bold whitish patches in the outer wing; barred tail lacks the red.

FERRUGINOUS HAWK

Buteo regalis

Coursing the contours of rolling, grassy hills, circling high above the landscape, or sitting alertly in a barren field, the Ferruginous Hawk is a bird of California's open country. This large grassland hawk spends much of its time perched low in a tree or on a fencepost watching for unsuspecting rodents. Hunting from the air, this powerful bird strikes unexpectedly, often swooping at its prey from great heights. • Ferruginous Hawks were once shot and poisoned because they were considered pests, but because their diet is composed mostly of rabbits, ground squirrels and gophers, they can actually be of service to ranchers and farmers. Conversion of pristine grasslands and rodent control campaigns have reduced and localized Ferruginous Hawks.

ID: *Light morph:* rusty-red upperparts; white underparts; dark rusty 'leggings'; pale head; pale tail is tipped with rust. *Dark morph:* rare; dark underparts; white tail; dark wing linings; pale flight feathers. *Immature:* lacks the noticeable dark on the legs. *In flight (light morph):* dark reddish-brown legs stand out against the white belly; mostly white underparts; holds wings in a shallow V while soaring.

Size: *L* 22–27 in; *W* 56 in.

Status: fairly common visitor from mid-September to early April (a few may appear in late August); extremely rare and very local occasional summer breeder.

Nesting: usually in a solitary tree, on a cliff, on the ground or on an artificial nesting platform; wide, massive nest of sticks, weeds and cow dung is lined with finer materials; female incubates 2–4 eggs for 32–33 days; male provides the food.

Feeding: captures prey it spots while soaring; hunts from a low perch or from the ground; eats primarily ground squirrels, rabbits and hares, mice and pocket gophers; also takes snakes and small birds.

Voice: generally silent; alarm call is a loud, squealing *kaaarr*, usually dropping at the end.

Similar Species: *Red-tailed Hawk* (p. 112): smaller; darker underparts; dark abdominal 'belt'; red (adult) or brown (immature) tail. *Swainson's Hawk* (p. 111): dark flight feathers contrast with light wing linings (dark forms are all dark underneath). *Rough-legged Hawk* (p. 114): dark 'wrist' patches and dark streaking on the breast; dark brown belly band or dark streaking on the belly.

ROUGH-LEGGED HAWK

Buteo lagopus

Each fall, arctic-nesting Rough-legged Hawks drift south in search of warmer, southern meadows and sagebrush habitat. The irregular annual abundance of Rough-legs in northern California results from the interplay of annual reproductive success, small mammal abundance and the vagaries of early winter weather. In years when the number of small mammals on the tundra is high, Rough-legs may produce up to seven young; in lean years, a pair may raise but a single chick. • Foraging Rough-legged Hawks can easily be identified at great distances—they are one of the few large hawks that routinely hover over prey. • The name *lagopus*, meaning 'hare's (or rabbit's) foot,' refers to this bird's distinctive feathered feet—an insulating adaptation for survival in cold climates.

immature

ID: large, bulky hawk; legs and feet are feathered to the toes. *Light morph:* white tail with a wide, dark subterminal band; wide, dark belly band; darkly streaked breast and head; dark upperparts. *Dark morph:* dark wing linings, head, body and underparts; light flight feathers and undertail; dark subterminal tail band. *Immature:* lighter streaking on the breast; bold belly band; white at the base of the upperwing flight feathers. *In flight:* light underwings with dark 'wrist' patches; long wings; frequently hovers.

Size: *L* 19–24 in; *W* 48–56 in.

Status: irregular and locally uncommon to fairly common visitor from mid-October to March; most common in the northeast and generally scarce in the northwest; a few birds occasionally appear earlier in fall or linger into late spring; ranges much more widely in irregular 'invasion' winters.

Habitat: open grasslands, savannah, sagebrush flats, coastal plains, agricultural fields, meadows, pastures and open river valleys.

Nesting: in northern Canada and Alaska.

Feeding: hunts from a perch or from the ground; eats mostly small rodents; occasionally captures birds, amphibians, reptiles and large insects.

Voice: seldom heard in northern California; alarm call is a cat-like *kee-eer*.

Similar Species: *Other buteo hawks:* rarely hover; adults lack the large dark 'wrist' patches and the dark subterminal band on an otherwise light tail. *Northern Harrier (p. 106):* slimmer; long tail; facial disc; cruises slowly over the ground.

GOLDEN EAGLE

Aquila chrysaetos

The high mountains, savannahs, rimrocks and rolling rural foothills of northern California provide a spectrum of varied habitats for this impressive hunter. During the summer months, observers might see a breeding pair of Golden Eagles hunting together or displaying breathtaking aerial acrobatics. Few people ever forget their first encounter with a Golden Eagle soaring overhead—the wingspan of adults exceeds 7 ft. During spring and fall, eagles breeding north of California can be seen soaring along the crest of the Sierra Nevada, often as specks in the sky, cruising at a height of over 15,000 ft! • Golden Eagles and Bald Eagles are not closely related— they share the name 'eagle' because of their immense size.

immature

ID: very large; all brown, with a golden tint to the neck and head; legs and feet are fully feathered; brown eyes; brown tail is slightly banded with grayish white; yellow feet; dark bill. *Immature:* dark terminal band on the white tail; white at the base of the under-wing flight feathers. *In flight:* long, large rectangular-shaped wings; soars expertly, holding wings in a shallow V.
Size: L 30–40 in; W 6$\frac{1}{2}$–7$\frac{1}{2}$ ft.
Status: locally rare to uncommon year-round resident; migrants and winter visitors may boost local populations seasonally.
Habitat: *Breeding:* open and semi-open woodlands from the lower foothills to the high alpine. *Non-breeding:* lower-elevation open and broken woodlands, grasslands, savannahs, chaparral, farmlands and alpine tundra.
Nesting: on a cliff ledge or in a tall tree overlooking open hunting habitat; nest is built of sticks, branches and roots and measures up to 10 ft across; site is often reused and may become stained white from droppings.

Feeding: swoops on prey from a soaring flight; very opportunistic feeder on small mammals and birds; often eats carrion; may also take lizards, snakes and some larger mammals.
Voice: generally quiet; rarely a short bark; yelps at the nest site.
Similar Species: *Bald Eagle* (p. 105): immature lacks the leg feathers, shows diffuse white in the wings rather than 2 discrete patches and has a larger head and heavier bill. *Red-tailed Hawk* (p. 112): much smaller; light flight feathers; hints of red in the tail. *Turkey Vulture* (p. 68): naked head (barely visible in flight); flight feathers are lighter than the wing linings; rocks and teeters constantly in flight. *California Condor* (p. 69): much larger; white underwing linings.

AMERICAN KESTREL
Falco sparverius

The American Kestrel is the smallest falcon in northern California, but it is not merely a miniature version of its relatives. Kestrels are more buoyant in flight, and they are not inclined toward the all-out aerial attacks that have made other falcons such revered predators. Kestrels often 'wind-hover' to scan the ground, flapping rapidly to maintain a stationary position while facing upwind. They also perch on telephone wires above roadsides and along open fields, peering intently into the grass—this is often the only clue needed to identify them.

This robin-sized predator routinely captures small rodents and birds, although large insects make up the majority of its summer diet. • The American Kestrel's species name, *sparverius*, is Latin for 'pertaining to sparrows,' even though sparrows are only an occasional prey item. Old field guides refer to this common bird as the Sparrow Hawk.

ID: small falcon; 2 distinctive facial stripes. *Male:* rusty back; blue-gray wings; blue-gray crown with a rusty cap; lightly spotted underparts. *Female:* rusty back and wings. *In flight:* frequently hovers; long, rusty tail; straightaway flight is accomplished with deep, swallow-like wingstrokes.

Size: L 7½–8 in; W 20–24 in.

Status: common year-round resident (seasonal movements occur with northern and high-elevation breeders); uncommon coastal migrant from mid-August to late November.

Habitat: open fields, oak woodlands, forest edges, grasslands, sagebrush flats, roadsides and agricultural areas with hunting perches; post-breeding birds may be seen up into mountain alpine areas.

Nesting: in a natural cavity or an abandoned woodpecker cavity; may use an old magpie or crow nest; pair incubates 4–6 darkly spotted, white to pale brown eggs for 28–31 days.

Feeding: swoops from a perch or hovers; eats mostly insects, including grasshoppers, crickets, dragonflies and beetles; will also eat mice, small birds, reptiles and amphibians.

Voice: loud, often repeated, shrill *KLEE! KLEE! KLEE!* when excited; female's voice is lower pitched.

Similar Species: *Merlin* (p. 117): slightly larger; darker; lacks the 2 bold facial stripes; dark-banded tail; does not hover. *Sharp-shinned Hawk* (p. 107): short, rounded wings; adults lack the rusty-red on the back; flap-and-glide flight. *Prairie Falcon* (p. 119): much larger; entirely sandy-brown upperparts; dark 'wing pits'; does not hover nor does it allow approach.

MERLIN
Falco columbarius

Although it is only slightly larger than a kestrel, the Merlin is another bird altogether. Sometimes mistaken for a Peregrine Falcon, the Merlin snatches other birds in mid-air at high speed, in classic falcon fashion. The main weapons of this small falcon—like all its falcon relatives—are speed and surprise. Their sleek body design, long, narrow tail and pointed wings increase aerodynamic efficiency in high-speed pursuits. • Merlins chiefly hunt small songbirds and shorebirds. Along the coast, where they are most commonly seen, Merlins make life exciting for such flocking birds as 'peep' sandpipers, Dunlins and blackbirds. • The scientific name *columbarius* is from the Latin for 'dove' or 'pigeon,' which the Merlin resembles in flight—this bird was formerly known as the Pigeon Hawk.

ID: heavily banded tail; heavily streaked underparts; no distinctive facial stripes; long, narrow tail. *Male:* blue-gray back and crown; rusty leg feathers. *Female:* brown back and crown. *In flight:* very rapid, shallow wing-beats; banded tail; pointed wings with a straight trailing edge.
Size: L 10–12 in; W 23–26 in.
Status: uncommon migrant and visitor from late September to mid-April; a few birds may arrive in late August and remain into early May.
Habitat: semi-open to open country with scattered lookout posts; estuaries, seacoast, open woodlands, savannah, windbreaks and hedgerows, pastures, and the edges of grasslands and agricultural fields.
Nesting: in the northwestern U.S., Canada and Alaska.
Feeding: stoops at or 'tail-chases' smaller birds, particularly flocking songbirds and shorebirds; in fall, sometimes captures large flying insects.
Voice: high-pitched *ki-ki-ki-ki-ki*; almost never heard in northern California.
Similar Species: *American Kestrel* (p. 116): smaller; more colorful; 2 bold stripes; often hovers; perches on roadside wires. *Peregrine Falcon* (p. 118): much larger; distinctive, dark 'helmet.' *Prairie Falcon* (p. 119): much larger; dark 'wing pits.' *Sharp-shinned Hawk* (p. 107) and *Cooper's Hawk* (p. 108): short, rounded wings; deeper wingbeats in a flap-and-glide flight pattern.

PEREGRINE FALCON
Falco peregrinus

The Peregrine Falcon's awesome speed and superior hunting skills were little defense against the insidious effects of chlorinated hydrocarbons (from the chemical DDT) from the 1940s to 1970s. The estimated California population of 100–300 pairs prior to 1940 steadily plummeted to two known breeding pairs by 1970. The ban on DDT in North America in 1972, followed by intensive conservation and reintroduction efforts, have brought about a strong and heartening recovery across much of this raptor's North American range. • While migrants and wintering birds commonly hunt waterfowl and shorebirds, summer peregrines typically concentrate on birds of the forest canopy, capturing all manner of species, from woodpeckers to warblers. • The scientific name *peregrinus* is Latin for 'wandering,' reflecting this species' great range over much of the globe.

immature

ID: blue-gray back; dark, broad 'mustache' joining with a dark 'helmet'; light underparts with fine, dark, transverse barring and spotting. *Immature:* similar patterning as an adult, but brown where the adult is blue-gray; heavier breast streaks. *In flight:* pointed wings; long, narrow, dark-banded tail.
Size: *Male:* L 15–17 in; W 37–43 in. *Female:* L 17–19 in; W 43–46 in.
Status: rare year-round resident; rare to uncommon migrant and visitor from early September to mid-May; scattered summer breeding.
Habitat: *Breeding:* seacoast, offshore islands and mountainous areas with cliffs for nesting and ready access to productive hunting grounds; also introduced to tall skyscrapers and bridges in urban areas. *Winter* and *In migration:* lakeshores, seacoast, estuaries and marshlands with an abundance of avian prey.
Nesting: usually on rocky cliffs or ridges; some use artificial nest sites on bridges and buildings; no material is added; nest sites are traditionally reused; female (mainly) incubates the 3 or 4 eggs for 32–34 days.
Feeding: often enters high-speed, diving stoops, striking birds in mid-air with clenched feet; prey are consumed where they fall or are taken to a pluck site; may also chase down birds on the wing; small birds are the primary prey.
Voice: generally silent away from the nest; loud, harsh, continuous *cack-cack-cack-cack-cack* near the nest site.
Similar Species: *Prairie Falcon* (p. 119): sandier-brown above; dark 'wing pits'; lacks the dark 'helmet.' *Merlin* (p. 117): much smaller; lacks the bold 'helmet.'

PRAIRIE FALCON
Falco mexicanus

Rocketing overhead like super-charged fighter jets, Prairie Falcons often seem to appear out of nowhere. During spring and summer, they often concentrate their hunting efforts over ground squirrel colonies, readily swooping over expanses of wind-swept grass to pick off naive youngsters. As summer fades to fall, large flocks of migrating songbirds often capture the attention of these pallid 'ghosts of the plains.' • Like any human pilot learning to fly a plane, freshly fledged falcons only get to keep their wings if they survive flight training—inexperienced and over-eager falcons risk serious injury or death when pushing the limits in early hunting forays. Swooping falcons can easily misjudge their flight speed or their ability to pull out of a dive. • Prairie Falcons commonly soar for long periods on updrafts or along ridgelines.

ID: brown upperparts; pale face with a dark brown, narrow 'mustache' stripe; underparts are white with brown spotting. *In flight:* diagnostic dark 'wing pits'; pointed wings; long, narrow, banded tail; quick wing-beats and direct flight.
Size: *Male: L* 14–15 in; *W* 37–39 in. *Female: L* 17–18 in; *W* 41–43 in.
Status: uncommon year-round resident; uncommon fall migrant and winter visitor.
Habitat: *Breeding:* river canyons, cliffs, rimrocks or rocky promontories in arid open lowlands or high intermontane valleys. *Winter* and *In migration:* open, treeless country, such as open fields, pastures, grass-lands and sagebrush flats.
Nesting: on cliff ledges, in crevices or on rocky promontories; rarely in abandoned nests of other raptors or crows; usually without nesting material; female mostly incubates 3–5 whitish eggs, spotted with brown, for about 30 days; male brings food to the female and young.

Feeding: high-speed strike-and-kill by div-ing swoops, low flights or chases on the wing; eats ground squirrels, small birds and small vertebrates; also takes some lizards and large insects; females consume more mammalian prey than do males.
Voice: generally silent; alarm call near the nest is a rapid, shrill *kik-kik-kik-kik*.
Similar Species: *Peregrine Falcon* (p. 118): lacks the dark 'wing pits'; dark, distinctive 'helmet.' *Merlin* (p. 117): much smaller; no contrasting 'wing pits.' *American Kestrel* (p. 116): much more colorful; smaller; 2 bold facial stripes; often hovers; lacks the dark 'wing pits.'

119

CHUKAR

Alectoris chukar

The Chukar is an Old World species that was first introduced to California as a gamebird in 1932. Since its introduction, it has become a well-established resident of northern California's hot, arid habitats. Fortunately, the introduction of this bird seems to have had little effect on our native species: the Chukar occupies an ecological niche largely unexploited by grouse and quails. • Part of the Chukar's success is its impressive reproductive capabilities: a female will typically produce 8 to 16 eggs, and will sometimes lay more than 20 in a single clutch! A female will lay eggs in two separate clutches, leaving one clutch to be incubated by the male. • In fall and winter, Chukars feed in groups of 5 to 40 family members (called 'coveys') and they use their typical *chuck* or *chuck-or* call to reassemble. During summer, this call may help disperse breeding pairs into separate territories.

♂

Nesting: on the ground in a shallow scrape lined with grass and feathers; female incubates 8–16 pale yellow to buff eggs, spotted with reddish-brown, for about 23 days.
Feeding: gleans the ground for weed and grass seeds; plucks green leaves from grasses and other plants; also takes berries and some insects, especially grasshoppers.

ID: grayish upperparts and breast; white cheeks and throat are bordered completely by black, forming a mask and 'necklace'; alternating black and white barring on the flanks; reddish-pink bill, eye ring and legs. *In flight:* rufous outer tail feathers.
Size: L 13 in.
Status: introduced; uncommon to locally fairly common year-round resident.
Habitat: rocky hillsides, arid foothills, canyons, dry sagebrush and hot, dry valleys below 7000 ft.

Voice: rapid, laughing *chuck-chuck-chuck.*
Similar Species: *Mountain Quail* (p. 126): 2 long, straight plumes on the head; chestnut throat is bordered by white; black-and-white barring on chestnut flanks. *California Quail* (p. 127): forward-curling head plume; white streaking on chestnut flanks; male has a black throat.

RING-NECKED PHEASANT
Phasianus colchicus

The spectacular Ring-necked Pheasant was introduced into North America from Asia in the mid-1800s mainly as quarry for hunters. Many other gamebirds have been introduced, but none has become as well established as this colorful pheasant. Despite widespread introduction programs, however, Ring-neck populations have been able to persist only locally under North America's diverse climatic conditions and intense hunting pressure. Some pheasant populations within northern California require annual replenishment through the stocking of hatchery-raised young. • Male pheasants are heard much more often than they are seen. Their distinctive, loud *krahh-krawk!* can be heard echoing near farmyards and brushy suburban parks. • The flight muscles of many gamebirds are not well developed for flight—pheasants are uninclined to fly long distances but will explode in bursts of flight to travel over small areas or to quickly escape a predator.

ID: long, barred tail; unfeathered legs. *Male:* green head; white collar; bronze underparts; naked, red face patch. *Female:* mottled brown overall; light underparts.

Size: *Male: L* 30–36 in. *Female: L* 20–26 in.

Status: introduced; locally common year-round resident; birds are released widely for hunting west of the Sierra Nevada, but these populations are not established.

Habitat: agricultural lands, brushy and weedy fields, stubble fields, croplands and shrubby, overgrown hillsides at lower elevations.

Nesting: on the ground; among grass or sparse vegetation or next to a log or other natural debris; in a slight depression lined with grass and leaves; female incubates 10–12 eggs for up to 25 days.

Feeding: in summer, gleans the ground and vegetation for weed seeds and terrestrial insects; in winter, eats mostly buds, seeds and waste grain.

Voice: male utters a loud, raspy, rooster-like *krahh-krawk!* promptly followed by muffled whirring of wings; flushed or running birds give a hoarse *ka-ka-ka, ka-ka.*

Similar Species: male is distinctive. *Sage Grouse* (p. 123): female has a black belly; feathered legs; darker overall. *Ruffed Grouse* (p. 122): female is smaller; has a shorter, fan-shaped tail; feathered legs. *Blue Grouse* (p. 124): female has a shorter, fan-shaped tail; feathered legs; grayer in color. *Greater Roadrunner* (p. 202): has a raised head crest; longer bill; colorful bare skin behind the eye; lacks the barring on the tail.

RUFFED GROUSE
Bonasa umbellus

When a male Ruffed Grouse is displaying nearby, he makes a sound that is felt more than heard: a forest drumbeat that reverberates in the chest. The male struts on a fallen log with his tail fanned and his neck ruffed, beating the air with accelerating wing strokes to proclaim his territory. 'Drumming' is primarily restricted to the spring courting season, but Ruffed Grouse may also drum for a few weeks in fall. • During winter, the feather bristles on the toes of these birds elongate, providing them with temporary snowshoes. • The Ruffed Grouse is named for the black ruffs on the sides of its neck. Displaying males erect these black patches to impress females. • The scientific name *Bonasa* is thought to refer to this grouse's drumming sound, which is apparently likened to the bellowing call of a bull aurochs (an extinct European wild cattle). The name *umbellus* refers to the 'sun-shade' appearance or function of this bird's black neck tufts.

rusty-brown morph

ID: small, ragged crest; mottled rusty-brown overall; black shoulder patches; barred tail is tipped with a dark band. *Female:* tail band is incomplete in the center.
Size: L 15–19 in.
Status: uncommon to rare, local year-round resident.
Habitat: moist coniferous forests, locally from near sea level to over 5000 ft; partial to damp deciduous regrowth, benches, disused roadways and hillside seeps.
Nesting: often beside logs, boulders and trees; in a shallow depression among leaf litter; female incubates 9–12 eggs for 23–25 days.

Feeding: gleans the ground and vegetation; eats terrestrial insects, other invertebrates and the buds of trees and shrubs.
Voice: *Male:* uses his wings to produce a hollow, drumming courtship sound of accelerating, hollow thumps. *Female:* utters rallying notes to the brood.
Similar Species: *Blue Grouse* (p. 124): paler band at the tip of the darker tail; lacks the small head crest and black shoulder patch.

SAGE GROUSE
Centrocercus urophasianus

In March and April, groups of Sage Grouse assemble at their courtship 'leks' at dawn to perform a traditional springtime dance. Males enter a flat, short-grass arena, inflate their pectoral sacs, spread their pointed tail feathers and strut with vigor to intimidate their peers and attract prospective mates. The most fit and experienced males are found at the center of the circular lek; immature males are generally poor strutters and are forced to the periphery. An impressive male can mate with up to 75 percent of the nearby females. • By late summer, Sage Grouse often migrate to higher elevations; some individuals have been sighted on both sides of the Sierran crest at over 10,000 ft. • Unfortunately, road construction, off-road vehicle use and overgrazing have all contributed to the destruction of leks and prime Sage Grouse habitat throughout their northern California range.

ID: *Male:* large grouse; black belly and bib; white breast; long, spiked tail; mottled brown back; yellow comb. *Female:* black belly; mottled brown plumage; very faint yellowish comb.

Size: *Male: L* 27–34 in. *Female: L* 18–24 in.

Status: year-round resident: uncommon, but very locally abundant during March and April courtship assemblages.

Habitat: treeless plains and rolling hills dominated by sagebrush, grasses and forbs.

Nesting: on the ground, usually under a sagebrush; in a shallow depression sparsely lined with leaves and grass; female incubates 6–9 eggs for up to 27 days.

Feeding: mostly sagebrush leaves; flowers, buds and terrestrial insects are taken during summer.

Voice: generally silent; flocks flush with a startling burst of wingbeats. *Male:* on breeding grounds, makes a unique hollow *oop-la-boop* sound as air is released from his jiggling air sacs. *Female:* issues a *quak-quak* call on breeding grounds.

Similar Species: *Ring-necked Pheasant* (p. 121): female lacks the black belly and has unfeathered legs. *Blue Grouse* (p. 124): fan-shaped tail; lacks the black belly.

BLUE GROUSE
Dendragapus obscurus

In the higher coniferous forests, the low, owl-like hooting of the male Blue Grouse carries indistinctly through conifer foliage that has yet to be visited by the northbound migrant birds. Male Blue Grouse sometimes begin their breeding calls while patches of snow still remain—their deep, courting notes are one of the earliest signs of spring. The male's voice is so deep that the human ear can detect only a fraction of the sounds actually produced. • Hormonal changes and food availability cause these birds to make seasonal migrations. Rather than moving latitudinally, however, Blue Grouse simply move altitudinally. During late summer, some birds move upslope to timberline on ridgetop balds before descending to lower elevations for the winter months. • *Dendragapus* is Greek for 'tree-loving.' Although these birds roost in coniferous trees, they spend much time on the ground. • Blue Grouse are often easily approached—a characteristic that has earned them the nickname 'fool hen.'

Nesting: on the ground, often near a fallen log or under a shrub; in a shallow depression lined with vegetation, such as leaves, twigs and needles; female incubates 7–10 buff-colored eggs for 25–28 days.

Feeding: leaves, berries, seeds and flowers; conifer needles and buds in winter; young birds eat grasshoppers and beetles.

Voice: from 5–8 extremely deep, ventriloqual 'hoots.'

ID: overall mottled brownish-gray coloration; white undertail coverts; broad gray band at the tail tip; feathered legs.
Male: blue-gray crown, nape, upper back and tail feathers; orange-red comb above the eye; inflated yellow throat patches surrounded by white feathers when displaying.
Female: blue-gray lower breast and belly; faint yellow comb.
Size: *Male:* L 17–19 in. *Female:* L 18–22 in.
Status: uncommon year-round resident.
Habitat: coniferous forests of higher foothills and mountains; ranges through the upper edge of foothill oak and conifer forest types.

Similar Species: *Ruffed Grouse* (p. 122): smaller; rusty brown; small head crest; black shoulder patch; banded tail. *Ring-necked Pheasant* (p. 121): female has lighter undersides and a longer, pointed tail.

WILD TURKEY
Meleagris gallopavo

Wild Turkeys are wary birds with acute senses and a highly developed social system. Members of foraging flocks cooperate to elude attacks by stealthy predators. • Although turkeys prefer to feed on the ground and travel by foot, they can fly short distances, and they often roost in trees during the night. • The Wild Turkey is the only native North American animal that has been widely domesticated—the wild ancestors of chickens, pigs, cows, horses, sheep and most other domestic animals all came from Europe, Asia or Africa. • The Wild Turkey was Benjamin Franklin's choice for America's national emblem, but his selection lost to the Bald Eagle by one ballot in a congressional vote. • The genus name *Meleagris* is a reference to the African Guinea-fowl, a bird that shares a vague resemblance to the Wild Turkey of North America.

♂

ID: very large; much like the domestic turkey; naked, red-blue head; dark, glossy, iridescent body plumage; copper tail is tipped with dirty white; unfeathered legs. *Male:* conspicuous central breast tuft; more colorful on the head and body; red wattles. *Female:* blue-gray head; less iridescent body; smaller.
Size: *Male:* L 48–50 in. *Female:* L 35–37 in.
Status: introduced; locally uncommon to common year-round resident.
Habitat: chiefly openings and forest edge within the oak-conifer zone of valley edges, rolling foothills and lower mountain slopes.
Nesting: on the ground; in open woods or along the edge of an opening; in a slight depression lined with grass and leaves;

female incubates 10–12 eggs for 25–31 days; female tends the young for several weeks.
Feeding: broadly omnivorous diet includes seeds, fruits, bulbs, leaves, acorns, berries and roots; also eats insects, snails and spiders; sometimes takes small amphibians and reptiles.
Voice: wide array of sounds: courting male gives a *gobble* series that is audible at up to 1 mi; alarm call is a loud *pert*; gathering call is a *cluck*; contact call is a loud *keouk-keouk-keouk*.
Similar Species: none.

125

MOUNTAIN QUAIL
Oreortyx pictus

As spring arrives, the leafing foothill and mountain slopes of northern California are touched now and again by a resonant, querulous report—the call of the male Mountain Quail. At other seasons, however, Mountain Quails are less readily detected. Family groups seem to vanish within a moment from the roadside, concealing themselves among dense brush and sheltering thickets. These birds prefer to move on foot, taking flight only when dangerous conflicts demand a speedy escape.
• Unlike most of California's birds, newly born quails begin to toddle about within minutes of hatching. After nesting, small family groups may move to lower elevations, traveling many miles on foot.

gray morph

♂

ID: 2 long, straight head plumes; chestnut throat is edged with olive-white; chestnut flanks, with large white bars; variable gray and brown breast and upperparts. *Immature:* shorter head plumes; white chin; lacks the chestnut in the throat.
Size: L 10$\frac{1}{2}$–11$\frac{1}{2}$ in.
Status: fairly common to common year-round resident; moves downslope in winter, especially in the Sierra Nevada.
Habitat: thickets, dense brush, chaparral, pine-oak woodlands and broken forest in wooded foothills and mountains; remains close to water in hot weather; found at and above the upper elevational limits of the California Quail where both occur.
Nesting: on the ground; in a shallow depression under the cover of grass, shrubs, thickets or logs; well-concealed nest is lined

with grass, leaves, conifer needles and feathers; adults may share the incubation of 9–10 buffy-white eggs over 24 days; young leave the nest soon after hatching.
Feeding: digs and scratches among leaf litter and climbs into trees and shrubs to glean food; eats seasonally available seeds, berries, bulbs, green leaves, flowers, acorns and some insects and fungi.
Voice: remarkable spring call of male is a resounding, upslurred *quee-YARK!*; contact call is a rising series of 4–10 querulous whistles.
Similar Species: *California Quail* (p. 127): forward-curling, teardrop-shaped plume; black throat; scaled belly; brown sides with white streaks.

CALIFORNIA QUAIL
Callipepla californica

California Quails spend most of their time scuttling about in tight, cohesive coveys. In fall and winter, these groups may include up to 200 birds. • In many of northern California's suburban parks and rural farmlands, coveys have succumbed to predation by feral cats and to severe habitat alteration. Even though they are rarely seen far from the protective confines of their brushland habitat, noisy scratching and soft vocalizations usually give them away. Unlike the Mountain Quail, these birds do not migrate. • During April and May, males advertise their courting desires by uttering a raucous *WHERE are YOU?* • The California Quail is our state bird.

♂

ID: drooping, forward-facing plume; gray-brown back; gray chest; white scales on the belly; unfeathered legs. *Male:* black throat; white stripes on the head and neck. *Female:* gray-brown face and throat.
Size: L 9¹/₂–11 in.
Status: fairly common to locally abundant year-round resident from sea level to 6000 ft; avoids dense forests; generally localized in regions of intensive monoculture.
Habitat: chaparral, brushland, oak woodlands, streamside woodlands and along the brushy edges of suburban parks, gardens and agricultural fields.
Nesting: on the ground; under a brushpile, shrub, log or debris; shallow depression is lined with leaves and grass; may nest above the ground, often in an abandoned nest of another species; female incubates 10–16

darkly marked pale-buff to dull-white eggs for 18–23 days; 2 females may lay eggs in 1 nest.
Feeding: gleans items from the ground while walking; may scratch at the ground and leaf litter; eats seeds, leaves, fresh plant shoots, berries, acorns, bulbs, flowers and some insects, waste grain and birdseed.
Voice: call is a loud, low-pitched *where are you?* or *chi-ca-go*; *cow* call is given by unmated males.
Similar Species: *Mountain Quail* (p. 126): 2 long, straight head plumes; chestnut sides, with black-and-white barring; chestnut throat.

BLACK RAIL

Laterallus jamaicensis

The sparrow-sized Black Rail is one of North America's most elusive and seldom-seen marshland birds. Its diminutive size and secretive, partly nocturnal habits leave most birdwatchers wondering if this bird really exists. Its voice—a repeated *ki-kee-der* from a male and a *who-whoo* from a female is often the only clue to its presence. Because the Black Rail is rarely seen and is practically impossible to observe for any extended period of time, much remains to be learned about its natural history and population dynamics. • Protection of marshland and critical rethinking of the consequences of draining and ditching fragile marshes will help to ensure the survival of this enigmatic creature. • Your best chance to see a Black Rail is among the saltwater marshes of San Pablo and San Francisco bays during the highest tides of December and January.

ID: tiny; short, black bill; small, stocky body; large feet; blackish upperparts with white flecking and a chestnut nape; dark grayish-black underparts with white barring on the flanks; red eyes.

Size: *L* 6 in.

Status: rare to locally fairly common year-round resident; recent summer breeder in northern Central Valley foothills.

Habitat: tidal saltwater marshes of pickle-weed, cordgrass and bulrush; also fresh-water cattail and bulrush marshes at lower elevations.

Nesting: cup-shaped nest of vegetation with a woven, domed canopy is located among dense vegetation above the water or the ground; nest entrance is connected to the ground or to the water's surface by a ramp of dead vegetation; pair incubates and probably helps raise the young; chicks leave the nest shortly after hatching.

Feeding: foraging behavior and diet are poorly understood; eats mostly insects, small crustaceans and seeds.

Voice: male's call-note is a repeated *ki-kee-der*; female's call-note is a deeper *who-whoo.*

Similar Species: *Virginia Rail* (p.130): reddish bill; rusty breast; gray cheek. *Sora* (p.131): much lighter coloration; yellow bill; black face mask.

CLAPPER RAIL
Rallus longirostris

The Clapper Rail characteristically flicks its tail as it walks through expanses of cordgrass and pickleweed. This bird's thin profile and long, spreading toes allow it to move quickly and efficiently through dense, squishy saltwater marshland. • For years, Clapper Rail habitat throughout North America has been under siege by humans hoping to convert 'inhospitable' marshland into airports, malls and landfills. In northern California, introduced Red Foxes have taken a heavy toll on these birds, extripating by 1980 the population in Elkhorn Slough in Monterey County. • Clapper Rails usually lay 5 to 12 eggs over the course of a few days, resulting in asynchronous hatching. Because young rails leave the nest within hours of hatching, adults must often split up: one stays on the nest to incubate any remaining eggs; the other moves to a nearby auxiliary nest where the vulnerable young are brooded in safety.

ID: long, slighty downcurved bill; 4 recognized subspecies differ in brightness of coloration; generally darker back feathers have lighter, pale edges; grayish-brown to cinnamon breast; gray to brown-and-white barring on the flanks; grayish face.
Size: L 14½ in.
Status: very local, fairly common year-round resident; very rare in marginal habitat.
Habitat: tidal saltwater marshes of pickleweed and cordgrass; often feeds along marshy tidal channels during low tide.
Nesting: pair builds a cup nest of vegetation in dense cover above or near the water; nest usually includes a domed canopy and an entrance ramp; young leave the nest within hours of hatching.

Feeding: aquatic insects, crustaceans and small fish are caught by probing, snatching or gleaning from the water, ground or vegetation; seeds, amphibians, worms and other small items may also be eaten.
Voice: call is a series of 10 or more loud, harsh *kek* notes, accelerating at first, then slowing toward the end; 1 calling bird will often cause an entire marsh to erupt with the widely scattered 'chime-ins' of other unseen rails.
Similar Species: *Virginia Rail* (p. 130): much smaller; brown back feathers, gray face and red bill. *Least Bittern:* solid black back feathers lack the lighter edging; buffy-orange wing patches and face; not normally in the same habitat.

VIRGINIA RAIL
Rallus limicola

The best way to meet a Virginia Rail is to sit alongside a wetland marsh, clap your hands three or four times and wait patiently. At best, this slim bird may reveal itself for an instant, but most often the bird's voice is all that betrays its presence. • When pursued by an intruder or predator, a rail will scurry away through dense, protective vegetation, rather than risk exposure in a getaway flight. • Rails are remarkably narrow birds built with modified feather tips and flexible vertebrae, which allow them to squeeze through the narrow vegetative confines of their marshy homes with ease. The saying 'as thin as a rail' may have been coined in reference to these thin wetland inhabitants.

ID: rusty breast; barred flanks; gray cheeks; long, downcurved, reddish bill; very short tail. *Immature:* much darker overall; light bill. *In flight:* floppy wingbeats and dangling legs; chestnut wing patch.
Size: *L* 9–11 in.
Status: fairly common year-round resident; migrants and winter visitors greatly swell resident populations from November to late March; rare to locally fairly common summer breeder.
Habitat: freshwater wetlands, especially in cattail, bulrush and tule marshes; also in flooded riparian woodlands and coastal saltwater marshes (especially in winter). *In migration:* will resort to nearly any wetland with appropriate overhead cover.
Nesting: concealed in emergent marsh vegetation, usually suspended just over the water; loose basket nest of coarse grass, cattail stems or sedges; pair incubates the

spotted, pale buff eggs for up to 20 days; both adults feed and tend the young.
Feeding: probes into soft substrates for soft-bodied invertebrates, such as earthworms, beetles, snails, spiders, insect larvae and nymphs; often snatches prey from vegetation; may also eat seeds and small fish.
Voice: call, given day or night, is an often repeated, telegraph-like *kik, kik, ki-dik, ki-dik, ki-dik, ki-dik*; also gives an accelerating series of grunts that trail off in pitch and energy.

Similar Species: *Sora* (p. 131): short, yellow bill; black mask. *Clapper Rail* (p. 129): much larger; dark back feathers are edged in gray; lacks the reddish bill and the chestnut wing patch.

SORA

Porzana carolina

Halfway between a crazed laugh and a horse's whinny, the call of a Sora hidden deep within a marsh puzzles the uninitiated. Despite being the most common and widespread rail in North America, the Sora is seldom seen. Its elusive habits require most would-be observers to detect it by its characteristic call. • The Sora habitually flicks its short, stubby tail. This odd gesture is thought to distract prey into believing that the Sora's tail is actually the bird's head. • Athough its feet are not webbed, this inhabitant of marshy areas swims quite well over short distances. • Some Soras overwinter in the southern U.S., and many spend the colder months in the West Indies.

breeding

ID: short, yellow bill; front of the face is black; gray neck and breast; long, greenish legs. *Immature:* brown overall; dark bill; yellow legs.

Size: L 8–10 in.

Status: rare to uncommon year-round resident; uncommon to common migrant and visitor from mid-August to mid-April; rare to uncommon summer breeder.

Habitat: freshwater marshes with standing water and abundant emergent vegetation to about 7000 ft; grassy or marshy borders of streams, lakes and ponds; saltwater and brackish coastal marshes in winter; fall migrants may drop into gardens, large parking lots, etc.

Nesting: usually over water, but occasionally in a wet meadow; under concealing vegetation; well-built basket nest of grass and aquatic vegetation; pair incubates 10–12 brown-spotted, buff eggs for up to 20 days; both adults feed the young.

Feeding: gleans and probes vegetation for seeds, plants, aquatic insects and mollusks.

Voice: alarm call is a sharp *keek*; courtship song begins *or-Ah or-Ah*, descending quickly in a cackling, yet fluid, *we-wee-wee-wee-weee!*

Similar Species: *Virginia Rail* (p. 130): long, reddish, downcurved bill. *Clapper Rail* (p. 129): much larger; long, downcurved bill. *Black Rail* (p. 128): smaller; very dark overall; thin, black bill.

COMMON MOORHEN
Gallinula chloropus

The Common Moorhen is a curious mix of comedy and confusion. This member of the rail family appears to have been assembled by committee: it has the bill of a chicken and the body of a duck, and its long legs and huge feet are in full heron form. • Although Moorhens might look gangly and awkward, their strides are executed with a poised determination. As the moorhen strolls around a wetland, its head mirrors the movement of its legs. With each step, its head bobs back and forth in synchrony, producing a comical, chugging stride. This bird is a capable swimmer and occasional diver, although its feet are not webbed and it lacks lobed toes. • Besides building nests, Common Moorhens construct a number of other platforms on which adults might roost or brood their young.

breeding

ID: brown-tinged, gray-black body; white streak on the sides and flanks; white undertail coverts; reddish bill and forehead shield; yellow-tipped bill; long, yellow legs. *Breeding:* brighter bill and forehead shield. *Juvenile:* browner plumage; duller legs and bill; whitish throat.
Size: L 12–15 in.
Status: uncommon to fairly common year-round.
Habitat: large freshwater marshes with standing water and broken stands of tall emergent vegetation.
Nesting: pair builds a platform or a wide, shallow cup of bulrushes, cattails and reeds in shallow water or along the shoreline; often built with a ramp leading down to the water; pair incubates 8–11 eggs for 19–22 days; both adults, and sometimes older siblings, feed the young.
Feeding: gleans prey while swimming, tipping, diving, walking on land or clambering through marsh vegetation; omnivorous diet of aquatic vegetation, berries, fruits, tadpoles, insects, snails, worms and spiders; may take carrion and eggs.
Voice: various sounds include chicken-like clucks, screams, squeaks and a loud *cup*; courting males give a harsh *ticket-ticket-ticket*.
Similar Species: *American Coot* (p.133): white bill; lacks the white streak on the flanks.

AMERICAN COOT

Fulica americana

The distinctive calls of American Coots are commonly heard echoing across wetlands throughout the summer months. Coots are easily identified when they swim because their head pumps back and forth. • All rails can dive and swim, but American Coots are especially adapted to water. They spend much of their time on open water, and, with the exception of the breeding season, they are highly sociable. American Coots are constantly squabbling. They can often be seen running across the surface of the water, charging rivals and attempting to intimidate them. • Coots are colloquially known as 'Mud Hens,' and few non-birders know that they are not a species of duck.

ID: gray-black, duck-like bird; white, chicken-like bill with a reddish spot on the forehead shield; unusually long, green-yellow legs with lobed toes; white undertail coverts; red eyes. *Immature:* lighter body color; darker bill and legs.

Size: L 13–16 in.

Status: common to abundant year-round resident; northern and higher-elevation breeders may retreat to milder areas for winter; influx of wintering birds from September to April greatly increases populations.

Habitat: freshwater marshes, ponds and wetlands with open water and emergent vegetation; many use coastal saltwater marshes and estuaries in winter; also found in city parks, on golf courses and locally on inshore kelp beds.

Nesting: in emergent marsh vegetation; floating nest, built by the pair, is usually made of cattails and grass; pair incubates 8–12 grayish to buff eggs with brown spots

for 21–25 days; both adults feed and tend the young.

Feeding: often gleans the water's surface for algae, aquatic vegetation and invertebrates; also eats submerged water plants; sometimes dives for tadpoles and fish; grazes in flocks on cropped or grazed grass.

Voice: in summer, calls frequently through the day and night: *Pete Warren, Pete Warren;* also a hollow, clipped *kup.*

Similar Species: *Common Moorhen* (p. 132): base of the bill and nasal shield are red; bill has a yellow tip; white streaking on the flanks. *Ducks* (pp. 76–102): all lack the chicken-like, white bill and uniformly black body color. *Grebes* (pp. 41–46): swim without pumping their heads back and forth; rarely seen on land; do not graze lawns.

SANDHILL CRANE
Grus canadensis

Deep, resonant, rattling croaks betray the approach of a flock of migrating Sandhill Cranes. These migrations can entertain a birder for an entire fall morning, as flock after flock sail effortlessly overhead. The expansive, V-shaped lines suggest flocks of geese, but the cranes' loud calls are distinctly different from the honking of geese. • Sandhill Cranes are wary and reclusive when nesting, and they prefer to raise their young in areas that are isolated from human disturbance and development. It is unlikely that a birder would unknowingly stumble across a crane nest; ever-vigilant parents noisily announce the presence of any apparent threat. • Cranes mate for life, reinforcing their pair bond each spring with an elaborate courtship dance, in which the partners bow before each other after leaping high into the air with their wings half spread.

ID: very large bird; long legs; long neck; pale gray plumage (often becomes stained rusty from iron oxides in the water); naked red crown; long, straight bill; 'bustle' of shaggy feathers hangs over the rump of a standing bird. *Immature:* lacks the red crown; reddish-brown plumage may appear patchy. *In flight:* neck and legs are fully extended with the feet visible beyond the tail; slow downbeat; quick upstroke.
Size: L 40–50 in; W 6–7 ft.
Status: locally common migrant and visitor from late September to early April; locally uncommon to fairly common breeder from March to September.
Habitat: *Breeding:* open, but isolated, wet grassy meadows and shallow marshlands. *Winter* and *In migration:* agricultural fields, grasslands, mudflats and shorelines of freshwater lakes and rivers.
Nesting: on a large mound of aquatic vegetation in the water or along a shoreline; pair incubates 2 olive-splotched eggs for 29–32 days; young hatch asynchronously; young remain with adults into migration.

Feeding: probes and gleans the ground for insects, soft-bodied invertebrates, berries, waste grain, shoots and tubers; frequently takes amphibians, reptiles, small mammals and nesting birds.
Voice: unforgettable, loud, resonant, rattling croak: *gu-rrroo gu-rrroo gurrroo,* sometimes raised to an excited chorus for long moments.
Similar Species: *Great Blue Heron* (p. 61): flies with its neck folded back over its shoulders; lacks the red forehead patch. *Whooping Crane:* exceedingly rare throughout North America; all-white plumage with black flight feathers. *White-faced Ibis* (p. 67): long, down-curved bill; deep brown wings and tail. *Great Egret* (p. 62): all white.

BLACK-BELLIED PLOVER

Pluvialis squatarola

During winter, Black-bellied Plovers can be seen darting along sea beaches, mudflats and plowed fields, foraging with a sedate, robin-like run-and-stop technique. • Although they are usually dressed in plain gray for their sunny California retreat, some Black-bellied Plovers sport their summer tuxedo plumage through spring and fall. • These plovers are common in coastal and Central Valley areas of northern California from September to May, with migrational peaks in April and May, and again in September and October. A few non-breeding birds linger on coastal mudflats of major estuaries through summer.

non-breeding

ID: short, stout, black bill; relatively long, dark legs. *Female:* lighter than the male. *Breeding:* black face, breast and belly; light gray crown; white shoulders; black back is spangled with white; white undertail coverts. *Non-breeding:* gray-brown upperparts; lightly streaked, pale underparts. *Juvenile:* like the non-breeding adult, but with boldly spotted upperparts. *In flight:* black 'wing pits'; whitish rump; white wing linings; travels in large, open flocks.
Size: L 10½–13 in.
Status: fairly common to common migrant from late March to mid-May and from late July to mid-October; common visitor from October to early April; a few non-breeders may remain over summer.
Habitat: sandy ocean beaches, estuarine mudflats; may use breakwaters, exposed reefs, flooded and freshly plowed fields, pastures, sod farms and extensive lawns.
Nesting: in the Arctic.

Feeding: forages using a run-and-snatch technique; picks from the surface; winter diet consists of mollusks, crustaceans, insects and marine worms; consumes mostly insects in summer; may eat some plant material.
Voice: call is a plaintive, slurred, 3-note whistle: *pee-oo-ee!*
Similar Species: *Willet* (p. 146): larger; longer bill and legs; does not run and stop; not as plump. *Pacific Golden-Plover* (p. 136) and *American Golden-Plover:* bold, white eyebrows are contrasted by the dark crown and face in breeding plumage; darker overall in winter; upperparts are flecked with gold in breeding plumage.

135

PACIFIC GOLDEN-PLOVER

Pluvialis fulva

Over the years, the taxonomic classifications of the Pacific Golden-Plover and its close relative, the American Golden-Plover, have changed several times. Until recently, both the Pacific and American golden-plovers were known collectively as the Lesser Golden-Plover to distinguish them from their Eurasian relative, the Greater Golden-Plover. Before being assigned the 'Lesser' name, the two North American relatives were simply known as the American Golden-Plover. Future scientific changes to the nomenclature of these birds may inspire confused birders to simply refer to them as the 'Notorious Name-Changing Plovers.'
• Although both golden-plovers pass through northern California in small numbers each spring and fall, only the Pacific has been recorded wintering along our coastline. While a very few transients move through from mid-April to late May, most occur from September to mid-November.

non-breeding

ID: compact plover shape; dark back is speckled with gold; straight, black bill; long, black legs. *Breeding:* black face and underparts; white stripe across the forehead and through the shoulders. *Non-breeding:* buffy golden breast and neck with dark streaking. *Juvenile:* like winter adult, but without prominent streaking on the breast.
Size: L 10–11 in.
Status: very rare migrant from mid-April to late May; rare to locally uncommon migrant from late August to mid-November; locally rare to uncommon visitor from November to late April.
Habitat: estuaries, drier tidal mudflats and the upper waveslope of sandy ocean beaches; also seen inland on pastures, extensive lawns, plowed fields and other areas with short grasses.
Nesting: in Alaska.
Feeding: non-breeding diet includes crustaceans, mollusks, insects and some berries; eats mostly insects in the breeding season.

Voice: call is a loud, whistled *chu-leet*; courting flight display is a repeated, whistled *teee-chewee*.
Similar Species: *American Golden-Plover:* white rather than buffy eyebrows; non-breeding birds have overall darker upperparts with whitish rather than gold speckling. *Black-bellied Plover* (p. 135): slightly larger; heavier bill; black and white; lacks the golden speckling on the back; non-breeding birds are much lighter and drabber in color; contrasting black 'wing pits.'

SNOWY PLOVER
Charadrius alexandrinus

The Snowy Plover is an inconspicuous year-round patron of our remaining undisturbed coastal beaches and a summer breeder among the barren shorelines of interior alkali lakes. Snowy Plovers were at one time found along much of the northern California coastline, but human development now restricts this threatened species to a few undisturbed protected areas. For most of the year, this plover blends unseen into its surrounding environment, moving like a ghost over isolated coastal dunes, open sandy beaches and blazing white alkali pans. Although it may be tempting to search for Snowy Plovers, this activity is likely not in the best interest of the bird: its nesting activities can be easily disrupted by well-intentioned birders who inadvertently keep the parent bird away from its nest for prolonged periods. This bird's nest is also notoriously difficult to spot and might easily be crushed under a carelessly placed foot. For these reasons, Snowies should only be sought out in the non-breeding season, when human disturbances are minimized and when their population is boosted by the arrival of nesters that have retreated to the coast or southward for winter.

ID: white underparts; light brown upperparts; thin, black bill; variable dark patches on the ear, shoulder and forehead; slate gray legs. *Juvenile:* lacks the dark patches.
Size: L 6–7 in.
Status: uncommon to fairly common, local year-round resident; resident populations are boosted by migrants and visitors from October to late March; rare to locally fairly common breeder from April to early October; California populations are small and considered threatened.
Habitat: coastal birds use sandy beaches (especially those backed by dunes), sand spits and the drier shoreline areas of tidal estuaries, bayshore sandflats and salt-evaporation ponds; interior birds use the shorelines of alkaline lakes.
Nesting: on bare ground; lines a shallow scrape with pebbles, shells, grass and other debris; may be located near a grass clump or piece of driftwood; pair incubates 3 pale buff eggs dotted with black for 26–32 days; young leave the nest within hours of hatching.

Feeding: run-and-stop foraging technique used to catch tiny crustaceans, mollusks, marine worms and some insects; inland birds prey more on insects.
Voice: flight call is a soft, whistled *ku-wheat* or *chu-wee*; also gives a low *krut*.
Similar Species: *Semipalmated Plover* (p. 138): darker back; complete breast band; bicolored bill; orangish legs. *Killdeer* (p. 139): 2 black breast bands; much larger; darker back; rusty tail.

SEMIPALMATED PLOVER
Charadrius semipalmatus

During their seasonal marathon flights, small flocks of Semipalmated Plovers routinely touch down on northern California shorelines. During a brief stop-over or an extended winter stay, these stocky birds perform wind sprints across mudflats intermixed with teetering, foraging probes. • Shorebird plumage is generally categorized in two forms: cryptic and disruptive coloration. Most sandpipers have cryptic coloration, which blends into the background of their preferred habitat. Disruptive coloration is the patterning exhibited by most plovers. Heavy, distinctive banding breaks the form of the bird into unrecognizable pieces. Like the stripes of a zebra, the contrast between dark and light makes it difficult for predators to pinpoint the bird's form. • The scientific name *semipalmatus* refers to the partial webbing between the toes of this plover.

non-breeding

ID: dark brown back; white breast with 1 black, horizontal band; orange legs; stubby, black-tipped, orange bill; white face patch above the bill; white throat and collar; brown head; black band across the forehead; small white eyebrow.
Immature: dark legs and bill; brown banding.
Size: *L* 7 in.
Status: fairly common to common migrant from late March to mid-May and from late July to mid-October; uncommon to fairly common winter visitor; a few non-breeders may remain over summer; most numerous and widespread along the coast.
Habitat: drier areas of coastal mudflats and estuaries; upper waveslope of ocean beaches; also uses shorelines of interior lakes, rivers and marshes.

Nesting: in northern Canada and Alaska.
Feeding: run-and-snatch feeding, picking from the surface; usually on shorelines and beaches; eats crustaceans, worms and insects.
Voice: exclamatory, high-pitched, 2-syllabled, rising whistle: *chu-WEE!*
Similar Species: *Killdeer* (p. 139): larger; 2 black bands across the breast. *Snowy Plover* (p. 137): much paler upperparts; darker legs and bill; neck band does not connect across the breast; dark forehead band on breeding birds does not connect to the eyes.

KILLDEER
Charadrius vociferus

The Killdeer is among the most widely distributed of all North American shorebirds. Unlike most members of its family, it is often found in habitats many miles from water. The Killdeer is often the first shorebird a beginning birder will identify, and its boisterous *kill-deer* call is easy to recognize. • If its nest site is approached, this bird will feign injury and fan its bright rusty tail to lure the intruder away from its eggs or young. Although the Killdeer is well known as a master of deception, several species of ducks and many other shorebirds also practice this defense strategy. • The Killdeer's scientific name *vociferus* means 'loudly vocal.'

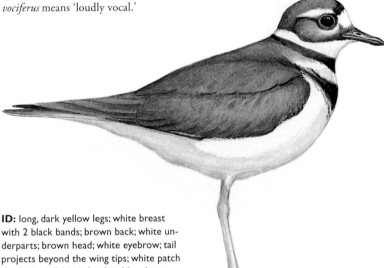

ID: long, dark yellow legs; white breast with 2 black bands; brown back; white underparts; brown head; white eyebrow; tail projects beyond the wing tips; white patch above the bill; black forehead band; rusty rump. *Immature:* downy; only 1 breast band.
Size: L 9–11 in.
Status: fairly common to common year-round resident; northern and higher-elevation summer breeders may retreat to milder areas for winter; migrants and winter visitors boost resident populations from late August to May.
Habitat: open environments, such as lawns, fields, lakeshores, sandy beaches, mudflats, gravel streambeds, wet meadows and grasslands from sea level to the mountains; most numerous at lower elevations.
Nesting: usually on any piece of open ground, including shorelines, beaches, fields and lightly traveled gravel roads; in a shallow depression, usually unlined but sometimes lined with pebbles, grass bits or debris; pair incubates 4 darkly blotched eggs for 24–28 days; occasionally has 2 broods per season.

Feeding: run, stop and snatch feeder; mostly eats insects, but may also eat some seeds.
Voice: loud and distinctive *kill-dee kill-dee kill-deer* and variations, including *deer-deer-deer-deer.*
Similar Species: *Semipalmated Plover* (p. 138): adult is smaller and has only 1 breast band; usually present only in migration and over winter. *Snowy Plover* (p. 137): much smaller; paler upperparts; dark neck band does not connect across the breast; dark forehead band on breeding birds does not connect to the eyes; restricted to extensive sand or alkali-flat habitats.

BLACK OYSTERCATCHER
Haematopus bachmani

A frequent accompaniment to the background roar of surf and the cries of Western Gulls are the piercing flight calls of Black Oystercatchers. The entirely sooty-blackish plumage and sedate behavior of these birds often causes them to remain undetected until they betray their presence among rocky tidepools with long-continued calls. • Throughout the year, oystercatchers spend their time within the intertidal zone, searching for marine worms, crabs and exposed mollusks. This bird's long, narrow, blood red bill is well adapted for prying open the tightly sealed shells of mussels and other shellfish. • Rocky offshore islands rich with intertidal life and free from predators and human disturbance are well populated with breeding oystercatchers. Owing to their territoriality and the spotty distribution nature of their preferred habitat, Black Oystercatchers are limited in numbers.

ID: all-black plumage; long, blood red bill; red eye ring; pinkish legs.
Size: L 16¹/₂–18¹/₂ in.
Status: uncommon year-round resident; rare to uncommon fall and winter visitor.
Habitat: rocky shorelines, islands, sea stacks, breakwaters, jetties and reefs; mudflats close to rocky areas outside of breeding season; bathes at freshwater outfalls.
Nesting: on the ground well above the high-water mark; pair builds a slight scrape lined with pebbles and shells; pair may mate for life; pair incubates 2–3 olive to buff eggs with dark scrawls and spots for 24–29 days.
Feeding: forages at low tide on rocky mussel beds; pries open shells; limpets, mussels and other shellfish form bulk of diet; also takes sea urchins, marine worms, crabs and other invertebrates.
Voice: call is a very loud, far-carrying *wheep* or *whick* repeated in prolonged series in flight; similar single-note calls are uttered in the vicinity of the nest.
Similar Species: none.

BLACK-NECKED STILT

Himantopus mexicanus

The Black-necked Stilt strides daintily around coastal and interior wetlands on long, gangly legs. This bird is usually found throughout much of northern California, but its seasonal abundance varies dramatically depending on the specific locality. • Whether this bird is wandering along a smelly sewage lagoon or wading in a white salt-evaporation pond, the stilt's dignity adds a sense of subtle glory to the bleak landscape it is most often associated with. • On hot summer days, adult Black-necked Stilts routinely take turns sheltering their eggs from the warmth of the hot sun. Adults might even be observed wetting their belly feathers in order to cool off their encased young during their next incubation duty. • Proportionately, this bird has the longest legs of any North American bird, and is truly deserving of the name 'stilt.'

♂

ID: very long, orange legs; dark upperparts; clean white underparts; long, straight, needle-like bill; small, white eyebrow; male is blacker above than the female.

Size: L 14–15 in.

Status: locally rare to common year-round resident; rare to locally very common migrant and breeder from early April to October.

Habitat: *Breeding:* along the margins of freshwater, brackish and saltwater marshes and on the marshy shorelines of lakes, ponds and tidal mudflats; also forages in flooded agricultural fields and salt-evaporation ponds.

Nesting: in a shallow depression on slightly raised ground near water; nest is lined with shells, pebbles or vegetative debris; pair incubates 4 darkly blotched, buff eggs for about 25 days; both adults tend the precocial young.

Feeding: picks prey from the water's surface or from the bottom substrate; primarily eats insects, crustaceans and other aquatic invertebrates.

Voice: not vocal during migration; loud, sharp *yip-yip-yip-yip* in summer; *kek-kek-kek-kek* in flight.

Similar Species: *American Avocet* (p. 142): upturned bill; lacks the black on the head.

AMERICAN AVOCET

Recurvirostra americana

An American Avocet in full breeding plumage might just be the most elegant bird in North America. To some birders, its curvy features, graceful movements and striking colors are unmatched. • During courtship, the female avocet extends her dainty bill forward and lowers her chin until it just clears the water's surface. The male struts around his statuesque mate until conditions are perfect; then he jumps atop the still female and the pair quickly mate. After the male dismounts, the pair cross their slender bills and walk away in unison, reinforcing their new bond. • Avocets are easily identified at a distance by their habit of whisking their long, recurved bills back and forth through shallow water when feeding.

breeding ♂

ID: long, slim, upturned, black bill; long, pale gray-blue legs; black wings with wide, white patches; white underparts; female's bill is slightly more upturned and shorter than the male's. *Breeding:* peachy-red head, neck and breast. *Non-breeding:* grayish head, neck and breast. *In flight:* long, skinny legs and neck; black-and-white wings.

Size: *L* 17–18 in.

Status: uncommon to locally abundant year-round resident; uncommon to locally abundant migrant from early March to early May and from mid-July to early November; uncommon to locally abundant visitor from October to March; locally common breeder from mid-March to September.

Habitat: lakeshores, interior alkaline wetlands, exposed mudflats, coastal estuaries, shallow lagoons, salt-evaporation ponds and shallow freshwater sloughs and ponds.

Nesting: semi-colonial; in a shallow depression along a dried mudflat, exposed shoreline or open area, always near water; pair builds a shallow scrape or a mound of vegetation lined with pebbles or other debris; pair incubates 4 darkly blotched eggs for 23–25 days.

Feeding: sweeps its bill from side to side through the water's surface; picks up small crustaceans, aquatic insects and occasionally seeds; males sweep lower in the water column than females; occasionally swims and tips-up like a duck.

Voice: loud, shrill *PLEEK, PLEEK, PLEEK*.

Similar Species: *Black-necked Stilt* (p. 141): straight bill; mostly black head; red legs. *Willet* (p. 146): straight, heavy bill; flashy flight pattern suggests an avocet but is grayish overall.

GREATER YELLOWLEGS

Tringa melanoleuca

The Greater Yellowlegs often performs the role of lookout among mixed flocks of shorebirds. At the first sign of danger, this large sandpiper begins calling, bobbing its head and moving slowly away from danger. Along with the Killdeer, this shorebird is often heard before it is seen. When faced with a threatening situation, the Greater Yellowlegs usually retreats into deep water before becoming airborne as a last resort. • Many shorebirds, including the Greater Yellowlegs, roost while standing on one leg. These stubborn 'one-leggers' may be mistaken for crippled individuals, but this stance is an adaptation for thermoregulation: two exposed feet needlessly emit precious warmth to the external environment. • Most Greater Yellowlegs are observed in northern California from July to late April. These birds are often seen singly, but concentrations occur in large expanses of good habitat. • The scientific name *melanoleuca* is Greek for 'black and white,' a straightforward reference to this bird's plumage.

non-breeding

ID: long, bright yellow legs; slender, dark bill is noticeably longer than the head width. *Breeding:* brown-black back and wing coverts; fine, dense, dark streaking on the head and neck; dark barring on the breast often extends onto the belly; subtle, dark eye line; light lore. *Non-breeding:* gray overall; fine streaks on the breast.
Size: *L* 13–15 in.
Status: fairly common migrant from mid-March to mid-May and from late June to early November; locally common winter visitor; a very few non-breeders may remain over summer.
Habitat: margins and shorelines of fresh-water and saltwater marshes, lagoons, ponds, lakes, sloughs, tidal estuaries and rivers; also uses mudflats, tidal channels and flooded agricultural fields.

Nesting: in northern Canada and Alaska.
Feeding: usually wades knee-deep in water; occasionally runs a few steps to snatch prey from the water's surface; commonly sweeps its bill from side to side; primarily eats aquatic invertebrates but will also eat small fish.
Voice: alarm call is a piercing series of whistled *tew-tew-tew-tew-tew* notes, usually 3–5 notes per series; spring migrants may utter a rhythmic song of 'weedle-cory' notes.

Similar Species: *Lesser Yellowlegs* (p. 144): smaller; shorter bill; generally calls in pairs of *tews. Willet* (p. 146): black-and-white wings in flight; grayish legs; darker neck and sides; heavier bill.

LESSER YELLOWLEGS

Tringa flavipes

The lovely Lesser Yellowlegs is a medium to small shorebird, best known to the varied members of the fall sandpiper flocks with which it mingles—and to the birders who watch them. Remaining in touch with one another by giving infrequent 'tew' or 'kew' calls, scattered Lesser Yellowlegs walk steadily through muddy shallows, picking small invertebrates from the surface. • From early March to early May and again from early July to early October, migrants descend from the night skies to forage in shallow pools and quiet backwaters along the California coast. • Lesser Yellowlegs and Greater Yellowlegs are similar birds, and both occur in migration throughout northern California. The Lesser's bill is not noticeably longer than the width of its head and is thinner than the Greater's longer bill. The Greater's bill is also slightly upturned—so slightly that it can be noticed one moment and not the next. If the species cannot be distinguished, it is respectable to simply write 'yellowlegs' in your field notes.

non-breeding

ID: bright yellow legs; dark bill is not noticeably longer than the head width; brown-black back and wing coverts; fine, dense, dark streaking on the head, neck and breast; lacks barring on the belly; subtle, dark eye line; light lore.

Size: L 10–11 in.

Status: rare to uncommon migrant from early March to early May; much more numerous, sometimes locally common migrant from early July to early October; rare winter visitor.

Habitat: freshwater and saltwater marshes, lagoons, estuaries, tidal mudflats, ponds and flooded agricultural fields.

Nesting: in northern Canada and Alaska.

Feeding: snatches prey from the water's surface; frequently wades in shallow water; primarily eats aquatic invertebrates, but will also take small fish and tadpoles.

Voice: flat, high-pitched *tew* or *kewk-kewk*; seldom more than 2 calls in the series; lacks the harsh, arresting quality of Greater Yellowlegs.

Similar Species: *Greater Yellowlegs* (p. 143): larger; slightly upturned bill is noticeably longer than the head width; dark barring on the belly in breeding plumage. *Solitary Sandpiper* (p. 145): darker backed; white eye ring; greenish legs. *Willet* (p. 146): larger; black-and-white wings in flight; grayish legs; heavier bill.

SOLITARY SANDPIPER

Tringa solitaria

No other shorebird has such an unusual nesting site: a tree! The Solitary Sandpiper's nesting strategy remained undiscovered by early ornithologists because they never thought to look for this bird's eggs in an abandoned songbird nest. • Shorebirds lay eggs that are large relative to their bodies, and the incubation period is correspondingly long. When more time is spent developing inside the egg, a chick's chance of survival is often increased. Shortly after sandpiper chicks hatch, they begin to feed on their own. Such highly developed hatchlings, known as precocial young, must learn quickly to fend for themselves. (The hatchlings of many songbirds are born naked and helpless; they are called altricial young.) • True to its name, the Solitary Sandpiper is somewhat reclusive and is frequently seen alone or in small groups, bobbing its body like a dancer. • Most Solitary Sandpipers are seen in northern California from early April to early May and from early August to late September; they are absent in winter.

breeding

ID: dark, elegant shorebird; white eye ring; short green legs; brown-gray, spotted back; white lore; brown-gray head, neck and breast have fine white streaks; dark upper-tail feathers have black-and-white barring on the sides. *In flight:* dark underwings; spirited, swallow-like flight.

Size: L 7¹/₂–9 in.

Status: rare to locally uncommon migrant from early April to late May and from late July to late October.

Nesting: in northern Canada and Alaska.

Feeding: stalks shorelines, picking up aquatic insects and other aquatic invertebrates; occasionally stirs the water with a foot to spook out prey.

Voice: high, thin *peet-wheet* or *wheet wheet wheet* during summer, suggesting the Spotted Sandpiper.

Similar Species: *Lesser Yellowlegs* (p. 144): larger; no eye ring; bright yellow legs. *Spotted Sandpiper* (p. 148): paler upperparts; incomplete eye ring; very spotted breast and orange, black-tipped bill in breeding plumage; white eyebrow and clean white throat and foreneck in winter plumage.

MIGRANT ONLY

WILLET
Catoptrophorus semipalmatus

If you spot a Willet slowly walking along the shore of a wetland, there is little to alert you to this bird's spirited character. This large shorebird cuts a rather dull, gray figure when it is grounded on northern California shorelines, but the instant it takes flight, its wondrous black-and-white wings flash in harmony with its loud, rhythmic call. It is widely believed that the bright, bold flashes of the Willet's wings might serve as a warning to other shorebirds. These flashes might also intimidate predators during a Willet's dive-bombing defense of its young. • 'Willet' is an onomatopoeic description of this bird's common call. The genus name *Catoptrophorus* is a Latinized form of 'mirror-bearing,' a reference to the flashy white patches on its otherwise dark wings.

breeding

ID: large, grayish shorebird; plump; heavy, straight, black bill; light throat and belly; dull bluish-gray legs. *Breeding:* intricate dark streaking and barring overall. *Non-breeding:* lightly mottled, gray-brown plumage. *In flight:* eye-catching black-and-white wing pattern.
Size: L 14–16 in.
Status: fairly common to common migrant from early April to mid-May and from late June to mid-October; fairly common to common winter visitor; fairly common local breeder from April to August.
Habitat: *Breeding:* wet grassy meadows, usually adjacent to lakes, in high plateau country. *Winter:* coastal tidal mudflats, exposed ocean beaches, estuaries, rocky coastal reefs, breakwaters, lagoons, saltwater marshes and ponds. *In migration:* wet fields and shores of marshes, ponds and lakes.

Nesting: in a shallow depression in tall grass, lined with finer grass; pair incubates 4 brown-blotched, olive-buff to grayish eggs for 22–29 days; precocial young tended by both adults until the female departs.
Feeding: feeds by probing muddy areas; also gleans the ground for insects; occasionally eats shoots and seeds.
Voice: flocks converse with hectic, harsh call-notes; loud, rollicking *pill-will willet* is heard on breeding grounds.
Similar Species: *Marbled Godwit* (p. 151): warm brown; larger and much longer, slightly upturned bill is orange or pinkish, with a black tip. *Greater Yellowlegs* (p. 143): smaller; long, yellow legs; lacks the bold wing pattern; paler neck and sides.

WANDERING TATTLER
Heteroscelus incanus

Named for their migratory prowess and for their piercing alarm notes, Wandering Tattlers touch northern California jetties and tidepools with the subtle romance of seasonal passages as yet unfinished. Some may reach tropical Pacific beaches in winter, a realm unlike their northerly nesting sites. • The breeding behavior of this bird was discovered in 1912, when a nest was found on a gravel bar along a Yukon stream. Subsequent observations have revealed its preference for nesting along mountain streams above treeline from Denali National Park to Prince William Sound.

non-breeding

ID: horizontal posture; dark bill is much longer than the width of the head; short, yellow legs; bobs its tail fluidly while walking. *Breeding:* gray upperparts; underparts have dense, dark barring. *Non-breeding:* all gray except for the white belly. *In flight:* all upperparts are unmarked and evenly gray.
Size: L 10–10½ in.
Status: uncommon to fairly common migrant from late March to mid-May and from early July to mid-October; rare to uncommon visitor from October to March.
Habitat: *Breeding:* along mountain streams above treeline. *Winter:* on rocky coastlines, jetties and breakwaters. *In migration:* occasionally appears on the lower waveslope of sandy beaches and, exceptionally, on estuarine mudflats.
Nesting: in northwestern British Columbia, the Yukon and Alaska.
Feeding: diet includes crustaceans, mollusks, marine worms and other invertebrates; creeps about intertidal rocks and reefs.
Voice: distinctive flight call is a short series of rapid-fire whistles all on one pitch; silent while feeding or at rest.
Similar Species: *Surfbird* (p. 154): chunkier; stubby bill is shorter than the width of the head; lower mandible has a yellow base; dark breast; dark spots on the belly; white on the wings and tail in flight. *Rock Sandpiper* (p. 161): shorter, slightly decurved bill; dark breast; flecking on the belly and sides; thin but apparent white wing stripe in flight. *Black Turnstone* (p. 153): squat, black bill is shorter than the width of the head; black breast, head and upperparts; complex pattern of white on the back, wings and tail in flight.

147

SPOTTED SANDPIPER
Actitis macularia

This diminutive shorebird breeds nearly throughout northern California in summer and is a year-round resident of larger streams. Unlike many shorebirds that move in large flocks, the Spotted Sandpiper is usually seen alone, in solitary pairs or in family groups. • Although its breast spots might not be seen from a distance, this bird is easily recognized by its bobbing behavior and by its stiff-winged, quivering flight as it buzzes along pebbly shorelines. • It wasn't until 1972 that the unexpected truths about the Spotted Sandpiper's breeding activities were finally understood. Similar to phalaropes, female Spotted Sandpipers defend their territories and leave the males to tend the nest, eggs and hatched young. This unusual nesting behavior—polyandry, from the Greek for 'many men'—is found in only about one percent of all bird species.

breeding

ID: short-legged shorebird.
Breeding: white underparts are heavily spotted with black (slightly more so in the female); yellow-orange legs; yellow-orange, black-tipped bill; white eyebrow.
Non-breeding and *Juvenile:* pure white breast, foreneck and throat; brown bill; dull yellow legs. *In flight:* flies close to the water's surface with very rapid, shallow wingbeats; white upperwing stripe; often heard before it is seen.
Size: L 7–8 in.
Status: uncommon migrant from mid-March to mid-May; common migrant from late July to mid-October; uncommon breeder from May to August; uncommon winter visitor.
Habitat: *Breeding:* beaches and gravel bars along the shores of freshwater streams, lakes, ponds and estuaries; also along the margins of wet meadows. *Non-breeding:* debris-littered or pebbly shores of lakes, ponds, streams and estuaries, protected ocean beaches, rocky coastline, reefs, breakwaters and boat basins.

Nesting: usually well above the water's edge, among logs or under bushes; in a shallow depression lined with grass; male almost exclusively incubates the 4 eggs and tends the precocial young; eggs are buff-colored, blotched with brown.
Feeding: picks and gleans along shorelines for terrestrial and aquatic invertebrates; also snatches flying insects from the air.
Voice: shrill, penetrating *eat-wheat, eat-wheat, wheat-wheat-wheat-wheat!* often given in long series in flight and upon landing.
Similar Species: *Solitary Sandpiper* (p. 145) and *Lesser Yellowlegs* (p. 144): lack the spotted breast; streaking on the neck year-round. *Other sandpipers:* all lack the spotted breast; none bob and teeter as continuously.

WHIMBREL
Numenius phaeopus

During spring and fall, a wide scattering of Whimbrels may be seen on expansive mudflats, along undisturbed ocean waveslopes or in large plowed fields. Each bird pursues its meal in individual wanderings, yet remains in contact with others of its kind, ever prepared to take flight as a flock. • Currently, the Whimbrel enjoys an widespread distribution much like that of the Ruddy Turnstone: this bird nests across northern North America and Eurasia and spends its winters on the shores of six continents. • Unlike its smaller relative, the Eskimo Curlew—which is now widely believed to be extinct—the Whimbrel was able to escape the ravages of reckless 19th-century hunters. • Birders who have traveled to the Arctic might remember wandering into Whimbrel territories and suffering an intimidating aerial attack by defensive parents. • The scientific name *Numenius*, from the Greek word *neos*, meaning 'new,' and *mene*, meaning 'moon'—was given to the Whimbrel and other curlews because of resemblance of the shape of their bills to the crescent moon.

ID: large, rangy sandpiper; long, downcurved bill; striped crown; dark eye line; mottled brown body; long legs. *In flight:* even-colored, dark underwings.
Size: L 17½ in.
Status: fairly common to abundant migrant from mid-March to mid-May; fairly common migrant from late June to late September; rare to fairly common winter visitor; uncommon non-breeding summer visitor.
Habitat: coastal shoreline habitats, including beaches, mudflats, estuaries, rocky shores, saltwater marshes, reefs and breakwaters; also uses lawns, flooded fields, freshwater marshes and the margins of lakes and rivers during migration.
Nesting: in northern Canada and Alaska.

Feeding: insects, crustaceans, other invertebrates and berries are picked up from the ground or probed from just under the surface.
Voice: series of hollow, single-pitched whistles: *pip pip pip*; northbound birds in spring may give snatches of a breeding 'song.'
Similar Species: *Long-billed Curlew* (p. 150): lacks the striped crown; much longer bill; warm orange-cinnamon underwing linings.

149

LONG-BILLED CURLEW
Numenius americanus

Armed with a bill that reaches more than 7 in long, the Long-billed Curlew—North America's largest sandpiper—is an imposing and remarkable bird indeed. Its long, downcurved bill is a dexterous tool designed for picking grasshoppers from dense prairie grasslands or extracting buried mollusks from soft, penetrable mud. • Long-billed Curlews breed primarily on undisturbed grasslands, which in northern California are restricted to the extreme northeastern plateau country. Male curlews engage in spectacular displays over their nesting territory: they give loud, ringing calls while fluttering high and then gliding down in an undulating flight. • Over the years, decimation by gun and by plow have led to a decline in this curlew over most of its range. The future of the Long-billed Curlew is largely tied to the adoption of conservative range and grassland management strategies. Recent studies have indicated that returning individuals occupy and defend winter foraging territories in successive years.

ID: very large, long-necked sandpiper; very long, downcurved bill (slightly longer in the female); buff-brown underparts; mottled brown upperparts; unstriped head; long legs; orange-cinnamon underwing linings.
Size: *L* 20–26 in.
Status: rare to locally abundant migrant and visitor from late June to mid-May; uncommon to locally fairly common breeder from April to August.
Habitat: *Breeding:* grasslands interspersed with lakes or marshes. *Non-breeding:* tidal mudflats, estuaries, saltwater marshes and tidal channels; often grasslands and agricultural fields with short grasses.
Nesting: in a slight depression sparsely lined with grass and other debris; pair incubates 4 buff eggs spotted with brown and olive for 27–30 days; precocial young leave the nest soon after hatching.
Feeding: probes grasslands for insects, including grasshoppers and beetles; probes

shorelines and coastal mudflats for mollusks, crabs, crayfish, marine worms and insects; may eat nestling birds, eggs and some berries.
Voice: most common call is a loud whistle: *cur-lee cur-lee cur-lee*; also a melodious, rolling *cuurrleeeuuu*.
Similar Species: *Marbled Godwit* (p. 151): often found among or near curlews along coast; shorter, slightly upturned, bicolored bill. *Whimbrel* (p. 149): smaller; much shorter, downcurved bill; dark and pale striping on the head; unmarked, white belly.

MARBLED GODWIT

Limosa fedoa

As the sun winks briefly from beneath a broad brow of cloud to the west and sinks into the Pacific beyond Humboldt Bay, hundreds of Marbled Godwits gather restlessly at their cramped high-tide roosting islets in preparation for a nighttime migratory flight. The form of a passing raptor silhouetted against the overcast sky sends the mob of large shorebirds into a sudden uproar of combined voice, causing the day's last joggers and dog-walkers to pause and wonder. Finally, there comes the moment when the swarm of godwits departs northward for distant nesting grounds. In a rush, the flock peels from the roost, assembles into wedges and lines and heads upward into the onshore breeze. • Marbled Godwits breed in two highly disjunct regions: on the prairies of the northern U.S. and southern Canada and in coastal western Alaska. In our region, they may be found singly or in flocks among other migrant and wintering shorebirds in estuaries and along the ocean beaches. Their large size, warm-brown color and long, slightly upturned, pink-based bills make them easy to recognize.

non-breeding

ID: long, upturned, pinkish bill with a dark tip; long neck and legs; buffy-brown throughout; dark-and-light pattern on the back. *Breeding:* finely barred with dark across the underparts. *Non-breeding:* plainer beneath, with only slight streaks. *In flight:* flashes cinnamon-orange wing linings.

Size: L 16–20 in.

Status: uncommon to locally abundant migrant and visitor from July to late May; smaller numbers winter in the interior; a few linger through early summer at larger estuaries.

Habitat: tidal mudflats, ocean beaches, plowed fields, lakeshores and rain-pooled pastures.

Nesting: on the northern Great Plains and Canadian prairies and locally in coastal western Alaska.

Feeding: picks grasshoppers and beetles from grass; probes deeply in soft substrates for worms and invertebrate larvae; takes mollusks and crustaceans along the coast; may also eat the tubers and seeds of aquatic vegetation.

Voice: unique; resonant, anxious cries of *ka-REK* while foraging or taking flight; members of flocks gathered at roosts utter a rollicking *RADica-RADica-RADica!*

Similar Species: *Long-billed Curlew* (p. 150): slightly larger; longer, downcurved bill. *Willet* (p. 146): stout, straight, all-dark bill; black-and-white wing pattern in flight. *Whimbrel* (p. 149): decurved bill; striped head; lacks the cinnamon-orange panel in the underwing.

151

RUDDY TURNSTONE

Arenaria interpres

Although most of us are given but a glimpse into the life of a Ruddy Turnstone, its harlequin markings, singular foraging behavior and profoundly transient lifestyle cause us to ponder this bird's charisma. • Ruddy Turnstones are circumpolar sandpipers, breeding in the High Arctic and wintering far southward along the world's temperate shorelines. In northern California, they are found singly or in small groups along wrack-edged ocean beaches, in rocky tidepools, around lower-estuarine boat basins and on breakwaters, piers and jetties. Generally uncommon along the West Coast, Ruddy Turnstones become most numerous during the extended southward movement, which takes place from July through September. During migratory peaks, flocks of as many as several dozen birds feed on estuarine mudflats littered with seaweed and other debris. A few may be found in winter among flocks of Black Turnstones at harbor entrances. • As their name implies, turnstones search for food by nosing among and flipping over pebbles, shells, bits of wood and other objects, exploiting a niche unused by other shorebirds.

non-breeding

Nesting: in the Arctic.

Feeding: forages by gleaning from the ground, probing in mud or under turned-over objects; takes mostly insects, mollusks and crustaceans; broadly omnivorous, also eating carrion, seeds, berries, sea urchins, spiders, moss, fish, eggs, worms and human food.

Voice: harsh, chuckling rattle calls are more muted and distinctly lower pitched than the insistent, hectic chatter of the Black Turnstone.

Similar Species: *Black Turnstone* (p. 153): deep blackish overall in breeding plumage except for a white 'teardrop' at the front of the face and a white belly and undertail; non-breeding plumage has an even margin of dark and light on the breast; legs and feet are duller, seldom appearing bright orange.

ID: squat, plover-like shorebird; white belly; black bib curving up to the shoulder; short, stout, slightly upturned, black bill; short, orange-red legs and feet. *Breeding:* strikingly patterned; ruddy upperparts; black-and-white face; black collar; dark, streaky crown. *Non-breeding:* deep brownish above; indistinct suggestion of summer pattern on the breast. *In flight:* flashes a complex dark-and-white pattern.

Size: *L* 9¹/₂ in.

Status: uncommon to fairly common migrant from mid-April to mid-May and from mid-July through September; uncommon visitor from late July to mid-May.

Habitat: sand or cobble beaches with shells, pebbles and abundant wrack and debris; estuarine mudflats; tidepools, rocky marine contructions; rare inland.

BLACK TURNSTONE
Arenaria melanocephala

During much of the year, Black Turnstones may be seen searching the barnacle- and seaweed-covered rocky outcroppings of coastal shores. Turnstones creep in tight flocks among exposed lower-intertidal rocks, methodically inspecting the nooks and crevices of surf-pounded rocks for mollusks, marine worms and other intertidal invertebrates. They do much of their foraging by probing and, like other turnstones, gain notice for their novel technique of flipping over small, loose objects to expose concealed food items. The turnstone's bill reflects form related to function, as it is short, fine-tipped and slightly upturned.

non-breeding

ID: stout, slightly upturned bill; blackish upperparts; white belly; dark to dingy orange legs and feet. *Breeding:* cream white 'teardrop' between the eye and bill; white eyebrow and lore. *In flight:* boldly marked black-and-white pattern.

Size: *L* 9–9¹/₂ in.

Status: fairly common migrant and visitor from early July to early May; a few non-breeders may remain over summer.

Habitat: rocky shorelines, breakwaters, jetties and reefs; may also use sandy beaches with seaweed wracks; occasionally visits mudflats, gravel bars and pasture rainpools.

Nesting: in Alaska.

Feeding: forages on rocks or other substrates; pries open shells with its bill or hammers to crack open; finds prey by flipping over rocks; eats mostly barnacles, limpets and other crustaceans and mollusks; insects and some seeds and berries are taken during the breeding season.

Voice: call is a remarkably shrill, high-pitched *skirrr*; flocks erupt from intertidal boulders with a hectic mass chatter.

Similar Species: *Surfbird* (p. 154): larger; mottled; yellowish-green legs; terminal black band on its white tail. *Wandering Tattler* (p. 147): teeters and bobs as it feeds; light gray overall; larger. *Ruddy Turnstone* (p. 152): rust color in its wings and back. *Black-bellied Plover* (p. 135): breeding bird has white on its crown, neck and undertail coverts.

SURFBIRD
Aphriza virgata

Wreathed in mist from yet another dying Pacific roller, a Surfbird treks stolidly through a crazed landscape of tidepools and treacherous rocky shores. Although it is attuned to the swell and swoon of tons of seawater, there nevertheless comes the moment when wings carry this small bird to safety, and what looked like three or four individuals reveal themselves to have been but a portion of the greater flock. The spangled dark plumage worn by these 'rockpipers' causes their chubby forms to blend into the backdrop of dark and glistening seaweeds and mussels that encrust the boulders. • Surfbirds are a minority at many sites, but they may outnumber Black Turnstones during the southward migration of adults following breeding in July. They defend foraging and bathing sites from intrusive turnstones with a buff display featuring broadly flared wings.

non-breeding

ID: chunky; stout, yellow-based bill with a swollen tip; variably heavy chevron spotted on the underparts; short, yellow legs. *Non-breeding*: boldy streaked head and neck; dense black chevrons on the breast and sides; dull-orange centers to the shoulder feathers. *In flight*: suggests turnstones, but pattern of white on dark is limited to a wing stripe and white-based tail.
Size: L 9–9¹/₂ in.
Status: uncommon to locally common migrant from late March to early May and from mid-July to early October; uncommon to fairly common visitor from mid-September to mid-May.
Habitat: rocky intertidal habitats with abundant invertebrate life; tidepools, headlands, reefs, older jetties and breakwaters at harbor entrances; occasionally forages at the waveline on short sandy beaches; visits offshore islands and rocks.
Nesting: in Alaska and the Yukon.
Feeding: with a sideways jerk of the head, pries marine invertebrates from rocks with its bill; gleans items from marine algae and crevices; routinely forages in the company or vicinity of Black Turnstones, Wandering Tattlers and Black Oystercatchers.
Voice: a single or 2-noted *key-week*; less prone to excited group chatter than turnstones.
Similar Species: *Black Turnstone* (p. 153): slightly smaller; blacker above; lacks the extensive spotting on the underparts; flashy black-and-white pattern in flight. *Rock Sandpiper* (p. 161): in non-breeding plumage suggests a pint-sized Surfbird, but has a slender, slightly drooping sandpiper bill; lacks the Surfbird's banded tail.

RED KNOT
Calidris canutus

Here and there among flocks of dowitchers and Dunlins one may distinguish several Red Knots. Although only locally numerous, a few migrant Red Knots may appear almost anywhere along the northern California coast, consorting with more abundant species. • In fall and winter, dull-colored Red Knots are particularly difficult to distinguish from other migrating and overwintering shorebirds. As spring progresses, Red Knots make their annual journey northward, having molted into distinctive robin-like attire. While the Red Knot's drab winter plumage blends well with the uniform grays and browns of sandy beaches and mudflats, its bright summer wardrobe helps it to avoid detection by predators in a sea of rust-tinged arctic grasses, sedges, small shrubs and wildflowers. • Larger estuarine mudflats and long sandy beaches attract their share of Red Knots, but for the most part, they are seldom seen unless pointedly searched for among mixed flocks of shorebirds. • Some migrating knots wander as far south as Australia and South America in winter.

non-breeding

ID: chunky, round-bodied, mid-sized shorebird. *Breeding:* rusty face, breast and underparts; brown, black and chestnut upperparts. *Non-breeding:* pale gray upperparts; white underparts with some faint streaking in the breast; white wing stripe; faint grayish barring on the white rump. *Immature:* buffy wash on the breast; finely scaled upperparts.
Size: L 10½ in.
Status: uncommon to locally common migrant from early April to mid-May and from late July to early October; rare to uncommon visitor from October to March.
Habitat: tidal mudflats, estuaries and saltwater marshes with tidal channels; may also use rocky shorelines, breakwaters and sandy beaches.

Nesting: in the Arctic.
Feeding: feeds by probing in the mud or snatching prey from the ground; insects, mollusks, crustaceans, worms and a variety of plant materials are consumed.
Voice: generally silent; when flushed softly calls its name: *knot*.

Similar Species: *Long-billed Dowitcher* (p. 164) and *Short-billed Dowitcher* (p. 163): much longer bills (at least 1½ times longer than width of the head); white lower back; distinctive call-notes.

155

SANDERLING
Calidris alba

As the wavefront spills in and out on sandy beaches, lines of lively Sanderlings sprint up and back, running and cavorting in the surf. These leggy, pallid sandpipers rush to exploit crustaceans that are active within the fluid-sand zone, often lifting from the lip of an oncoming wave in unison, calling in snappy notes. They feed at times on wet mudflats, doing so in a manner more typical of the shorebird family. • Sanderlings are among the world's cosmopolitan creatures. They breed across the Arctic in Alaska, Canada and Asia, spending winters running up and down sandy shorelines in more temperate climes on every continent but Antarctica.

non-breeding

ID: straight, sturdy, black bill; black legs. *Breeding:* rusty head and breast with dark spotting or mottling. *Non-breeding:* quite pale; white underparts; pale gray upperparts; black shoulder patch (often concealed). *Juvenile:* white-edged, blackish upperparts; conspicuous buffy wash on the upper breast.

Size: L 7–8¹/₂ in.

Status: common to abundant migrant from mid-April to late May and from early July to mid-September; common to abundant visitor from July to late May; a few nonbreeders usually remain over summer.

Habitat: lower waveslope of sandy ocean beaches; also uses rocky shorelines, breakwaters, tidal mudflats and estuaries; occasionally on inland freshwater shorelines and mudflats.

Nesting: in the Arctic.

Feeding: diet in winter is mainly coastal invertebrates, including sand crabs, marine worms, amphipods, insects and small mollusks; may eat carrion; diet in summer includes mostly insects and some leaves, seeds and algae.

Voice: generally vocal; flocks converse and flush with electric *twik!* notes, sometimes continued in an irregular series.

Similar Species: *Least Sandpiper* (p.158): smaller and browner. *Dunlin* (p.162): darker backed and dark breasted; slightly downcurved bill. *Red Knot* (p.155): larger; whitish rump barred with gray; breeding adult has rufous underparts. *Western Sandpiper* (p.157) and *Semipalmated Sandpiper:* smaller; dark shoulder marks; lack the uniformly copper-colored head and upper breast in spring and summer; sandy upperparts in winter.

WESTERN SANDPIPER
Calidris mauri

The Western Sandpiper is one of the 'peep' sandpipers—a small sandpiper in the genus *Calidris*. Members of this group can be notoriously difficult to identify. If the subtleties of plumage and calls are not of particular interest, moments spent appreciating the grace and wonderment of these exuberant migrants offer a calm apart from cares. • Western Sandpipers breed only in Alaska but fan out broadly across the continent in migration, wintering as far southeast as Florida. They are present in great numbers on larger mudflats in Northern California from the last days of June through the balance of the year until the following early May. Western Sandpipers commonly feed, roost and travel in large flocks, and the great swarms of small shorebirds wheeling over estuarine tideflats in July and August are dominated by this species.

non-breeding

ID: small sandpiper; long, black, slightly downcurved bill; black legs. *Breeding:* rusty crown, ear and wing patches; lines of chevron spots form streaks on the upper breast and flanks; white lower breast and belly. *Non-breeding:* pale gray upperparts; white underparts; white eyebrow. *In flight:* narrow, white wing stripe; black line splits the white rump.
Size: *L* 6–7 in.
Status: common to abundant migrant from early April to early May and from early July through September; very uncommon (northward) to very common in coastal lowlands and interior in winter; a few may remain over summer.
Habitat: tidal mudflats, estuaries, saltwater marshes with tidal channels, lagoons, sandy beaches, flooded fields, shallow sloughs and pools and the shorelines of freshwater lakes, ponds and marshes; common inland, but greatest numbers concentrate on tidal mudflats.
Nesting: in Alaska.
Feeding: gleans the substrate and probes quickly into soft mud and shallow water; occasionally submerges its head while probing; eats primarily aquatic insects, worms, small mollusks and crustaceans.
Voice: flight call is a squeaky, high-pitched *cheep* or *chir-eep;* flocks produce a constant subdued din of conversational chatter.
Similar Species: *Sanderling* (p. 156): larger; thicker, relatively shorter, straighter bill; bold white upperwing stripe in flight. *Dunlin* (p. 162): larger; black belly in breeding plumage; longer bill is thicker at the base; gray-brown breast wash or streaking in winter plumage. *Least Sandpiper* (p. 158): smaller; light-colored legs; darker breast wash in all plumages.

LEAST SANDPIPER
Calidris minutilla

This short-billed, brownish sandpiper is the smallest North American shorebird, but its tiny size doesn't preclude impressive migratory feats. As with most other 'peeps,' some individuals migrate much of the length of the globe twice each year, from the Arctic to South America and back again. • Shorebirds must optimize their breeding efforts during the brief arctic summer. While they move north, female Least Sandpipers are already developing massive eggs, and when they nest, the entire clutch may weigh more than half the weight of the female! The precocial young hatch in an advanced state of development and get an early jump on life. Their first order of business is to fatten, learn to fly and prepare for the fall migration south.

non-breeding

ID: short, often pale-based, black bill; yellowish or greenish legs; dark, mottled back; buff-brown breast, head and nape; light breast streaking. *Juvenile:* like the adult, but the feathers of the upperparts are richly patterned with dark centers and pale edges; dim streaks across a warm, brownish breast.
Size: L 5–6¹⁄₂ in.
Status: common to abundant migrant from mid-March to mid-May and from mid-July to late October (most common along the coast); fairly common to common visitor from mid-July to mid-April; a few non-breeders usually remain over summer.
Habitat: tidal mudflats, estuaries, saltwater marshes with tidal channels, lagoons, sandy beaches with kelp wracks, flooded fields, shallow sloughs and pools and the shorelines of freshwater streams, lakes, ponds and marshes.
Nesting: in northern Canada and Alaska.

Feeding: probes or pecks the substrate in short grass, on beaches, on mudflats or in shallow pools; eats mosquitoes, beach fleas, amphipods, gastropods, flies, small snails, marine worms, other aquatic invertebrates and occasionally seeds; more inclined to feed on drying mud than to wade.
Voice: thin, high-pitched *kree-eep* or *kreeet* (the long-e tone is distinctive).

Similar Species: *Other 'peeps':* dark legs; generally larger; paler breasts. *Sanderling* (p. 156) and *Western Sandpiper* (p. 157): lack the dark wash on the breast in winter plumage.

BAIRD'S SANDPIPER
Calidris bairdii

The Baird's Sandpiper is a modest-looking bird with extraordinary migratory habits. Like many shorebirds, the Baird's Sandpiper remains on its arctic breeding grounds for a very short time. As soon as newly hatched chicks are able to fend for themselves, the adult birds abandon their nests and flock together to begin their southward migration in July. A few weeks after the parents have departed, the young form a second wave of southbound migrants. • Most Baird's Sandpipers seen in northern California are juveniles and are observed from late July through September. • This elegant wader was named after Spencer Fullerton Baird, an early director of the Smithsonian Institution who organized several natural history expeditions across North America.

non-breeding

juvenile

ID: small, long-winged, brown sandpiper; black legs and bill; fine dark streaks across a buffy-brown breast. *Juvenile:* feathers of the upperparts appear 'scaly,' with pale fringes and dark centers.

Size: L 7–7 1/2 in.

Status: very rare migrant from mid-March to early June; uncommon to locally fairly common migrant from late July into October; most common along coast.

Habitat: upper ocean beach waveslope, drier estuarine and freshwater mudflats, damp alkali flats and the margins of sewage ponds.

Nesting: in the Arctic.

Feeding: alone or in loose company of other sandpipers; walks slowly along, picking insects and other invertebrates from the water's surface; rarely probes; much less inclined to wade than other sandpipers of similar appearance and habitat.

Voice: soft, reedy, rolling *creeep creeep*, often repeated in flight; ordinarily silent while foraging.

Similar Species: *Pectoral Sandpiper* (p. 160): striped, rather than scaly, upperparts; usually has dull yellowish legs. *Least Sandpiper* (p. 158): smaller; streakier upperparts; paler leg color. *Dunlin* (p. 162): longer bill with a downcurved tip; distinct upperwing stripe in flight; wades in water. *Western Sandpiper* (p. 157) and *Sanderling* (p. 156): both lack the noticeably long-winged look; generally in large, busy flocks in or near water.

MIGRANT ONLY

PECTORAL SANDPIPER
Calidris melanotos

This widespread traveler has been observed in every state and province in North America during its epic migrations. In northern California, these sandpipers are most commonly seen from mid-August to late October at grass-dotted mudflats in the coastal lowlands as they rest and refuel during their journey to southern South America. • The Pectoral Sandpiper is one of the few birds that exhibits sexual dimorphism: the female is only two-thirds the size of the male. • The common name 'pectoral' refers to the prominent air sacs on the breast of the male. These sacs are inflated as part of the courtship ritual or when a predator approaches. The scientific name *melanotos* is Greek for 'black back.'

non-breeding

juvenile

ID: pale-based, dark, slightly downcurved bill; rusty, dark brown crown; brown breast streaks end abruptly at the edge of the white belly; white undertail coverts; dull yellowish legs; streaked or finely lined, pale-edged, dark upperparts.
Size: *L* 9 in. (female is slightly smaller).
Status: rare migrant from late March to mid-May; uncommon migrant from July to early November; most common along coast, but small concentrations may occur in excellent habitat, both coastally and at inland mudflats and marshes.
Habitat: grassy borders of estuaries, bays and lagoons, drier areas of mudflats, flooded fields and the shorelines of shallow fresh-water ponds, marshes and streams.
Nesting: in the Arctic.
Feeding: walks about very slowly, probing and pecking the ground, searching primarily

for small insects and crustaceans, including flies, beetles, amphipods and larvae; may also take spiders and some seeds.
Voice: often heard as it flushes, uttering a low-pitched, reedy *krrick* or *krrick-krrick*.
Similar Species: *'Peeps'*: smaller; all lack the well-defined light belly and dark pectoral region. *Least Sandpiper* (p. 158): half the size; short neck. *Baird's Sandpiper* (p. 159): half the size; scaled, rather than streaked upperparts; wing tips extend beyond the tail tip; black legs. *Sharp-tailed Sandpiper*: rich, peachy-buff breast without streaks; broader, flaring, white eyebrow; flatter and distinctly rustier chestnut crown.

MIGRANT ONLY

ROCK SANDPIPER
Calidris ptilocnemis

This marvelously camouflaged bird is best seen between early November and late March as it forages along northern California's rocky shorelines among larger, more conspicuous and much more numerous Surfbirds and Black Turnstones. The Rock Sandpiper's mottled, dark gray appearance makes it difficult to distinguish and keep in view among the gray rocks and splashing surf of the outer coast. • This sandpiper detects most of its food by sight, often while perilously close to crashing ocean waves. • In its winter plumage, the Rock Sandpiper looks very similar to the Purple Sandpiper (*C. maritima*) of the Atlantic coast and the eastern Canadian Arctic islands.

non-breeding

ID: yellowish legs; longish, thin, slightly drooping bill. *Breeding:* black bill; black patch on the lower breast; reddish-brown edges on the back and crown feathers. *Non-breeding:* base of the bill is greenish-yellow; gray head and neck; mottled gray back, wings and breast. *In flight:* thin but conspicuous white wing stripe; dark center stripe on the rump and tail.

Size: *L* 8–9 in.

Status: rare visitor from late October to mid-April.

Habitat: rocky shores, tidepools and rock jetties along ocean coast.

Nesting: in western Alaska and eastern Siberia.

Feeding: small crustaceans, mollusks, insects and other marine invertebrates form bulk of winter diet; may also eat algae, moss, berries, seeds and other plant material.

Voice: generally silent in winter; rarely issues a short *tweet* call.

Similar Species: *Non-breeding Surfbird* (p. 154): much larger; solid gray head and breast; shorter, thicker bill with pale base; wide, dark, subterminal tail band in flight. *Non-breeding Black Turnstone* (p. 153): short, slightly upturned bill; lacks the extensive spotting or streaking below; white back patch and wide, dark, subterminal tail band in flight.

DUNLIN
Calidris alpina

This small shorebird's social behavior is so remarkable that, from a distance, synchronized flocks of thousands of Dunlin appear as a swarm of flying insects. Outside the breeding season, Dunlins are communal creatures that form dynamic, swirling clouds of individuals flying wing tip to wing tip, all changing course simultaneously. These tight flocks are generally more exclusive than many other shorebird troupes, and Dunlins frequently mass in flocks composed mostly or entirely of their own kind. They are among the swiftest of the shorebird migrants—a flock was once observed passing a small plane at 110 mph. • Dunlins are most commonly seen from mid-September to mid-May along the northern California coast. They nest on the high arctic tundra and winter on the coasts of North America, Europe and Asia. • This bird was originally called the 'Dunling' (meaning 'a small brown bird'), but with the passage of time the 'g' was dropped.

non-breeding

ID: stout; larger than the similar 'peeps'; longish, slightly downcurved, black bill; black legs. *Breeding:* black belly; streaked white underparts; rusty wings and crown. *Non-breeding:* whitish underparts with gray wash across the breast; dark mousy-gray upperparts. *In flight:* thin, white wing stripe. **Size:** L 7½–9 in.
Status: common to locally abundant migrant from late March to mid-May and from mid-September to mid-November; common to locally abundant visitor from mid-September to mid-May.
Habitat: tidal mudflats and saltwater marshes, estuaries, lagoon shorelines, flooded fields and muddy edges of freshwater marshes, ponds and lakes.
Nesting: in the Arctic.
Feeding: gleans from the water's surface, probes in mud or performs rapid probing, called 'stitching,' in shallows in winter; eats mostly invertebrates, including crustaceans, mollusks, marine worms and rarely small fish; feeds mostly on insects in summer.
Voice: call is a rather low-pitched, raspy *drzeerp* or *cheezp.*
Similar Species: *Least Sandpiper* (p.158): much smaller; darker brown upperparts; shorter, yellowish legs; seldom wades or probes in open water. *Sanderling* (p.156): paler; stout, straight bill; usually seen running at the edge of the surf. *Western Sandpiper* (p.157) and *Semipalmated Sandpiper:* smaller; lack the black belly and the grayish upper breast; paler backs in winter. *Rock Sandpiper* (p.161): breeding adult has a black patch on the lower breast; yellowish legs; dark ear patch; streakier below in winter.

SHORT-BILLED DOWITCHER

Limnodromus griseus

During spring and fall, the expansive estuarine mudflats left exposed by the ebb tide are sprinkled throughout with scattered assemblages of migrant shorebirds. The most open, featureless stretches of mud are favored feeding grounds for legions of Short-billed Dowitchers. Flocks sometimes numbering in the hundreds or even thousands forage during low water in northern California's bays and then concentrate in crowded, mixed-species roosts when the high tide washes across the flats. • Lacking long legs, dowitchers feed on mud or in shallow pools but can reach hidden invertebrate prey several inches down. The vigorous sewing machine-like rhythm that so characterizes the foraging behavior of both species of dowitcher is helpful for long-range field identification. • Distinguishing this dowitcher from its close relative, the Long-billed Dowitcher, may be difficult for even experienced birders. Although most people are content to simply call them dowitchers, some birders insist on attempting to separate them even though they are extremely similar in their dull winter plumage.

non-breeding

ID: stocky, medium-sized sandpiper; straight, long, dark bill; white wedge on the lower back in flight. *Breeding:* dull cinnamon reddish overall; dark upperparts; fine black spotting on the sides and flanks; largely white belly. *Non-breeding:* gray upperparts; dirty white underparts; white eyebrow; pale tail bars are wider than the dark ones; best identified by voice in winter.
Size: L 11–12 in.
Status: fairly common to locally abundant migrant from mid-March to mid-May and from late June to late September; fairly common to locally abundant visitor from early July to mid-May.
Habitat: mudflats, estuaries and sparsely vegetated saltwater marshes; uses lakeshores, shallow marshes, ponds and flooded fields during migration.
Nesting: in northern Canada and Alaska.
Feeding: wades in shallow water or on mud; eats seasonally available aquatic

invertebrates; may eat seeds, aquatic plants and grasses.
Voice: generally silent while feeding; flight call is a very rapid, toneless, metallic *tutututu*, given most often when flocks flush.
Similar Species: *Long-billed Dowitcher* (p. 164): pale tail bars are no wider than the darker ones in flying winter birds; breeding birds have fine white barring on the red underparts; overall darker upperparts; reddish extends through the belly. *Red Knot* (p. 155): stockier; shorter bill; unmarked, red breast in summer; winter birds lack the barring on the tail and the white wedge on the back in flight. *Common Snipe* (p. 165): boldly striped head; streaked upperparts; rusty tail; lacks the white wedge on the lower back.

LONG-BILLED DOWITCHER

Limnodromus scolopaceus

Almost any freshwater mudflat or short grass marsh will occasionally host these snipe-like shorebirds during their spring and fall migrations or in winter. As a group, dowitchers are easy to recognize: they are large, plump sandpipers that forage in tight flocks along wet shorelines, probing deliberately into mudflats in an up-down motion much like a sewing machine. • Both species of North American dowitchers occur at various times and places in northern California. They coexist by using different habitats but are sometimes found near each other. Attention to their calls and study of the details in their plumage should enable the two species to be distinguished. As a rule, Long-billed Dowitchers are birds of freshwater habitats, frequenting lakeshores, flooded pastures, grass-dotted marshes and the mouths of brackish tidal channels. They appear in greatest numbers inland, leaving the broad tidal mudflats to the Short-bills.

non-breeding

ID: stocky, medium-sized sandpiper; very long, straight, dark bill (longer in the female); white wedge on the lower back in flight; white eyebrow. *Breeding:* thoroughly reddish underparts; lightly barred flanks; dark, mottled upperparts. *Non-breeding:* gray upperparts; dirty white underparts; white eyebrow; dark tail bars are wider than the pale ones; best identified in winter by voice.
Size: L 11–12½ in.
Status: common to locally abundant migrant from early April to mid-May and from late July to late October (most common along coast); common to locally abundant visitor from late July to early May; very rare visitor from late May to late July.
Habitat: along lakeshores, shallow marshes and freshwater mudflats.
Nesting: in the Arctic.
Feeding: probes in shallow water and on mudflats with a quickly repeated up-down

motion of the bill; frequently plunges its head below the water; eats larval flies, worms and other soft-bodied invertebrates; also eats mollusks, worms, crustaceans and seeds of aquatic plants.
Voice: note is a single, loud, piping *keek*, sometimes given in loose series; calls frequently both in flight and while foraging;
Similar Species: *Short-billed Dowitcher* (p. 163): bill is very slightly shorter; pale bars on the tail are wider than the dark bars (seen in flight in winter); dark barring on a usually whitish belly and flanks in breeding plumage. *Common Snipe* (p. 165): heavily striped head; rusty tail; lacks the white wedge on the lower back; seldom found in flocks well out in the open.

COMMON SNIPE

Gallinago gallinago

The eerie, hollow, ascending winnowing of the Common Snipe is a special night sound heard at 'high-quality' northern California freshwater wetlands. Specialized outer tail feathers vibrate like saxophone reeds as this bird performs springtime courtship dives high above its marshland habitat. • Common Snipes are both secretive and well camouflaged, so they generally remain unnoticed until they flush suddenly from beneath a nearby tussock. Taking to the air, a snipe performs a series of evasive zig-zags designed to deter predators. • The Common Snipe's bill is a wonderfully dexterous tool: the tip is semi-flexible and sensitive, allowing the bird to feel and extract soft-bodied earthworms and larval insects buried deep within the mud. • The name *gallinago* is derived from the Latin *gallina*, meaning 'a hen.'

ID: brownish overall; long, sturdy, dark grayish bill; relatively short legs; heavily striped head and back; dark eye stripe; large, dark eyes; unmarked white belly; streaked breast; barred sides and flanks; rusty tail. *In flight:* quickly zig-zags as it takes off, often 'towering' high into the air and then dropping rapidly back into the marsh.

Size: *L* 10$^1/_2$–11$^1/_2$ in.

Status: fairly common migrant and visitor from late August to early May; locally uncommon to fairly common breeder from late April to mid-October.

Habitat: grassy edges of freshwater marshes, ponds, lakes, rivers and streams, 'beaver-ground,' wet meadows and flooded grassy fields; most numerous at sites affording frequent overhead cover.

Nesting: usually in dry grass, often under vegetation; nest is made of grass, moss and leaves; female incubates 4 olive-buff to brown eggs, marked with dark brown, for about 20 days; both parents raise the young, often splitting the brood.

Feeding: probes soft substrates for soft-bodied invertebrates, mostly larvae and earthworms; also eats mollusks, crustaceans, spiders, small amphibians and some seeds.

Voice: eerie, accelerating courtship 'song': *woo-woo-woo-woo-woo-woo* with an abrupt end; often sings a clipped, deliberate *wheat wheat wheat* from an elevated perch; alarm call is a raspy, nasal *scaip!*

Similar Species: *Long-billed Dowitcher* (p. 164) and *Short-billed Dowitcher* (p. 163): white wedge up the lower back; lack the heavy striping on the head and back; usually seen in flocks in the open.

WILSON'S PHALAROPE
Phalaropus tricolor

Not only are phalaropes among the most intensely colorful of North American shorebirds, their breeding strategies are also the most unusual. All phalaropes practice polyandry, in which each female mates with several males. A female defends the nest site while leaving her mate to incubate the eggs and tend to the precocial young. • In June, July and early August of every year, more than 100,000 Wilson's Phalaropes typically arrive on Mono Lake to undergo a partial molt before they continue on their southward migration. This species does not occur at sea but instead migrates through the Great Plains and Great Basin en route to and from wintering grounds in southern South America.

breeding

ID: slender, leggy shorebird; dark, needle-like bill; variably dark above and whitish below; white eyebrow; black legs. *Breeding female:* very sharp colors; gray cap; chestnut throat; black eye line extends down the side of the neck to the back. *Breeding male:* duller overall; dark cap. *Non-breeding:* all-gray upperparts; white eyebrow; gray eye line; white underparts; dark yellowish legs. *Juvenile:* like the breeding male, but with conspicuously pale-edged upperparts and wash of buff across the breast.
Size: L 8¹/₂–9¹/₂ in.
Status: rare (in northwest) to locally abundant migrant from late March to early June and from mid-June to mid-September; locally uncommon to common breeder from May through July; rare winter visitor.
Habitat: *Breeding:* boggy ponds, grassy marshes and wet meadows up to 6900 ft. *In migration:* alkaline lakes, sewage ponds, freshwater shorelines, flooded fields, estuaries and saltwater marshes.
Nesting: near water; in a depression lined with grass and other vegetation; nest is often well concealed; male incubates the

4 brown-blotched buff eggs for 18–27 days; male also rears the young.
Feeding: whirls in tight circles in water to stir up prey from substrate; picks aquatic insects, worms and small crustaceans from the water's surface or just below it; on land, walks slowly with foreparts lowered, making short jabs to pick up invertebrates.
Voice: surprisingly deep, grunting *work work*, heard most often on breeding grounds.
Similar Species: *Red-necked Phalarope* (p. 167): more compact; shorter bill; streaked back; red stripe down the side of the neck in breeding plumage; dark cap and bold, black mark behind the eye in fall; generally uncommon inland. *Red Phalarope* (p. 168): more compact; shorter, thicker bill; all-reddish neck, breast and underparts in breeding plumage; dark nape and mark behind the eye in fall and winter; rarely seen inland. *Lesser Yellowlegs* (p. 144): larger; bright yellow legs; streaked neck; mottled upperparts.

RED-NECKED PHALAROPE

Phalaropus lobatus

Tiny, buoyant mites seeming all but lost among the troughs, Red-necked Phalaropes enliven the open sea with hectic activity. Phalaropes swim and rapidly dab in tight circles, stirring up zooplankton, the community of tiny larval crustaceans, mollusks and other aquatic invertebrates that live in the upper layer of seawater. As prey funnel toward the water's surface, phalaropes select items daintily with their needle-like bills. • Most of these arctic breeders migrate north and south along the coast or many miles seaward. Small flocks regularly appear well inland along the shores of lakes, reservoirs and larger freshwater marshes. • Like grebes and coots, phalaropes have individually webbed toes, an adaptation enabling life on the open ocean or upon the tundra. • 'Phalarope' is a translation of the Greek words for 'coot's foot.'

breeding

ID: small, delicate bird; black, needle-like bill; long, black legs; slim neck. *Breeding female:* chestnut stripe down the side of the neck onto the upper breast and throat; white chin; blue-black head; incomplete white eye ring; white belly; buff stripes on the upper wings. *Breeding male:* white eyebrow; less intense colors than the female. *Non-breeding:* sharply contrasting white underparts; buff-streaked, dark gray back; black cap and bold, black mark from eye to ear.

Size: *L* 7 in.

Status: fairly common to locally abundant migrant from late March to late May and from late June to mid-October; a few may remain over summer.

Habitat: open ocean, from the surfline to well offshore; harbors, estuaries, lagoons, saltwater marshes with tidal channels and pools, salt-evaporation ponds, alkaline lakes, sewage ponds and open freshwater marshes.

Nesting: in the Arctic.

Feeding: whirls in tight circles in shallow or deep water, picking insects, small crustaceans and small mollusks from the water's surface or just below it; on land, totters jerkily about, lunging with short jabs to pick up invertebrates in open areas.

Voice: vocal when in flocks, uttering snappy, single- or double-noted *plik* calls, especially in flight.

Similar Species: *Wilson's Phalarope* (p. 166): usually seen inland in freshwater habitats; never at sea; larger; longer legs; more needle-like bill; female has a gray cap and a black eye line extending down the side of the neck and onto the back in breeding plumage. *Red Phalarope* (p. 168): slightly chunkier; somewhat heavier bill; unstreaked, pale gray upperparts in winter; strikingly reddish below in spring.

MIGRANT ONLY

RED PHALAROPE
Phalaropus fulicaria

The phalarope's reversal of 'traditional' gender roles is also manifested in a reversal of typical plumage characteristics—females are more brightly colored than their male counterparts. Even John J. Audubon misunderstood the phalarope's breeding habits and odd coloring; he mislabeled the female and male birds in all his phalarope illustrations. • The bulk of Red Phalarope migration in spring and fall takes place miles at sea. Few are seen along the coast in spring, but heavy weather in November and December may cause dramatic 'wrecks,' during which thousands are driven onshore. At such times, the beaches, coastal ponds, wet fields and even large parking lots harbor exhausted phalaropes. Wintering Northern Harriers and Merlins act quickly to benefit from these events. • Red Phalaropes have occasionally been observed tending surfaced whales, quickly snatching parasites living on their backs.

breeding

ID: *Breeding female:* odd and striking; chestnut red neck and underparts; white face; black on the crown and around the base of the bill; stout, yellow bill is tipped with black. *Breeding male:* suggests the female but has a mottled brown crown and generally duller colors. *Non-breeding adult:* white head, neck and underparts; gray upperparts; black bill, nape and 'phalarope mark' extending from eye to ear. *Immature:* duller, buffy version of the breeding male.
Size: *L* 8–9 in.
Status: common to abundant migrant from late April to early June and from early July to mid-November; common to abundant, irregular visitor from about mid-November to early January; smaller numbers may occur from January to mid-April.
Habitat: open ocean waters well away from shore, preferring upwellings and current edges; occasionally seen at more inshore locations, such as bays, lagoons, estuaries, tide-rips and salt-evaporation ponds; rarely seen well inland.
Nesting: in the Arctic.
Feeding: gleans from the water's surface, usually while swimming in tight spinning circles; winter diet is poorly known; summer diet includes small crustaceans, mollusks, insects and other invertebrates; rarely takes vegetation or small fish.
Voice: calls include a shrill, high-pitched *wit* and a low *clink clink.*
Similar Species: *Red-necked Phalarope* (p. 167): more petite; winter adult has a darker back and a thinner bill; dark nape extends over the crown; white V on the upper back in flight. *Sanderling* (p. 156): lacks the wide, dark eye patch extending to the ear; sprints back and forth at the edge of the surf.

POMARINE JAEGER
Stercorarius pomarinus

Jaegers are powerful, swift pirates of the limitless skies that stretch across tundra or open ocean. Only during the high arctic breeding season do jaegers seek the solid footing of land. • During much of the year, lone birds and small groups may be encountered at sea. Most jaegers concentrate over the nutrient-rich, prey-abundant borders of prominent ocean currents and upwellings, passing shore points regularly only in modest numbers. Late fall storms occasionally push a 'Pom' into a harbor entrance or even to a large, inland lake. • Jaegers are aggressive in defense of eggs and young. Adults attack intruders with stooping parabolic dives or tail-chase pursuits.

light morph breeding

dark morph breeding

ID: falcon-like seabird; long central tail feathers are spoon-shaped and twisted; black cap or 'helmet.' *In flight:* wings are broad based; comparatively heavy, powerful wingbeats; white flashes from the base of the under primaries. *Light morph:* mottled or barred with 'chocolate-on-cream' across the breast, sides and flanks; dark vent. *Dark morph:* all-dark body except for a white flash in the wing. *Juvenile:* pointed central tail feathers barely project from the rest of the tail; conspicuous white flash at the base of the upper primaries; variable amounts of dark barring on the underwings and underparts; lacks the adult's extensive black cap.
Size: *L* 20–23 in; *W* 4 ft.
Status: fairly common pelagic migrant from mid-April to late May and from early August to mid-November; rare to fairly common pelagic visitor from mid-November to mid-April.
Habitat: open ocean, often miles offshore; regularly detected from land in small numbers during periods of migration.
Nesting: in the Arctic.

Feeding: snatches fish from the ocean surface; harrasses other birds into ultimately dropping their food; will chase and gulp down small birds; may also eat carrion and pick from refuse.
Voice: generally silent; may give a sharp *which-yew*, a squealing *weak-weak* or a squeaky whistled note during migration.
Similar Species: *Parasitic Jaeger* (p. 170): more petite; longer, pointed tail feathers; lacks the mottled sides and flanks; immature and subadult have barred underparts; short, pointed tail streamers. *Long-tailed Jaeger:* very long, thin, pointed tail; lacks the breast band and the barring on the underparts; has a 2-toned pattern above; juvenile has stubby, rounded tail points but more solid dark markings on the throat and upper breast; very little white on the upperwing primaries; both adult and subadult lack the white on the base of the underwing primaries; lacks the very dark vent.

PARASITIC JAEGER
Stercorarius parasiticus

Alert, speedy and able 'turn on a dime,' Parasitic Jaegers intimidate gulls and terns. If incapable of eluding the pirate's maneuvers, a hapless victim may drop or cough up a hard-earned meal. Parasitic Jaegers are most commonly encountered wherever other sea-going birds are successful in finding food. 'Kleptoparasitism' is the behavioral term for the jaeger's thieving ways. Although 'jaeger' is derived from a German word for hunter, 'parasitic' more aptly describes this bird's foraging habits while on northern California waters. During the breeding season, Parasitic Jaegers have been known to follow people (including birders!) and hunting mammals in the hopes of snatching eggs and young that may have been left unattended by fleeing adult birds of other species. • Of the three jaegers that migrate along the northern California coast, the Parasitic is the species most widely and regularly seen from shore points.

*light morph
breeding*

ID: long, pointed, dark wings; slightly projecting, pointed central tail feathers; brown upperparts; dark cap; pale flash in the outer wing. *Light morph:* pale underparts; white to cream-colored collar; dark brown breast band. *Dark morph:* entirely brown underparts and collar. *Juvenile:* barred underparts; pointed central tail feathers extend just past the end of the tail.
Size: L 15–21 in; W 36 in.
Status: fairly common migrant from early April to mid-May and from mid-July to mid-October; a few may occur through to early December and some oversummer.
Habitat: chiefly ocean waters from the outer surf zone out across the continental shelf; some birds, mostly juveniles, enter estuaries and harbors, especially in fall; rare migrant at inland lakes and reservoirs.
Nesting: in the Arctic.

Feeding: small schooling fish initially captured by such birds as Bonaparte's Gulls and Elegant and Common terns provide much of diet along the coast; varied small animals and eggs are taken during summer on tundra.
Voice: generally silent in our area; sudden uproar from a tern flock often signals the appearance of a jaeger.
Similar Species: *Pomarine Jaeger* (p. 169): more robust; broader-winged; adult has shorter, spoon-shaped central tail feathers; dark mottled sides and flanks. *Long-tailed Jaeger:* light-morph adult is entirely pale below; much longer, pointed central tail feathers; lacks the dark neck band; usually miles offshore.

MIGRANT ONLY

BONAPARTE'S GULL
Larus philadelphia

Those birder-naturalists who feel disdain for gulls will discover that time spent appreciating the many graces of Bonaparte's Gulls is a sure remedy. Delicate in both plumage and behavior, these gulls avoid landfills, preferring to pick food items from the surface of lakes, marshes and ocean swells. • This small, energetic gull migrates through northern California in compact flocks that generally draw little attention. Their thousands become briefly evident during the peak of migration in April, however, when small flocks and lines may pass through the surf zone and just offshore for hours. Here and there throughout the California coastal lowlands, lingering flocks of Bonaparte's Gulls make themselves at home throughout the winter months. • Unlike nearly all other gulls, Bonaparte's choose to nest in trees, typically in the boreal forests of Canada and Alaska. • This small gull was not named for the French emperor, but rather for his nephew, zoologist Charles Lucien Bonaparte.

non-breeding

breeding

ID: small, elegant gull; thin, black bill; pale gray mantle; white eye-arcs; white underparts. *Breeding:* black head; orange-red legs. *Non-breeding:* white head; neat, round, dark ear patch. *1st winter:* suggests the adult, but has much dark trim on the upperwing, including a dark border on the leading edge of the primaries; thin, complete, dark terminal tail band. *In flight:* recognizable at long range by the conspicuous white wedge in the outer wing.
Size: *L* 12–14 in; *W* 33 in.
Status: fairly common to locally abundant migrant from early April to late May and from early September to late November; uncommon to fairly common winter visitor; rare to uncommon but regular non-breeding summer visitor.
Habitat: protected coastal waters, estuaries, boat basins, beaches, lagoons, sewage ponds, water-management channels and impoundments, reservoirs and open ocean.

Nesting: in Canada and Alaska.
Feeding: dabbles and tips-up for aquatic invertebrates, small fish and tadpoles while swimming; gleans the ground for terrestrial invertebrates; also pursues flying insects; plunges to the surface to fish.
Voice: annoyed, harsh *eer eer* while feeding in flocks; single birds are ordinarily silent.
Similar Species: *Franklin's Gull:* breeding adult has a darker back, a reddish bill and a prominent subterminal white area in the outer wing. *Sabine's Gull* (p. 181): large black, white and gray triangles on the upperwings; forked tail; yellow-tipped, dark bill; pelagic.

HEERMANN'S GULL

Larus heermanni

Recognizing the distinctive Heermann's Gull is refreshing for novice coastal birders who may struggle to identify many of the region's gulls. • The Heermann's Gull is an exception to the rule that most gulls migrate north to breed and return south for winter. Instead, the Heermann's Gull travels south to sun-baked Isla Raza in the Sea of Cortez to raise its chicks and then moves north for the balance of the warmer months. • Heermann's Gulls are kleptoparasitic, pirating food items of every description from the bills of Brown Pelicans and other associates. Pelicans are especially victimized, and in summer each floating juvenile pelican never gets far from its attendant Heermann's. • Adult Heermann's Gulls begin appearing in April, increasing in late spring, and juveniles arrive in early summer. Numbers decrease in September as the flow of migrants through the inshore waters reverses itself.

non-breeding

ID: *Breeding:* unique; red bill is tipped with black; ashy-gray body; white head; white-tipped, black tail; black legs; dark eyes. *Non-breeding:* pale gray head. *1st winter:* very dark gray-brown body and wings; black legs.
Size: *L* 16–19 in; *W* 51 in.
Status: common to locally abundant post-breeding visitor from mid-June to mid-December; irregularly lingers over winter and into spring; occasional nesting attempts in San Francisco Bay and Monterey Bay.
Habitat: coastal ocean waters, usually close to shore, including bays, harbors, beaches, offshore islands, lagoons and coastal creek outfalls.

Nesting: on islands in the Sea of Cortez; has attempted to breed on the central California coast.
Feeding: dips to the water's surface to snatch items while in flight; often pirates food from other birds; small fish form the bulk of the diet; also takes crustaceans, mollusks, insects, eggs, carrion and some human food-waste; uses garbage dumps locally.
Voice: calls include a whiny, high-pitched *weeee* and a nasal, far-carrying *kawak*; argumentative in 'feeding frenzies.'
Similar Species: *California Gull* (p.175): 1st-winter bird is larger and has a mottled brown body and dull pink legs and feet.

MEW GULL
Larus canus

The appearance of Mew Gulls each fall coincides with the heavy southward migration of waterfowl and raptors. The first few birds around river mouths and over the breakers in October increase to many thousands by late fall. Winter storms allow Mew Gulls to expand from their usual open coast estuary habitats into flooded fields and pastures. Joining other gulls and shorebirds, flocks of dozens or hundreds walk with quick steps, searching for earthworms and other invertebrates driven to the surface. • The Mew Gull is the smallest of the typical 'white-headed' gulls, but adults in summer plumage are seldom seen here; they breed in Canada and Alaska and have largely departed their wintering areas by April. • The small, short bill, large eyes and conspicuous single subterminal white patch in the black wing tips make the adult an easily identified gull.

non-breeding

ID: dainty; small, thin bill; wings extend well beyond the tail at rest; rapid walking stride. *Non-breeding adult:* greenish-yellow bill (variable) with a dark smudge on the lower mandible; medium gray back; variable dusky streaking or clouding on the head, neck and upper breast; noticeable white area in the black wing tips; pale green-yellow legs and feet. *1st winter:* dingy gray-brown with a grayish back; dark-tipped, pink bill; slightly darker brown outer primaries.
Size: *L* 15–16 in; *W* 43 in.
Status: chiefly near-coastal, occuring sparingly inland; fairly common to common visitor from October to mid-April; a few may remain over summer along the northern coast.
Habitat: mostly waters of tidal influence, ranging from the upper reaches of estuaries out to sea; forages widely along the open coast; concentrates in fields and harbors and on mudflats and ocean beaches.
Nesting: in Alaska, northwestern Canada and along the British Columbia coast.

Feeding: opportunistic; captures fish, crustaceans and other invertebrates by plunging to the water's surface, plucking from wave-wash or picking from the ground; normally avoids garbage dumps.
Voice: members of flocks at feeding or roosting sites utter a high-pitched cough, *queeoh*; not particularly vocal while in our area.
Similar Species: *Ring-billed Gull* (p. 174): paler gray above; distinctly black-ringed, yellow bill; pale eyes; lacks the eye-catching white wing tip area; less dusky-headed in winter. *California Gull* (p. 175): much larger; red-and-black marks on the lower mandible of yellowish or dull blue-gray bill; lacks the Mew Gull's wing tip pattern.

173

RING-BILLED GULL
Larus delawarensis

At home in an increasingly humanized world, flocks of Ring-billed Gulls are a routine sight not only in unmanaged habitats but at shopping mall parking lots, athletic fields and garbage dumps. • Most of these gulls breed outside California, but variable numbers appear at larger lakes and in estuaries nearly throughout the year, with May and June the period of comparative scarcity away from nesting colonies. • Strongly preferring freshwater or upper-estuarine environments, Ring-billed Gulls are uncommon along the outer coast and avoid extensive rocky shorelines. While in California, Ring-bills frequent plowed fields, croplands, large wetlands and tidal mudflats in addition to pursuing handouts of bread in city parks. • Adults are known by their very pale upperparts and clean white or lightly freckled heads, ringed bills and clear yellow eyes.

non-breeding

ID: rather small gull. *Non-breeding adult*: pale eyes; boldly black-ringed yellow bill; very pale gray back and wings; mostly black wing tips; yellowish legs; head is lightly grizzled or flecked with brownish. *Breeding adult*: clean head; brighter bill and leg color; narrow ring of orange-red skin around the eyes. *1st winter*: grayish back; brownish wings; white tail with a neat black band at the tip; pale underparts; black-tipped, pinkish bill.
Size: L 18–20 in; W 48 in.
Status: common to locally abundant migrant and visitor from mid-July to mid-May; local breeder from April to October; rare to fairly common non-breeding summer visitor.
Habitat: uses a wide spectrum of open-country foraging environments within commuting distance of water; common at garbage dumps.

Nesting: colonial; on open beaches, islands or shorelines; on the ground in a shallow scrape lined with plants, nearby debris, grass and sticks; pair incubates 2–4 brown-blotched, gray-to-olive eggs for 23–28 days; both adults feed the young.
Feeding: opportunistic; gleans practically any edible item from the ground or water's surface; flycatches in wide aerial sallies for winged ants, termites and dragonflies in warmer weather; scavenges for carrion, waste crops and human leftovers.
Voice: high-pitched, plaintive squeals and shrieks; an argumentative bird.
Similar Species: *California Gull* (p. 175): distinctly larger; longer, heavier bill; slightly darker gray mantle; greenish-yellow or gray-greenish legs and feet; dark eyes. *Mew Gull* (p. 173): smaller; non-breeding adult has a slightly darker gray mantle and more concentrated white spots in the black wing tips; usually has darker eyes; doesn't 'hang out at the mall.'

CALIFORNIA GULL
Larus californicus

Despite this bird's name and its abundance along the coast and at lakes nearly throughout the state, the California Gull was originally celebrated for consuming hordes of crop-threatening grasshoppers in Utah in 1848 and 1855. A monument in Salt Lake City honors this interior prairie-and-basin nester, which was made the Utah state bird. • Most California Gulls breed inland, but small numbers of subadults linger in wintering areas through spring and early summer. Adults returning to northern California appear in July and August, and their growing legions are soon augmented by dispersing migrant juveniles. • The world's largest colony of California Gulls at Mono Lake suffered mixed fortunes in recent decades: water diversions caused Negit Island to become a predator haunted peninsula.

breeding

ID: dark eyes. *Breeding adult:* clean white head; narrow reddish ring of skin around the eye. *Non-breeding adult:* dark gray mantle; white spots on the black wing tips; greenish-gray legs and feet; bill has both a red and a black spot on the lower mandible. *1st winter:* dark brown, becoming paler on the underparts; black-tipped, pink bill; dull pink legs; long wing tips.
Size: L 18–20 in; W 48–54 in.
Status: common to locally abundant migrant and visitor from late July to early May; uncommon non-breeding summer visitor; locally common to abundant breeder from late March to early October.
Habitat: lakes, marshes, croplands, estuaries, cities, garbage dumps and the open ocean to miles offshore; widespread in migration.
Nesting: colonial; on open beaches or shorelines, often on islands; usually on the ground in a shallow scrape lined with plants, grass, feathers and small sticks; pair incubates 2–3 eggs for 23–27 days; brown-and-gray blotched eggs may be olive,

brown, gray or buff colored; both adults feed the young.
Feeding: gleans the ground for invertebrates; scavenges for carrion and the eggs and young of other birds; 'surface tips' for aquatic invertebrates and small fish; feeds at garbage dumps.
Voice: high-pitched, quarrelsome, braying cries, heard mostly at breeding sites and at 'feeding frenzies' involving numbers of competitive gulls.
Similar Species: *Ring-billed Gull* (p. 174): slightly smaller, with a stubbier bill; paler-mantled; pale eyes. *Herring Gull* (p. 176): pink legs and feet; pale eyes; more extensively streaked on the head and breast in winter. *Western Gull* (p. 178): larger, with (usually) a slightly darker gray mantle; extensive gray 'shadow' in the trailing portion of the underwing; pink legs and feet; lacks the head or breast streaking.

HERRING GULL
Larus argentatus

Several species of large 'pink-footed' gulls visit northern California in fall, winter and spring. With experience, an adult Herring Gull may be distinguished from among these highly similar species by its pale eyes, dark-streaked head, neck and upper breast, and by the high contrast between its black wing tips and very pale gray 'mantle.' • Although Herring Gulls are aggressive and opportunistic, they find themselves outcompeted by Western Gulls at many coastal feeding sites. Therefore, they are generally more common well up in the larger estuaries and at landfills beyond the normal foraging range of the saltwater-loving Western Gulls. • The identification of large gulls is not as simple as many standard field guides might lead one to believe. These birds require slightly more than three years to assume full adult plumage, molting through many confusing intermediate stages in the process.

non-breeding

ID: large gull; pinkish legs; yellow bill; red spot on the lower mandible tip; light eyes; light gray back; black wing tips with white spots. *Breeding:* white head; white underparts. *Non-breeding:* variably heavy dark streaking on the head, neck and upper breast; wing tips are black above and below. *1st winter:* dark nearly throughout, paler on the trailing portion of the mid-wing; heavy, dark bill is variably pink-based.
Size: *L* 23–26 in; *W* 58 in.
Status: uncommon to locally common migrant and visitor from late September to early May.
Habitat: frequents food sources generally in the vicinity of water; concentrates at landfills, river mouths and in agricultural land; migrates in detectable numbers along beaches and through the surf zone.
Nesting: in Canada, Alaska, the northern Midwest and the northeastern U.S.

Feeding: omnivorous and opportunistic, picking nearly any edible item from the ground or water; scavenges carrion and garbage; captures small fish, crustaceans and mollusks; eats small mammals and the eggs and young of other birds in summer.
Voice: adults in northern California utter argumentative calls and squealing chatter while feeding.
Similar Species: *Non-breeding Thayer's Gull* (p. 177): pale underwing tips; slightly darker gray mantle; slightly shorter and slimmer bill; most have dark eyes. *Western Gull* (p. 178): darker mantle; larger bill; unstreaked or very nearly unstreaked head, neck and upper breast; only large gull common in summer. *California Gull* (p. 175): generally smaller; darker gray mantle; dark eyes; greenish or yellowish legs; red-and-black spot on the lower mandible.

THAYER'S GULL

Larus thayeri

The Thayer's Gull was first described in 1925, and for decades it was considered to be a subspecies of the Herring Gull. It wasn't until 1973 that it was elevated to full species status by the American Ornithologists' Union. Today a majority of gull students argue that the Thayer's is more closely allied to the Iceland Gull than to the Herring Gull. It is widely felt that these creatures represent the more strongly pigmented portion of the highly variable Iceland Gull spectrum. • Thayer's Gulls breed in the eastern Canadian Arctic and migrate southwestward in late summer and fall, occurring in northern California between October and April. The greatest numbers are typically encountered mixed in among throngs of feeding or loafing gulls well inside the San Francisco Bay system. Single birds may show up anywhere along the coast, at sea, or on lakes and reservoirs well inland. Most of our Thayer's Gulls are either in their first winter of life or are adults.

non-breeding

breeding

ID: *Non-breeding adult*: pink feet; pale gray mantle; dark eyes; red spot near the tip of the lower mandible; variably heavy streaking on the head, neck and upper breast; black upperwing tips with a few white spots; underwing tip is entirely pale except for dark tips to most outer primaries.
1st winter: pale gray-brown; slim, all-dark or nearly all-dark bill; primaries are slightly darker than the upperparts; pale-based outer tail feathers.
Size: L 22–25 in; W 55 in.
Status: uncommon to locally fairly common migrant and visitor from mid-October to mid-April.
Habitat: disperses widely from night roosts and concentrates at landfills, harbors, river mouths, plowed fields and pastures.
Nesting: on islands of the eastern Canadian Arctic.

Feeding: omnivorous and opportunistic, consuming almost any edible item by gleaning from the ground or snatching from the water's surface.
Voice: seldom heard in northern California; argumentative calls are given by birds at 'feeding frenzies.'
Similar Species: *Herring Gull* (p. 176): slightly larger; wing tips are black with white 'mirrors' both above and below; slightly longer, heavier bill; pale yellow eyes. *Glaucous-winged Gull* (p. 179): larger; wing tips lack blackish; longer, heavier bill. *California Gull* (p. 175): slightly darker mantle; black on both the upper- and underwing tips; greenish or pale yellowish legs and feet; bill has both a red and a black spot near the tip of the lower mandible.

WESTERN GULL

Larus occidentalis

Western Gulls are the classic, dark-backed 'seagulls' familiar to anyone who has spent time along northern California beaches or coastal waters. Big and bold, they are among the most dramatic and conspicuous birds wherever they occur, whether sitting atop pilings, splashing in stream outfalls or kiting on stiff breezes above coastal bluffs. • Although many similar species of large, pink-footed gulls appear along the West Coast during the year, the Western is the only species that nests on the outer coast between the Columbia River and Mexico. Their world headquarters is Southeast Farallon Island, where about one-third of the entire population of some 50,000 pairs breeds. • Human development and alteration of the landscape has caused a change in the feeding patterns of Western Gulls. Once oceanic and intertidal feeders, they now regularly visit industrial waterfronts and city parks, snatching scraps of garbage or awaiting a handout. • Adult Western Gulls are robust and powerful scavengers—their thickset build, brutish behavior and sheer force of numbers cause gulls of smaller species to avoid feeding at sites where these birds are numerous.

breeding

ID: thick, long bill; pink feet; dark gray mantle; from below, flight feathers look deep grayish well in toward the body from the black wing tips. *1st winter:* deep brown nearly throughout; all-dark bill; whitish rump.
Size: L 24–26 in; W 58 in.
Status: common, locally abundant resident along coast; occasional inland.
Habitat: open ocean, shores, estuaries, garbage dumps, waterfronts and coastal cities.
Nesting: singly or colonially; on offshore islands and protected mainland cliffs; pair builds a vegetation-lined nest in a shallow scrape; pair incubates 3 eggs (usually) for 29–32 days; pair feeds the young by regurgitation.

Feeding: takes any remotely edible item by gleaning, picking from the water's surface, plunging from the air or by theft.
Voice: male territorial 'long call' is an extended series of shouted *h'yah!* notes; anxious *kuk kuk kuk* near the nest or fledglings; argumentative squalling at 'feeding frenzies.'
Similar Species: *Glaucous-winged Gull* (p. 179): hybridizes with Western Gull farther north; Glaucous-winged and hybrids are similar at all ages, but paler where Western Gull is darker. *Herring Gull* (p. 176): much paler-mantled, with highly contrasting black wing tips. *California Gull* (p. 175): smaller; greenish or yellowish legs and feet; extensive streaking on the head and the sides of the upper breast in winter.

GLAUCOUS-WINGED GULL

Larus glaucescens

Among the crowds of Western Gulls gathered along the open coast and in estuaries are paler-backed adult gulls with noticeably whitish wings. Glaucous-winged Gulls, like most large gull species, show small white spots, or 'mirrors,' in the wing tips. However, these mirrors are inconspicuous, contrasting only slightly because they are set within pale gray, rather than black, outer primaries. • Glaucous-wings are most numerous in northern California from late fall into early spring. Scattered immature birds remain throughout the warmer months each year, their drab first-winter plumage becoming visibly worn and faded by late spring. • Glaucous-winged Gulls frequent the same habitats as Western Gulls, but unlike their darker-mantled relatives, they also exhibit a strong tendency to move up estuaries and river systems well beyond the influence of the tides. • This species routinely hybridizes and backcrosses with the Western Gull in Oregon and Washington. Mixed mating has produced a confusing spectrum of intergrades possessing characteristics of both parent species. Identifying large gulls on the West Coast demands the ability to recognize these individuals—a skill acquired only with much practice and experience.

non-breeding

ID: pink legs and feet; long, heavy bill. *Non-breeding adult:* most have dark eyes; pale gray back and wings; small white spots within slightly darker grayish wing tips; yellow bill with a red spot near the tip of the lower mandible; typically has a uniformly dingy head, neck and upper breast; winter 'streaking' on the breast. *1st winter:* uniformly drab grayish-brown; all-dark bill.
Size: *L* 24–27 in; *W* 58 in.
Status: common visitor from mid-October to late April; a few non-breeders may remain over summer.
Habitat: beaches, bays, harbors, estuaries, lagoons, garbage dumps and rarely inshore lakes.
Nesting: along the coast from northern Oregon to Alaska.
Feeding: forages by walking, wading, swimming or plunging; omnivorous diet

includes a variety of fish, mollusks and crustaceans, nestling birds, carrion, human food-waste and some plant matter.
Voice: variable calls; typical sound is a bold *kow kow.*
Similar Species: *Herring Gull* (p. 176): pink feet; yellow eyes; black wing tips. *Western Gull* (p. 178): dark back; dark wings; yellow eyes; black wing tips. *Ring-billed Gull* (p. 174) and *California Gull* (p. 175): black wing tips; yellow-green feet. *Thayer's Gull* (p. 177): smaller; slightly darker wing tips; thinner bill. *Glaucous Gull* (p. 180): whiter primary feathers; heavier build. *Mew Gull* (p. 173): much smaller; darker mantle; black in the wing tips.

GLAUCOUS GULL

Larus hyperboreus

Glaucous Gulls are arctic birds, wintering southward only sparingly into temperate latitudes. They are capable of making a living through scavenging but are also powerful predators, taking small mammals and birds during the northern summer. Adults often linger farther north in winter than do immatures, so that most of the modest total of Glaucous Gulls seen each year in northern California are in subadult plumages. The function of the 'mortality curve' dictates that first-winter birds will outnumber older subadult age classes (fewer of which will have survived to their second or third winters), hence the reason Glaucous Gulls in our region tend to represented by individuals in their first year of life. • Despite their inexperience with the competitive rigors of a gull's world, first-winter Glaucous Gulls wintering in northern California are notable among gulls of their age class for their ability to defend food sources. Teetering atop a mound of freshly bulldozed garbage, a gull secures a chosen food item through an intimidating 'mantling' of widespread wings and by the well-aimed, no-nonsense jabs of a snapping bill.

non-breeding

ID: large and stout; white wing tips.
1st winter: pale, often whitish; long, heavy, pinkish bill, tipped with black; subtle, broken white eye-arcs on darker individuals; undertail coverts are barred with dusky.
Non-breeding adult: very pale gray mantle; pale eyes; pure white wing tips; yellow bill with a red spot near the tip of the lower mandible; variable head and neck streaking.
Size: *L* 27 in; *W* 60 in.
Status: rare but regular visitor along the outer coast from mid-October to April; exceptionally rare from late spring into early fall.
Habitat: chiefly marine and estuarine habitats, including ocean, river mouths, beaches, industrial waterfronts and garbage dumps.

Nesting: in the Arctic.
Feeding: omnivorous, foraging in the manner of most other large gulls; snatches almost any edible item, living or dead.
Voice: similar to that of other large gulls; seldom heard in northern California.
Similar Species: *Glaucous-winged Gull* (p. 179): 1st-winter bird has an all-dark bill and nearly uniformly dingy gray-brown flight feathers; adult usually has dark eyes and pale gray wing tips with poorly contrasting, small white 'mirrors.' *Other large gulls:* most are smaller and have at least some black or blackish in the wing tips.

SABINE'S GULL
Xema sabini

I t is unfortunate that few people other than birders, commercial fishermen and residents of the Far North are aware of the existence of Sabine's Gulls. They truly are stunning and wondrous birds, earning admiration whenever they are seen. • The Sabine's Gull exemplifies the 'pure transient' species. Breeding in the Arctic and wintering south of the Equator, it appears along the West Coast only in spring and fall migration. It is notable for avoiding the coastline or nearshore waters, traveling north or south well out over the continental shelf or beyond. Experienced birders occasionally detect single birds or small flocks from shore points with the aid of a spotting scope, most often in May and September. • Sabine's Gulls tend to fly well above the surface of the ocean, passing slowly in loose lines and in open, dispersed flocks. Their easy buoyance, willowy wingstrokes and dramatic upperparts pattern make them as distinctive a gull as any. • In odd contrast to the habits of most of their kind, a very few immature Sabine's sometimes appear inland in fall.

breeding

ID: small; slightly forked tail. *Breeding adult*: sooty hood with a black lower margin; black outer primaries; white secondaries and inner primaries; gray back and coverts comprise a triangular mosaic on the upper surface of the back and wings; yellow-tipped, black bill; black legs and feet.
1st fall: scaly gray-brown back; dusky crown; dark terminal tail band.
Size: *L* 13–14 in; *W* 36 in.
Status: uncommon to fairly common migrant from late April to early June and from late July to October; exceptional inland in spring.
Habitat: pelagic; the bulk of the population remains well out at sea during migration.
Nesting: in the Arctic.
Feeding: dips or swoops to the water's surface to snatch food items; gleans while swimming; occasionally found onshore, walking about and picking from the surface of mud or sand; small fish and pelagic crustaceans may comprise much of the diet while in passage at sea.
Voice: call is a harsh, short, grating cry.
Similar Species: *Black-legged Kittiwake* (p. 182): narrow wings; lacks the forked tail; flies with shallower downstrokes; dark, diagonal band across the pale inner upperwing. *Bonaparte's Gull* (p. 171): more tern-like, with a narrow but flashing wedge of white in the forewing; immatures have dark-margined wings and a thin, dark carpal bar; tends to bunch up in tight flocks; usually migrates very near the ocean's surface.

MIGRANT ONLY

BLACK-LEGGED KITTIWAKE
Rissa tridactyla

Kittiwakes are small, highly marine gulls that breed along coastlines at higher latitudes and spend the balance of the year on the open ocean. In northern California, Black-legged Kittiwakes are most often seen from coastal headlands or from boats in fall, winter and spring. • Following strong 'kittiwake years,' immature birds may spend the entire summer at sea off California. Late fall and winter storms that persist for several days may tire these small gulls; the nearshore ocean then becomes flecked with not only seafoam but with abundant, scattered kittiwakes! • During migration and in winter, one may find a few of these birds standing among hordes of larger gulls on exposed ocean beaches. In such situations, their small size, rather lowslung posture and short legs make them look as if they are seated. • Black-legged Kittiwakes are open-ocean scavengers and fishers. Unlike most gulls, they do not join in 'feeding frenzies' at garbage dumps. Kittiwakes cruise high over the waves, darting downward in an instant to snap up a food item. They are exceptionally rare away from the ocean, scarce even in the lower reaches of estuaries.

1st winter

non-breeding

breeding

ID: small gull; pale gray mantle; black wing tips, legs and feet. *Non-breeding*: pale gray back and wings; jet-black wing tips; unmarked, green bill; gray nape and smudge behind the eye. *1st winter*: flashy underwing pattern; square-ended or slightly notched white tail with a black terminal band; black bill; dark half-collar.
Size: L 16–18 in; W 36 in.
Status: irregularly uncommon to abundant migrant and visitor from October to mid-May; a few younger birds sometimes linger into or throughout summer.
Habitat: maritime, preferring open ocean along the edge of the continental shelf or over upwellings.
Nesting: along the Alaskan coast and Bering Sea islands; on the eastern coast of Canada.

Feeding: dips to the water's surface in flight or gleans while swimming; takes small fish, pelagic crustaceans, worms, mollusks and small squid.
Voice: stacatto calls uttered near nest site; almost never heard in northern California.
Similar Species: *Adult Mew Gull* (p. 173): slightly darker mantle; bold, irregular white area in the black wing tips; lacks the discrete dark head markings. *1st-fall Sabine's Gull* (p. 181): upperpart pattern is more dramatic, with secondary coverts dark throughout; dusky crown, nape and sides of the breast.

CASPIAN TERN
Sterna caspia

The robust size, eye-catching whiteness and commanding voice of Caspian Terns cause their presence to be readily known to the most casual observer. They are the largest terns in North America, and their heavy bills, deliberate flight and broad spread of wings seem, somehow, to span a conceptual gap between the smaller terns and the larger gulls. • Unlike gulls, Caspian Terns are strictly fish-eating. They spend their foraging time searching for surface-swimming prey, beating their wings with shallow, fluid strokes while cruising over lakes, larger reservoirs, estuaries and nearshore ocean. Because of their need for live prey, Caspian Terns may be distinguished at a glance from the larger, paler-mantled gulls by noting that their bills are held consistently downward, betraying their vigilance in scanning the surface of the water. • These terns enjoy a tremendous global distribution, breeding in isolated colonies at many sites from the tropics into the Northern Hemisphere. While some Caspian Terns nest in northern California, the bulk of the thousands seen passing along the coast each spring and fall are likely headed to or from the world's largest colony, which is situated in the lower Columbia River.

ID: black cap, with white in winter; heavy, dagger-like, blood red bill; very pale gray upperwings; extensive blackish on the underwing tips; white underparts; black legs; short, shallowly forked, white tail. *Juvenile:* vividly scaled with dark edgings and margins to the feathers of the back, coverts and tail; duller orangish bill.
Size: L 19–23 in; W 50–55 in.
Status: uncommon to locally abundant migrant and breeder from mid-March to late October; local visitor from November to March; most numerous in coastal migration from early April to mid-May and from late August to October.
Habitat: nearshore ocean, open coast, estuaries, rivers, freshwater lakes and reservoirs.
Nesting: pair builds a shallow scrape on bare sand, dirt or rocks; nest is sparsely lined with vegetation, rocks or twigs; pair incubates 1–3 brown- or black-spotted, pale buff eggs for 20–22 days; both adults feed the young.

breeding

Feeding: hovers over water and plunges headfirst after small fish, tadpoles and aquatic invertebrates; rarely gleans while swimming.
Voice: adults utter a very loud, harsh *kruh-RAUW*; dependent juveniles contact adults with high-pitched, quavering *tee-a-wee*.
Similar Species: *Elegant Tern* (p. 184): smaller; more slender; obvious wedge of blackish in the leading edge of the upperwing; long, orange 'carrot bill.' *Forster's* (p. 187), *Common* (p. 185) and *Arctic* (p. 186) terns: lack the heavy red bill; quicker, darting wingbeats.

ELEGANT TERN
Sterna elegans

Following their early spring breeding efforts in subtropical waters, flocks of Elegant Terns move up the Pacific coast into northern California. Their incursions are an annual event, yet the northward extent of the movement and the numbers involved varies yearly. The warming of nearshore ocean water during strong El Niño events has resulted in visitations by Elegant Terns to coastal Oregon and Washington and even southwestern British Columbia. • The first main influx of birds dispersing northward from breeding colonies in the Sea of Cortez and along the southern California coast appears in northern California in late spring. These birds are adults, many of which briefly retain the entirely black crown of the early breeding season. Later returnees swelling the ranks in June and July include legions of white-forecrowned adults and whatever crop of juveniles may have been produced. When Elegant Terns arrive en masse in an estuary or about a harbor entrance, they are highly conspicuous as they fly back and forth high over the water in every direction.

non-breeding

ID: long, slender bill; slicked-back black crest. *Non-breeding:* pale gray upperparts with restricted dark wedge in the outer primaries; white forecrown; black crown and nape; slightly shaggy crest; carrot-like, slender orange bill; forked white tail. *Breeding adult:* entirely black crown; subtle pinkish blush on the underparts. *Juvenile:* feathers of the upperparts are thoroughly tipped or edged with dusky; bill is sometimes yellow. *In flight:* flies quite rapidly, with a jabbing downstroke to each wingbeat.
Size: L 16–17 in; W 34 in.
Status: irregularly numerous and widespread non-breeding visitor along the coast in late spring, summer and early fall; may be absent from the northernmost coast in some years; very rare in winter.
Habitat: strictly coastal, frequenting inshore ocean, estuaries, coastal freshwater and salt lagoons, river mouths and creek outfalls; exceptional anywhere inland.
Nesting: on islands in the Sea of Cortez and along the coast of southern California.
Feeding: cruises and hovers above the water, plunges or swoops after small fish near the surface, including northern anchovy, various smelts and similar small schooling fish.
Voice: adults utter a repeated, 3-note *Ker-ou-ac!* in flight; argument note is a peevish *zar-zar-zar-zar*; semi-dependent juveniles contact adults with a wheezy, whistled call.
Similar Species: *Caspian Tern* (p. 183): twice the size; heavy, red bill; all-white upperwings. *Forster's* (p.187), *Common* (p.185) and *Arctic* (p. 186) *terns:* smaller; smaller bills; different voices. *Royal Tern:* very rare; slightly larger; heavier, red-orange bill.

COMMON TERN
Sterna hirundo

Wheeling about in mid-air to a stationary hover, the Common Tern dives headfirst into the water, emerging with a small fish caught in its thin, dagger-like bill. • Common Terns are occasionally observed patrolling the shorelines of northern California's inland lakes and rivers, but they are most likely to be seen along the seacoast or well offshore. In northern California, peak numbers of terns are seen from mid-April to mid-May and from mid-August to mid-October. • Terns are effortless fliers and they are among the greatest migrants. Recently, a Common Tern banded in Great Britain was recovered in Australia—a record distance for any bird.

breeding

ID: *Breeding:* black cap; thin, red, black-tipped bill; light gray wing coverts; red legs; white rump; mostly white tail; white under-parts. *Non-breeding:* black nape; lacks the black cap. *In flight:* shallowly forked tail; long, pointed wings with a darkish wedge in the outer primaries; dark shoulder bar.
Size: *L* 13–16 in; *W* 30 in.
Status: uncommon to fairly common coastal migrant from early April to late May and from mid-July to early November.
Habitat: offshore open ocean, coast, bays, harbors and lagoons; rarely on interior freshwater lakes, reservoirs and rivers; frequently encountered well offshore.
Nesting: in the extreme northern and eastern U.S. and in Canada east of the Rocky Mountains.

Feeding: hovers over the water and plunges headfirst after small fish and aquatic invertebrates.
Voice: high-pitched, drawn-out, rasping *key-are* is most commonly heard at colonies, but also in foraging flights.
Similar Species: *Forster's Tern* (p. 187): more orangy-colored bill and legs; mostly gray tail; silver-tipped primaries; lacks the dark shoulder bar; black 'earpatches' in winter. *Arctic Tern* (p. 186): rare onshore in migration; all-red bill; dark-tipped, translucent outer primaries. *Caspian Tern* (p. 183): much larger; heavy, red bill with a faint black tip. *Elegant Tern* (p. 184): larger; long, orangish bill; shaggy head crest.

MIGRANT ONLY

ARCTIC TERN
Sterna paradisaea

This elegant bird is among the most accomplished of avian migrants, flying from the Arctic to the Antarctic each year—it occurs in northern California only during spring and fall passages. The best time to meet migrating Arctic Terns is from late April to early June or from mid-August to late September. They are seldom seen among mixed seabird assemblages along the coastline, but look for them from boats well offshore. • Because they experience 24 hours of daylight on their northern nesting grounds and long days of sunlight on southern wintering grounds, Arctic Terns perpetually avoid winter and experience more daylight in an average year than most creatures.

breeding

ID: *Breeding:* blood red bill and legs; short neck; black cap on the rounded head; translucent primaries with a thin, dark trailing edge on the underwing; even gray on the upperwings; white cheeks contrast with gray wash on the underparts; long, forked tail. *Non-breeding* and *Immature:* white shoulders; white underparts and forehead; black bill; shorter tail. *In flight:* short neck makes the head barely visible beyond the front of the wing tips.
Size: *L* 14–17 in; *W* 29–33 in.
Status: rare to uncommon migrant from late April to early June; uncommon to fairly common migrant from early July to late October, usually well offshore.
Habitat: open ocean in migration.
Nesting: in northern and eastern Canada and Alaska, primarily north of the Arctic Circle.

Feeding: hovers over water and then swoops to the surface or plunges for small fish and crustaceans; also takes insects, mollusks, other invertebrates and rarely berries.
Voice: calls include a harsh, raspy, high-pitched *kee-ya* and a repeated *key-key-key-key* or *keer, keer.*
Similar Species: *Common Tern* (p. 185): black-tipped bill; head is less rounded; longer neck; outer upperwing primaries and trailing edge of the underwings are gray; immature has dark gray shoulders.

Forster's Tern (p. 187): breeding adult has a thicker, black-tipped, orange bill; less rounded head; trailing edge of the underwing is not as dark; non-breeding and immature generally have a white nape.

MIGRANT ONLY

FORSTER'S TERN
Sterna forsteri

The Forster's Tern is the only northern California tern that lives exclusively in North America. This tern closely resembles the Common Tern, and for years ornithologists did not distinguish the two as separate species. • The Forster's Tern bears the name of a man who never actually visited North America: German naturalist Johann Reinhold Forster. He lived and worked in England, and, having examined tern specimens sent to him from the Hudson Bay region, he suggested that the Forster's was distinct from the very similar Common Tern. • Most terns are known for their extraordinary ability to catch fish in dramatic, headfirst dives. The Forster's Tern swoops gracefully above lakes and marshes, snatching insects from the water's surface.

non-breeding

breeding

ID: *Breeding:* black cap and nape; thin, orange, black-tipped bill; pale gray back; orange legs; white underparts; white rump; gray tail with white outer feathers. *Non-breeding:* white head except for black patches at the sides. *In flight:* forked tail; long, pointed wings.

Size: *L* 14–16 in; *W* 31 in.

Status: rare to locally common migrant from early March through May and from late July through October; locally uncommon to common visitor from October to March; locally fairly common to common breeder from April to August.

Habitat: ocean coast, estuaries, lagoons, large freshwater lakes, large rivers, alkaline lakes and diked ponds.

Nesting: occasionally colonial; platform of floating vegetation in freshwater or saltwater marshes or marshy lakes; pair builds the nest and incubates 3 olive to buff eggs, marked with brown, for about 24 days; both adults feed the young.

Feeding: hovers above the water and plunges headfirst after small fish and aquatic invertebrates.

Voice: call when flying is a nasal, short *keer keer*; also a grating *tzaap*; soft *tik* calls.

Similar Species: *Common Tern* (p. 185): wedge of dark in the primaries; darker red bill and legs; mostly white tail; call is longer and more drawn out. *Arctic Tern* (p. 186): red bill and legs; shorter neck; gray wash on the underparts. *Elegant Tern* (p. 184): shaggy head crest; very long, orangish bill.

187

LEAST TERN

Sterna antillarum

Persisting today at only a few places in California, Least Terns dramatize the impact human activities can have upon birds of the estuarine beaches. Development and disturbance have caused breeding habitat for this species to diminish to only one significant colony in San Francisco Bay. • As is true for many colonial waterbirds, breeding success varies annually in response to food supply, weather, predation and disturbance. Scattered observations indicate that Least Terns nesting in the East Bay commute across the Santa Cruz Mountains to and from Monterey Bay, suggesting the importance of a dependable marine fishery. These tiny terns may also migrate to and from San Francisco Bay via the overland route, as apparent migrants are rarely seen on the seaward side of the peninsula. Least Terns occasionally appear elsewhere along the coast, having been found as far north as Crescent City. They are very rarely found inland in northern California.

breeding

ID: *Breeding:* black cap and nape; white forehead; black-tipped, orange-yellow bill; orange-yellow legs; gray upperparts; white underparts; black wedge on the upper side of the outer primaries. *1st summer:* black bill, legs and eye line extending into the nape; grayish cap; white forehead. *Immature:* black eye line; white forehead; dark cap; yellow bill and feet. *In flight:* flies with dashing, rapid wingstrokes.
Size: *L* 9 in; *W* 20 in.
Status: rarely detected coastal migrant; very rare in most areas and away from saltwater influences; very local breeder from May to August; California population is considered endangered.
Habitat: waters and shores of San Francisco Bay and locally elsewhere along the ocean coast.
Nesting: colonial; on undisturbed, flat ground near water; nest is a shallow, scraped-out depression often lined with pebbles, grass or debris; pair incubates 1–3 eggs for 20–22 days and raise the young; chicks leave the nest shortly after hatching.
Feeding: typically forages by hovering above water before plunging to or below the surface; eats mostly fish, crustaceans and insects; may eat mollusks and other invertebrates; will take insects on the wing or snatch prey from the ground or water's surface.
Voice: call is a loud, high-pitched *chirreek!* and *kip kip kip.*

Similar Species: *Elegant* (p. 184), *Black* (p. 189), *Common* (p. 185) and *Forster's* (p. 187) *terns:* all are larger; breeding birds lack the white forehead and the yellow, black-tipped bill.

BLACK TERN
Chlidonias niger

Black Terns are less common in northern California than they were early in the 20th century. The fortunes of these birds are today tied closely to water management, whether it involves the acreage of flooded rice fields or the quality and quantity of impounded marshland. • A birder's first sighting of a flock of Black Terns is not quickly forgotten. The finest artwork or most revealing photograph can't prepare one for the zest and the surpassing grace of this bird. Plunging, fluid wingstrokes carry scattered Black Terns across expanses of freshwater marsh in the Klamath Basin, the Great Basin and in the Central Valley. • To spell this tern's genus name correctly, one must misspell *chelidonias*, the Greek word for 'swallow'—when the Black Tern was initially described and named, the 'e' was accidentally left out.

breeding

ID: *Breeding:* black head and underparts; gray back, tail and wings; white undertail coverts; black bill; reddish-black legs. *Non-breeding:* white underparts and forehead; molting fall birds may be mottled with brown. *In flight:* long, pointed wings; shallowly forked tail; uncommonly elegant flight.

Size: *L* 9–10 in; *W* 24 in.

Status: rare to locally common migrant from mid-April to early June and from late August to mid-October; rare to locally common breeder from April to late September; scarce coastally and almost unknown in many areas.

Habitat: primarily shallow, freshwater marshes, sloughs, ponds and lakes. *In migration:* flooded fields, estuaries, coastal lagoons and coastlines; occasionally encountered at sea in fall.

Nesting: singly or loosely colonial; on matted vegetation on water among emergent vegetation; pair builds a small platform of loose, dead vegetation; pair incubates 2–4 darkly blotched, buff to olive eggs for about 22 days.

Feeding: snatches insects from the air and from tall grass; fish and insects are taken from the water's surface; also takes small amphibians, earthworms, spiders, small crustaceans and leeches.

Voice: greeting call is a shrill, metallic *kik-kik-kik-kik-kik;* typical alarm call is *kreea.*

Similar Species: *Other terns:* all are light in color, not dark.

COMMON MURRE
Uria aalge

Common Murres are skilled divers and swimmers. Like all members of the auk family (Alcidae), they have small wings, webbed feet and sleek, waterproofed plumage designed for the capture of fish by underwater pursuit. • Common Murres nest in huge, tightly packed colonies on offshore islands. Some sites support tens of thousands of birds. In winter, they may travel miles out into the open North Pacific, disappearing from shore altogether. However, sudden mid-winter visits to breeding rocks by large numbers of birds suggests that many murres also winter fairly close to shore. • Juvenile murres literally 'get a jump on life,' leaping into the water while still tiny. Male parents then accompany them for weeks. • Many waterbirds share the countershading pattern of the murre. From above, the bird's dark back blends with the steely sea; from below, predators and prey may be slow to recognize this bird's light-colored underbelly against the shimmering, glinting surface. • Each year, the gillnets, long-line nets and discarded, ever-fishing 'ghost nets' of an international fleet drown innumerable alcids, shearwaters and albatrosses in the North Pacific.

breeding

ID: deep, sooty-brown upperparts; white underparts; slender, black bill. *Breeding:* dark brown head and neck. *Non-breeding:* white neck, chin and lower face.
Size: *L* 16–17 in.
Status: common to locally abundant year-round resident; resident populations may be boosted from late October to late May by visitors from northern areas.
Habitat: *Breeding:* on offshore islands, islets and rocks. *Foraging:* on the open ocean from just beyond the surf zone to miles offshore; father-and-chick pairs regularly visit the lower reaches of estuaries from July to September.
Nesting: highly colonial; on bare rock or a flat, rocky surface close to water; 1 variably marked and colored egg is incubated by both parents for 28–37 days; incubating adults are often within touching range in tightly packed colonies.

Feeding: dives to the surface for fish; also takes squid, marine worms and crustaceans.
Voice: adults utter a low, harsh *murrr*; dependent juvenile gives a high-pitched, quavering whistle: *FEED-me-now, feed-me-now, feed-me-now!*
Similar Species: *Murrelets* (pp. 192–94): half the size; much smaller bills; much more rapid wingbeats. *Scoters* (pp. 92–94): much bulkier; heavy, duck-like bills; shorter necks. *Common Loon* (p. 40): much larger overall; larger head; white underparts are not visible when floating. *Horned Grebe* (p. 42): smaller; longer neck; red eyes. *Western Grebe* (p. 45): longer, slimmer neck; pale bill.

PIGEON GUILLEMOT
Cepphus columba

Pigeon Guillemots are among the most widespread and commonly seen alcids along the Pacific coast. During the summer months, these seabirds forage just off northern California shores and nest in nooks, crannies and crevices on sea cliffs, steep banks and sometimes beneath docks. By late September, they disappear from local shores, not returning until early March. • The guillemot's black breeding plumage is punctuated by its radiant vermilion red mouth-lining and red feet. In their summer courtship rituals, these birds flaunt their scarlet mouths and wave their scarlet feet while peering down the throats of potential mates. • 'Guillemot' is derived from the French name for William. Both the scientific name *columba* and the common name 'pigeon' refer to this bird's similarities in size and body form to the Rock Dove.

breeding

ID: bright red feet and mouth; slender, black bill; long neck; white wing patch;. *Breeding:* black overall. *Non-breeding:* whitish head, neck and underparts; black eye patch; mottled gray-and-white back and crown.
Size: L 12–14 in.
Status: locally fairly common to common breeder from mid-March to early September; few winter around Monterey Bay.
Habitat: *Breeding:* on offshore islands, islets or along the mainland coastline where there are cliffs with holes, ledges, crevices or caves; may also use old buildings, docks, wharves or piers. *Summer:* nearshore ocean waters and lower reaches of estuaries. *Winter:* distribution incompletely understood.
Nesting: singly or in loose colonies; builds a shallow scrape in pebbles, dirt or shells inside a crevice, cave or burrow; may place the nest under debris or among large

rocks; pair incubates 1–2 eggs for 26–32 days; pale blue-green to creamy eggs have dark blotches concentrated near the larger end.
Feeding: forages underwater by diving and swimming; eats seasonally abundant fish, mollusks, crustaceans, worms and other marine invertebrates.
Voice: distinctive stuttering series of wheezy notes at nest sites; silent otherwise.
Similar Species: *Ancient Murrelet* (p. 194) and *Marbled Murrelet* (p. 192): smaller; lack the white wing patch. *Rhinoceros Auklet* (p. 196): more robust; thicker bill; lacks the white wing patch. *Common Murre* (p. 190): lacks the white wing patch; highly colonial nester.

MARBLED MURRELET
Brachyramphus marmoratus

Since the discovery of the first Marbled Murrelet nest in North America—in Santa Cruz County in 1974—much has been learned about this enigmatic seabird. Their entirely separate nesting and foraging habits represent the most spectacular life history dichotomy of any of our birds. Commuting from old-growth tracts to the open sea and back, the Marbled Murrelet is ordinarily the only inland-nesting species in North America never to touch land itself. • Perhaps once among the most abundant nearshore birds in northern California, more than a century of habitat destruction has diminished Marbled Murrelet numbers. • The straight-line flight of this bird low across the water is faster than that of any other northern California seabird—a useful identification tip at long range.

non-breeding

breeding

ID: small, stocky seabird. *Breeding:* mottled dark brown nearly throughout; paler on the throat and undertail coverts; appears flat headed on water. *Non-breeding:* black 'helmet'; narrow nape line, back and wings (both above and below); white stripe across the scapulars, throat and underparts. *Juvenile:* like the non-breeding adult, but is finely flecked with dark on the breast.
Size: L 9–10 in.
Status: fairly common throughout the year, less numerous south to Monterey Bay; uncommon to fairly common breeder from late April to mid-August; less frequently noted in winter.
Habitat: nearshore ocean and around harbor entrances, favoring sandy bottoms opposite rocky shores. *Breeding:* in dense, older conifer forest, particularly stands of old-growth coast redwood and Douglas-fir.
Nesting: solitary or semicolonial; single egg is laid in shallow depression on large limbs or on debris fans in foliage up to 150 ft above the ground; pair alternates incubation for about 4 weeks; adults bring single fish to chick at nest 3–8 times a day for another month.
Feeding: small fish, such as herrings, juvenile salmon, anchovies and various smelts, are captured during dives from the surface.
Voice: distinctive; piercing, loose series of high-pitched *keer* notes, given both on the water and in flight; *keer* calls and 'jet sounds' are heard in and over forests.
Similar Species: *Common Murre* (p. 190): much larger; longer body and bill; lacks the white scapulars. *Ancient Murrelet* (p. 194): black crown; gray back; lacks the white scapulars; very stubby, pale bill. *Craveri's Murrelet* and *Xantus' Murrelet* (p. 193): lack the white scapulars.

XANTUS'S MURRELET
Synthliboramphus hypoleucus

Newly hatched Xantus's Murrelets are extremely precocious: murrelet young are not fed on the nest; instead they are led out to sea by their parents only one or two nights after they hatch. • Colonies of murrelets nest on islands with tall, sheer sea cliffs, and flightless youngsters often perform freefalls of more than 200 ft to join their parents on the crashing surf below. • Xantus's Murrelets are rarely seen from the mainland, and even young fledglings are led far out to sea to be fed by their parents. • Field research has shown that breeding colonies are extremely sensitive to predation. Cats, rats, snakes and even deer mice will destroy large numbers of eggs and newly hatched young.

ID: bold, white, half eye ring; short, slender, black bill; bright white wing linings; black upperparts; white underparts.
Size: L 9¹/₂–10¹/₂ in.
Status: irregularly uncommon to fairly common visitor from August to April; pushes farther north in some 'warm winter' years.
Habitat: warmer offshore ocean waters, often well beyond the edge of the continental shelf; rarely detected from shore.
Nesting: from the Channel Islands south to the tip of the Baja Peninsula.
Feeding: dives underwater to forage; eats mostly small fish and some crustaceans; pairs often forage together.

Voice: call, given year-round, is a series of shrill, trilling whistles.
Similar Species: *Craveri's Murrelet:* slightly longer, thinner bill; dark half-collar; dusky gray-buff wing linings. *Ancient Murrelet* (p. 194): black chin and throat; much shorter, thicker, pale bill; may have white streaking on the head. *Cassin's Auklet* (p. 195): stubby bill; pale eyes; dark gray except for the belly and undertail coverts.

ANCIENT MURRELET
Synthliboramphus antiquus

This proficient mariner is 'ancient' because during the breeding season its feathery, white eyebrows and gray mantle give it a distinguished, aged look. Unfortunately, few birders will ever see the Ancient Murrelet in breeding plumage along the California coast. This murrelet is present along the northern California coast from early October to April, and the best time to observe it is from mid-November to mid-March. Once in a while a few birds may be seen lingering along our coastline through summer, especially after a large winter 'invasion.' • Unlike most members of the auk family, which raise a single nestling each year, Ancient Murrelets typically raise two youngsters in their single, annual brood.

breeding

ID: small, compact alcid; very short, dark-tipped, yellowish bill; gray back; bright white wing linings. *Breeding:* black chin, throat, crown, nape and sides; wispy white streaks on the crown and nape. *Non-breeding:* gray replaces black on the sides; lacks the bold white streaking on the crown. *Immature:* like non-breeding adult but lacks the black throat; some black streaking on the chin.
Size: L 9¹/₂–10¹/₂ in.
Status: irregularly rare to fairly common visitor from early October to late April; locally numerous during invasion years; very rare visitor inland.
Habitat: cool open ocean and inshore coastal waters; often seen from headlands, piers, breakwaters and beaches; occasionally seen in harbors and protected bays.

Nesting: in British Columbia, Alaska and northeast Asia.
Feeding: swims underwater for shrimp; very small fish and other crustaceans may be taken.
Voice: only occasionally heard in California; year-round calls include low chips and piping whistles; adults and young recognize each other by voice.
Similar Species: *Xantus's Murrelet* (p. 193): slender, black bill; white chin and throat. *Craveri's Murrelet:* slender, black bill; white chin and throat; mottled dark wing linings. *Cassin's Auklet* (p. 195): dark wing linings; pale eyes; uniformly grayish above.

CASSIN'S AUKLET
Ptychoramphus aleuticus

This small, stout, seafaring bird is easily distinguished from its alcid relatives by its rounded wing tips and gray neck and underwings, which are displayed in flight. • Their small size and ground-nesting habits make them extremely vulnerable to predators including foxes, weasels, cats and rats that are introduced to their remote island nesting colonies. • Cassin's Auklets are commonly seen feeding in large, dynamic flocks. Individuals briefly appear above the ocean surface in between lengthy dives up to 120 ft. • Like flightless penguins of colder climates, auklets, murrelets and puffins use their stubby wings to 'fly' underwater. Natural oils secreted by the uropygial gland help waterproof dense feathers against cold water. Waterproofed feathers, however, are useless against oil spills that coat and smother ocean-feeding birds. • The Latin genus *Ptychoramphus*, meaning 'a folded beak,' refers to the tiny ridges across this bird's bill.

ID: very small, plump alcid; bold, white crescents above and below the yellow eyes; dark sooty-gray upperparts fade to paler gray on the sides, flanks, throat, breast and underwings; white belly and undertail coverts; dark bill is pale at the base of the lower mandible.
Size: L 8–9 in.
Status: uncommon to locally very common visitor from mid-August to February; fairly common to locally abundant breeder from March to September; some 50,000 breed on Southeast Farallon Island.
Habitat: *Breeding:* offshore islands and grassy sea stacks. *Foraging:* ocean waters, especially over upwellings along the continental shelf; also forages over deeper water or near nesting islands.
Nesting: colonial; pair excavates an underground burrow in soil; may use a natural crevice; the same nest site may be used over many years; pair incubates 1 whitish egg for about 39 days.
Feeding: swims underwater to catch prey; may dive more than 120 ft; eats small crustaceans including copepods, amphipods and shrimp in the breeding season; may also feed on small fish and squid.
Voice: generally silent; weak croaking heard only at breeding colony.
Similar Species: *Xantus's* (p. 193), *Craveri's* and *Ancient* (p. 194) *murrelets:* all have a greater contrast between the darker upperparts and the white underparts; all have white in the neck and breast; more pointed wing tips.

RHINOCEROS AUKLET
Cerorhinca monocerata

Only during the breeding season, from February to June, does the Rhinoceros Auklet sport whispy, white facial plumes and a striking rhino-style horn at the base of its upper mandible. • These birds may be most common along the coast in winter, but the better weather conditions of spring and summer allow more dependable viewing near their scattered breeding sites. Typically from one to a half-dozen 'Rhinos' can be seen, swimming and diving on the ocean just beyond the breakers. • During winter storms, Rhinoceros Auklets drift on mountainous waves, seemingly unaffected by the chilling wind and ocean spray. Some birds will remain submerged underwater for up to two minutes while pursuing prey or attempting to evade surface disturbances. • In recent years, increased numbers have been detected at historic nest sites. Whether this signals a strengthening of the southern population or is simply a result of increased monitoring of seabirds remains uncertain.

breeding

ID: dark grayish upperparts and breast; whitish belly; stout, pale bill; short, thick neck. *Breeding:* fleshy, yellowish horn at the base of the bill; thin, white plumes originating from behind the eye and behind the bill.
Size: L 14–15¹/₂ in.
Status: uncommon to abundant migrant and visitor from mid-October to May; locally rare to uncommon breeder and non-breeding visitor from April to October; abundance and distribution near shore fluctuates considerably.
Habitat: *Breeding:* offshore islands, islets and sea cliffs with enough soil for nesting burrows. *Foraging:* along inshore coastal waters and widely in offshore open ocean; irregularly numerous off headlands and about harbor entrances.

Nesting: colonial; in an underground burrow up to 20 ft long; nest is a shallow cup of moss and twigs; pair incubates 1 egg for 39–52 days.
Feeding: captures food in its bill while swimming underwater; takes crustaceans and feeds on small schooling fish.
Voice: silent at sea; gives barks, growls, shrieks and groans at the nesting colony.
Similar Species: *Cassin's Auklet* (p. 195): much smaller; smaller, stubby bill; 2 thick, white crescents around the eyes. *Marbled* (p. 192), *Xantus's* (p. 193) and *Ancient* (p. 194) *murrelets:* smaller; more extensive white underparts; more rapid wingbeats. *Tufted Puffin* (p. 197): juvenile is darker overall and has a dark eye with a broad, gray stripe behind it; much less apt to be seen from land.

TUFTED PUFFIN
Fratercula cirrhata

Stubby wings propel this bird with surprising speed and agility when it swims underwater in pursuit of prey or when it retreats from predators. An advantage below the waves, however, results in awkwardness in the air—the Tufted Puffin and other alcids are easily recognized by their awkward take-off attempts and laborious flight pattern. For this reason, the Tufted Puffin is most likely to dive, rather than fly, when approached by a boat or an airborne threat.
• Breeding Tufted Puffins, clad like flamboyant clowns, are at best an uncommon sight along the northern California coast, making them a special and rare attraction. • In recent years puffins have had a tough time of it. They are extremely dependent on small fish of a very specific size, and it has been estimated that hundreds of the puffins living off the Pacific coast are drowned annually in fishermen's gillnets.

breeding

ID: *Breeding:* immense, bright red-orange bill; white face; long, yellow tufts behind the eyes; black crown, neck and body; yellow eyes. *Non-breeding:* large, laterally compressed, orangy bill; short, golden-gray eyebrow tufts; all-dark head and body. *Immature:* dark eyes; much smaller, all-black to yellow-green bill; may have white or dark underparts.
Size: *L* 14½–15½ in.
Status: locally rare to uncommon year-round resident; moves offshore outside the breeding season.
Habitat: *Breeding:* on offshore islands with soil burrows; upwellings near islands. *Winter:* deep, offshore ocean.
Nesting: colonial; 1 white egg with dark spots is incubated by both adults for about

45 days; nest chamber is in an underground burrow up to 20 ft long; both adults feed the young.
Feeding: small schooling fish are favored; forages by swimming underwater for up to 2 minutes; also takes crustaceans, mollusks, sea urchins and rarely marine algae.
Voice: generally silent; soft growls and grunts are occasionally given at nesting colony: *er err* or *eh-errr errr errr errr.*
Similar Species: *Rhinoceros Auklet* (p. 196): lacks the massive bill; juvenile is paler and has a shallower bill.

ROCK DOVE

Columba livia

Rock Doves are the wild, or 'feral,' version of the domestic pigeon. Introduced from Europe in the 17th century, Rock Doves have settled wherever there are cities, towns, farms or grain elevators. 'Wilder' members of this species occasionally live close to tall cliffs along the ocean coast or in the interior. • The Rock Dove was first domesticated from Eurasian birds in about 4500 B.C. as a source of meat. Since that time, Rock Doves have also been used by humans as message couriers—both Caesar and Napoleon used them—and as scientific subjects. Much of our understanding of bird migration, endocrinology, sensory perception, flight and other avian traits and biological functions derives from experiments involving Rock Doves. • No other 'wild' bird varies as much in coloration as the Rock Dove—a result of semi-domestication and extensive inbreeding over time.

ID: color is highly variable (iridescent blue-gray, red, white or tan); usually has a white rump and orange feet; dark-tipped tail. *In flight:* powerful, deep, irregular wingbeats; holds its wings in a deep V while gliding.
Size: *L* 12–13 in; male is usually larger.
Status: locally abundant year-round resident.
Habitat: urban and suburban areas, railroad yards, farms, ranches and grain terminals to about 8000 ft; wilder birds may be found on interior cliffs and sea cliffs.
Nesting: on ledges of barns, cliffs, bridges, buildings and towers; flimsy nest of sticks, grass and assorted vegetation; pair incubates 2 eggs for about 18 days; parents feed the young 'pigeon milk'; may raise up to 5 or more broods each year.
Feeding: gleans the ground for waste grain, seeds and fruits; occasionally eats insects.
Voice: soft, cooing *coorrr-coorrr-coorrr.*
Similar Species: *Band-tailed Pigeon* (p. 199): dark rump; pale band on a dark tail; yellow feet; white collar; adult shows no plumage variability among flocks.

BAND-TAILED PIGEON

Columba fasciata

Through much of its extensive range in the Americas—from nearly the southeastern tip of Alaska to northern Argentina—the Band-tailed Pigeon is a bird of the foothills and mountains. Band-tails are fond of acorns and generally are most numerous in forests with a strong oak component. Not surprisingly, they are found widely in northern California, ranging from sea level to the upper altitudinal limits of the oak zone. A retreat from higher elevations and from much of the northern interior is apparent in winter. Rugged canyons densely grown to oak and madrones often host flocks of these retiring pigeons. Clinging clumsily to twigs that may scarcely support their weight, they reach into adjacent foliage, plucking nuts and fruits. Often, their presence overhead is revealed only by the occasional heavy slapping of broad wings as foraging birds shift position within the canopy. Birdfeeders in suburban backyards edging stands of tall trees also support their share of Band-tails. • In spring, Band-tailed Pigeons utter a soft, low-pitched 'coo' of two or three notes; their hooting is so low and resonant that it is widely mistaken for an owl's.

ID: purplish head and breast; black-tipped, yellow bill; white half-collar on the iridescent green nape; dark gray tail is broadly tipped with a pale gray band.
Size: L 13–15 in.
Status: uncommon to locally common year-round resident; spring influx and fall departure are noted in many areas.
Habitat: mixed conifer-hardwood forests and woodlands, canyons and suburban-rural edge; will assemble in late summer and fall in large numbers in vicinity of mineral springs or salt licks.
Nesting: near the fork of a tree branch; fragile platform nest of sticks with minimal lining; pair incubates a single white egg for 18–20 days; both adults feed 'pigeon milk' to the young.
Feeding: gleans vegetation for nuts, especially acorns; also eats other seeds and insects during migration; most foraging is done in trees.
Voice: generally quite silent; very deep, hollow *Ooh, uh-WOO*, heard most frequently in spring, is given in slow, deliberate series from a high perch; wings make a loud slapping noise upon taking flight.
Similar Species: *Rock Dove* (p. 198): typically has a white rump and dark bill; lacks the gray band on the dark tail. *Mourning Dove* (p. 200): smaller and more slender; pale brown overall; longer, white-fringed tail; lacks the purple head and the glossy green nape; whistling wingbeats.

MOURNING DOVE

Zenaida macroura

The soothing, rhythmic coo of the Mourning Dove is a common sound that graces many of northern California's woodlands, farmlands and suburban parks and gardens. During the winter months, hundreds of Mourning Doves will congregate in large flocks around lowland watering holes, granaries and cattle pastures. • Mourning Doves are swift, direct fliers. When they burst into flight, their wing tips clap against each other and then whistle as the bird accelerates. • All members of the pigeon family (including doves) feed 'milk' to their young. Since birds lack mammary glands, it isn't true milk but a nutritious liquid produced by glands in the bird's crop. The chicks insert their bills into the adult's throat to eat the thick, protein-rich fluid. • This bird's common name reflects its sad song. The genus name *Zenaida* honors Zenaide, the Princess of Naples and wife of Charles Lucien Bonaparte (the nephew of the French emperor).

ID: sleek, buffy gray-brown plumage; small head; dark, shiny patch below the ear; dark bill; pale rosy underparts; long, white-trimmed, tapering tail; black spots on the upperwing; dull red legs. *Juvenile:* more rounded wing tips.
Size: *L* 11–13 in.
Status: uncommon to locally abundant year-round resident.
Habitat: varied; open woodlands, lowland forest edges, savannah, riparian woodlands, farmlands, ranches, cities, parks and suburban areas; avoids dense forests; has benefited from human-induced habitat change.
Nesting: in the fork of a shrub or tree, or occasionally on the ground; female builds a fragile, shallow platform nest from twigs supplied by the male; pair incubates 2 white eggs for 14 days; young are fed 'pigeon milk.'

Feeding: gleans the ground and vegetation for the seeds of agricultural crops, weeds and native vegetation; visits feeders.
Voice: mournful, soft *coo-AHH, coo, coo-coo.*
Similar Species: *Rock Dove* (p. 198): stockier; iridescent neck; white rump; broader tail. *Band-tailed Pigeon* (p. 199): stockier; yellow bill; white collar on the nape; iridescence on the back of the head; broader tail. *Yellow-billed Cuckoo* (p. 201): curved, yellow bill; long, rounded tail with white spots on the undersides; brown upperparts; white underparts.

YELLOW-BILLED CUCKOO

Coccyzus americanus

From deep within impenetrable riverside undergrowth emerges a jungle-like call: *ku-ku-ku-ku-ka-ka-kowk-kowk-kowk*. This strange, mysterious cry might be the only evidence of your meeting with one of northern California's rarest, elusive birds, the Yellow-billed Cuckoo. There were an estimated 70,000 breeding pairs in California in the late 19th century, but the degradation and destruction of the cuckoo's closed-canopy riparian forest habitat has claimed most of its population. Today, fewer than 300 cuckoos remain in California. Much of the state's last remaining cuckoo habitat exists in fragments along northern California's upper Sacramento River. The protection of this crucial habitat, and the restoration of other riparian areas, could help reverse the cuckoo's potentially dismal future. • Over some parts of their range, cuckoos are nicknamed 'Rain Crows,' because their mysterious cries are thought to forecast rain.

ID: slender; olive-brown upperparts; white underparts; slightly downcurved bill; black upper mandible; yellow lower mandible; long tail, with large, white spots on the underside; rufous in the wings is especially apparent in flight.
Size: *L* 11–13 in.
Status: very rare to very uncommon local breeder from mid-May to early September; exceptionally rare migrant.
Habitat: mixed old-growth willow-cottonwood riparian woodlands with a dense understory of tangles and thickets.
Nesting: on a horizontal branch in a willow; messy, loose structure of twigs is lined with roots and grass; pair incubates 3–4 pale bluish-green eggs for 9–11 days; both adults feed the young.

Feeding: often forages in riparian canopies, gleaning vegetation for insect larvae, especially hairy caterpillars; also eats berries, small fruits, small amphibians and lizards and occasionally the eggs of other birds.
Voice: long series of deep, hollow *koks*, slowing near the end: *kuk-kuk-kuk-kuk kuk kop kow kowlp kowlp.*
Similar Species: *Mourning Dove* (p. 200): short, straight, all-dark bill; pale rosy underparts; orange-pink feet; tapered tail. *California Thrasher* (p. 306): longer, all-dark, sickle-like bill; dark underparts; stays mostly close to the ground.

GREATER ROADRUNNER
Geococcyx californianus

Celebrated in legends and cartoons, the roadrunner lives up to its reputation as a speedy and spirited bird, commonly dashing along and across highways and gravel roads bisecting its brushy habitat. This large member of the cuckoo family spends much of its time on its long, spindly legs, chasing after insects, lizards and small rodents at speeds of up to 15 mph. Roadrunners seldom find the need to fly, and when they do resort to the air, they pass quickly and directly over short distances. • Roadrunner courtship is an energetic affair involving high-speed foot chases followed by long, breath-catching pauses. The male typically leads the performance by running away from his mate with both tail and wings held over his body, and after a few graceful bows and some affectionate tail wagging, both adults seal their bond by exchanging offerings of sticks or vegetation. • Through wildfire suppression and suburban sprawl, Roadrunner habitat has been diminished and fragmented, resulting in population decreases throughout much of its spotty northern California distribution.

ID: streaky, brown and whitish plumage; long, thick bill with a hooked tip; raised head crest; bare, blue-and-red skin patch through the eye; thick, scaly legs; short, rounded wings; very long tail.
Size: *L* 23 in.
Status: rare to uncommon year-round resident; formerly north to South Klamath Mountains.
Habitat: open chaparral and brushy areas around the edges of interior valleys; arid woodlands of pinyon pine and juniper, agricultural lands and suburbs up to 7500 ft.
Nesting: usually in a cactus, dense shrub or low tree; bulky platform of sticks, vegetation and feathers (may include snakeskin

and dried cow manure); pair incubates, although the male does more; breeding pair may mate for life and defend its breeding territory year-round.
Feeding: catches insects, small mammals, lizards, snakes and small birds by running them down; forages while walking quickly, suddenly dashing toward prey; may leap into the air to catch insects and small birds; also eats scorpions, snails, spiders, fruit and seeds.
Voice: descending, dove-like cooing; loud bill-clattering is often the first sign of this bird's presence.
Similar Species: *Ring-necked Pheasant* (p. 121): female lacks the raised head crest and the colorful bare skin behind the eye; shorter bill; barred tail; found in croplands.

BARN OWL
Tyto alba

The haunting look of this night hunter has inspired superstitions among many people. Naked faces and black, piercing eyes give downy nestling Barn Owls an eerie look. In truth, however, the dedicated hunting efforts of these northern California residents helps to keep farmlands and even city yards free from undesirable rodents. • Like the House Sparrow and Rock Dove, the Barn Owl has found success by associating with urban and agricultural areas. Its nocturnal habit, taste for small rodents and general tolerance of humans has allowed this adaptable bird to prosper on six continents. Unfortunately, the advent of monoculture and the loss of the urban-rural edge to development has diminished the Barn Owl's foraging habitat locally.

ID: heart-shaped, white facial disk; dark eyes; pale bill; golden-brown upperparts spotted with black and gray; creamy-white, black-spotted underparts; long legs; white undertail and underwings.
Size: L 12½–18 in; W 45 in.
Status: rare to locally common year-round resident.
Habitat: roosts and nests in cliffs, hollow trees, barns and other unoccupied buildings, mine shafts, caves, bridges, tree groves and riverbanks; requires open areas, including agricultural fields, pastures, lawns, marshy meadows, open beach edges or open streamside areas, for hunting.
Nesting: in a natural or artificial cavity, often in a sheltered, secluded hollow of a building; may dig a hole in a dirt bank or use an artificial nest box; no actual nest is built; female incubates 3–8 whitish eggs for 29–34 days; male feeds the incubating female.

Feeding: eats mostly small mammals, especially rodents; also takes small numbers of snakes, lizards, birds and large insects; rarely takes frogs and fish.
Voice: calls include harsh, raspy screeches and hisses; also makes metallic clicking sounds; often heard flying high over cities and residential areas late at night.
Similar Species: *Short-eared Owl* (p. 212): yellow eyes set in black sockets; vertical streaks on the breast and belly; black 'wrist' patches; erratic flight pattern. *Spotted Owl* (p. 209): much darker; white spots on the dark chest and belly; darker facial disk. *Barred Owl*: barred chest; streaking on the belly; darker facial disk.

203

FLAMMULATED OWL

Otus flammeolus

As the campfire settles into glowing embers, from beyond the edges of the clearing comes an odd, low-pitched sound: a Flammulated Owl has shaken off the torpor of summer daytime to begin the evening's hunt. • Because its diet is composed chiefly of large insects—a scarce commodity in mountain forests in winter—this owl migrates to Mexico or Central America. Birders searching for this elusive owl must plan their efforts during the warmer months. • A quick field identification mark for the Flammulated Owl is that it is the only small North American owl with dark eyes. • Once considered rare, increased 'owling pressure' by birders and raptor researchers in recent decades has indicated that these insectivorous night hunters are actually widespread and numerous in many areas. Northern California's vast expanses of semi-open pine and pine-oak forest offer the tree cavities and open ground this species prefers.

red morph

ID: dark eyes; small ear tufts; smeary-whitish inner fringe to the deep rusty facial disks; dark bill; white eyebrow; vertical breast streaks.
Size: *L* 6–7 in; *W* 15 in.
Status: locally common breeder from early April to late September; almost never detected in migration.
Habitat: broken or open montane forests composed of mixed oaks and conifers; strongly associated with ponderosa pine, Jeffrey pine and California black oak; absent from lowlands.
Nesting: usually in an abandoned woodpecker cavity, often lined with a few wood chips; female incubates 2–3 eggs for 21–24 days; male feeds the incubating female.

Feeding: most often gleans insects from foliage or from the ground while hovering; also swoops from a perch to catch moths, beetles and other insects in flight.
Voice: muffled, low-pitched, mellow hoot given about every 3 seconds; heard from twilight to dawn.
Similar Species: *Western Screech-Owl* (p. 205): larger; light-colored eyes; larger ear tufts; lacks rufous in the plumage. *Northern Pygmy-Owl* (p. 207) and *Northern Saw-whet Owl* (p. 213): lack the ear tufts; light eyes.

WESTERN SCREECH-OWL
Otus kennicottii

Despite its small size, the Western Screech-Owl is an adaptable hunter. It has a varied diet that ranges from insects, amphibians and small mammals to birds larger than itself. • These owls pass the daylight hours concealed in dense shrubs or roosting in hollow trees; they hunt from deep evening twilight until dawn. Western Screech-Owls demand little more than a secluded roosting site, a tree hollow for nesting, some woodland edge and semi-open ground that they can scout from low tree limbs. • Western Screech-Owls are most vocal in northern California between March and June. Their distinctive courting whistle percolates through both natural and suburban habitats at this time of year, briefly revealing this bird's otherwise secretive presence. Their bouncing-ball whistles are easily imitated, often drawing an owl into flashlight range. • Robert Kennicott, for whom this species is scientifically named, traveled and collected owl specimens across northern Canada and Alaska.

ID: ear tufts; heavy, vertical breast streaks; yellow eyes; dark bill.
Size: L 7–11 in; W 18–24 in.
Status: uncommon to abundant year-round resident.
Habitat: open or broken, lowland woodlands of oaks, conifers or a mix of deciduous and coniferous trees; riparian woodlands, pinyon pine–juniper woodlands, savannah, parklands, suburbs, towns, farms and ranches.
Nesting: in an abandoned woodpecker cavity, magpie nest, nest box or natural cavity; adds no nesting material; female incubates 2–5 white eggs for about 26 days; male feeds the incubating female; both adults feed the young.
Feeding: hunts at night; swoops from a perch to capture invertebrates, mice, voles, amphibians and occasionally songbirds; able to capture animals larger than itself.

Voice: distinctive series of soft, accelerating, evenly pitched whistles and notes, with a rhythm like that of a bouncing ball coming to a stop; pairs often appear to 'counter-sing'; agitated variations occur.
Similar Species: *Great Horned Owl* (p. 206): much larger; much longer tail; horizontal barring on the breast. *Long-eared Owl* (p. 211): tall ear tufts are set very close together; body is tall and narrow. *Northern Saw-whet Owl* (p. 213): lacks the ear tufts. *Flammulated Owl* (p. 204): dark eyes; very short ear tufts; rufous coloration in the facial disk; whitish eyebrows.

GREAT HORNED OWL
Bubo virginianus

The Great Horned Owl is the most widely distributed avian predator in the Western Hemisphere, and it is among the most formidable. • Like most owls, Great Horned Owls are quite capable of seeing and hunting during daylight hours, but they tend to hunt under low light conditions when their prey are more active. This bird uses its specialized hearing, powerful talons and human-sized eyes to hunt for an astonishingly wide diversity of prey, including small shrews, birds, amphibians, rabbits, ground squirrels, waterfowl and even hawks. It has a poorly developed sense of smell, however, which might explain why it consistently preys on skunks—molted Great Horned Owl feathers are occasionally identifiable by a simple sniff. • Because this large owl is not limited to a certain habitat, it is the most commonly seen owl in northern California.

Nesting: usually in a tree; also on cliffs in the abandoned stick nest of a hawk, crow, raven, eagle or heron; adds little material to the nest; female mostly incubates the 2–3 dull white eggs for 28–35 days; both adults feed the young.

Feeding: mostly nocturnal; also hunts by day in winter; usually swoops from a perch; detects prey with its ears and eyes; eats small mammals, insects, fish, amphibians, reptiles and birds.

Voice: male gives 5–6 deep hoots during the breeding season: *hoo, hoo-hoo HOO, Hoo*; female gives 6–8 hoots; dependent juveniles give harsh screams at intervals both day and night.

Similar Species: *Western Screech-Owl* (p. 205): much smaller; vertical breast streaks. *Long-eared Owl* (p. 211): vertical breast streaks; ear tufts are set very close together; much slimmer body. *Great Gray Owl* (p. 210) and *Barred Owl*: both lack the ear tufts.

ID: yellow eyes; tall ear tufts are set wide apart; fine, horizontal barring on the breast; facial disk is outlined in black and is often rusty-orange in color; white chin; heavily mottled, gray, brown and black upperparts; overall plumage color varies from light gray to dark brown.

Size: *L* 18–25 in; *W* 36–60 in.

Status: uncommon to fairly common year-round resident; may retreat from the highest elevations in winter.

Habitat: broken or open mixed forests and oak woodlands, riparian woodlands, densely wooded canyons with exposed cliffs, farmlands, towns and parks.

NORTHERN PYGMY-OWL
Glaucidium gnoma

Even when the Northern Pygmy-Owl is looking the other way, two dark 'false eyes' on the back of its head stare blankly toward you. Because larger birds and mammals are less likely to attack a bird that is apparently looking in their direction, the pygmy-owl is usually effective in 'guarding' its own back.
• This appropriately named bird is northern California's smallest owl, but it regularly catches prey that outweigh it. During fierce battles, this tiny owl might be dragged some distance before it is able to dispatch its prey.
• During daylight hours, the Northern Pygmy-Owl is often mobbed by angry gangs of chickadees or other songbirds. By imitating this owl's whistled call, birders may attract a similar group of agitated birds.

red morph

ID: long, narrow tail; thin, dark streaking on the whitish undersides; 2 black 'false eyes' on the nape; no ear tufts; light bill; small, yellow eyes; white chin and eyebrows; white spots on the dark forehead; gray and reddish color morphs.
Size: *L* 7 in; *W* 15 in.
Status: rare to uncommon year-round resident; generally more numerous with increasing forest cover.
Habitat: varied conifer and conifer-oak forests and woodlands with sufficient tree cavities; locally at sea level to the upper limit of forests.
Nesting: in an abandoned woodpecker cavity or natural tree hollow; nest is usually unlined; female incubates 3–4 white eggs for about 28 days; both adults raise the young.

Feeding: largely or entirely by day; swoops from a perch and chases birds in flight; eats small rodents, large insects, reptiles, amphibians and small birds.
Voice: mellow *toot* uttered once every 2 or 3 seconds, remarkably like a wooden recorder; series of 20–30 rapid-fire, decelerating *toots* when agitated; all calls are given at the same pitch.
Similar Species: *Northern Saw-whet Owl* (p. 213): chunkier; lacks the 'false eyes'; blurry, reddish streaking on the breast; dark bill; light streaking on the forehead. *Western Screech-Owl* (p. 205): ear tufts; larger, yellow eyes. *Flammulated Owl* (p. 204): ear tufts; dark eyes; active only at night.

BURROWING OWL
Athene cunicularia

The Burrowing Owl is the only owl in North America that nests in underground burrows. Despite its name, however, this owl does not usually excavate its burrow—in northern California, alcids, shearwaters and storm-petrels are the only burrowing birds—the extermination of burrowing mammals in northern California has reduced the availability of suitable nesting sites. Additionally, the conversion of native grasslands to croplands and residential areas has greatly diminished available habitat for these birds.
• During the day, these ground-dwelling birds can be seen atop fenceposts or rocks in open grassland habitat. When they perch at the entrance to their burrows, they can look very similar to the ground squirrels or prairie-dogs with which they closely associate.

ID: long legs; rounded head; no ear tufts; yellow bill; short wings; white spotting on the breast; dark barring on the belly; brown upperparts are flecked with white. *Immature:* dark breast and light belly are unmarked.
Size: L 8–9 in; W 20–24 in.
Status: rare to very uncommon local breeder or resident; rare migrant and winter visitor; scarce in northwestern California; resident population now much declined and fragmented owing to development.
Habitat: dry, open grasslands, rolling hills and ranchlands; barren ground with gullies, arid shrublands and occasionally along seacoast bluffs and rocky breakwaters.
Nesting: often loosely colonial; in abandoned ground squirrel, badger, hare or prairie-dog burrows; enlarges the burrow up to 7 ft deep with its talons; may add grass, sticks or other debris, such as dried cow dung to the nest site; female incubates 7–10 white eggs for 28–30 days; male feeds the incubating female.

Feeding: opportunistic; stalks prey, pounces from a mound or swoops down from flight or from a fencepost perch; eats mostly ground insects, such as grasshoppers, beetles and crickets; also eats small rodents, birds, amphibians and reptiles.
Voice: call is a harsh *chuk* or *QUEE! kuk-kuk-kuk-kuk-kuk*; rasping, rattlesnake-like warning call when inside its burrow. *Male:* mournful *coo-coo-roo* in courtship.
Similar Species: *Short-eared Owl* (p. 212): larger; heavy, dark streaking on the breast; short legs; long wings with dark 'wrist' marks; black eye sockets. *Barn Owl* (p. 203): larger; dark eyes; white facial disk; unmarked white underparts.

SPOTTED OWL
Strix occidentalis

Within the past few decades, the Spotted Owl has unwittingly become notorious as the prime icon of timberland management issues across its range in the Pacific Northwest. Long a bird of mystery, it was believed to be rare until the combined forces of owl surveyors, banders and radio telemetry technicians began to uncover hundreds of previously unknown pairs. • Although a large proportion of the California population makes do with a managed mosaic of second-growth and remnant older forest, long-term studies have suggested that the threatened northern subspecies, *S. o. caurinus*, does best where forest fragmentation is minimal. • Spotted Owls tolerate remarkably close human approach, although females will attack intruders at the nest site, and they respond readily to imitations of their distinctive hoots. Birders calling for these owls should keep the welfare of the bird foremost in mind, exercising restraint in their encounters with these marvelous birds.

ID: round head; no ear tufts; chocolate brown, white-tipped feathers produce a mottled look; dark eyes; indistinct, creamy blaze on the center of the upper breast.
Size: L 16½–19 in; W 45 in; female is slightly larger.
Status: rare to locally fairly common resident.
Habitat: old-growth coniferous and mixed conifer-hardwood forests; wanderers or dispersing juveniles are occasionally found well outside the typical habitat.
Nesting: on a shallow scrape in a tree hollow, broken top, abandoned stick nest or cave or cliff crevice; pair uses the same nest site for years or alternates between 2 or more sites; female incubates 2–3 whitish eggs for 28–32 days; male feeds the incubating female and defends the territory; pair may not nest each year.
Feeding: generally a nocturnal hunter except while breeding; eats mostly small mammals, but is an opportunistic hunter and diet is varied.
Voice: common call is the male's 4-note hoot, *hoo, Hoo-Hoo…HOOO*, which is audible at approximately 1 mile; female generally gives a similar 3-note hoot, which is hollower and higher pitched; abruptly upslurred contact whistle is given by each sex.
Similar Species: *Barred Owl*: slightly larger; grayer; contrast of horizontal barring on the upper breast and vertical dark streaking on the pale background of lower breast. *Barn Owl* (p. 203): tawny-buff above; white 'monkey face' and underparts; seldom seen in dense forests. *Great Gray Owl* (p. 210): much larger; small, yellow eyes; very broad facial disk; streaking on the breast and belly.

GREAT GRAY OWL
Strix nebulosa

A face shaped like a satellite dish and an ensnaring cluster of talons just may be the last look at life for a rodent scouted by a Great Gray Owl. This bird's great head swivels smoothly, focusing instantly on the slightest sound or movement beneath a carpet of snow or within a summer's growth of grass and wildflowers. When prey is detected, the owl launches itself in noiseless flight, gliding downward on fixed wings, punching through anything that may be in the way of its meal. • Although it is the largest North American owl, the Great Gray's seeming bulk is largely a mass of fluffy insulation—it is out-weighed by about 15 percent by both the Snowy Owl and the Great Horned Owl. • Great Gray Owls are widespread across the boreal forests of the Northern Hemisphere. Following the cool conifer forests southward via major mountain ranges, their extension into California is tenuous indeed, with the entire state population thought to number only a few dozen birds. A trek into one of its few traditional sites in the higher Sierra Nevada offers the best opportunity to see the legendary Great Gray Owl in California.

ID: gray plumage; large, rounded head; no ear tufts; small, yellow eyes; well-defined, concentric rings in the facial disk; black chin bordered by white; long tail.
Size: L 24–33 in; W 54–60 in; female is slightly larger.
Status: rare year-round resident.
Habitat: dense, old-growth coniferous forests of red fir, Jeffrey pine and lodgepole pine; often hunts along the edge of adjacent meadows.
Nesting: in an abandoned hawk, raven or eagle nest; occasionally nests in a broken-top tree or stub; adds little nest material;

female incubates 2–4 eggs for up to 36 days.
Feeding: listens and watches from a perch, then swoops to catch voles, mice, shrews, gophers, squirrels and small hares.
Voice: slow, deep, almost inaudible series of hoots.
Similar Species: *Great Horned Owl* (p. 206): ear tufts. *Snowy Owl:* white plumage. *Spotted Owl* (p. 209) and *Barred Owl:* smaller; dark eyes.

LONG-EARED OWL

Asio otus

Long-eared Owls will either inflate or compress their bodies in response to certain situations. To scare an intruder, this owl will expand its air sacs, puff its feathers and spread its wings to double its size in a threat display. To hide from an intruder or predator, it will compress itself into a long, thin, vertical form to blend into the stumps and branches that surround it. • This nocturnal predator hunts in open areas, but during the day it returns to dense stands of trees to roost. • Despite the common use of 'eared' in many owl names, the tufts on top of the Long-eared Owl's head are made only of feathers. • The secretive habits of Long-eared Owls causes them to remain a mysterious species over much of northern California.

ID: long ear tufts are relatively close together; slim body; vertical belly markings; light brown facial disk; mottled brown plumage; yellow-orange eyes; white around the bill.
Size: L 13–16 in; W 36–47 in.
Status: rare to locally uncommon year-round resident; status not well understood.
Habitat: dense, mixed forests and tall shrublands, usually next to open spaces, such as grasslands and meadows; may hunt over extensive semi-open terrain.
Nesting: often in an abandoned crow, magpie or hawk nest; occasionally in a natural tree cavity; female incubates 4–5 eggs for up to 25–30 days.

Feeding: nocturnal; flies low, pouncing on prey from the air; eats mostly voles and mice, occasionally shrews, pocket gophers and small rabbits; also takes small birds and amphibians.
Voice: breeding call is a low, soft *quoo-quoo*; alarm call is *weck-weck-weck*.

Similar Species: *Western Screech-Owl* (p. 205): smaller; ear tufts are farther apart; body is less compressed. *Great Horned Owl* (p. 206): much larger; ear tufts are farther apart; body is less compressed.

211

SHORT-EARED OWL
Asio flammeus

The Short-eared Owl flies so characteristically that after a first encounter with this bird it will be easy to identify one in flight from quite a distance. It beats its long wings slowly, similar in many ways to a butterfly, as it courses low over wet meadows, often by day. • Short-ears perform spectacular aerial courtship dances while clapping their wing tips together below their bodies. These birds typically inhabit open country where these courtship displays—called sky dances—are more effective than the usual 'hoot' for communicating. • This owl's life revolves around the population levels of voles, leading to nomadic movements in response to prey availability. Breeding populations have decreased significantly during the 20th century.

ID: yellow eyes in black sockets; heavy, vertical streaking on the buff belly; straw-colored upperparts; short ear tufts are rarely seen. *In flight:* dark elbow patches; deep wingbeats; long wings; very short tail.
Size: L 13–17 in; W 44 in.
Status: rare to uncommon year-round; most regular from October to March.
Habitat: open country, including grasslands, wet meadows and cleared forests. *In migration:* frequently in alpine meadows; occasionally encountered miles at sea in fall. *Breeding:* occasionally in coastal estuaries where conditions are prime.
Nesting: on the ground; in a slight depression sparsely lined with grass; female incubates 4–7 eggs for 26–37 days.
Feeding: uses hearing, vision and flight adaptations to forage low over marshes, wet meadows and tall vegetation; pounces from the air; eats mostly voles and other small rodents, as well as insects, small birds and amphibians; suffers kleptoparasitism by the Northern Harrier.
Voice: generally quiet; produces a soft *toot-toot-toot* during the breeding season; sneezy, squalling 'bark' may be heard at dusk as wintering birds become active.

Similar Species: *Burrowing Owl* (p. 208): much longer legs; shorter tail; shorter wings. *Long-eared Owl* (p. 211): long ear tufts; shorter wings; rarely hunts during the day.

NORTHERN SAW-WHET OWL

Aegolius acadicus

Northern Saw-whet Owls are opportunistic hunters that take whatever they can, whenever they can. When temperatures are below freezing, these small owls may choose to catch more than they can eat at a single sitting. The extra food is usually stored in trees, where it quickly freezes. When new hunting efforts fail, a hungry owl can return to thaw out its frozen cache by 'incubating' it as it would a clutch of eggs. • The common name 'saw-whet' comes from one of this owl's calls: its steady, whistling notes are thought to be similar to the sound of a large mill saw being sharpened, or 'whetted.' Heard far more than they are seen, Saw-whets usually only call in the dark of night. • Saw-whets can be encountered in forested areas throughout northern California from mid-winter well into early spring. • The scientific name *acadicus* is Latin for 'from Acadia' (New Brunswick, Nova Scotia and Maine), the region where this bird was first collected.

ID: small owl; large, rounded head; light, unbordered facial disk; dark bill; vertical, rusty streaks on the underparts; brown, white-spotted upperparts; lightly streaked forehead; short tail. *Immature:* white between the eyes; rich brown upperparts; buff-brown underparts.
Size: L 7–9 in; W 18 in.
Status: rare to locally uncommon year-round resident; non-breeding areas often support migrants and visitors from late September through March.
Habitat: open and broken woodlands that are purely coniferous, deciduous or mixed.
Nesting: in abandoned woodpecker cavities and natural hollows in trees; may use artificial nest boxes; female incubates 5–6 white eggs for 27–29 days; male feeds the incubating female.

Feeding: nocturnal; swoops from a perch; eats mostly mice and voles; occasionally takes large insects, small bird, shrews and amphibians; may occasionally cache food.
Voice: distinctive by its repetition; single, evenly spaced (about 100–130 per minute), whistled *whew-whew-whew-whew*; continuous and easily imitated; notably ventriloqual; doesn't call during the day.
Similar Species: *Northern Pygmy-Owl* (p. 207): light-colored bill; proportionately longer tail; dark 'false eye' patches on the nape; white spots on a dark forehead; fewer dark streaks on the underparts. *Flammulated Owl* (p. 204): dark eyes; small ear tufts.

LESSER NIGHTHAWK
Chordeiles acutipennis

With a distinctive, erratic flight, the Lesser Nighthawk flies low over open fields at dusk, feeding efficiently on a diet of flying insects. • Shaped like a boomerang with an added head and tail, the nighthawk zigzags across darkening skies, occasionally uttering its trilling call. • Aside from their quick, manic flight, nighthawks are equipped with a very wide mouth gape, fringed with feather shafts to increase the chance of catching insects. • The Lesser Nighthawk is one of three members of the goatsucker family found in northern California.

ID: mottled brown upperparts; buffy underparts with faint dark barring; small bill; wing bar is buffy in the female. *In flight:* long, pointed wings; pale bar across the 'wrists'; white throat; long, rectangular tail; male has a broad white tail band.
Size: *L* 8–9 in.
Status: local, rare to uncommon breeder from late March to early October.
Habitat: drier lowland valleys with sparse brush or scrub vegetation; prefers gravelly areas for nesting.
Nesting: on open, barren ground, sometimes shaded by a small shrub; 2 white-to-pale gray eggs with fine brown, gray and lavender dots are incubated, mostly by the female, for 18–19 days; pair feeds the young by regurgitation.

Feeding: insects are scooped up in the wide, gaping mouth during flight; usually forages at dusk, but may also feed during the day or night; often seen feeding on insects that are attracted to bright outdoor lights.
Voice: distinctive call is a soft, rapid, tremulous trill.
Similar Species: *Common Poorwill* (p. 216): shorter, rounded tail and wings; bulkier neck; corners of the tail are tipped with white. *Common Nighthawk* (p. 215): forked, triangular-shaped tail (male has a thin, white tail band); darker overall; whitish underparts have prominent dark bars; white bar on the primaries is farther from the wing tip; call is a nasal *peent*.

COMMON NIGHTHAWK

Chordeiles minor

The Common Nighthawk is mild-mannered by day as it rests on the ground or on a horizontal tree branch, its color and shape blending perfectly with the texture of the bark. At dusk, however, this bird takes on a new form as a dazzling and erratic flier, catching insects in flight. • To many people, the sound of a nighthawk is the sound of spring and summer evenings at a favorite campground. During courtship, the male flies high above open woodlands and forest clearings; then, from a great height, he dives swiftly toward the ground. As he strains to pull out of his death-defying dive, he thrusts his wings forward in a hard, braking action, producing a deep, hollow *vroom* sound with the feathers of his wings. • Nighthawks are generally less nocturnal than other members of their family, but they still spend many daylight hours resting on tree limbs or on the ground. They have very short legs and tiny feet, and unlike most birds that perch, nighthawks sit lengthwise or diagonally on branches.

ID: intricately cryptic, mottled light and dark plumage; barred underparts. *Male:* white throat. *Female:* buff throat. *In flight:* bold white 'wrist' patches on long, pointed wings; shallowly forked, barred tail; flight is erratic.
Size: L 8¹/₂–10 in.
Status: irregular distribution; uncommon migrant and rare to locally common breeder from late May to mid-September; rare from late September to mid-October; more numerous northward and at higher elevations.
Habitat: *Breeding:* city rooftops, broken coniferous forests. *Foraging* and *In migration:* open woodlands, meadows, savannahs, sagebrush flats, larger rivers and lakes, townsites and suburban areas.
Nesting: on bare ground covered with rocks, pebbles, gravel or very short vegetation; no actual nest is built; mostly the female incubates the 2 well-camouflaged eggs for about 19 days; both adults feeds the young.
Feeding: primarily crepuscular, but will also feed during the day and night; catches insects in flight; may fly around street lights at night to catch prey attracted to the light; eats mosquitoes, beetles, flying ants, moths, termites and other flying insects.
Voice: unique, frequently repeated, nasal *peent*; also makes a deep, hollow *vrooom* with its wings.
Similar Species: *Common Poorwill* (p. 216): lacks the white 'wrist' patches; shorter, rounder wings; tail has white or buff-colored outer corners.

215

COMMON POORWILL

Phalaenoptilus nuttallii

In 1946, the scientific community was surprised by the discovery of a Common Poorwill that appeared to be hibernating through winter in a rock crevice. It was cold to the touch and had no detectable breath or heartbeat. Although poorwills do not enter true hibernation like some mammals, they will enter a short-term torpor in which their body temperature drops as low as 43°. It is suspected that some poorwills survive in northern California as year-round residents by entering torpor during cold spells, but most poorwills probably migrate to warmer climates for winter. • The 1946 discovery was clearly not the first suggestion of this strange habit in poorwills: in 1804, Meriwether Lewis found a mysterious 'goatsucker … to be passing into the dormant state,' and the Hopi had named this bird *Holchoko*, 'the sleeping one,' in an earlier era.

♂

ID: cryptic, mottled plumage; light to dark-brown overall; pale throat; finely barred underparts. *Male:* white tail corners. *Female:* buff tail corners. *In flight:* moth-like or bat-like fluttering; rounded wings and tail.
Size: L 7¹/₂–8¹/₂ in.
Status: not completely known; rare to locally common migrant and breeder from late March to late October; some birds are residents that enter torpid state during winter.
Habitat: arid, open, grassy environments, pinyon-juniper woodlands, chaparral, brushy slopes, sagebrush flats and open shrublands in the foothills; occasional in logging clearcuts.

Nesting: on bare ground; no actual nest is built; pair incubates 2 white eggs for 20–21 days; both adults feed the young.
Feeding: feeds at dawn and dusk and on moonlit nights; catches a variety of flying insects on the wing; eats mostly moths and beetles.
Voice: *poor-will* is frequently heard at dusk and through the night; at close range, a hiccup-like sound can be heard at the end of the phrase.
Similar Species: *Common Nighthawk* (p. 215): long, pointed wings with white 'wrist' patches; longer tail; often feeds during daylight hours.

BLACK SWIFT

Cypseloides niger

The fast-flying Black Swift is the largest of the North American swifts. It forages high in the air when skies are clear; periods of rain or low overcast bring it closer to the ground. Swifts hunt insects on the wing for much of the day, but as the sun sets they rocket back home to spend the night atop their nests. • In northern California, small, isolated, semi-colonial groups of Black Swifts nest exclusively on steep, vertical walls behind inland waterfalls and on ocean sea cliffs. Few observers are lucky enough to see a Black Swift nest: not only are these birds limited by their distribution, but their nests are well-concealed within tight rock crevices or behind sheets of cascading spray. Swifts cast a characteristic boomerang silhouette in flight. They are shaped much like swallows—long, tapering wings, small bills, wide gape and long, sleek bodies—but swifts and swallows are not closely related.

ID: black overall; slender, sleek body; whitish-tipped feathers around the forehead; very small legs. *In flight:* long, tapering wings angle backward; fairly long, slightly forked tail; variably slow to rapid, shallow wingbeats; often glides in broad circles.
Size: *L* 7 in.
Status: locally rare to uncommon from early May to late September; most migrants are detected along the coast from mid-May to early June; breeds at widely scattered sites; total population is small.
Habitat: *Breeding:* steep, usually wet cliffs in interior canyons and along the ocean coast. *Foraging* and *In migration:* over forests, woodlands, canyons, valleys, savannah and even cities.
Nesting: semi-colonial; on a cliff in a crevice, in a cavity or on a ledge, often near or behind a waterfall; nest is made of moss, mud and algae; pair incubates 1 white egg for 24–27 days; both adults feed the young.
Feeding: on the wing; eats flying insects, especially stoneflies, caddisflies and mayflies; often seen feeding high in the sky during daylight hours.

Voice: high-pitched *plik-plik-plik-plik*; not often heard away from the vicinity of nest sites.
Similar Species: *Vaux's Swift* (p. 218): smaller; lighter color overall; pale throat and rump; short, stubby tail. *White-throated Swift* (p. 219): white underneath from the chin to the vent; white flank patches; white tips to the secondaries.

VAUX'S SWIFT
Chaetura vauxi

In late summer and early fall, increasingly large flocks of Vaux's Swifts circle above towns and cities in tight groups prior to plunging collectively into chimneys. Some birders know Vaux's as 'town birds.' • Migrating flocks of hundreds, sometimes thousands, of swifts appear along the coast in spring, when fog and low cloud-cover cause them to become more detectable. • When not flying, swifts use their small, strong claws to cling to vertical surfaces. • John Kirk Townsend named this bird after William Sansom Vaux, an eminent mineralogist. Although Vaux was deserving of the honor, it is ironic that one of America's most aerially inclined birds is named for a man whose passion was for earth-bound treasures.

ID: brownish-gray overall; paler throat and rump. *In flight:* brown-gray upperparts; lighter underparts; pale throat; short, squared-off tail; long wings taper backward.
Size: *L* 5 in.
Status: uncommon to locally common migrant from late March to mid-May and from mid-August into October; locally fairly common breeder from early April to September; extremely rare and sporadic local winter visitor.
Habitat: *Breeding:* coastal coniferous forests of coast redwood and Douglas-fir or interior forests of mixed oaks and conifers. *Foraging* and *In migration:* over forest openings, burned-over forests, meadows, rivers and lakes; in migration may roost in chimneys or crevices in buildings.
Nesting: in a natural tree cavity, such as a woodpecker hole, burned-out hollow or broken-off top; uses chimneys widely; pair uses sticky saliva to glue sticks, twigs and conifer needles to the inner wall of the cavity; pair incubates 4–5 white eggs for 18–19 days; both adults feed the young.
Feeding: long-sustained cruises on the wing, often just above treetops; feeds almost entirely on flying insects, including flies, moths, ants and aphids; often seen feeding high in the sky in the company of Violet-green Swallows.
Voice: call is a clipped, chittering *id-id-id-IS-ziz!*
Similar Species: *Black Swift* (p. 217): black; much larger overall; longer, shallowly forked tail. *White-throated Swift* (p. 219): light and dark patterning on the underparts. *Bank Swallow* (p. 273): dark breast band on the white underparts. *Northern Rough-winged Swallow* (p. 272): dirty white underparts; heavier wings; larger tail.

WHITE-THROATED SWIFT

Aeronautes saxatalis

This avian marvel is one of the most ambitious frequent fliers in California skies. Only brief, cliff-clinging rest periods and annual nesting duties keep this bird out of the air—the White-throated Swift feeds, drinks, bathes and even mates while flying. • White-throated Swifts ask little more than persistently fair skies and a vertical or even overhanging rock face in which to nest. Southerly coastal cliffs, Sierran canyons and Great Basin rimrocks all support swifts, as do the concrete canyons of the urban wilderness. • During its lifetime, the average White-throated Swift is likely to travel more than a million miles—enough to take it around the earth more than 40 times! It is also considered the fastest North American swift, timed at up to 200 mph. At that speed, this native Californian would certainly rank among the fastest birds in the world.

ID: slender, sleek body; dark upperparts; white throat tapering to the belly; black flanks with white patches. *In flight:* long, tapering wings angle backward; slightly forked tail is often held in a point.

Size: L 6–7 in.

Status: rare to locally abundant breeder from mid-March to mid-October; uncommon to fairly common visitor from mid-October to mid-March; some are resident and some are probably highly transient.

Habitat: forages widely over a variety of open habitats. *Breeding:* on cliffs and canyon walls in the mountains and foothills; also on tall buildings, freeway overpasses and under bridges.

Nesting: colonial; in a crack or crevice on a cliff face; shallow saucer of twigs and conifer needles is glued together with saliva; pair incubates 4–5 eggs for 18–19 days.

Feeding: on the wing, flying perhaps hundreds of miles each day; feeds almost entirely on flying insects.

Voice: loud, shrill, descending laugh: *skee-jee-ee-ee-ee-ee-ee-ee*.

Similar Species: *Vaux's Swift* (p. 218) and *Black Swift* (p. 217): lack the white underparts and flanks. *Bank Swallow* (p. 273): all-white underparts except for the dark collar; broader wings. *Violet-green Swallow* (p. 271) and *Tree Swallow* (p. 270): all-white underparts; broader wings.

219

BLACK-CHINNED HUMMINGBIRD
Archilochus alexandri

A suburban Central Valley garden bursting with nectar-rich native wildflowers and sheltering trees would certainly be heaven for the Black-chinned Hummingbird. Add a hummingbird feeder that is regularly cleaned and stocked with a fresh sugarwater mixture (4 parts water, 1 part sugar), and your backyard could become a summer hummingbird attraction. • The Black-chinned Hummingbird is the western counterpart of the Ruby-throated Hummingbird of the East. The females of these two species are virtually indistinguishable in the field. • Naturalist and hummingbird taxonomist H.G.L. Reichenbach was deeply influenced by Greek mythology. He named several hummingbird genera after Greeks—Archilochus was a notable Greek poet. The species name *alexandri* honors a doctor who collected specimens in Mexico.

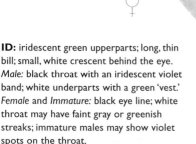

ID: iridescent green upperparts; long, thin bill; small, white crescent behind the eye. *Male:* black throat with an iridescent violet band; white underparts with a green 'vest.' *Female* and *Immature:* black eye line; white throat may have faint gray or greenish streaks; immature males may show violet spots on the throat.

Size: L 3–3 1/2 in.

Status: rare to common migrant and breeder from April to September.

Habitat: *Breeding:* in lowland riparian woodlands, orchards and shrub-filled canyons. *In migration* and *Post-breeding:* may feed in gardens and meadows in the foothills and mountains.

Nesting: tiny cup nest of plant down and spider webs is saddled atop a branch; female incubates 2 eggs for up to 16 days.

Feeding: hovers in the air and probes flowers for nectar; eats small insects and takes sugarwater from feeders.

Voice: soft, high-pitched, warbling courtship songs; buzz and chip alarm calls; male's wings buzz in flight.

Similar Species: *Broad-tailed, Rufous* (p. 224), *Allen's* (p. 225) and *Calliope* (p. 223) *hummingbirds:* females and immatures have rufous or peach color on the sides and flanks. *Costa's Hummingbird* (p. 222): male's violet gorget extends onto the crown and down sides of the throat; female has more white at the tail tip and has a shorter bill and a different call. *Anna's Hummingbird* (p. 221): female has more gray and green on the underparts and red spotting on the throat.

ANNA'S HUMMINGBIRD
Calypte anna

Northern California residents meet a wide variety of hummingbirds, and the male Anna's Hummingbird stands out in the crowd: no other male hummingbird has its head and neck draped in a rose-red splendor. • Anna's Hummingbirds nest in cities, backyard gardens, chaparral, oak woodlands and orchards. Following the mid-winter to early-spring nesting period, most Anna's undergo a post-breeding movement northward or to higher elevations to take advantage of the abundant blooms of late spring. In late summer, most Anna's retreat to warmer lowlands where they will spend the remainder of the year. Anna's is the only hummingbird common in northern California during winter.

ID: iridescent emerald green upperparts; pale grayish underparts; long, thin bill. *Male:* rosy-pink throat and head; deep greenish wash across the lower breast and belly. *Female:* green crown; rose-flecked throat; light green flanks.

Size: L 3¹/₂–4 in.

Status: uncommon to abundant year-round resident at middle and lower elevations; increasingly common southward; local east of the Cascade-Sierra, sometimes in winter.

Habitat: warmer, semi-open, lightly wooded country outside of high mountains; retreats to lowlands and towns in winter.

Nesting: on a tree branch, in a shrub, among vines or under sheltered eaves; female builds a small cup of plant fibers, spider webs and lichen that is lined with plant down and occasionally feathers; female incubates 2 white eggs for 14–19 days; female feeds the young.

Feeding: probes for nectar while hovering at flowers; also takes some insects and sugarwater.

Voice: unique; male utters a squeaky, rambling song that suggests a cricket in the shop for a tune-up; call is an incisive *chick*.

Similar Species: male is distinctive. *Allen's Hummingbird* (p. 225) and *Rufous Hummingbird* (p. 224): females have rufous-brown flanks. *Costa's Hummingbird* (p. 222) and *Black-chinned Hummingbird* (p. 220): females are whiter below, have unmarked or finely spotted throats and are smaller; male Costa's has a dark violet head and an extended gorget that does not completely encompass the eye.

221

COSTA'S HUMMINGBIRD

Calypte costae

Among the ripple effects of suburban sprawl in northern California has been the subtle northward advance of Costa's Hummingbirds into the region. Once restricted to desert washes and dry hillsides, these tiny birds are now increasingly attracted to the exotic flowering trees and shrubs common in parks and neighborhoods. Spring, late summer and even winter sightings have been recorded as far north as Del Norte and Siskiyou counties.

ID: small; green upperparts; pale underparts. *Male:* amethyst purple crown and throat, extending down the shoulders. *Female:* whitish beneath; unmarked throat; white tips on the tail corners.

Size: L 3–3¹/₂ in.

Status: local, rare to uncommon breeder from mid-March to late September; occurs rarely in most of northern California, generally as an occasional visitor at feeders.

Habitat: dry slopes of chaparral or coastal sage scrub as well as suburban parks and gardens with a variety of flowering plants.

Nesting: fairly close to the ground on a horizontal branch in a shrub or small tree, often in a yucca or cactus; female builds a tiny cup of plant fibers, flowers, leaf bits, feathers and spider webs; female incubates 2 white eggs for 15–18 days.

Feeding: probes for nectar while hovering at flowers; also takes some insects and sugarwater; favors native desert plants.

Voice: call-note is a short *tsik* or a high, metallic *tink* or *pit,* often issued in rapid, twittering series; displaying male also gives a high, thin *zing* or whiny whistle that sounds like an old-fashioned brass ring-whistle.

Similar Species: *Anna's Hummingbird* (p. 221): larger; dingier gray-green underparts; male has a rose-red crown and a throat gorget that encompasses the eye. *Rufous Hummingbird* (p. 224): male has a red-orange throat, back and tail; female has rusty flanks and a finely spotted throat. *Calliope Hummingbird* (p. 223): male has a green crown and a distinctive 'candy-striped' gorget pattern. *Black-chinned Hummingbird* (p. 220): female is almost indistinguishable from female Costa's.

CALLIOPE HUMMINGBIRD

Stellula calliope

Glistening in the slanting rays of sunlight announcing dawn in a Sierran meadow, the iridescent gorget of the male Calliope Hummingbird suggests nectar dripping from the bird's needle-like bill. • As females dance and feed among clusters of spring wildflowers, males compete for attention by flashing their seductive *haute couture* between dazzling high-speed dips and dives. • This is North America's smallest bird, and it is also the smallest long-distance migrant: individuals routinely travel up to 5000 miles in a year. Contrary to myth, hummingbirds never hitch rides on the backs of eagles or geese. • Novice birdwatchers often ponder the pronunciation of this bird's name. It is generally accepted as 'kuh-LYE-o-pee.'

ID: miniscule; iridescent green upperparts; rather short bill; at rest, tail-tip falls just short of the wing tips. *Male:* narrow, candy red gorget streaks extend down the otherwise white throat from the bill; white breast and belly; light green flanks. *Female:* white underparts; peach-colored flanks; fine, dark green spots on the throat; shortish bill and tail.
Size: *L* 3¹/₄ in.
Status: rare to locally common breeder from late March to early September; scarce to locally uncommon spring migrant in lowlands; very rare coastally.
Habitat: mountain meadows, streamside thickets, regenerating burned areas, and shrubby hillsides interspersed among montane and subalpine forests between 4000 and 9000 ft.
Nesting: saddled on a branch under foliage or on an overhanging conifer branch; tiny cup nest is made of plant down, moss, lichen and spider webs; often builds over previously used nests; female incubates 2 eggs for up to 16 days.

Feeding: probes flowers for nectar while hovering; also eats small insects and takes sugarwater from feeders.
Voice: high-pitched, chattering *tsew* note.
Similar Species: *Rufous Hummingbird* (p. 224) and *Allen's Hummingbird* (p. 225): slightly larger overall; longer tail and bill; female often has red spotting on the throat. *Broad-tailed Hummingbird:* noticeably larger overall; longer tail and bill; female shows rufous in the tail. *Costa's* (p. 222), *Anna's* (p. 221) and *Black-chinned* (p. 220) hummingbirds: females lack the peach-colored flanks.

RUFOUS HUMMINGBIRD
Selasphorus rufus

The tiny Rufous Hummingbird is, like the Western Tanager and Townsend's Solitare, the northernmost representative of a family with mostly tropical affiliations. This hummingbird breeds as far north as southern Alaska, extending southward throughout most of the Pacific Northwest. In northern California, the Rufous Hummingbird is known only as a migrant. It may nest along the northernmost California coast, but the great similarity of this species to the Allen's Hummingbird makes it difficult to be sure. • Male hummers are aggressively territorial. This behavior underlies the remarkable fiestiness so evident wherever hummingbirds gather about a concentrated food source. • Males abandon females at the onset of nesting and drift inland to higher elevations beginning as early as mid-May. Females and immatures follow, with the entire population ultimately moving southward through the late-blooming mountain meadows and brushlands toward Mexico.

ID: long, thin, black bill; mostly rufous tail. *Male:* orange-brown back, tail and flanks; iridescent orange-red throat; green crown; white breast and belly; some have green backs. *Female:* green back; red-spotted throat; rufous sides and flanks contrast with the white underparts.

Size: L 3¹/₄–3¹/₂ in.

Status: fairly common to abundant migrant from early February to late April, with a peak in March; reappears at higher elevations in late spring, remaining until September; a few individuals linger well into early winter at lowland hummingbird feeders.

Habitat: nearly any habitat offering abundant flowers.

Nesting: saddled on a drooping conifer bough; tiny cup nest of plant down and spider webs is covered with lichens; female incubates 2 eggs for up to 14 days.

Feeding: probes mostly red flowers for nectar while hovering; also eats small insects, sap and sugarwater.

Voice: call is a low *chewp chewp*; also utters a rapid and exuberant confrontation call, *ZEE-chuppity-chup!*

Similar Species: *Allen's Hummingbird* (p. 225): male has a green back; female is indistinguishable. *Calliope Hummingbird* (p. 223) and *Broad-tailed Hummingbird*: much less rufous in the tails; much paler sides and flanks; females lack the red spotting on the throat. *Anna's Hummingbird* (p. 221): green back and flanks; male is slightly larger and has a rosy crown and gorget.

MIGRANT ONLY

ALLEN'S HUMMINGBIRD

Selasphorus sasin

Most Allen's Hummingbirds arrive in northern California between mid-January and mid-March, timing their appearances to coincide with the first flowering of native shrubs. To attract pollinators (insects and hummingbirds), plants produce colorful flowers with sweet, energy-rich nectar. • Male Allen's Hummingbirds are quick to establish territories among coastal scrub, chaparral, eucalyptus and cypress groves, as well as in parks and gardens. These small, pugnacious birds perch high atop shrubs and trees, surveying their territories from a commanding station. • The drab-colored female incubates the eggs in a nest no greater in diameter than a silver dollar. Tiny, well-concealed hummingbird nests are seldom seen unless they are built in a backyard garden.

♂

ID: iridescent green head and back; long, dark bill; red flanks. *Male:* bright orange-red throat; white breast; rufous vest. *Female:* red-spotted throat; white underparts.
Size: *L* 3¹/₄–3¹/₂ in.
Status: uncommon to common migrant from late-January to mid-April and from mid-July through August; common breeder from March to June.
Habitat: nearly any well-vegetated area with plenty of flowers; coastal sage scrub, mixed coastal forests, soft chaparral, riparian woodlands, canyons and ravines, oak woodlands and suburban parks and gardens.
Nesting: on a tree branch or shrub; female builds a small cup of plant fibers, mosses, lichen and spider webs lined with plant down; may improve and reuse old nests;

female incubates 2 white eggs for 17–22 days; female feeds the young.
Feeding: probes for nectar while hovering at flowers; also takes some insects and sugarwater; favors red tubular flowers, such as salmonberry, tree tobacco and paintbrush.
Voice: call is series of *chup* notes and an excited chatter.
Similar Species: *Anna's Hummingbird* (p. 221): male has a rose throat and crown; female has grayish flanks and a rose-spotted throat. *Rufous Hummingbird* (p. 224): migrant; male usually has a rufous back; female is indistinguishable.

BELTED KINGFISHER
Ceryle alcyon

N ever far from rivers, lakes, or coastal waterways, the Belted Kingfisher is generally found perched on a bare branch that extends over a productive patch of water. This bird is easily identified by its outsized head and bill, shaggy, blue crest and distinctive, rattling call. As its name suggests, the kingfisher preys primarily on fish. With a precise headfirst dive, it can catch fish up to 2 ft beneath the water's surface. • During the breeding season, a pair of kingfishers will typically share the effort in excavating a nest burrow. They use their bills to chip away at the soil and then kick loose material out of the tunnel with their tiny feet. • Female kingfishers maintain a traditional avian role in reproduction, but they are more colorful than their male counterparts. • Alcyon (Halcyone) was the daughter of the wind god in Greek mythology; she and her husband were transformed into kingfishers.

ID: shaggy, blue crest; blue breast band; white collar; long, dagger-shaped bill; very short legs; blue upperparts; white underwings; small, white patch in front of the eye. *Female:* rust-colored 'belt'. *Male:* no 'belt.' *In flight:* ragged, flopping flight.
Size: L 11–14 in.
Status: uncommon year-round resident; uncommon to locally fairly common migrant and visitor from late August to April; widespread in summer.
Habitat: most freshwater and saltwater habitats with shoreline perching sites; requires nearby earthen banks or cliffs for summer nesting.
Nesting: in a cavity at the end of an earth burrow; pair dig up to 7 ft deep with their bills and claws; pair incubates 6–7 eggs for up to 24 days.

Feeding: dives headfirst, either from a perch or from a hover 10–50 ft above the water; eats mostly small fish and aquatic invertebrates.
Voice: fast, repetitive rattle *crrrr-crrrr-crrrr-crrrr*, like a teacup shaking on a saucer.
Similar Species: none.

LEWIS'S WOODPECKER

Melanerpes lewis

This northern California resident is unique among its woodpecker relatives not only for its green-and-pink coloration, but because it does much of its foraging as flycatchers do, catching insects on the wing. It frequently perches alone in semi-open country at the tops of oaks or pines or atop poles and snags. • Lewis's Woodpeckers often fly in a crow-like fashion, crossing the sky with slow, floppy wingbeats. • Competition with European Starlings and the loss of extensive snag habitat through modern wildfire supression has greatly diminished this woodpecker's numbers. Fall and winter concentrations still occur in areas with abundant oak mistletoe, a favored cold-weather berry source. • These large, dark woodpeckers are named for Meriwether Lewis, co-leader of the western 'Expedition of Discovery' in the early 1800s. Although Lewis was not formally trained as a naturalist, his diary details a great many concise and original observations of natural history.

ID: dark green upperparts; dark red face; pale gray breast and collar; pinkish belly; dark undertail coverts; sharp, stout bill. *Immature:* brown head and face; brown breast; lacks red in the face and in the light gray collar.

Size: *L* 11 in.

Status: complex; rare to locally fairly common resident; irregular, in many locales present some years and absent others.

Habitat: broken or burned-over pine forests, pinyon pine–juniper and gray pine–oak woodlands, open riparian woodlands, ranch windbreaks and isolated groves.

Nesting: excavates a cavity in a dead or dying tree; pair incubates 6–7 white eggs for about 15 days.

Feeding: flycatches for flying invertebrates; probes into cracks and crevices for invertebrates; eats acorns and mistletoe berries locally in winter.

Voice: nearly silent away from the nest; utters a harsh series of *chur* notes.

Similar Species: *Other woodpeckers:* none is dark green in color; all fly with pronounced undulations.

227

ACORN WOODPECKER
Melanerpes formicivorus

The highly social Acorn Woodpecker is well known for its unique, communal lifestyle. These woodpeckers live in cohesive family groups of up to 16 birds, which commonly stay together year-round to protect communal food-storage and nesting sites. During the breeding season, only one or two pairs will actually mate and produce eggs, which are laid in a single, large nest cavity. Non-breeding members of the group remain with the breeding couples to help incubate the eggs, raise the young and protect their communal feeding territory. • The Acorn Woodpecker eats a variety of food items, but almost half its diet consists of acorns that are harvested by the family group and stored in hole-studded 'granary trees' for later consumption. An ancient, standing, dead valley oak or sycamore serving as a larder may be perforated with up to 50,000 holes. • When it comes time to diversify its palate, the Acorn Woodpecker prefers to glean insects from tree bark or catch them on the wing during short, swooping flights.

♂

ID: primarily glossy black upperparts; clown-like white patches on the face, throat, rump and upperside of the wings; throat is often yellowish; black breast and streaking on the otherwise white underparts; pale eyes. *Male:* red crown and nape. *Female:* red only on the nape.

Size: L 9 in.

Status: uncommon to locally abundant year-round resident throughout most of wooded northern California; very local in the northeast.

Habitat: closely associated with many species of oak; also found in riparian woodlands and parks.

Nesting: all members of the group help to excavate a cavity in a dead tree or branch; nesting groups include up to 7 breeding males, 3 breeding females and various non-breeding relatives; both breeders and helpers incubate the eggs and raise the young in rotating shifts.

Feeding: omnivorous diet consists primarily of acorns and insects; acorns are harvested in fall and stored in holes drilled into bark or standing dead wood; insects (especially ants) are gleaned from bark and foliage or are caught on the wing; may eat fruit and seeds; may also visit sapsucker wells for insects and sap.

Voice: call is a raucous *Jay-cup, Jay-cup, Jay-cup*, often becoming a chorus.

Similar Species: *White-headed Woodpecker* (p. 235): white face and throat; black underparts and rump.

WILLIAMSON'S SAPSUCKER

Sphyrapicus thyroideus

In most woodpeckers the sexes look very much alike, but they are so different in the Williamson's Sapsucker that for years confused naturalists described them as separate species. • Woodpeckers' feet are specially designed to allow them to move vertically up and down tree-trunks: two toes face forward, another toe points off at a 90-degree angle, and the small hind toe (which is missing in three-toed woodpeckers) generally points backward. Sapsuckers hitch effortlessly up and down tree-trunks in search of sap, adult insects and larvae, their stiff, pointed tail feathers propping them upright. • In most parts of their range, Williamson's Sapsuckers are confined to higher-elevation forests where pines, true firs and aspen are prevalent. • This sapsucker is named in honor of Robert S. Williamson, a topographical engineer and U.S. Army lieutenant who lead the Pacific Railroad Survey across Oregon and northern California during the mid-1800s.

ID: *Male:* black overall; white 'mustache' and eyebrow; broad white wing patch; yellow belly; red chin; black-and-white flanks. *Female:* brown head; brown-and-white barring on the back and wings; black bib; yellow wash on the belly. *In flight:* both sexes show a white rump.
Size: *L* 9 in.
Status: uncommon to locally fairly common year-round resident; most apparent from April to October.
Habitat: montane and subalpine forests from 5200–9800 ft (particularly where lodgepole pines are abundant); may use a variety of forest types and pinyon pine stands at lower elevations during winter.
Nesting: male excavates a cavity in a tree-trunk or a dead tree limb; often uses the same tree, but a different cavity, the following year; pair incubates 4–6 eggs for 12–14 days.

Feeding: hammers a series of small, square wells in living trees; eats sap and insects from sapwells; occasionally eats berries and flycatches for insects.
Voice: loud, shrill *chur-cheeur-cheeur;* tapping is irregular and slow, with a Morse code rhythm.
Similar Species: *Red-breasted Sapsucker* (p. 231): all-red head. *Red-naped Sapsucker* (p. 230): red crown and nape patch. *Northern Flicker* (p. 237): red underwings; large dark spots on the underparts. *Other woodpeckers:* lack the bold, white wing patch, red chin and yellow belly wash.

RED-NAPED SAPSUCKER
Sphyrapicus nuchalis

The Red-naped Sapsucker has adopted a variation of the typical woodpecker foraging strategy: it drills lines of parallel 'wells' in the bark of living trees and shrubs. Sapsuckers are quick to make their rounds once the wells are filled with pools of sap, collecting trapped bugs and oozing fluid from various sites. Sapsuckers don't actually suck sap; they lap it up with a long tongue that resembles a frayed paintbrush. This deliberate foraging practice has convinced some people that this bird is capable of planning. • Some people worry that the activities of this sapsucker will kill ornamental trees and shrubs, but most healthy plants can withstand a series of sapsucker wells. • Kinglets, warblers, waxwings and hummingbirds are known to feed from sapsucker wells.

♂

ID: red forehead; red patch behind the ear; black-and-white striped head; black bib; yellow wash on the breast; black-and-white wings and back; white rump; light yellow upper back with fine black streaking. *Male:* red chin and throat. *Female:* white chin; red throat.
Size: *L* 8¹/₂ in.
Status: rare migrant and visitor from late October to early March; uncommon to locally fairly common breeder from March to October.
Habitat: *Breeding:* aspen stands, pine-aspen forests, montane riparian woodlands and tall willows at 4500–9500 ft. *Winter* and *In migration:* lower-elevation riparian woodlands, orchards, tree groves and shade trees.
Nesting: excavates a cavity in a living deciduous tree; occasionally uses the same tree for 2 years, making a new hole; cavity is lined with wood chips; pair incubates 4–5 eggs for 13 days.

Feeding: hammers a series of small, square wells in living trees; eats the sap and insects from the wells; frequently catches flying insects.
Voice: call is a cat-like *meow*; tapping is irregular and Morse code–like.
Similar Species: *Hairy Woodpecker* (p. 234) and *Downy Woodpecker* (p. 233): lack the red forehead and black bib. *Williamson's Sapsucker* (p. 229): male lacks red on the crown and nape. *Red-breasted Sapsucker* (p. 231): all-red head and breast.

RED-BREASTED SAPSUCKER

Sphyrapicus ruber

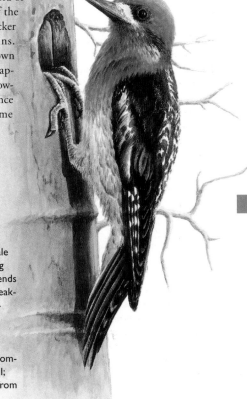

B old in appearance, yet shy and inconspicuous in nature, the Red-breasted
Sapsucker is a woodpecker most birders desire to meet. • Sapsuckers drill rows
of small holes in the trunks of trees and tall shrubs, later collecting oozing sap
and trapped insects. They also dine on the soft cambium layer growing beneath the
bark. • Birdwatchers from the East who meet
a Red-breasted Sapsucker in the Sierra or
Coast Ranges are often reminded of the
similar-looking Red-headed Woodpecker
found east of the Rocky Mountains.
• The Red-breasted Sapsucker is known
to interbreed with the Red-naped Sapsucker. These two species and the Yellow-
bellied Sapsucker of the East were once
considered various forms of the same
species.

ID: red head, chin, throat and breast; pale
yellow to whitish belly; large, white wing
patch; long, white 'mustache' stripe extends
from the base of the forehead; dark streaking on the sides and flanks; black upperparts; dark back is marked with white;
white rump. *Juvenile:* browner overall.
Size: L 8^1/$_2$ in.
Status: irregular, uncommon to fairly common visitor from October to early April;
uncommon to fairly common breeder from
April to September.
Habitat: *Breeding:* moist coastal coniferous
forests, interior coniferous forests and
broken mixed woodlands, often close to
riparian areas. *Winter and In migration:* in a
wide variety of lowland woodlands, parks,
gardens and exotic tree plantations.
Nesting: excavates a cavity in a tree, often
deciduous, where the heartwood has been
softened by fungus; 3–6 white eggs are
incubated for 12–13 days.
Feeding: hammers a series of small, square
wells in living trees; eats the sap and insects
from the wells; may also flycatch for insects.

Voice: loud spring call is a hoarse, descending *QUEEoh*! in series; drumming is a short
burst followed by irregular Morse code–like
beats; softer *cheer* calls are frequent.

Similar Species: *Red-naped
Sapsucker* (p. 230): black-
and-white striping on the
head; black breast band.
Williamson's Sapsucker
(p. 229): white striping
on a black head; black
breast.

231

NUTTALL'S WOODPECKER
Picoides nuttallii

The Nuttall's Woodpecker is a permanent resident in foothill and valley-bottom woodlands throughout much of the interior and near the Pacific Coast from Sonoma County southward. Only in northern Baja California and around Lake Tahoe does its range extend beyond California. • Hopping acrobatically on the undersides of branches and deftly scaling tree-trunks, the Nuttall's Woodpecker probes in crevices and flakes off bark in search of wood-boring insects, insect eggs and ants. Although it has a preference for mature oak forests, individuals are occasionally encountered in evergreen and deciduous woodlands. • This energetic woodpecker was named for one of America's early naturalists, Thomas Nuttall. Nuttall was primarily a botanist, but he traveled widely across the country, observing all aspects of natural history. Nuttall's many contributions to ornithology include his *Manual of Ornithology of the United States and Canada,* the first field guide ever written about North American birds.

ID: black-and-white barring on the back; black cheek; dark spots on the flanks.
Male: rich red cap on the back of the head.
Female: no red cap.
Size: L 7–7^1/$_2$ in.
Status: uncommon to very common year-round resident.
Habitat: oak and streamside woodlands; in fall, migrates to higher elevations where pine-oak woodlands dominate below 6000 ft.
Nesting: in a cavity in a live or dead tree, excavated mostly by the male; uses a new cavity every year; may excavate a hole in a fencepost, utility pole or large shrub; pair incubates 3–4 white eggs for about 14 days; both adults feed the young.
Feeding: eats mostly insects taken from trees and shrubs; may also take fruits, nuts, seeds and berries; often forage in pairs.

Voice: calls are a high-pitched whinny and a loud, 2-syllable *pitik;* drums even taps for 1–2 seconds.
Similar Species: *Acorn Woodpecker* (p. 228): all-black back. *Downy Woodpecker* (p. 233) and *Hairy Woodpecker* (p. 234): lack the barring on the back. *Williamson's Sapsucker* (p. 229): male has an all-black back; female has a brown head and a dark breast patch. *Black-backed Woodpecker* (p. 236): all-black back; prefers coniferous habitat.

DOWNY WOODPECKER

Picoides pubescens

A regular patron of backyard suet feeders, the Downy Woodpecker is often the first woodpecker a novice birdwatcher can identify with confidence. It is the smallest and most familiar North American woodpecker, and is the most likely species to be found in neighborhood ravines and wooded city parks. Like many other small birds, Downies are generally approachable and tolerant of humans. Once you become familiar with its dainty appearance, it's not long before you recognize it by its soft taps and brisk staccato calls as it gleans the limbs of neighborhood trees. • This woodpecker's small bill is amazingly effective at poking into tiny crevices and extracting dormant invertebrates and wood-boring grubs. Like many woodpeckers, it has feathered nostrils to filter out the sawdust it produces while hammering. To cushion the shock of years of hammering, woodpeckers have a flexible, reinforced skull, strong neck and bill muscles, and a brain that is tightly packed in a protected cranium.

ID: clear white to ashy-white belly and back; black wings are barred with white; black eye line and crown; short, stubby bill; mostly black tail; white outer tail feathers are spotted with black. *Male:* small, red patch on the back of the head. *Female:* no red patch.
Size: L 6–7 in.
Status: uncommon to fairly common year-round resident.
Habitat: most wooded environments below 6000 ft, especially riparian woodlands; sometimes city parks, suburban gardens and orchards; avoids higher forests and dense stands of large conifers.
Nesting: pair excavates a cavity in a dying or decaying trunk or limb over more than 2 weeks; cavity is lined with wood chips; incubates 4–5 eggs for 11–13 days.
Feeding: forages on trunks and especially on branches; chips, taps and probes for insect eggs, cocoons, larvae and adults; also eats nuts and seeds; often attracted to suet feeders.
Voice: spring 'song' is a brief, thin, descending stutter; call-note is a weak *pik*.
Similar Species: *Hairy Woodpecker* (p. 234): larger; bill is as long as the head is wide; no spots on the white outer tail feathers. *Nuttall's Woodpecker* (p. 232): black spots on the sides; dark barring on the flanks; lacks the white back patch.

233

HAIRY WOODPECKER

Picoides villosus

A second or third look is often required to confirm the identity of the Hairy Woodpecker, which is easily confused with its smaller relative, the Downy Woodpecker. In a backyard that offers a generous supply of tasty suet (usually a mixture of fat, small nuts and seeds) it is not uncommon to see both species vying for a position at the feeder—a convenient situation that will allow you to make a sight and sound comparison. • The secret to a woodpecker's wood-boring ways is hidden in its bill. Most woodpeckers have very long tongues, in some cases more than four times the length of the bill. Such a long tongue is made possible by twin structures that wrap around the perimeter of the skull and store the tongue in much the same way that a measuring tape is stored in its case. Also, the tip of the tongue is sticky with saliva, and it is finely barbed to seize reluctant wood-boring insects.

ID: white to ashy-white belly; black wings are spotted with white; black cheek and crown; bill is about as long as the head is wide; black tail with white outer feathers. *Male:* small red patch on the back of the head. *Female:* no red patch.

Size: L 7^1/$_2$–9^1/$_2$ in.

Status: very common year-round resident.

Habitat: most wooded environments (especially coniferous forests) below 8500 ft; occasionally found up to 10,000 ft in the central Sierra Nevada.

Nesting: pair excavates a nest site in a live or decaying trunk or limb over more than 2 weeks; cavity is lined with wood chips; pair incubates 4–5 eggs for up to 12 days.

Feeding: forages on trunks and branches; chips, hammers and probes bark for insects, insect eggs, cocoons and larvae; also eats nuts, fruit and seeds; attracted to feeders, particularly suet.

Voice: loud, sharp *peek!;* harsh, ragged trill: *keek-ik-ik-ik-ik-ik.*

Similar Species: *Downy Woodpecker* (p. 233): smaller; bill is shorter than the width of the head; dark spots on white outer tail feathers. *Nuttall's Woodpecker* (p. 232): lacks the white back patch; black spots on the sides; dark barring on the flanks.

WHITE-HEADED WOODPECKER

Picoides albolarvatus

T he White-headed Woodpecker is a reclusive specialty of the mountain pine-and-fir forests of the western United States. Pine seeds are an important element of its diet, so this woodpecker forages chiefly among old or maturing forests supporting three-needle or five-needle pines. • The relatively low water content of pine seeds means that these birds must remain close to a reliable source of drinking water. • In spring, both the male and female can be heard engaging in territorial drumming. Throughout most of the year, their habit of quietly tapping the flaking loose bark high on trunks and out among the limbs causes them to remain less easily detected than their relatives.

ID: all-black plumage except for the white head, throat and wing patch; dark eyes; male has a red nape patch.

Size: *L* 9 in.

Status: uncommon to locally fairly common year-round resident.

Habitat: mountain pine forest; may also forage among red and white firs, incense-cedar, Douglas-fir and sequoia.

Nesting: adults take turns excavating a new nest cavity in a standing dead tree (usually a pine or fir); may create new holes in the same tree for many years; pair incubates 4–5 white eggs for 14 days; both parents feed the young.

Feeding: pries open cones for seeds and chips large flakes of bark for insects; gleans from trunks and needle clusters; eats mostly pine seeds and insects; also eats ants, spiders and wood-boring beetles.

Voice: call is a sharp, rattling *tea-deek* or *tea-dee-deek*.

Similar Species: *Acorn Woodpecker* (p. 228): black chin; yellowish throat; white forehead; yellow eyes are surrounded by black; rear half of the body is white except for the black tail.

BLACK-BACKED WOODPECKER
Picoides arcticus

L
ike the Great Gray Owl, the Black-backed Woodpecker reaches the southern limit of its North American range in the Sierra Nevada. The cool, fir-crowded, high-elevation forests of the Sierra Nevada echo the flavor of the Black-back's preferred habitat in Canada and Alaska. • During courtship, the Black-backed Woodpecker perches on a dead, hollow tree and drums noisily. Don't hesitate to approach this busy bird if you find one—the yellow-capped males are often so focused that they could scarcely be bothered by a passing human. • These woodpeckers are most active in recently burned forest patches where wood-boring beetles thrive under the charred bark of lodgepole pines. In years when food is scarce, a few of these birds may drift to lower elevations, rarely showing up in timbered foothill parks. • Black-backs, unlike other woodpeckers, have only three toes. • The species name *arcticus* reflects this bird's largely northern distribution.

ID: solid black back; white underparts; black barring on the sides; predominantly black head with a black 'mustache' and a single white line below the eye; 3 toes; black tail with pure white outer feathers.
Male: yellow crown.
Female: black crown.
Size: L 9–10 in.
Status: rare to uncommon local year-round resident.
Habitat: subalpine coniferous forests, particularly stands of lodgepole pine and red fir, at 7500–9000 ft; occasionally found as low as 4000 ft or up to 10,000 ft.
Nesting: excavates a cavity in a dead or dying conifer trunk or limb; excavation may take up to 12 days; pair incubates 4 eggs for up to 2 weeks.
Feeding: gleans under bark flakes for larval and adult wood-boring insects; occasionally eats berries.

Voice: call is a sharp *pik*; drums in a prolonged series of steady bursts.
Similar Species: *Williamson's Sapsucker* (p. 229): male has a red chin, black breast, white rump and large white wing patch. *Hairy Woodpecker* (p. 234): large white back patch; lacks the dark barring on the sides; male has red on the back of the head. *Nuttall's Woodpecker* (p. 232): white barring on the back; male has red on the head. *Three-toed Woodpecker:* white back with black, horizontal barring; one accepted record for California.

NORTHERN FLICKER
Colaptes auratus

Northern Flickers spend much of their time on the ground, feeding on ants and other land insects. They appear almost robin-like as they hop about in swinging strides on grassy meadows, fields, roadsides or forest clearings. • Flickers often bathe in dusty depressions (the dust particles absorb oils and bacteria), but to clean themselves more thoroughly, they preen themselves with captured ants. Ants contain formic acid, which can kill small parasites on the skin and feathers. • There are two forms of the Northern Flicker in North America: the 'Red-shafted Flicker' (red wing and tail linings and a red 'mustache' in the male) occurs in California and most areas west of the Continental Divide; the 'Yellow-shafted Flicker' (yellow wing and tail linings and a black 'mustache' in the male) typically occurs east of the divide and in the North. Intergrades with the Yellow-shafted Flicker are commonly seen in northern California from September to April. • Native peoples of the Sierra Nevada prized the salmon-red wings and tail of this bird. The bright feathers were woven together with shells and other items to be incorporated into robes and ceremonial head-dresses.

'Red-shafted Flicker'

ID: brown, barred back and wings; spotted underparts; black bib; red wing and tail linings; white rump; long bill; gray face; brown crown. *Male:* red 'mustache.' *Female:* no 'mustache.'
Size: L 13 in.
Status: common resident, migrant and winter visitor throughout northern California.
Habitat: most broken or open forests, woodlands, forest edges, fields and meadows, riparian woodlands and suburban parks and gardens to 10,000 ft; retreats from the highest elevations in winter.
Nesting: pair excavates a cavity in a dead or dying deciduous tree; builds a new cavity annually; may use nest boxes; cavity is lined with wood chips; pair incubates 5–8 eggs for up to 11 days.
Feeding: forages on the ground for ants and other terrestrial insects; also eats berries, fruits and nuts; probes bark;
sometimes flycatches; frequently visits seed and suet feeders.
Voice: spring call is a loud, laughing, rapid *wick-wick-wick-wick-wick-wick* of up to 50 notes.
Similar Species: *Female Williamson's Sapsucker* (p. 229): all-brown head; lacks the red wing and tail linings and black spots on the underparts.

PILEATED WOODPECKER
Dryocopus pileatus

With its flaming red crest, breathtaking flight and maniacal call, this impressive deep-forest dweller is successful at stopping most hikers in their tracks. Considering its laugh and quirky looks, it is no surprise that this bird once inspired a cartoon character.
• Using its powerful, dagger-shaped bill, the Pileated Woodpecker chisels out rectangular cavities in an unending search for grubs and ants. These large woodpeckers are not as frequently encountered as smaller species, because they require extensive areas in which to forage: a pair of breeding Pileated Woodpeckers generally requires more than 100 acres of mature forest to survive and successfully raise its young.
• As a primary cavity nester, the activities of the Pileated Woodpecker are essential to many other creatures: Common Mergansers, Wood Ducks, small falcons, owls and some small mammals all rely on woodpecker cavities for nesting sites. • There is no real consensus on whether this bird's name is pronounced 'pie-lee-ated' or 'pill-e-ated'—it's generally a matter of preference, sparking good-natured debate.

ID: crow-sized; predominantly black; flashy, white wing linings are visible in flight; flaming red crest; yellow eyes; stout, dark bill; white stripe running from the bill to the shoulder; white chin. *Male:* red 'mustache'; red crest extends from the forehead. *Female:* no 'mustache'; red crest starts on the crown. *Juvenile:* short, pinkish crest.
Size: L 16–19 in.
Status: uncommon but widely distributed year-round resident.
Habitat: old-growth or maturing mixed and coniferous forests from near sea level to 7500 ft; may also use lowland riparian woodlands; prefers stands with large, dead and dying trees.
Nesting: pair excavates a cavity in a dead or dying tree-trunk; excavation can take 3–6 weeks; cavity is lined with wood chips; pair incubates 4 eggs for 15–18 days.
Feeding: often hammers the base of rotting trees, creating fist-sized rectangular holes; eats carpenter ants and wood-boring beetle larvae; fond of berries and nuts.
Voice: loud, fast, laughing, rolling *yucka-yucka-yucka-yucka* that carries great distances; arresting series-call is given from a high perch; resonant, irregular *wuk…wuk-wuk…wuk* is given in flight or when anxious.
Similar Species: none.

PASSERINES

asserines are also commonly known as songbirds or perching birds. Although these terms are easier to comprehend, they are not as strictly accurate, because some passerines neither sing nor perch, and many non-passerines do sing and perch. In a general sense, however, these terms represent passerines adequately: they are among the best singers, and they are the birds most often seen perching.

It is believed that passerines, which all belong to the order Passeriformes, make up the most recent evolutionary group of birds. Theirs is the most numerous of all orders, representing nearly three-fifths of all living birds worldwide.

Passerines are grouped together based on the sum total of many morphological and molecular similarities, including such things as the number of tail and flight feathers and reproductive characteristics. All passerines share the same foot shape—three toes face forward and one faces backward—and no passerines have webbed toes. Also, all passerines have a tendon that runs along the back side of the bird's knee and tightens when the bird perches, giving it a firm grip.

Some of our most common and easily identified birds are passerines, such as the Red-winged Blackbird and House Sparrow, but the passerines also include some of the most challenging and frustrating birds to identify, until their distinct songs and calls are learned.

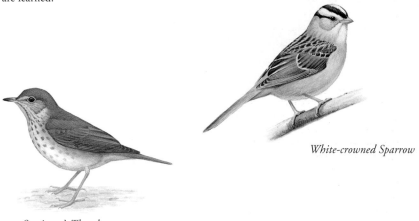

Warbling Vireo

White-crowned Sparrow

Swainson's Thrush

Golden-crowned Kinglet

OLIVE-SIDED FLYCATCHER
Contopus cooperi

During the summer breeding season, Olive-sided Flycatchers prefer to reside well up in the forest canopy where they have easy access to the plentiful flying insects that inhabit the sunny forest heights. • This flycatcher's enthusiastic call makes it a favorite with many birders: *Quick-three-beers* it cries, loudly and clearly. It's a good thing this feisty little bird has such a distinctive call, because its drab plumage and preference for treetops can make it difficult to observe. In late summer it changes its tune to a subdued but persistent *pip-pip, pip*. • Flycatchers perch with a distinctive, upright and attentive profile. Their ready-and-waiting stance allows them to quickly launch out and snatch insects that fly past. • The scientific name *Contopus* means 'short foot.'

ID: dark olive-gray 'vest'; light throat and belly; olive-brown upperparts; white rump patches; large, dark bill; no eye ring.
Size: L 7¹/₂ in.
Status: uncommon migrant from mid-April to mid-June and from August to mid-October; uncommon to locally fairly common breeder from May to August.
Habitat: *Breeding:* extensive conifer forests and stands from near sea level to 9000 ft (occasionally up to 10,500 ft); may also use exotic cypress or eucalyptus groves. *In migration:* wide variety of habitats, requiring only full-crowned trees.
Nesting: in a conifer; usually on a horizontal branch far from the trunk; nest of twigs and plant fibers is bound with spider silk; female incubates 3 eggs for 14 days.

Feeding: flycatches for insects by 'sallying,' typically from an upper-canopy or tip-top perch.
Voice: male's call is a loud, liquid *quick-three-beers*, with the 2nd note highest in pitch; position call is a snappy single-pitched *pip-pip, pip*.
Similar Species: *Western Wood-Pewee* (p. 241): smaller; lacks the white rump tufts.

WESTERN WOOD-PEWEE
Contopus sordidulus

This bird's burry, down-slurred call will usually lead you to a forest edge or clearing, where the songster sings persistently throughout the hot hours of a summer afternoon. • Wood-Pewees launch themselves into aerobatic, looping foraging ventures in search of flying insects, often returning straightaway to the same perch. • The nest of the Western Wood-Pewee is well camouflaged by both its shape and color: the completed structure resembles a mere bump on a horizontal limb. When cryptic concealment doesn't provide enough protection against predators, this flycatcher will vigorously defend its nest by chasing hawks, jays and chipmunks. • The scientific name *sordidulus* refers to its dusky, 'dirty' color.

ID: dark olive-brown upperparts; light underparts with a blurrily dark-vested look; 2 faint white wing bars; no eye ring; pale throat; slightly peaked hind-crown; dark lower mandible; light undertail coverts.
Size: L 5–6 in.
Status: uncommon to abundant migrant from early-April to early June and from mid-August to late September; widespread, common breeder from early May to August.
Habitat: most semi-open woodland and forest habitats up to 11,000 ft, including riparian and oak woodlands, mixed oak-coniferous forests and more open coniferous forests.
Nesting: on a horizontal limb in a tree; small cup nest of plant fibers is bound with spider silk; female incubates 3 eggs for 12–13 days.
Feeding: flycatches for insects.

Voice: plaintive whistle, *purREER*, that drops off at the end; song is *oom-VLIVVIT…purREER*.
Similar Species: *Olive-sided Flycatcher* (p. 240): larger; 2 white rump tufts. *Dusky* (p. 245), *Hammond's* (p. 243), *Pacific-slope* (p. 246) and *Cordilleran* (p. 247) *flycatchers*: smaller; shorter wing tips; white eye rings. *Willow Flycatcher* (p. 242): paler lower mandible; paler underparts; browner upperparts. *Gray Flycatcher* (p. 244): paler underparts are often tinged with yellow; rounder head profile; grayer overall; dips its tail persistently.

WILLOW FLYCATCHER
Empidonax traillii

As the spring movement of northern California's songbirds wanes in mid-May, Willow Flycatchers begin to appear in vernal wetlands and sapling-dotted hollows. Most of these birds ultimately pass through the area, but small numbers remain past mid-June to nest. Except for the nighthawk and Black Swift, the Willow Flycatcher is the latest of all migrants in spring. • A loss of willow habitat has led to a great decline in this bird's population: a scant 200 breeding pairs are estimated to remain in California. • The Willow Flycatcher and the Alder Flycatcher were once lumped as one species, the Traill's Flycatcher. Thomas Stewart Traill was an Englishman who helped John James Audubon find a British publisher for his book *Ornithological Biography*.

ID: olive-brown upperparts; 2 whitish wing bars; no eye ring; white throat; yellowish belly; pale olive breast.

Size: L 5 3/4 in.

Status: rare to uncommon migrant from mid-May to mid-June; locally uncommon to fairly common migrant from late July to late September; local, rare breeder from early June to late August; California populations have declined to federal Endangered status in recent years.

Habitat: riparian woodlands and thickets along streams, rivers, floodplains and at moist mountain meadows, springs and seepage areas.

Nesting: small cup nest is built in a fork of a small shrub; female incubates 3–4 eggs for 13 days.

Feeding: flycatches for insects; also gleans vegetation for invertebrates.

Voice: male's call is a quick, sneezy *fitz-bew* (up to 30 times a minute), with accent on the 1st note; position call is a liquid *wit*.

Similar Species: *Western Wood-Pewee* (p. 241): gray-olive upperparts; darker lower mandible; peaked crown. *Hammond's* (p. 243), *Dusky* (p. 245), *Pacific-slope* (p. 246) and *Cordilleran* (p. 247) *flycatchers*: fully discernable, pale eye rings. *Gray Flycatcher* (p. 244): paler gray overall; dark tip on the lower mandible; dips its tail persistently.

HAMMOND'S FLYCATCHER

Empidonax hammondii

This retiring, diminutive flycatcher makes its home beneath the shady, dense canopy of mature mountain conifers throughout the winter snowpack zone of northern California. • The Hammond's Flycatcher is easily confused with the very similar-looking Dusky Flycatcher, which often inhabits forest edges nearby. Fortunately, there are a few clues birders can use to distinguish the two. The Dusky Flycatcher prefers sun-drenched brushfields and scattered young conifers, but the Hammond's 'closets-up' within the shady, humid inner canopy of firs and pines. The Hammond's has a darker breast and a shorter tail, which is held almost vertically when the bird is perched; Dusk-ies tend to have a darker tail that contrasts with a lighter-colored rump, and it is usually held at an angle. • William Hammond, after whom this bird is named, was an army surgeon who sent animal specimens from western North America to the Smithsonian Institution for scientific classification.

breeding

ID: olive-grayish upperparts; 2 white wing bars; distinct, light eye ring; gray face; tiny, all-dark bill; light gray throat; thin, dark tail with a gray outer edge.
Size: L 5½ in.
Status: rare to locally common migrant from early April to late May and from late August to mid-October; locally common breeder from May to August.
Habitat: *Breeding:* dense mixed coniferous forests at 4000–8000 ft (especially forests supporting red fir in the Sierra, and mature Douglas-fir in the northwest). *In migration:* a variety of habitats ranging from chaparral and riparian woodlands to suburban parks and deciduous forests.
Nesting: on a limb in a coniferous tree; small cup nest of plant fibers, leaves and grass is lined with feathers and grass; female incubates 3–4 eggs for up to 15 days.

Feeding: flycatches and hover-gleans vege-tation for insects, generally well within the mid-canopy.
Voice: song is low and spiritless *dissup... wassup;* call is a soft, but incisive *peep* or *bik.*
Similar Species: *Dusky Flycatcher* (p. 245): bill and tail are slightly longer; white edges on the outer tail feathers. *Western Wood-Pewee* (p. 241) and *Willow Flycatcher* (p. 242): larger; no eye ring. *Pacific-slope Flycatcher* (p. 246) and *Cordil-leran Flycatcher* (p. 247): pale yellowish chin; yellower underparts; longer, broader bills have conspicu-ously pale lower mandibles. *Gray Flycatcher* (p. 244): paler gray overall; slightly longer, pale-based bill; dips its tail persistently.

GRAY FLYCATCHER
Empidonax wrightii

Fragrant, pine-dotted sagebrush flats of the Great Basin and the pinyon pine–juniper woodlands of the adjoining Sierran east slope are the summer home of the pale Gray Flycatcher. This bird favors a mixture of scattered dry-site conifers and an extensive growth of tall sagebrush or bitterbrush. • Helping to distinguish this *Empidonax* from its nearly identical relatives—the Dusky and Hammond's flycatchers—are the Gray's deliberate downward tail-bobbing, slender proportions and tendency to drop to the ground frequently in pursuit of insects, a useful foraging strategy in a country where frosts may occur nightly. • Spencer Fullerton Baird named this distinctly western species in honor of Charles Wright, a botanist who accompanied the Pacific Railroad's Exploratory Team during the mid-1800s.

breeding

ID: drab grayish upperparts; whitish underparts; faint eye ring; 2 thin, white wing bars; pale lower mandible with a dark tip; long tail with a thin, white border. *In fall:* olive-tinged; often sallies from a perch to the ground and back.
Size: L 5¹/₄–6 in.
Status: locally common migrant from early April to late May and from late August to early October; locally uncommon to fairly common breeder from April to mid-August.
Habitat: *Breeding:* above 4000 ft on sagebrush flats and in pine or juniper woodland; avoids dense forests; migrants commonly appear in varied habitats.
Nesting: may form loose colonies; nests in a vertical fork of a sagebrush branch or on a horizontal branch of pinyon pine or juniper; female builds a deep, bulky cup nest of grass, twigs and strips of bark; lines the nest with feathers, fur and plant down; female incubates 3–4 creamy white eggs for about 14 days.

Feeding: insects are taken by hawking or hovering.
Voice: *chawip seeahl* song is often followed by an aspirated *whea* or liquid *whilp*; call is a loud *whit*.
Similar Species: *Dusky Flycatcher* (p. 245): usually darker and plumper overall; darker lower mandible; more contrast between the upper- and underparts; does not dip its tail. *Hammond's Flycatcher* (p. 243): darker; more 'vested'; plumper; tiny, all-dark bill; often flicks its wings and short, thin tail. *Willow Flycatcher* (p. 242): browner upperparts; lower mandible is entirely pale; bolder wing bars. *Pacific-slope Flycatcher* (p. 246) and *Cordilleran Flycatcher* (p. 247): bolder eye ring; dark olive-green upperparts; yellowish underparts; lower mandible is entirely pale.

DUSKY FLYCATCHER
Empidonax oberholseri

Many novice birders might wonder why three virtually identical-looking birds, the Dusky, Hammond's and Gray flycatchers, are not just lumped together as a single species—after all, why make life so confusing? It's not surprising that even prominent ornithologists of the past considered the Dusky Flycatcher to be a subspecies of the Gray Flycatcher. However, closer inspection of collected specimens, DNA analysis and detailed studies of bird behavior and habitat requirements have revealed that these birds indeed deserve a distinct status. • The scientific name *oberholseri* honors Dr. Harry Oberholser, one of the finest 20th-century ornithologists. He worked for the U.S. Fish and Wildlife Service and the Cleveland Natural History Museum.

breeding

ID: olive-brown upperparts; 2 faint, white wing bars; light-colored eye ring; dark bill with orange at the base of the lower mandible; white throat; long, dark tail is trimmed with white.
Size: L 5–6 in.
Status: rare (coast) to fairly common migrant from mid-April to late May and from late August to September; uncommon to locally very common breeder from early May to mid-August.
Habitat: *Breeding:* montane chaparral, sapling-dotted forest openings, brushy meadows from 3000–8000 ft. *In migration:* variety of open woodland habitats, riparian woodlands and chaparral.
Nesting: in the fork of a small shrub; small cup nest of weeds, plant fibers, feathers, grass and fur; female incubates 3–4 eggs for 15–16 days.

Feeding: flycatches for aerial insects; also gleans and hover-gleans leaves, limbs and bark for larval and adult insects.
Voice: male's call is a quick, whistled *PREE-tick-preet*, rising at the end; summer song is a repeated *du…DU-hic*; call-note is a flat *wit*.
Similar Species: *Hammond's Flycatcher* (p. 243): bill and tail are slightly shorter; lacks the white edges on the outer tail feathers; prefers shady forest habitat. *Western Wood-Pewee* (p. 241) and *Willow Flycatcher* (p. 242): no eye ring. *Pacific-slope Flycatcher* (p. 246) and *Cordilleran Flycatcher* (p. 247): yellow underparts; longer, broader bill has an all-pale lower mandible. *Gray Flycatcher* (p. 244): paler gray overall; slightly longer bill; dips its tail persistently.

245

PACIFIC-SLOPE FLYCATCHER
Empidonax difficilis

Fortunately for birders, the Pacific-slope Flycatcher's song is much more distinct than its plumage. When you enter any moist woodland during spring, this flycatcher's snappy, rising *pawee!* or *tink* call is always one of the first sounds you'll hear. • This common songbird was formerly grouped with the Cordilleran Flycatcher into a single species, the Western Flycatcher. • Like other members of its family, the Pacific-slope Flycatcher hunts primarily by 'hawking'—after launching from an exposed perch, it seizes a flying insect in mid-air and then loops back to alight on the same perch it vacated moments earlier. 'Hawking' and 'sallying' are words used interchangeably with the term 'flycatching.'

ID: olive-green upperparts; yellowish throat; yellow-green underparts; almond-shaped, white eye ring; 2 pale wing bars (buffy in the juvenile); dark bill with orange lower mandible; dark wings and tail.
Size: *L* 5–6 in.
Status: common to abundant migrant from mid-March to mid-May and from late July to early October; rare winter visitor; fairly common to abundant breeder from April to late August.
Habitat: moist woodlands, mixed forests, low- to middle-elevation coniferous forests, shady, steep-walled canyons and ravines; demands full shade.
Nesting: in a crevice, on a rocky streamside ledge, in a tree cavity, on a stump, under a bridge or among the roots of an upturned tree; female builds a cup of grass, moss, rootlets, bark, leaves and lichen, lined with hair, feathers and soft plant fibers; female incubates 3–4 eggs for about 14–15 days.
Feeding: insects are taken by hawking, hovering or occasionally gleaning from branches or foliage; may also take spiders and caterpillars.
Voice: dawn song is insect-like: a series of 3 high-pitched, repeated phrases *siLEEK...tup...P'SEET!*; male's call is a single, upslurred *sweeet* or *fe-oo-eet!*; female's call is a brief, high-pitched *tink*.
Similar Species: *Willow Flycatcher* (p. 242): no eye ring; song is a reedy *fitz-bew*. *Western Wood-Pewee* (p. 241): no eye ring; dusky-colored. *Olive-sided Flycatcher* (p. 240): much larger; dark vest; song is a whistled *quick-three-beers*. *Gray Flycatcher* (p. 244) and *Dusky Flycatcher* (p. 245): lack the yellowish throat; found in sunny sites. *Hammond's Flycatcher* (p. 243): very small, all-dark bill; lacks the yellowish throat. *Cordilleran Flycatcher* (p. 247): identical song and appearance in the field; male's call is a 2-part upslurred *swee-deet* or *wee-eee*.

CORDILLERAN FLYCATCHER

Empidonax occidentalis

The Cordilleran Flycatcher and the Pacific-slope Flycatcher were formerly lumped together into one species, the Western Flycatcher. Although they are now regarded as distinct species, their similar field characteristics remain a troubling issue that perpetuates their uncertain status. • Cordilleran Flycatchers are thought to arrive in northern California around the same time as their Pacific-slope relatives, but much remains to be learned about this species' distribution and migration. • *Empidonax* is a wonderful name for this confusing, but endearing, group of flycatchers. It means 'king of the gnats'—a reflection of their amazing insect-catching abilities. • The scientific name *occidentalis* is Latin for 'western.'

ID: olive-green upperparts; yellowish throat; yellow-green underparts; almond-shaped, white eye ring; 2 pale wing bars (buffy in the juvenile); dark bill with orange lower mandible; dark wings and tail.
Size: L 5¹/₂ in.
Status: imperfectly known; uncommon to rare migrant and summer breeder from April to September.
Habitat: coniferous and riparian woodlands or shady deciduous forests, often near seepages and springs.
Nesting: in a cavity in a small tree, bank, bridge or cliff face; cavity is lined with moss, lichens, plant fibers, bark, fur and feathers; female incubates 3–4 eggs for 15 days.

Feeding: flycatches for insects.
Voice: male's call is a chipper whistle: *swee-deet.*
Similar Species: *Pacific-slope Flycatcher* (p. 246): identical song and appearance in the field; male's call is a single, upslurred *sweeet* or *fe-oo-eet. Willow Flycatcher* (p. 242) and *Western Wood-Pewee* (p. 241): no eye ring. *Hammond's Flycatcher* (p. 243) and *Dusky Flycatcher* (p. 245): lack the almond-shaped eye ring and the completely orange lower mandible; songs are very useful in field identification.

247

BLACK PHOEBE
Sayornis nigricans

The dark, handsome Black Phoebe is a routine resident of shady streamsides and other semi-open, moist habitats at lower and middle elevations throughout northern California. • An expert flycatcher, this phoebe is able to capture just about any insect that zips past its perch. Black Phoebes are seen most often sitting alert on exposed, low perches, such as fences, posts, stumps and the eaves of buildings. • In the manner of other phoebes, Black Phoebes collect a large proportion of their invertebrate prey by delicate sallies from perch to ground. In eroded streambeds without overhanging tree limbs, they resort to flycatching from stones, ranging in size from larger boulders to streamside cobble. • During cold weather, Black Phoebes tend to concentrate in protected lowlands, often around houses, outbuildings and on southern exposures. They scatter throughout suburban and urban areas in winter, occurring in greatest numbers about small lakes, ponds, parks and gardens.

ID: mostly black; white belly and undertail coverts; thin white edgings to the tail. *Immature:* dark brown upperparts; cinnamon wing bars and rump are retained well into fall.
Size: L 6³/₄ in.
Status: locally uncommon to very common year-round resident near water; retreats from higher elevations somewhat in winter.
Habitat: semi-open habitats near water, including riparian woodlands, steep-walled canyons, cities, farmlands with wet areas; occurs from sea level to 4000 ft (some wander to 10,000 ft).
Nesting: on cliffs, bridges, buildings and culverts; cup-shaped or semi-circular nest, built from vegetation, animal hair and mud,

is usually placed on a flat surface or vertical face with shelter from above; female incubates eggs; pair raises the young; may return to the same nest site over successive years.
Feeding: flycatches for aerial insects; gleans from plant foliage by fluttering or snatching; commonly takes insects from the ground or from the water's surface; regurgitates indigestible parts of prey as pellets.
Voice: song is an exclamatory *f'BEE, f'BEER!*; call-note is a penetrating *tsip!* or *tsee.*
Similar Species: none.

SAY'S PHOEBE

Sayornis saya

Unlike its close relative the Black Phoebe, this flycatcher is partial to dry environments. Say's Phoebes thrive in sun-parched grassy valleys and hot, dry canyons. Ranches straddled along northern California's grassy interior foothills provide this sweet songster with all the amenities: abandoned buildings provide a secure, sheltered nesting site that can be reused every year, and livestock conveniently stir up insects that the phoebe 'hawks' from a fencepost or other low perch. • The Say's Phoebe is the only bird whose genus and species names are derived from the same person, Thomas Say. A versatile naturalist, his primary contributions were in the field of entomology. • The name 'phoebe' comes from the call of a close relative, the Eastern Phoebe.

ID: apricot-buff belly and undertail coverts; dark tail; brown-gray breast and upperparts; dark head; no eye ring; very faint wing bars; constantly bobs its tail.

Size: *L* 7¹/₂ in.

Status: complex; locally rare to fairly common year-round; among the earliest-arriving migrants east of Cascade-Sierra.

Habitat: hot, dry canyons, ravines, rimrocks, valleys and gullies dominated by grasses and shrubs; may also use agricultural areas, scrublands; grassy coastal bluffs in winter.

Nesting: in a niche on a cliff face or beneath an eave or bridge; nest of grass, moss and fur; female incubates 4–5 eggs for up to 17 days.

Feeding: flycatches for aerial insects; also gleans buildings, vegetation, streamsides and the ground for insects; sometimes runs short distances in pursuit of prey.

Voice: song is *pitseedar*; call is a softly whistled *pee-ur.*

Similar Species: *Other flycatchers*: all lack the apricot belly.

249

ASH-THROATED FLYCATCHER
Myiarchus cinerascens

The hot midday air in the foothills of northern California often may be broken by only three sounds: distant human noises, the droning of annual cicadas and the shrill, whistled calls of Ash-throated Flycatchers. In the mind of a birder, the infrequent burry sounds from somewhere in the shadows of the heat-hazed oaks represent the voice of the dry woodlands and tall chaparral. • These flycatchers are found widely in the Pacific states and in the Southwest, yet they seem perhaps most abundant and most at home in California's broad array of arid and semi-arid oak and conifer woodlands. • Though they may spend the summer in junipers, pines or oaks, Ash-throated Flycatchers show a fondness for tree stands at lower and middle elevations, favoring communities offering an abundance of possible nest cavities. Ash-throated Flycatchers are as opportunistic as any other secondary cavity nester, using a bluebird box, junked machinery or an unused mailbox if a tree cavity cannot be found.

ID: gray-brown upperparts; gray throat and breast; yellow belly and undertail coverts; stout, dark bill; fluffy crown; 2 whitish wing bars; no eye ring; dark brown tail shows rufous in the webbing.
Size: L 7–8 in.
Status: uncommon to fairly common migrant from late March to late May and from mid-August to early October; uncommon to locally common breeder from early May to mid-August.
Habitat: *Breeding:* taller mixed chaparral, oak groves and woodlands, and riparian corridors with large old trees. *In migration:* wide variety of tree and shrub associations.
Nesting: in a natural or artificial cavity; pair amasses a nest of soft vegetation, hair and feathers; female incubates 4–5 creamy white eggs blotched with lavender and brown for about 15 days; both adults feed the young.

Feeding: forages by flying out from an inconspicuous perch to snatch prey; rarely catches prey in mid-air; tends to forage low among trees and shrubs; eats mostly insects; will take fruit, rarely small lizards and even mice.
Voice: song is a series of similar calls; distinctive *prrrt* call; also issues a burry *ka-BREER!* or a harsh, abrupt *ka-brick*; general quality of its voice vaguely suggests a referee's whistle.
Similar Species: *Western Kingbird* (p. 252): slightly larger; pale gray head; black tail with white outer edges; lacks the wing bars. *Cassin's Kingbird* (p. 251): gray head; dark tail lacks the reddish highlights; bright yellow belly; very pale wing bars are usually inconspicuous.

CASSIN'S KINGBIRD
Tyrannus vociferans

Although it is by no means a commonly seen bird in the dry interior valleys of northern California, the Cassin's Kingbird certainly makes itself known. When this bird decides to claim its territory of grassy ranchland or farmyard tree groves, it belts out a loud, tirelessly repeated call. Bold and fiesty, Cassin's Kingbirds work in pairs to defend their nesting territory, attacking larger birds, such as hawks, ravens, crows and magpies. • Assuming you are able to overlook their noisy nature, a pair of Cassin's Kingbirds nesting in your yard can be a blessing. Experts at catching pesky flying insects, kingbirds can help you to enjoy summer evening barbecues without requiring you to bathe in insect repellent first. • The scientific name *vociferans* was given to this bird in recognition of its loud calls.

ID: dark blue-gray upperparts; whitish chin; black bill; yellow belly and undertail coverts; dark wings; brown tail with thin, pale tipping; no wing bars.

Size: L 8–9 in.

Status: rare, local breeder from late March to early August, becoming somewhat more numerous southward; a few may remain over winter.

Habitat: open woodlands, dry savannahs interspersed with small tree groves and shrubby windbreaks adjacent to agricultural fields.

Nesting: well above the ground on a horizontal branch of a large tree, such as an oak, pine or cottonwood; bulky cup nest of twigs, leaves, feathers, hair and other debris is lined with plant fibers and other soft materials; female incubates 3–4 eggs for about 18 days; both adults feed the young.

Feeding: eats mostly insects caught by hawking or gleaned from the ground or foliage while hovering; also takes some berries and small fruits.

Voice: common year-round call is a loud *chick-weeer* or *chi-bew*; also issues an excited *kideedeedee* or *ki-dear ki-dear ki-dear*; loud, rising 'dawn song' is *burg-burg-burg-BURG*.

Similar Species: *Western Kingbird* (p. 252): lighter head, throat and upper breast; white outer tail feathers; calls *whit-ker-whit*. *Tropical Kingbird*: much longer bill; olive-yellow upper breast; seen in fall and early winter only; distinctive call is a rapid, twittering *pip-pip-pip-pip*.

251

WESTERN KINGBIRD
Tyrannus verticalis

The tumbling aerial courtship display of the Western Kingbird is sure to enliven a tranquil spring scene. Twisting and turning all the way, the male flies about 60 ft into the air, stalls, and then tumbles, flips and twists as he plummets to earth. • Western Kingbirds are commonly seen surveying for prey from fenceposts, barbed wire and powerlines. Once a flying insect is spotted, a kingbird quickly gives chase. When elusive prey requires a persistent hunt, a kingbird will not hesitate to chase an insect for 40 ft or more. • The scientific name *verticalis* refers to this bird's hidden, red crown patch, which is flared in courtship displays and in combat with rivals, but is not easily seen. People who have witnessed this bird's brave attacks against much larger birds might appreciate the origin of the name 'kingbird.'

ID: gray head and breast; white chin; black bill; ashy gray upperparts; dark gray mask; concealed orange-red crown; yellow belly and undertail coverts; white outer feathers on a square-ended, dark brown tail.

Size: *L* 8–9 in.

Status: common migrant from mid-March to late May and from August to early October; uncommon to common breeder from late March to mid-August.

Habitat: open habitats, including grasslands, savannah, sagebrush flats, shrubby margins of agricultural areas, suburban edge, and along the edges of oak and riparian woodlands.

Nesting: on a branch near the trunk of a deciduous tree; frequently on barns, towers and telephone pole crossbeams and behind transformer boxes; cup nest is lined with fur, twigs, roots and feathers; female incubates 4–5 eggs for 14 days.

Feeding: flycatches for aerial insects, such as bees, wasps, butterflies and moths; occasionally eats berries.

Voice: chatty, twittering *whit-ker-whit*; also *pkit-pkit-pkeetle-dot*; fiesty and argumentative.

Similar Species: *Cassin's Kingbird* (p. 251): darker breast and upperparts; lacks the white outer tail feathers. *Ash-throated Flycatcher* (p. 250): tail has rufous coloration; lacks the white outer feathers; browner head and back. *Empidonax flycatchers* (pp. 242–47): much smaller; eye rings; wing bars.

EASTERN KINGBIRD
Tyrannus tyrannus

When you think of a tyrant animal, images of a large carnivorous dinosaur are much more likely to come to mind than a little bird. True as that might be, no one familiar with the pugnacity of the Eastern Kingbird is likely to refute its scientific name, *Tyrannus tyrannus*. This kingbird is a bold brawler, and it will fearlessly attack crows, hawks and even humans that pass through its territory. Intruders are often vigorously pursued, pecked and plucked for some distance, until the kingbird is satisfied that there is no further threat. • Eastern Kingbirds rarely walk or hop on the ground; instead, they prefer to fly, even for very short distances. • The red crown, for which the kingbird is named, is rarely seen outside the courtship season.

ID: dark gray to blackish upperparts; white underparts; broadly white-tipped tail; black bill; concealed orange-red crown; no eye ring; black legs.
Size: *L* 8¹/₂ in.
Status: extremely rare to very rare migrant and transient from mid-May to September; extremely rare and local summer breeder.
Habitat: *Breeding:* large trees or shrubs adjacent to freshwater streams, ponds or lakes. *In migration:* riparian woodlands, tree groves in agricultural areas, scattered trees on coastal headlands, in parks, cemeteries and golf courses.
Nesting: on a horizontal limb in a small tree or shrub; also in cavities and human-made structures; pair builds the cup nest with plant fibers, grass, roots, feathers and fur; female incubates 3–4 eggs for up to 14 days.
Feeding: flycatches aerial insects; infrequently eats berries.
Voice: call is a quick, loud, chattering *kit-kit-kitter-kitter*; also a buzzy *dzee-dzee-dzeeb*.
Similar Species: *Tree Swallow* (p. 270): smaller; more streamlined; smaller bill; lacks the dark gray to blackish back and the white-tipped tail. *Olive-sided Flycatcher* (p. 240): 2 white rump patches; lacks the white-tipped tail and the all-white underparts.

LOGGERHEAD SHRIKE

Lanius ludovicianus

Although the Loggerhead Shrike shares the same coloration and many of the same markings as the Northern Mockingbird, this masked songbird differs greatly in its dietary preferences and hunting abilities. The Loggerhead Shrike possesses keen vision, and it often perches atop shrubs and small trees while it searches for prey. Like other members of its family, the Loggerhead Shrike impales its prey—including voles, mice, shrews, large insects, lizards, frogs and small snakes—on thorns and barbs as a means of storage. Shrikes seem to have an uncanny memory for the location of their food caches, and they have been known to find prey that has been stored for up to eight months. • Unfortunately, habitat destruction and pesticide use have caused declines in Loggerhead Shrike populations across much of North America. • This bird is called 'Loggerhead' because of its large head.

ID: black tail and wings; gray crown and back; extensive black mask extends above the all-dark, hooked bill; white underparts; barred flanks. *Juvenile:* gray barring on the crown, back, rump and underparts. *In flight:* white wing patches; white-edged tail.
Size: *L* 9 in.
Status: locally rare to fairly common (but declining in some areas) year-round resident; scarce spring and fall migrant.
Habitat: open country adjacent to dense brush, including savannah, oak woodlands, sagebrush plains, pinyon-juniper woodlands, ranches and some suburbs.
Nesting: in a low fork in a shrub or small tree; bulky cup nest of twigs and grass is lined with fine materials; female incubates 5–6 eggs for 15–17 days.

Feeding: swoops down from a perch or attacks prey in pursuit; regularly eats small birds, rodents, shrews and insects; also eats carrion, small reptiles and amphibians.
Voice: male's call in summer is a bouncy hiccup, *hugh-ee hugh-ee*; infrequently a harsh *shack-shack*.
Similar Species: *Northern Shrike* (p. 255): larger; adult has fine barring on the sides and breast; immature has brownish barring below, a paler, less well-defined mask and unbarred, light-brown upperparts; mask does not extend above the bill; present only from October to April. *Northern Mockingbird* (p. 304): slim bill; no mask; slimmer overall; much different behavior.

NORTHERN SHRIKE

Lanius excubitor

At the end of the breeding season, Northern Shrikes retreat from the Arctic to overwinter in southern Canada and the northern United States. Each year, a small number of these predatory songbirds migrate into northern California, where they perch like hawks upon exposed treetops to survey semi-open hunting grounds.

• Despite its robin-like size, the Northern Shrike can quickly kill small birds, rodents, reptiles and amphibians. Its macabre habit of impaling its prey has earned it the name 'butcher bird.' This gruesome act is simply a means of storing food for later consumption, out of the reach of scavengers.

• This shrike is distributed throughout the Northern Hemisphere; it is also found in Scandinavia, Asia, Britain and Japan.

ID: black tail and wings; pale gray upperparts; light underparts; fine barring on the sides and breast; black mask does not extend above the pale-based, hooked bill. *Immature:* faint mask; light brown upperparts; brown barring on the underparts; more frequently seen than adults in northern California. *In flight:* white wing patches; white-edged tail.

Size: *L* 10 in.

Status: irregular; rare to very uncommon visitor from mid-October to early April.

Habitat: broken woodlands, semi-open country, sagebrush plains, croplands with scattered trees and shrubs, pinyon-juniper woodlands, orchards, farmyards and ranches; frequently in dunelands or scrub near the seacoast.

Nesting: in northern Canada and Alaska.

Feeding: swoops down on prey from a perch or chases prey vigorously through the air and among vegetation; regularly eats small birds, shrews, rodents and insects; may also take lizards, snakes and frogs; dead prey may be impaled on a thorn or barb for later consumption.

Voice: usually silent; infrequently calls a grating *shek shek* during migration; may sing a grating, jabbering song by late winter.

Similar Species: *Loggerhead Shrike* (p. 254): smaller; darker gray; adult's mask extends above the bill and onto the forehead; juvenile has gray barring on the crown and back in late summer. *Northern Mockingbird* (p. 304): slim bill; no mask; slimmer overall; much different behavior.

CASSIN'S VIREO

Vireo cassinii

Distinct white 'spectacles' set against a gray head readily distinguish this compact yet nimble bird from other forest inhabitants. • Cassin's Vireos breed exclusively west of the Continental Divide and along the Pacific coast. Some birders have reported that this vireo is a fearless nester, often allowing brief close-range observations when it is incubating eggs. • The American Ornithologists' Union has given support to the notion that what was once called the Solitary Vireo actually constitutes three species. The Cassin's Vireo, along with the Blue-headed Vireo of the eastern deciduous and northern boreal forests and the Plumbeous Vireo of southwestern interior mountains and deserts, are now considered distinct species.

ID: gray head; bold white 'spectacles'; whitish underparts; brown-olive back and rump; yellowish sides and flanks; 2 white wing bars; short, hook-tipped bill.
Size: L 5–6 in.
Status: fairly common migrant and breeder from late March to mid-October; a few birds linger along coast into winter.
Habitat: drier, mixed deciduous and pine-oak woodlands, oak woodlands and riparian growth in shaded canyons. *Breeding:* from sea level well into the mountains.
Nesting: semi-pendant, open pouch hung from a horizontal fork in a tree; nest is made of grass, roots, plant down and spider webs; pair incubates 3–5 whitish eggs for about 12–14 days.
Feeding: forages slowly and deliberately along branches and foliage in the upper-parts of trees; may hawk or hover; eats mostly insects, but also takes spiders, berries and small fruits; turns its head in mechanical increments while pausing on a perch.

Voice: song is a series of high-pitched phrases: *See me?...Detroit...Surreal*; call is a harsh, drawling scold.
Similar Species: *Hutton's Vireo* (p. 257): yellowish underparts; blurry 'spectacles.' *Warbling Vireo* (p. 258): whitish eyebrow; no wing bars. *Ruby-crowned Kinglet* (p. 294): thinner bill; lacks the bold white lores; buffy-yellow underparts; different song; more constant wing-flicking.

HUTTON'S VIREO
Vireo huttoni

In early spring, male Hutton's Vireos sing continuously throughout the day, waging vocal battles in an attempt to defend their nesting territories. Their song is an oscillating *zuWEEM, zuWEEM, zuWEEM*. • Unlike their vireo relatives, Hutton's are year-round residents of northern California's oak and pine-oak woodlands. • Birders can attract a Hutton's Vireo with persistent 'pishing' or a convincing rendition of a Northern Pygmy-Owl call. Odds of seeing one are in your favor—this sprite of deep live-oak shadows is far more numerous than inexperienced birders might imagine. • The drab Hutton's Vireo closely resembles kinglets, *Empidonax* flycatchers and even a few warblers. • John Cassin named this bird after William Hutton, a field collector who first obtained this bird for scientific study.

ID: gray-green upperparts; short, slim, hook-tipped bill; incomplete eye ring; pale loral smudge; white wing bars.

Size: L 4¹/₂–5 in.

Status: locally uncommon to common year-round resident; high-elevation breeders may move to lower elevations over winter; some evidence of limited spring and fall migration is apparent.

Habitat: mixed conifer and oak forests and woodlands; strongly partial to live-oaks and tanoak, especially as consistent understory.

Nesting: well above the ground in the fork of an oak or on a conifer twig; pair builds a softball-sized open cup of grass, lichens, moss and bark fibers bound with spider webs and lined with fine grass; outer surface is covered with whitish plant down and spider egg cases; pair incubates 4 eggs for 14–16 days.

Feeding: hops from twig to twig in the inner canopy of trees and shrubs to glean or hover for insects; takes caterpillars, spiders, berries and small fruits.

Voice: monotonous song is a nasal, buzzy series of tirelessly repeated, 2-syllable notes: *zuWEEM, zuWEEM, zuWEEM*; routine call is a stuttered, *dzee? zeed-eed-eet!*

Similar Species: *Ruby-crowned Kinglet* (p. 294): smaller overall; smaller head and tail; thin, dainty black bill. *Warbling Vireo* (p. 258) and *Orange-crowned Warbler* (p. 311): both lack the wing bars. *Empidonax flycatchers* (pp. 242–47): all have longer tails and bodies; longer, flatter bills; erect posture.

257

WARBLING VIREO
Vireo gilvus

The Warbling Vireo is common and widespread in northern California, but you might still have to search to find one. It is difficult to spot among the dappled shadows of its wooded background because it is slow, deliberate and lacks any splashy field marks. This bird ranks high among California's songsters, however, and the oscillating, warbled quality of its squeaky song delights all listeners. The phrases end on an upbeat as if asking a question of the wilds. Once the velvety, hidden voice of the Warbling Vireo is learned, auditory encounters will soon abound. Searching the treetops for inconspicuous birds may literally be 'a pain in the neck,' but the satisfaction in a first visual confirmation of this bird is exceptionally rewarding.

breeding

ID: slender body; creamy-white eyebrow and sub-ocular crescent; no wing bars; olive-gray upperparts; yellowish wash on the flanks; light underparts; gray crown.
Size: *L* 5½ in.
Status: fairly common to common migrant from early March to mid-May and from early August to mid-October; uncommon to locally abundant breeder from mid-March to mid-August.
Habitat: *Breeding:* varied riparian woodlands and mixed deciduous-coniferous forests from sea level to 10,500 ft. *In migration:* almost any stand of trees, preferring hardwoods.
Nesting: in a horizontal fork in a deciduous tree or shrub; hanging, basket-like cup nest is made of grass, roots, plant down, spider silk and a few feathers; pair incubates 4 eggs for 12 days.

Feeding: gleans foliage and twigs for invertebrates; occasionally hovers and plucks insects from beneath leaves.
Voice: male's song is a squeaky but appealing musical warble: *I love you I love you Ma'am!* or *iggly wiggly iggly piggly iggly eeek!*; females occasionally sing from the nest; both sexes give an annoyed, peevish 'sneer' note.
Similar Species: *Red-eyed Vireo:* black eye line extends to the bill; blue-gray crown; red eyes. *Cassin's Vireo* (p. 256): bold white 'spectacles'; white wing bars. *Hutton's Vireo* (p. 257): broken white eye ring; white wing bars. *Orange-crowned Warbler* (p. 311): more yellowish-green throughout.

GRAY JAY
Perisoreus canadensis

There are few birds in California that rival the Gray Jay for boldness. Small family groups glide slowly and unexpectedly out of coastal and mountain coniferous forests, attracted by the slightest commotion or movement in the woods. These birds are surprisingly confiding, and they will quickly endear themselves to any passers by. • Gray Jays lay their eggs and begin incubation as early as late February. Their nests are well insulated to conserve heat, and nesting early means the adults will be feeding their quickly growing nestlings when the forests are full of fresh spring food. In preparation for tough times, Gray Jays often store food. To preserve their cache, they coat the food with a sticky mucus from specialized salivary glands. • Gray Jays have a restricted range within the northernmost mountains of California, but they are widely distributed throughout the Rocky Mountains, the Pacific Northwest, Canada and Alaska. In other parts of their range they may be known as 'Camp Robbers,' 'Canada Jays' or 'Whiskey Jacks.'

ID: fluffy, pale gray plumage; long tail; light forehead; darker on the crown and nape; dark gray upperparts; light gray underparts; white cheek; dark, stubby bill. *Immature:* dark sooty-gray overall.
Size: L 11½ in.
Status: locally rare to rather common resident.
Habitat: coastal and higher mountain coniferous forests.
Nesting: in the fork of a conifer; bulky, well-insulated nest is made of plant fibers, roots, moss, twigs, feathers and fur; female incubates 3–4 eggs for 17 days.

Feeding: searches the ground and vegetation for insects, fruit, songbird eggs and nestlings, carrion and berries; stores food items; carries off unguarded human food.
Voice: complex vocal repertoire; soft, whistled *quee-oo*; chuckled *cla-cla-cla*; also imitates other birds, especially the Northern Pygmy-Owl.
Similar Species: *Clark's Nutcracker* (p. 263): larger; heavy black bill; black-and-white wings and tail. *Loggerhead Shrike* (p. 254) and *Northern Shrike:* (p. 255) black mask; black-and-white wings and tail; live in open country.

259

STELLER'S JAY
Cyanocitta stelleri

The stunning Steller's Jay is a resident jewel common throughout northern California's forests. This crested bird generally presents itself as noisy and pugnacious, but in the vicinity of its nest, it suddenly becomes silent, cautious and cleverly elusive.
• Steller's Jays are most common in coniferous and evergreen hardwood forests and are normally absent only from the Central Valley and the sagebrush plains. They regularly visit foothill and lowland backyards. • Steller's Jays are inquisitive and bold, and, like other corvids, they will not hesitate to steal food scraps from inattentive picnickers. During winter they often descend upon feeders in search of peanuts and sunflower seeds.
• Georg Wilhelm Steller, the first European naturalist to visit Alaska, collected the 'type' specimen of this species.

ID: glossy, deep blue plumage; black head, nape and back; large, black crest; bluish forehead streaks; wings and tail are barred.
Size: *L* 11 1/2 in.
Status: widespread resident throughout forested northern California; irregular visitor to the lowlands, most often in fall and winter.
Habitat: deciduous oak woodlands, mixed woodlands and coniferous forests to 8500 ft; occasionally wanders up to 10,000 ft; some occupy townsites and exotic tree plantations.

Nesting: in the fork of a conifer; bulky stick and twig nest is lined with mud, grass and conifer needles; female incubates 4 eggs for 16 days.
Feeding: searches the ground and vegetation for insects, small vertebrates and other food items; forages in treetops for nuts, berries and other birds' eggs; visits feeders during winter.
Voice: harsh, far-carrying *shack-shack-shack*; grating *kresh, kresh*.
Similar Species: *Western Scrub-Jay* (p. 261) and *Pinyon Jay* (p. 262): lack the crest, the barring on the tail and wings and the black head, nape and back. *Gray Jay* (p. 259): silhouette against the sky looks longer-tailed and rounder-winged; slow glides.

WESTERN SCRUB-JAY

Aphelocoma californica

This slender jay is often seen foraging among leaf litter or surveying its tree-dotted habitat from a perch atop a tall shrub. • Oak mast is a staple of the Western Scrub-Jay's winter diet. Each fall, these jays harvest fallen acorns and store them individually in holes that they have dug in the ground with their strong bills. This intelligent bird often uses a rock or concrete slab as an 'anvil' to assist in cracking open the acorn's shielding coat. At the end of winter, uneaten acorns are not wasted—many germinate, regenerating the stand. • The Western Scrub-Jay has recently been granted full species status. It was formerly grouped into a single species with the Florida Scrub-Jay and the Island Scrub-Jay, which is endemic to southern California's Santa Cruz Island.

ID: slim body; gray back; otherwise sky blue upperparts; long, unmarked tail; streaked, white throat is bordered by a bluish 'necklace'; light gray underparts; dark, heavy bill; dark cheek patch; faint, white eyebrow.
Size: L 11½ in.
Status: common year-round resident.
Habitat: chaparral and dry, brushy, open areas of oak and pinyon-juniper woodlands, mixed oak-coniferous forests, broken mixed deciduous-coniferous woodlands and riparian woodlands; also found in suburban parks and gardens, urban shrubbery and roadside tree plantations to 8000 ft; may wander to 11,000 ft.

Nesting: in a small conifer or shrub; pair builds a bulky stick nest, usually with an inner cup lined with moss, grass and fur; female incubates 3–6 eggs for 15–17 days.
Feeding: forages on the ground for insects and small vertebrates; also eats other birds' eggs and nestlings, as well as acorns, pinyon nuts and many fruits.
Voice: perch call is a harsh, repetitive *ike-ike-ike*; in flight, utters a rough, frequently repeated *quesh quesh quesh*.

Similar Species: *Pinyon Jay* (p. 262): blue back and underparts; shorter tail. *Steller's Jay* (p. 260): large, black crest; dark head, nape and back; blue underparts; barred wings and tail.

261

PINYON JAY
Gymnorhinus cyanocephalus

The Pinyon Jay is a loud and highly gregarious bird that behaves much like the American Crow. Outside the breeding season, Pinyon Jays forage in enormous flocks that consist of many smaller family groups. While foraging, Pinyon Jays adhere to an orderly social structure: some take turns acting as look-out, while others concentrate on feeding. • Nesting takes place in late winter, with loose colonies of up to 150 birds. Pinyon pines and junipers (and occasionally oaks) are preferred nesting sites, and a single tree can support up to three nests. Cached seeds and nuts help to supplement freshly harvested foods when it comes time to feed growing young. Pinyon Jays might nest again in late summer depending on pinyon pine seed crops. When the pinyon crop fails, these jays become nomadic and disperse widely in search of other food.

ID: all-gray-blue plumage; light streaks on the throat; long, dark, pointed bill; short tail.
Size: L 9–11 1/2 in.
Status: uncommon to fairly common year-round resident.
Habitat: *Breeding:* pinyon-juniper forests and woodlands from 4000–7500 ft; ranges among stands of ponderosa pine; rare visitor elsewhere. *Foraging:* sagebrush flats, montane chaparral and forests of pine and tall sagebrush.
Nesting: in loose colonies in pinyon pines, junipers and shrubs; large, bulky nest is made of sticks, twigs and fibers; female incubates 4–5 eggs for up to 17 days.

Feeding: searches the ground and vegetation for pinyon nuts, seeds and insects; also eats berries and other birds' eggs and nestlings.
Voice: warning call is a low *krawk-krawk-krawk*; flight call is a high, piercing *mew* or laughing *hah-hah*.
Similar Species: *Western Scrub-Jay* (p. 261): light gray underparts; gray back; long tail. *Steller's Jay* (p. 260): large, black crest; dark head, nape and back; barred wings and tail.

CLARK'S NUTCRACKER
Nucifraga columbiana

Raucous and gregarious, Clark's Nutcrackers break the profound hush of mid-afternoon at timberline with conversational rasps. Inhabiting the higher ridges of the major ranges, they are often encountered in campgrounds and public day-use areas. Clark's Nutcrackers become bold when they learn that inattentive picknickers may provide a quick meal. • In fall, Clark's Nutcrackers spend much of their time using their long, sturdy bills to pry apart the cones of whitebark pine and Jeffrey pine. A special pouch at the base of the tongue allows mass transport of many seeds to storage spots. Small, scattered seed caches might be found up to 8 mi or more apart, with a combined stash of over 30,000 seeds! Over winter and throughout the nesting cycle, nutcrackers use memory to locate cache sites, which are often hidden under deep snow. • When Western explorer Captain William Clark, of the Lewis and Clark expedition, first sighted this bird, its large, straight bill misled him into believing it was a woodpecker—the Clark's Nutcracker was originally categorized in the genus *Picicorvus*, meaning 'woodpecker-crow.'

ID: light gray head, back and underparts; large, black bill; black wings with flashy, white secondaries. *In flight:* black central tail feathers; white outer tail feathers; stoops and tumbles unerringly along the upper slopes of tall peaks.

Size: *L* 12–13 in.

Status: fairly common year-round resident; erratic, irruptive westward movements in fall.

Habitat: *Breeding:* subalpine coniferous forests above 8000 ft; occasionally in pinyon-juniper forests above 7200 ft. *Non-breeding:* commonly appears in alpine areas; may move to lower elevations in winter.

Nesting: on a horizontal conifer limb; twig and stick platform nest is lined with grass and strips of bark; pair incubates 2–4 eggs for 16–22 days; nesting begins in March, with the eggs laid in April.

Feeding: forages on the ground and among trees for pine seeds and pinyon nuts; hammers cones and nuts with its bill; also eats insects; stores food for winter.

Voice: loud, unpleasant, grating *kra-a-a-a*, delivered mostly from a perch.

Similar Species: *Gray Jay* (p. 259): smaller; gray wings and tail; shorter bill. *Northern Mockingbird* (p. 304): much smaller; smaller bill; lighter underparts; white wing patch on the primary flight feathers; common in valleys and foothills.

BLACK-BILLED MAGPIE
Pica pica

The saying 'familiarity breeds contempt' is well illustrated by the Black-billed Magpie and the Yellow-billed Magpie in California. Magpies are among North America's loveliest birds, but they are too often discredited because of their aggressive demeanor. Many Californians are jaded by the omnipresence of magpies, but visitors to the region are often captivated by this bird's exceptional beauty and approachability. • A skilled architect, the Black-billed Magpie constructs an elaborate domed nest in a tree or on an iron bridge. Built of sticks and held together with mud, the nest conceals and protects the eggs and young from cold weather and predators. Abandoned nests remain in trees for years—their collapsed bulk often serves as nest sites for hawks or for non-builders, such as owls. Black-billed Magpies do not normally occur in eastern North America, but they are widely distributed throughout Europe, North Africa, Arabia and Asia.

ID: long, black tail; black head, breast and back; rounded, black-and-white wings; black undertail coverts; black bill; white belly.
Size: L 18–22 in.
Status: fairly common year-round resident.
Habitat: open agricultural areas, farmlands, cattle range and sagebrush flats.
Nesting: near the center of a tree or tall shrub; domed stick and twig nest is built on a base of mud and manure and lined with grasses, weeds and hair; female incubates 5–8 eggs for up to 24 days.

Feeding: omnivorous; forages on the ground for insects, carrion, human food-waste, nuts, seeds and berries; picks insects and ticks from large ungulates; occasionally eats bird eggs; routinely scavenges vehicle-killed animals, including magpies.

Voice: loud, nasal, frequently repeated *queg-queg-queg*; also many other vocalizations.
Similar Species: *Yellow-billed Magpie* (p. 265): yellow bill and eye patch; restricted to the Central Valley.

YELLOW-BILLED MAGPIE

Pica nuttalli

The long, iridescent tail of the Yellow-billed Magpie might leave most first-time admirers guessing that this bird has tropical origins. Its home, however, lies exclusively within the interior valleys of California west of the Sierra Nevada. • Foraging magpies spend much of their time on the ground—in a determined search for food, they use their sturdy bills to flip over rocks, bark, leaves and dry cow dung. They commonly feast on carrion, and, should the opportunity arise, they will steal food from other magpies. These birds often store left-over food and acorns in cache sites. • This magpie's Black-billed relative is rarely seen in the same range, preferring to live to the east in sage-brush country, ranchlands and riparian areas above 4000 ft.

ID: black-and-white body; wings and extremely long tail are iridescent; bright yellow bill; yellow around the eyes.

Size: L 16–18 in, including a 9–10 in tail.

Status: locally uncommon to very common year-round resident; extirpated from the peninsula south of San Francisco and other localities.

Habitat: open oak savannahs, ranches, pastures and streamside groves; prefers large open areas interspersed with trees; readily spotted along Interstate 5.

Nesting: colonial; far out on a high tree limb; both adults build a large, bulky domed nest of sticks and twigs with a mud base;

nest is lined with soft plant material; 4–8 darkly marked, olive-buff eggs are incubated 16–18 days by the female; male feeds the incubating female.

Feeding: omnivorous diet of seasonally available plants and animals; readily eats carrion, grasshoppers and acorns; often forages on the ground.

Voice: similar to Black-billed Magpie, but is generally quieter; calls include a harsh, raspy *chek-chek-chek* and a whiny, inquisitive *mahg?*

Similar Species: *Black-billed Magpie* (p. 264): virtually identical except for the black bill and the lack of yellow around the eyes; almost never occurs in the Yellow-bill's range.

AMERICAN CROW
Corvus brachyrhynchos

American Crows are wary, intelligent birds that have flourished despite considerable efforts by humans to reduce their numbers. Crows are opportunistic feeders, and much of their survival strength lies in their ability to adapt to a variety of habitats, food resources and environmental conditions. • In coastal and moist lowland areas of northern California, crows remain year-round and show a particular affinity for farmlands and urban areas. Populations that breed at high elevations and along the northern extremes of the state usually flock together in late summer or fall before moving to warmer locations. Flocks can be composed of hundreds of individuals—these impressive gatherings (known as 'murders') are merely get-togethers in preparation for evening roosts or preambles for the fall exodus. • *Corvus brachyrhynchos*, despite sounding cumbersome, is Latin for 'raven with the small nose.'

ID: all-black body; fan-shaped tail; black bill and legs; slim, sleek head and throat.
Size: L 17–21 in; W 37 in.
Status: common to locally common year-round resident; common breeder from April to September.
Habitat: open and broken woodlands in valleys and on rolling hills, in trees among agricultural fields, along rural windrows, in orchards and in urban and suburban parks and gardens to about 5000 ft.
Nesting: in coniferous or deciduous trees; large stick and branch nest is lined with fur and soft plant materials; female incubates 4–6 eggs for up to 18 days.

Feeding: opportunistic omnivore; feeds on carrion, small vertebrates, other birds' eggs and nestlings, berries, seeds, invertebrates and human food-waste.
Voice: distinctive, far-carrying, repetitive *caw-caw-caw*; boisterous yakking of flocks is familiar.
Similar Species: *Common Raven* (p. 267): larger; wedge-shaped tail; shaggy throat; heavier bill; commonly soars; prefers backwoods.

COMMON RAVEN

Corvus corax

Whether stealing food from a flock of gulls, harassing a Golden Eagle or scavenging from a carcass, the Common Raven is worthy of its reputation as a clever bird. Glorified in many cultures as a magical being, the raven does not act by instinct alone: when it is executing tumbling aerobatic feats, performing complex vocalizations or playfully sliding down a snowbank on its back, this bird exhibits behaviors that many people think of as exclusively human. • Few birds boast the Common Raven's immense distribution—this bird lives on coastlines, in deserts, on mountains and in the bitter winter cold and darkness of the arctic tundra. Aside from larger valley floors, it is a common resident nearly throughout northern California from sea level to the Sierra Nevada. • Breeding ravens maintain lifelong pair bonds, enduring everything from harsh weather and food scarcity to the raising of young.

ID: all-black plumage; heavy, black bill; wedge-shaped tail; shaggy throat; broad, blunt-pointed wings.
Size: *L* 24 in; *W* 50 in.
Status: common year-round resident.
Habitat: most habitats from low elevations to over 14,000 ft; tends to avoid habitats occupied by crows, such as urban parks, farmyards and orchards; forages in towns and cities locally, especially along the north coast.
Nesting: on steep cliffs, ledges, bluffs, power poles and tall conifers; large stick and branch nest is lined with fur and soft plant materials; female incubates 4–6 eggs for 18–21 days.

Feeding: opportunistic omnivore; feeds on carrion, small vertebrates, other birds' eggs and nestlings, berries, invertebrates and human food-waste.
Voice: deep, far-carrying, croaking: *craww-craww* or *quork quork*; also many other vocalizations; juveniles contact adults with a falsetto caricature of the adult's croak (a very familiar forest sound from mid-June to August).
Similar Species: *American Crow* (p. 266): smaller; fan-shaped tail; slim throat; slimmer bill; call is a higher-pitched *caw*; seldom soars high.

267

HORNED LARK

Eremophila alpestris

Horned Larks are uniquely patterned, small ground birds that are nearly always encountered in treeless, open country. Widespread across the plains and steppes of the Northern Hemisphere, they live throughout North America outside regions of extensive forest. • Many Horned Larks live permanently in northern California, while migrants and winter visitors may occur here during the colder months. • To escape the eye of predators, Horned Larks rely on their disruptive light-and-dark coloring, their creeping or 'strolling' foraging technique and a low profile among the scattered grass-tufts. They may not be detected until closely approached, whereupon the entire flock flushes and scatters on the breeze, to reassemble elsewhere in the vicinity. • Horned Larks are easy to see but nearly too close to identify when they flush just in front of a vehicle on rural gravel roads. They usually change course an instant before a fatal collision, briefly showing their distinctive white-bordered tail feathers.

ID: *Male:* strikingly patterned; small, black 'horns' (not always apparent); black line extending beneath the eye from the bill to the cheek; pale yellow or whitish face; brown upperparts; black breast band; dark tail with white outer tail feathers. *Female:* similar to male, but with less distinctive head patterning; duller plumage overall. *Juvenile:* dark and finely spotted above; paler and streaked below; often confuses the inexperienced.
Size: L 7 in.
Status: uncommon to common resident, migrant and summer breeder; locally abundant visitor from mid-October to early February.
Habitat: extensive barren-ground and short grass habitats from sea level to over 12,000 ft.

Nesting: well-concealed cup nest is placed in a shallow depression, often next to a rock or dried manure; nest is lined with grass, plant fibers and roots; female chooses the nest site and incubates 3–4 eggs for up to 12 days.
Feeding: gleans the ground for seeds; feeds insects and other small terrestrial invertebrates to its young.
Voice: delicate song is a lilting, upward-spiraling tinkle of soft notes: *TEEP, tip, TOOP-pit-tip-pit-tip-pit-ittle-EEE*; flight call is a thin *seet* or *see-dirt.*
Similar Species: *Sparrows* (pp. 326–41), *Lapland Longspur* (p. 343) and *American Pipit* (p. 308): all lack the distinctive facial pattern, the 'horns' and the solid black breast band.

PURPLE MARTIN

Progne subis

At scattered localities across northern California, mild-mannered Purple Martins attempt to hold their ground against pushy European Starlings and House Sparrows. Purple Martins once had their pick of natural nesting cavities and, at one time, Native Americans even erected hollow gourds to serve as nesting sites for these beneficial insectivorous birds. Nest site usurpation, along with the loss of snags through fire suppression and logging, however, has diminished the Purple Martin population—remaining birds are largely confined to snags along ridgetops and in commercial timberland. A population of Purple Martins nests in subterranean lava caves in Lava Beds National Monument in Modoc County. A very few persist coastally and in urban areas. • The scientific name of our largest swallow, *Progne*, refers to Pandion's daughter Procne, who, according to Greek mythology, had been transformed into a swallow.

ID: dark blue, glossy body; slightly forked tail; broad yet pointed wings; small bill. *Male:* dark underparts. *Female:* sooty gray underparts.
Size: L 7–8 in.
Status: very rare to locally uncommon migrant from late March to mid-May and from August to early October; locally rare to uncommon breeder from April to August.
Habitat: *Breeding:* riparian woodlands, oak woodlands, partially logged, broken or burned coniferous forests and montane mixed forests; requires large, cavity-filled trees close to open foraging areas of water or land. *In migration:* over rivers, reservoirs and agricultural areas.
Nesting: communal; nest is usually built in a tree cavity or in crevices under a bridge; locally in bird houses; nest materials

include feathers, grass, mud and vegetation; female incubates 4–5 eggs for 15–16 days.
Feeding: mostly while in flight; usually eats flies, ants, bugs, dragonflies and mosquitoes; may also toddle on the ground, taking insects and rarely berries.
Voice: song is a vibrant, congested warble, often uttered high in the sky; call is a rich, fluty, far-carrying *chew…chew, chew,* often heard in flight.
Similar Species: *European Starling* (p. 307): longer bill (yellow in summer); lacks the forked tail. *Barn Swallow* (p. 275): deeply forked tail; creamy brown underparts. *Phainopepla* (p. 310): prominent head crest; red eyes; white wing patches. *Black Phoebe* (p. 248) white belly; lacks the forked tail. *Tree Swallow* (p. 270): white underparts.

269

TREE SWALLOW
Tachycineta bicolor

Nesting Tree Swallows typically perch beside their fencepost nest boxes. When conditions are favorable, busy Tree Swallows are known to return to their summer nesting site to feed their young 10 to 20 times an hour (about 140 to 300 times a day!). This nearly ceaseless activity provides observers with plenty of opportunities to watch and photograph these birds in action. • Cavity nesters, such as the Tree Swallow, benefit greatly when landowners and progressive foresters allow dead trees to remain standing in backyards, gardens and cutblocks. In areas where natural tree cavities are scarce, nest boxes have proved a useful substitute for the Tree Swallow. • Unlike other North American swallows, female Tree Swallows do not acquire their full adult plumage until their second or third year. • In the bright spring sunshine, the back of the Tree Swallow appears steely blue; prior to fall migration it appears green.

ID: iridescent blue-green head and upperparts; white underparts; no white extending onto the cheek; dark rump; small bill; long, pointed wings; shallowly forked tail. *Female:* slightly duller. *Immature:* brownish above; white below; may have a dingy breast.
Size: L 5¹/₂ in.
Status: fairly common to abundant migrant from late January to early May and from late July to early October; uncommon to locally abundant breeder from March to early September; locally rare to common visitor from October to March.
Habitat: *Breeding:* natural cavities in trees or stumps located near freshwater lakes, ponds, marshes, sloughs, rivers or streams; may also use 'bluebird' nest boxes. *Winter* and *In migration:* over open meadows, lakes, ponds, fresh and saltwater marshes, sloughs, lagoons and rivers.

Nesting: in a tree cavity or nest box; nest of weeds, grass and feathers; female incubates 4–6 eggs for up to 19 days.
Feeding: catches flies, beetles, ants and termites on the wing; also takes stoneflies, mayflies and caddisflies over water; occasionally eats berries.
Voice: common call is a liquid, gurgly *klweet*; song is a crowded sequence of these notes.
Similar Species: *Violet-green Swallow* (p. 271): white cheek; white rump patches; different song. *Purple Martin* (p. 269): larger; female has sooty gray underparts; male has dark blue underparts. *Eastern Kingbird* (p. 253): larger; white-tipped tail; longer bill; dark gray to blackish upperparts; not highly aerial.

VIOLET-GREEN SWALLOW
Tachycineta thalassina

Because of its affinity for cliffs, open areas, natural tree cavities and nest boxes, the Violet-green Swallow is able to inhabit most of northern California's diverse habitats. • Swallows are swift and graceful fliers, routinely traveling at speeds of 30 mph. Violet-greens are often distinguished by their habit of foraging at 1000–2000 ft, far higher than other swallows normally feed. • Swallows occasionally eat mineral-rich soil, egg shells and exposed shellfish fragments, possibly to recoup the minerals lost during egg formation. In this way, non-living minerals and ancient clam beds are slowly being recycled and incorporated into the living tissues of these birds. • The scientific name *thalassina* is Latin for 'sea green,' a tribute to this bird's body color.

ID: iridescent greenish and purplish plumage; white underparts; white on the cheek; white rump patches; small bill; long, pointed wings; shallowly forked tail; small feet. *Female:* duller and more bronze than the male; brownish face.
Size: L 5¹/₄ in.
Status: fairly common to common migrant from mid-February to late April and from late August to mid-October; very uncommon to locally abundant breeder from late February to August; rare to uncommon, local winter visitor.
Habitat: open areas, including meadows, agricultural lands, edges of freshwater bodies and over forest canopies from sea level to timberline and beyond. *Breeding:* above treeline in cliffs.
Nesting: semi-colonial at times; in a tree cavity, cliff crevice, nest box or a crack in a

building; nest of weeds, grass and feathers; female incubates 4–6 eggs for up to 15 days.
Feeding: catches flying insects, such as flies, ants and wasps; drinks on the wing; may forage overhead at the limit of human vision.
Voice: exuberant, irregular chatter *ch-ch-ch-ch-chairTEE, chairTEE-ch-ch.*
Similar Species: *Tree Swallow* (p. 270) and *Purple Martin* (p. 269): lack the white cheek and rump patches. *Bank Swallow* (p. 273) and *Northern Rough-winged Swallow* (p. 272): brown upperparts; lack the white cheek. *Cliff Swallow* (p. 274): brown and blue upperparts; lacks the white cheek.

NORTHERN ROUGH-WINGED SWALLOW
Stelgidopteryx serripennis

Rough-winged swallows are almost the same color as the earthen banks in which they live. These semi-colonial, low-flying aerialists nest in burrows along streams and in roadcuts, often reusing abandoned burrows excavated by kingfishers, rodents or other swallows. They don't mind joining a crowd when foraging, and they often reappear nearby in mixed flocks of swallows that are hawking insects over a river or lake. • An early 20th-century ornithologist once caught a Northern Rough-winged Swallow and released it 30 miles from its nest. He immediately drove back to the site where he had captured the bird, only to find it feeding its nestlings. • Unlike other northern California swallows, male Northern Rough-wings have curved barbs along the outer edge of their primary wing feathers. The purpose of this sawtoothed edge remains a mystery. The ornithologist who initially named this bird must have been very impressed with its wings: *Stelgidopteryx* (scaper wing) and *serripennis* (saw feather) both refer to this unusual characteristic.

ID: earth brown upperparts; pale underparts except for the dusky throat; small bill; dark cheek; dark rump. *In flight:* long, pointed wings; notched tail.

Size: L 5¹/₂ in.

Status: uncommon to common migrant from early March to early May and from late July to late September; locally common breeder from March to July; very rare in winter.

Habitat: *Breeding:* requires near-vertical banks or bridges, culverts, dams and freeway overpasses with burrow holes, excavated cavities or crevices. *Foraging* and *In migration:* open lowland areas, grassy expanses, freshwater lakes, rivers and marshes.

Nesting: in single pairs or occasionally in small colonies; at the end of a burrow lined with leaves and dry grass; sometimes reuses kingfisher and rodent burrows and other natural or artificial crevices; pair incubates 4–8 white eggs for up to 16 days.

Feeding: catches flying insects on the wing; occasionally eats insects from the ground; drinks on the wing; generally does not forage at any great height.

Voice: low, ripping *brrrt*, ordinarily given in a loose series of 3–6 calls.

Similar Species: *Bank Swallow* (p. 273): dark breast band; colder-brown upperparts. *Tree Swallow* (p. 270): female has green upperparts and a clean white breast. *Violet-green Swallow* (p. 271): female has green upperparts, white cheek and rump patches and a white breast. *Cliff Swallow* (p. 274): brown-and-blue upperparts; buff forehead and rump patch; square tail.

BANK SWALLOW
Riparia riparia

A breeding colony of Bank Swallows seems to be in a constant flurry of activity as adults fly back and forth delivering mouthfuls of insects to their insatiable young. Not surprisingly, all this activity tends to attract predators, although few are able to catch these swift and agile fliers. Most nestlings are safe in their nest chamber, which may be located up to 5 ft into an earthen bank or bluff. Skunks and badgers have been known to reach the defenseless young. • In medieval Europe, it was believed that swallows spent winter in mud at the bottom of swamps, since they were not seen during that season. In those earlier days, it may have been beyond imagining that these birds fly south for the winter. • *Riparia* is from the Latin word for 'riverbank,' which is a common nesting site for this bird. If you approach a colony by canoe, they will usually burst from their burrows in the hundreds and circle nervously above until the river carries you away.

ID: brown upperparts; light underparts; white throat; dark cheek; distinct brown breast band; long, pointed wings; shallowly forked tail.
Size: L 5¹/₄ in.
Status: rare to uncommon migrant from early April to late May and from late July to mid-September (a few may remain into November); locally very rare to abundant breeder from mid-April to mid-August; colonies are widely scattered; populations have severely declined in the last 30 years.
Habitat: *Breeding:* earthen banks and bluffs to 7000 ft. *In migration:* open lowland areas, including meadows, farmlands, sewage ponds and freshwater lakes, rivers and marshes.

Nesting: colonial; in a burrow in a steep earthen bank; pair excavates a cavity and incubates 4–5 white eggs for up to 16 days.
Feeding: catches flying insects; drinks on the wing.
Voice: rough, brittle, twittering chatter: *speed-zeet speed-zeet.*
Similar Species: *Northern Rough-winged Swallow* (p. 272): warmer brown; lacks the dark breast band. *Violet-green Swallow* (p. 271): green upperparts; white cheek and rump patches; lacks the dark breast band. *Tree Swallow* (p. 270): lacks the dark breast band; greenish upperparts. *Cliff Swallow* (p. 274): lacks the dark breast band; brown-and-blue upperparts; buff forehead and rump.

CLIFF SWALLOW
Petrochelidon pyrrhonota

If the Cliff Swallow were to be renamed in the 20th century, it would probably be called the 'Bridge Swallow,' because almost every river bridge in western North America seems to have a colony of Cliff Swallows under it. Dramatic clouds of these birds will sometimes swirl up along either side of a bridge, especially when the colony is in the process of nest building. If you stop to inspect the underside of a bridge, you may see dozens or hundreds of gourd-shaped mud nests stuck to the pillars and structural beams. Unfortunately, years of high run-off and prolonged rains and floods have been known to wipe out entire nesting colonies of Cliff Swallows. • Cliff Swallows are brood parasites within their own colonies—females often lay one or more eggs in the temporarily vacant nests of neighboring Cliff Swallows. Upon returning to a parasitized nest, adults seem to accept the new deliveries and give the foreign eggs the same attention they give to their own.

ID: buff rump and forehead; blue-gray head and wings; rusty cheek, nape and throat; buff breast; white belly; spotted undertail coverts; squared tail.

Size: L 5¹/₂ in.

Status: common migrant from mid-March to late April and from late July to mid-September; locally uncommon to abundant breeder from April to late July.

Habitat: *Breeding:* cliffs, caves, rimrocks, ocean bluffs, bridges, buildings, tunnels, dams, viaducts and mine shafts to 9000 ft. *In migration:* open lowland areas, including meadows, farmlands, pastures, golf courses, sea beaches and freshwater lakes, rivers and marshes; may wander to 12,000 ft.

Nesting: colonial; under bridges and on cliffs, buildings and other similar sites; pair builds a gourd-shaped mud nest with a small opening on the bottom; pair incubates 4–5 eggs for up to 16 days.

Feeding: catches flying insects on the wing; drinks on the wing.

Voice: twittering chatter: *churrr-churrr*; also an alarm call: *nyew*.

Similar Species: *Barn Swallow* (p. 275): deeply forked tail; dark rump; rust-colored underparts and forehead. *Other swallows:* lack the buff forehead and the rump patch.

BARN SWALLOW
Hirundo rustica

The Barn Swallow has found success throughout most of the Northern Hemisphere through a welcomed affiliation with human beings. Once a cliff nester, this bird has come to exploit the potential afforded by buildings and other structures: high walls sheltered by overhanging eaves provide nestlings with protection from terrestrial predators and inclement weather. In such locations, the reproductive cycle of this two- or three-brooded species can be easily observed and studied. Unfortunately, not everyone appreciates the craftsmanship of the Barn Swallow's mud nest. Each year, many Barn Swallow families are callously extinguished just as the nesting season has begun. Such a course of action is all the more regrettable because these natural pest controllers are more beneficial alive than dead.

ID: long, deeply forked tail; rust-colored throat and forehead; blue-black upperparts; rust- to buff-colored underparts; long, pointed wings.

Size: *L* 7 in.

Status: very common migrant from early March to May and from late July to mid-October; locally uncommon to abundant breeder from April to mid-September; rare visitor from December to February.

Habitat: *Breeding:* rural and suburban buildings and other structures to 5000 ft (occasionally up to 8000 ft); also locally uses sea cliffs and caves. *In migration:* varied open lowland areas, including meadows, farmlands, parks, freshwater lakes, rivers, marshes, estuaries and beaches.

Nesting: on a vertical or horizontal building structure under a suitable overhang; on a bridge or in a culvert or cave; half-cup or full-cup nest of mud; pair incubates 4–7 eggs for 12–17 days.

Feeding: catches flying insects on the wing; bulk of foraging is done by sweeping low over the ground.

Voice: song is a long-sustained outpouring of busy chatter interspersed with gutturals; call is single or repeated *kvik* notes.

Similar Species: *Cliff Swallow* (p. 274): squared-off tail; buff rump and forehead; light-colored underparts. *Purple Martin* (p. 269): larger; shallowly forked tail; male is completely blue-black; female has sooty-gray underparts.

BLACK-CAPPED CHICKADEE
Poecile atricapillus

Black-capped Chickadees can be found in the extreme northwestern corner of California, where they build their nests and forage among willows and alders in lower-elevation woodlots and at forest edges. Although largely restricted to a narrow coastal range, they nevertheless offer a flock 'nucleus' for migrant and wintering kinglets and warblers in Humboldt and Del Norte counties. They only infrequently visit seed feeders in northern California. • When foraging, Black-capped Chickadees often swing upside-down on the tips of twigs, gleaning insects or plucking berries. Throughout much of the year, these birds are often found in the company of kinglets, nuthatches, creepers, Downy Woodpeckers and Chestnut-backed Chickadees. • Most songbirds, including Black-capped Chickadees, have both songs and calls. The chickadee's whistled song is delivered primarily during courtship to attract mates and to defend territories. The *chick-a-dee-dee-dee* call, which can be heard year-round, is used to keep flocks together and to maintain contact among flock members.

ID: black cap and bib; white cheek; plain gray back and wings; white underparts; light buff sides and flanks; dark legs.
Size: *L* 5–6 in.
Status: locally uncommon to fairly common year-round resident.
Habitat: red alder- and willow-dominated riparia, forest regrowth and dune-hollow thickets in coastal lowlands.
Nesting: in a natural cavity or an abandoned woodpecker nest; can excavate a cavity in soft, rotting wood; nest is lined with fur, feathers, moss, grass and cocoons; female incubates 6–8 eggs for up to 13 days.

Feeding: gleans vegetation, branches and the ground for small insects and spiders; also eats conifer seeds and invertebrate eggs; will locally visit feeders.
Voice: song is a simple, whistled *swee-tee* or *fee-bee-bee-bee*; call is a chipper, whistled *chick-a-dee-dee-dee*.
Similar Species: *Mountain Chickadee* (p. 277): white eyebrow; black eye line; gray sides. *Chestnut-backed Chickadee* (p. 278): rusty back and flanks; dark brown cap.

MOUNTAIN CHICKADEE
Poecile gambeli

This year-round resident of high-elevation forests spends much of its time feeding on seeds and insects high in a canopy of conifers. During winter, harsh weather can cause Mountain Chickadees to freeze or starve, and many move to lower elevations in search of warmer temperatures and abundant food sources. • The Mountain Chickadee breeds at higher elevations than other chickadees. It routinely nests in subalpine conifers at 8000–10,000 ft and is often seen foraging up to treeline. • The scientific name *gambeli* honors William Gambel, a 19th-century ornithologist who died of typhoid fever in the Sierra Nevada at the age of 28. • 'Chickadee' is an onomatopoeic derivation of this bird's call.

ID: white eyebrow through the black cap; white cheek; black bib; gray upperparts and tail; light gray underparts.
Size: L 5¼ in.
Status: uncommon to locally abundant year-round resident.
Habitat: montane coniferous forests and lower portions of subalpine forests at 2400–10,500 ft (occasionally up to 12,000 ft); irregular downslope flights to various woodland types in coastal and interior lowlands and foothills.
Nesting: in a natural cavity or an abandoned woodpecker nest; can excavate a cavity in soft, rotting wood; nest is lined with fur, feathers, moss and grass; incubates 5–9 eggs for up to 14 days.

Feeding: gleans vegetation, branches and the ground for small insects and spiders; visits backyard feeders for seeds; also eats conifer seeds and invertebrate eggs.
Voice: song is a sweet, clear, whistled *fee-bee-bay*; call is a drawling *chick a-day, day, day.*
Similar Species:
Black-capped Chickadee (p. 276): lacks the white eyebrow; buffy sides.
Chestnut-backed Chickadee (p. 278): rusty back and flanks; dark brown cap.

CHESTNUT-BACKED CHICKADEE
Poecile rufescens

Chestnut-backed Chickadees are among the common resident birds of many forests and woodlands from southern Alaska to the southern California coast. Truly tiny birds, their minute size allows them to nest in the tight quarters of nearly any tree cavity. Their habit of foraging widely within the canopy—from the lowermost boughs of trees to the tips of their crowns—allows most of northern California's forests to support them. In spring and early summer, Chestnut-backed Chickadees are found in pairs and, later, in straggling family groups. These assemblages gradually coalesce into larger winter flocks, which serve as a nucleus for associated kinglets, Townsend's Warblers, Red-breasted Nuthatches, Brown Creepers and Hutton's Vireos. • When intruders approach a chickadee nest, both parents remain nearby, fluttering their wings and sometimes hissing loudly at the perceived threat. • Tree cavities are attractive to chickadees in search of a nesting site, and they occasionally also function as insect magnets—bumblebees intent on establishing a new hive have been known to invade a chickadee cavity, chasing the small bird from its nest.

ID: dark brown cap; black bib; rich chestnut brown back and sides; white cheek; pale underparts; dark grayish wings and tail.
Size: L 4³/₄ in.
Status: locally uncommon to abundant year-round resident; among the most widespread species in shady forests over much of its range in northern California.
Habitat: coniferous, hardwood and mixed forests of any kind; common in oak woodlands lacking conifers; avoids oak savannah and drier pine forests; in residential areas, uses varied native and exotic tree plantings, gardens and tree clumps.
Nesting: excavates a cavity in a soft, rotting tree-trunk or limb stub, or uses a natural cavity or abandoned woodpecker nest; cavity is lined with fur, feathers, moss and grass; incubates 6–7 eggs for up to 15 days.

Feeding: gleans vegetation, chiefly among outer tree crowns and occasionally on the ground; takes insects, larvae, spiders, other invertebrates and seeds; a regular visitor to seed and suet feeders wherever adjoining cover of trees is available.
Voice: talkative quality of flocks suggests other chickadee species, but this species' calls are raspy and husky, lacking clear and sharp *dee-dee-dee* phrasing.

Similar Species: *Mountain Chickadee* (p. 277): white eyebrow; grayish overall, lacking any brown or rusty color. *Black-capped Chickadee* (p. 276): black cap; gray back; buffy flanks.

OAK TITMOUSE
Baeolophus inornatus

The nasal *tsick-a-dee-dee* call of the Oak Titmouse is a sound characteristic of the sprawling oak woodlands of interior northern California, west of the Cascade-Sierra. This little bird might be ordinary looking, but an oak forest would seem empty without its subtle presence. • The Oak Titmouse nests in natural cavities, rotted-out stumps and occasionally in abandoned woodpecker nests. It may even partially excavate a cavity in a soft, decaying tree. It lines its nesting cavity with fur, moss and other soft materials. • The Oak Titmouse frequently pairs with the same mate throughout its short life, which seldom exceeds five years.

ID: gray-brown back, tail and wings; small, pointed crest; gray underparts.
Size: *L* 5–5 1/2 in.
Status: locally uncommon to abundant year-round resident.
Habitat: mixed oak woodlands, riparian woodlands and residential plantings.
Nesting: female selects a natural cavity or an abandoned woodpecker cavity in a tree, stump, pole, nest box or fencepost; may use a crevice in a building; nest of vegetation is lined with feathers and hair; female incubates 6–8 eggs for 14–16 days; both adults feed the young.

Feeding: hops about trees and shrubs or hangs from foliage or bark; eats insects, seeds and nuts; also takes berries, small fruits and suet; often uses feeders.
Voice: song is a clear, whistled *teewee teewee teewee* or *weety weety weety*; chickadee-like calls include *tsik-a-dee-dee* or *tsik-a-deer*.
Similar Species: *Juniper Titmouse* (p. 280): gray overall. *Bushtit* (p. 281): smaller; relatively longer tail. *Hutton's Vireo* (p. 257): white wing bars; faint eye ring; lacks a crest.

JUNIPER TITMOUSE
Baeolophus griseus

Despite the Juniper Titmouse's plain, somber plumage, its disposition is bright and cheerful. This titmouse is a denizen of pinyon-juniper woodlands, and it often acknowledges visitors with an inquisitive raise of its head crest. • Juniper Titmice spend much of their time dangling upside-down among green foliage, pecking at bark or prying into every little crack or crevice in a search for aphids, leafhoppers, caterpillars, beetle larvae, spiders, seeds and berries. In winter, they are common at sunflower seed feeders. • Until recently, the Juniper Titmouse and the similar Oak Titmouse of western California were considered one species, the Plain Titmouse. • 'Titmouse' is a term that reflects these birds' high-pitched calls and their mouse-like, scurrying habits.

ID: uniform gray plumage; small, pointed crest; dark eye; no wing bars or eye ring.
Size: L 5¾ in.
Status: fairly common to common year-round resident.
Habitat: mature pinyon-juniper woodlands of the foothills and mountains.
Nesting: excavates a cavity in soft, rotting wood or uses a natural cavity or an abandoned woodpecker nest (chosen by the female); cavity is lined with fur, feathers, moss and grass; female incubates 6–8 eggs for 14–16 days.
Feeding: gleans vegetation, branches and the ground for small insects and spiders; also eats seeds.

Voice: song is a clearly whistled *witt-y witt-y witt-y*; call is a chickadee-like *tsick-a-dee-dee*.
Similar Species: *Oak Titmouse* (p. 279): less gray overall; smaller bill; prefers oak woodlands west of the Sierra. *Bushtit* (p. 281): no crest; brown cheek patch; darker legs. *Mountain Chickadee* (p. 277): black cap; white eyebrow; black bib. *Blue-gray Gnatcatcher* (p. 295): white eye ring; longer tail; white outer tail feathers; no head crest. *Phainopepla* (p. 310): female is much larger, and has a longer tail and red eyes.

BUSHTIT
Psaltriparus minimus

It is often said that the quality of the home reflects the character of its occupant. If this is true, then the tiny Bushtit is a noble resident. The intricate weave and elaborate shape of its hanging nest is an example of splendid architecture that is worthy of admiration and respect. • Intruders that violate the sanctity of a nest site may force the resident Bushtits to switch mates, desert the nest or build a new one in a different location. • The Bushtit is best described as a hyperactive, tiny, gray cottonball with a long, narrow tail. It seems to be constantly on the move, bouncing from one shrubby perch to another, looking for something to keep its hungry little engine running. • When they are not fully engrossed in the business of raising young, Bushtits travel in bands of up to 40 birds, filling the brushlands and woodlands with their charming bell-like tinkles. • *Psaltriparus* is derived from the Greek word *psaltris*, meaning 'player of the lute' (or zither), and *parus*, the former Latin generic name for a titmouse.

ID: uniform gray plumage; light brown cheek patch; long tail; no crest; coastal birds have a brown cap. *Male:* dark eyes. *Female:* pale eyes.
Size: L 4¹/₂ in.
Status: uncommon to common year-round resident at lower and middle elevations.
Habitat: a variety of brushlands and woodlands including pinyon-juniper-mahogany woodlands, riparian thickets, open oak woodlands, oak savannahs and both 'hard' and 'soft' chaparral to about 8000 ft; postbreeders might wander to 9000 ft.
Nesting: pair builds a sock-like, hanging nest, woven with moss, lichens, cocoons, spider silk, fur and feathers, which can take up to 50 days to complete; pair incubates 5–7 eggs for 12 days.

Feeding: gleans vegetation for insects; also eats small seeds; found in constantly roving, cohesive flocks during most of the year.
Voice: excited lisping notes; trilled alarm call.
Similar Species: *Oak Titmouse* (p. 279) and *Juniper Titmouse* (p. 280): small crest; relatively shorter tail; lighter-colored legs; lack the brown cheek patch. *Ruby-crowned Kinglet* (p. 294): greenish; distinct wing bars and eye ring; persistently flicks its wings.

RED-BREASTED NUTHATCH

Sitta canadensis

Red-breasted Nuthatches are often willing to join in on bird waves—warblers, chickadees, kinglets, titmice and small woodpeckers moving in mixed flocks through the forest—while foraging in winter and during migration. The nuthatch's chubby body form, loud, nasal cries and headfirst descents down tree-trunks easily set them apart from the other songbirds. • While building its nest, the Red-breasted Nuthatch smears the entrance of its nesting cavity with sap. It is thought that this sticky doormat might inhibit ants and other animals from entering the nest chamber. Invertebrate parasites can be the most serious threat to nesting success, because they can transmit diseases and emaciate nestlings. • The Red-breasted Nuthatch's distinctive, nasal *yank-yank-yank* calls are heard more often as spring arrives. • The scientific name *canadensis* plainly means 'of Canada'—in reference to this bird's extensive northern nesting distribution.

ID: rusty underparts; gray-blue upperparts; white eyebrow; black eye line; black cap; straight bill; short tail; white cheek. *Male:* deeper rust on the breast; black crown. *Female:* light red wash on the breast; dark gray crown.
Size: L 4¹/₂ in.
Status: fairly common year-round resident; uncommon to fairly common migrant outside of breeding habitat; irregularly numerous winter visitor, including to Central Valley floor in 'invasion' winters.
Habitat: *Breeding:* coniferous forests from sea level to 10,000 ft. *Non-breeding:* may appear in almost any stand of trees.
Nesting: excavates a cavity or uses an abandoned woodpecker nest in a tree; cavity is lined with bark, grass and fur; usually smears the entrance with sap; female incubates 5–6 eggs for 12 days.

Feeding: probes under loose bark for larval and adult invertebrates while creeping along boughs or moving headfirst down tree-trunks; eats many pine and spruce seeds during winter; often visits feeders for seeds and suet.
Voice: slow, continually repeated, nasal *yank-yank-yank*, accelerating in alarm or anxiety.
Similar Species: *White-breasted Nuthatch* (p. 283): larger; lacks the black eye line and the reddish underparts. *Pygmy Nuthatch* (p. 284): smaller; brown cap; lacks the bold black eye line. *Mountain Chickadee* (p. 277): black bib; lacks the reddish breast.

WHITE-BREASTED NUTHATCH

Sitta carolinensis

Nuthatches make their gravity-defying, headfirst struts look incredibly easy. These birds forage on tree-trunks upside down: a White-breasted Nuthatch will frequently pause in mid-descent, arch its head at a right angle to the trunk to survey its surroundings and call noisily to the world, all without losing its foothold. • Unlike wood-peckers and creepers, nuthatches do not use their tails to brace themselves against a tree-trunk; nuthatches clutch the trunk through foot power alone. • White-breasted Nuthatches are regular visitors to many backyard feeders, but they rarely stay long. Most zoom onto a feeder, quickly pick up a seed, then flutter off to hide their stash in a bark crevice. • White-breasted Nuthatches prefer either open, mature pine stands or well-developed oak woodlands. • The scientific name *carolinensis* means 'of Carolina'—an indication that the first scientific speci-men was collected in the mountains of the southeastern U.S.

ID: white underparts; white face; gray-blue back; rusty undertail coverts; short tail; straight bill; short legs. *Male:* black cap. *Female:* dark gray cap.
Size: *L* 5³/₄ in.
Status: fairly common year-round resident locally from near sea level to 10,000 ft.
Habitat: pine forests, oak woodlands and Sacramento River riparia.
Nesting: in a natural cavity or an aban-doned woodpecker nest in a large decidu-ous tree; cavity lined with bark, grass, fur and feathers; female incubates 5–8 eggs for up to 14 days.

Feeding: forages headfirst down tree-trunks in search of larval and adult inverte-brates; also eats many nuts and seeds; regularly visits feeders for seeds and suet.
Voice: frequently repeated *yarnk-yarnk-yarnk*; spring song is made of rapid notes on the same pitch.

Similar Species: *Pygmy Nut-hatch* (p. 284): brown cap; buff-colored underparts; light nape patch. *Red-breasted Nuthatch* (p. 282): black eye line; rusty underparts. *Chickadees* (pp. 276–78): all have a black bib.

PYGMY NUTHATCH

Sitta pygmaea

The Pygmy Nuthatch is one of the most energetic residents of northern California's mountains. During daylight hours it hops continuously among the limbs and twigs of pines, probing and calling incessantly. Its piping, high-pitched voice is quite unlike the nasal, rhythmic calls of the other nuthatches. • With a body designed mainly for foraging among clumps of needles, the Pygmy Nuthatch seems barely capable of keeping itself airborne as it awkwardly flutters between adjacent trees. • Pygmy Nuthatches are quietly gregarious, usually appearing in small flocks that increase in size during fall and winter. At night, Pygmy Nuthatches retreat to communal roosts in tree and building cavities. Although smaller groups seem to be the norm, up to 100 birds have been recorded snuggling together in a single roosting site. Pygmy Nuthatches are even sociable during the nesting season: a breeding pair might have up to three unmated male 'helpers' looking after their nestlings.

ID: brown cap bordered by a black eye line; white cheek and throat; gray-blue back and short tail; pale buff underparts; straight bill.
Size: L 4¹/₄ in.
Status: uncommon to common year-round resident.
Habitat: pine and pine-fir forests from sea level to 9000 ft; post-breeding movement may occur to 10,300 ft.
Nesting: often in an abandoned woodpecker cavity; occasionally excavates its own nest; cavity is lined with soft plant material, wood chips, fur and feathers; female incubates 6–8 eggs for 15–16 days.
Feeding: forages in the outer limbs of trees for adult and larval invertebrates; also eats pine seeds and suet; spends comparatively little time foraging on trunks.
Voice: high-pitched, piping *te-dee te-dee*, unlike the other nuthatches.
Similar Species: *White-breasted Nuthatch* (p. 283): larger; black crown; white above the eyes; rusty undertail coverts. *Red-breasted Nuthatch* (p. 282): black eye line; reddish underparts. *Chickadees* (pp. 276–78): all have a black bib and a longer tail.

BROWN CREEPER

Certhia americana

Brown Creepers are among the most incon-spicuous birds in North America. Embrac-ing sizable stands of larger trees during much of the year, they often go unnoticed until a flake of bark suddenly appears to come alive. • The Brown Creeper forages by spiraling methodically up tree-trunks. Once it reaches the upper branches of a fully investigated tree, the creeper darts down to the base of a neighboring tree to begin another foraging ascent. The long, stiff, pointed tail feathers help to prop this bird against vertical trunks as it hitches its way skyward. • Like the call of the Golden-crowned Kinglet, the thin whistle of the Brown Creeper is so high pitched that birders frequently fail to hear it. • There are many spe-cies of creepers in Europe and Asia, but the Brown Creeper is the only one in North America.

ID: brown back is heavily streaked with grayish white; white eyebrow; white under-parts; thin, downcurved bill; long, pointed tail feathers; rusty rump.
Size: L 5¹/₄ in.
Status: fairly common year-round resident throughout forested northern California; appears outside its breeding habitat in fall and winter.
Habitat: *Breeding:* varied forests and woodlands with large or rough-barked trees. *Winter* and *In migration:* also in any type of natural or exotic woodland at lower elevations.
Nesting: suspended under loose bark; sickle-shaped nest of grass and conifer needles is woven together with spider silk; female incubates 5–6 eggs for 15–17 days.
Feeding: hops slowly up tree-trunks and large limbs, probing loose bark for adult and larval invertebrates; may use the white breast as a light-reflecting aid in foraging.

Voice: song is a soft, quavering, high-pitched *trees-trees-beautiful-trees*; call is a single high *tseee*.
Similar Species: *Nuthatches* (pp. 282–84): all have a gray-blue back and a straight or slightly upturned bill; creep down tree-trunks. *Woodpeckers* (pp. 227–38): much larger; lack the brown back streaking; all have a straight bill.

285

ROCK WREN
Salpinctes obsoletus

Well-camouflaged plumage, secretive habits and echoing songs and calls can make it difficult to spot this endearing, mysterious bird among its rocky habitat. Singing male Rock Wrens are experts in the art of bouncing their buzzy, trilling songs off surrounding rocks to maximize the range and aural effect of the sound while remaining comfortably concealed from onlookers. • Rock Wren nests are generally built in a sheltered, rocky crevice, in an animal burrow or even in a crack of concrete or wood on an abandoned building. The entrance to each nest is typically 'paved' with a few small pebbles, bones and other debris, although some welcome mats have been documented to contain up to 1500 small items. The exact purpose of this paving is unclear: it might protect the nest from moisture, or it may make the nest easier to find in confusing rocky terrain. • Rock Wrens are typically identified at long range by their habit of bobbing atop prominent boulders. • *Salpinctes* is from the Greek word for 'trumpeter,' in reference to this bird's exclamatory call. The scientific name *obsoletus* is Latin for 'indistinct,' in reference to the bird's dull, cryptic plumage.

ID: blue-gray to gray-brown upperparts with intricate light and dark flecking; cinnamon rump and tail; light underparts; finely streaked, white throat and breast; slender bill; short, white eyebrow; tail is trimmed with buff-colored tips.

Size: L 6 in.

Status: rare to locally very common year-round resident; high-elevation breeders often move to milder areas for winter; most common east of the Cascade-Sierra; occasional in migration far from breeding areas.

Habitat: talus slopes, scree, outcrops, stony barrens and similar substrate with abundant crevices.

Nesting: in a crevice, hole or burrow; often places small stones at the opening; nest of grass and rootlets is lined with a variety of items; incubates 5–6 eggs for up to 14 days.

Feeding: forages among rocks, boulders, logs and on the ground for insects and spiders.

Voice: repeated, accented, 1–2-note phrases: *tra-lee tra-lee tra-lee*; alarm call is *tick-EAR.*

Similar Species: *Canyon Wren* (p. 287): clean, white throat; brown underparts; no eyebrow; very long bill. *House Wren* (p. 289): much smaller; brown upperparts lack the flecking; shorter bill. *Bewick's Wren* (p. 288): gray-brown upperparts and rump; bold, white eyebrow bordering a dark eye line; clean, white throat and breast.

CANYON WREN
Catherpes mexicanus

The lively song of the Canyon Wren is heard far more often than the bird itself is seen. The song, which echoes hauntingly across broad canyons, ripples and cascades downward in pitch as if it were recounting the action of tumbling boulders. • Because of its somewhat flattened body shape, the Canyon Wren is able to pass easily through narrow crevices. This small bird forages tirelessly, even during the hottest parts of the day, searching nooks and crevices with great vigilance for hidden insects and spiders. Its quick, gliding movements suggest a small rodent. • While foraging and moving about its territory, a Canyon Wren will quickly raise and lower its hindquarters every few seconds, giving birders a clue to the bird's identity. • *Catherpes* is the Latinized form of the Greek word *katherpein*, meaning 'to creep.'

ID: gray-streaked crown; clean white throat and upper breast; cinnamon belly; black-and-white flecking on the upperparts and flanks; long, downcurved bill; no eyebrow; thin, black barring on the tail.
Size: L 5³/₄ in.

Status: uncommon to locally common year-round resident; most common in and east of the Sierra Nevada.
Habitat: precipitous cliffs, steep-walled streamside canyons, boulder piles and rocky slopes and outcroppings; post-breeding birds may move up to 12,000 ft; much more partial to vertical cliffs than the Rock Wren.
Nesting: in a crevice under rocks, on a ledge or on a shelf in a cave; cup nest of moss, twigs and spider silk is lined with fur and feathers; female incubates 5–6 eggs for up to 18 days; both parents feed the young.

Feeding: gleans rocks, exposed ground and vegetation for insects and spiders.
Voice: song is a startling, descending, whistled *dee-ah dee-ah dee-ah dah-dah-dah*; call is a flat *jeet*.
Similar Species: *Rock Wren* (p. 286): lightly streaked throat and upper breast; faint, white eyebrow; blue-gray to gray-brown upperparts; light underparts. *Other wrens:* all have much shorter bills and a prominent eyebrow.

287

BEWICK'S WREN
Thryomanes bewickii

This charming, year-round resident seems to investigate all the nooks and crevices of its territory with endless curiosity and exuberant animation. As the Bewick's Wren briefly perches to scan its surroundings for sources of food, its long, narrow tail flits and waves from side to side, occasionally flashing with added verve as the bird scolds an approaching intruder. • Bewick's Wren populations in the West are better off than those of the East, where numbers are declining because of a loss of habitat. • John James Audubon chose to honor Thomas Bewick in the name of this spirited bird. A respected friend of Audubon, Bewick was an exceptionally talented wood engraver and the author and illustrator of *A History of British Birds*.

ID: long, bold, white eyebrow; long tail is trimmed with white spots; rich brown or gray-brown upperparts; clean, whitish underparts; slender, downcurved bill.
Size: *L* 5¼ in.
Status: uncommon to fairly common year-round resident at lower and middle elevations.
Habitat: chaparral, riparian thickets, dense vines and shrubby tangles bordering woodlands, parks and gardens, brush piles, shrublands within pinyon-juniper woodlands and oak woodlands.
Nesting: often in a natural cavity or an abandoned woodpecker nest; also in bird boxes; nest of sticks and grass is lined with feathers; female incubates 5–7 eggs for up to 14 days.

Feeding: gleans vegetation for insects, especially caterpillars, grasshoppers, beetles and spiders.
Voice: bold and clear *chick-click, for me-eh, for you*; alarm call is a peevish *dzeeeb* or *knee-deep*.
Similar Species: *Marsh Wren* (p. 291): heavy white streaking on a black back; shorter tail; more brown overall. *House Wren* (p. 289) and *Winter Wren* (p. 290): shorter tail; faint, buff eyebrow. *Rock Wren* (p. 286): dark and light flecking on the upperparts; lacks the long, bold, white eyebrow; cinnamon rump and tail; light streaking on the throat and breast.

HOUSE WREN
Troglodytes aedon

The House Wren's bubbly song and spirited disposition make it a welcome addition to any neighborhood. A small cavity in a standing, dead, backyard tree or a custom-made nest box is usually all it takes to attract this feathered charm to most backyards. Sometimes even an empty flowerpot, a vacant drainpipe, an abandoned vehicle or a single, forlorn shoe is chosen as a suitable nest site. Occasionally, however, you may find that your nest site offering is packed full of twigs and left abandoned without any nesting birds in sight. This nest cavity has become one of many partially constructed 'dummy' nest sites built by the male and disregarded by the female in favor of another location. In such a case, your only course of action should be to clean out the cavity and hope that another pair will find your offering more appealing. • In Greek mythology, Zeus transformed Aedon, the queen of Thebes, into a nightingale; the wonderfully bubbling call of the House Wren is somewhat similar to a nightingale's.

ID: unstreaked, brown upperparts; faint eyebrow; short 'cocked' tail is finely barred with black; faint eye ring; throat is lighter than the underparts.
Size: L 4³/₄ in.
Status: complex; common breeder from early April to late August; rare winter visitor.
Habitat: *Breeding:* riparian, oak, mixed oak-coniferous and almost pure coniferous woodlands and forests with tree cavities; occasionally up to 9000 ft. *Winter* and *In migration:* open woodlands, farmhouse gardens, suburban parks, brushy margins of agricultural areas and riparian thickets.
Nesting: often in a natural cavity or abandoned woodpecker nest; also in bird boxes and crevices; nest of sticks and grass is lined with feathers, fur and other soft materials; incubates 6–8 eggs for up to 19 days.
Feeding: gleans the ground and vegetation for insects, especially caterpillars, beetles, spiders and grasshoppers.

Voice: smooth, running, bubbly warble, lasting about 2–3 seconds: *tsi-tsi-tsi-tsi oodle-oodle-oodle-oodle*; alarm call is a low, churring scold.
Similar Species: *Winter Wren* (p. 290): shorter tail; darker overall; conspicuous barring on the flanks. *Bewick's Wren* (p. 288): long tail; long, bold, white eyebrow; gray-brown upperparts. *Rock Wren* (p. 286): much larger; blue-gray to gray-brown upperparts with light and dark flecking; longer bill. *Marsh Wren* (p. 291): heavy, white streaking on a black back; bold, white eyebrow.

WINTER WREN
Troglodytes troglodytes

The Winter Wren boldly announces its claim to a patch of moist coniferous forest, and then makes its home among the soft green moss and upturned roots of decomposing trees that carpet the forest floor. • The long, melodious, bubbly song of the Winter Wren distinguishes it from other forest birds—few singers in northern California can sustain their song for up to 10 seconds. When it's not singing, the Winter Wren can be observed skulking within the dense shrub layer, probing for food in myriad nooks and crannies. • While the female incubates the eggs and raises the young, the male helps out by delivering food. Once evening arrives, he sleeps apart from his family in his own unfinished nest. • The Winter Wren also breeds across Europe and Asia.

ID: very short, 'cocked up' tail; dark brown upperparts; light brown underparts; fine, light eyebrow; dark barring on the flanks.
Size: L 4 in.
Status: uncommon to common year-round resident; abundant in the north, sparingly southward to Monterey County; very rare to uncommon migrant and visitor from September to March outside breeding areas; rare east of the Cascade-Sierra.
Habitat: *Breeding:* dense, humid coniferous forests with dense undergrowth tangles and mossy, log-strewn floors; also uses deep, shady canyons with mixed oak-coniferous woodlands and dense riparian thickets; generally occurs to 6200 ft, but occasionally at 8000–12,200 ft. *Winter* and *In migration:* riparian thickets, canyon tangles, chaparral and backyard gardens at lower elevations.
Nesting: in a natural cavity, under bark or under upturned tree roots; bulky nest is made of twigs, moss, grass and fur; male

frequently builds up to 4 'dummy' nests prior to egg-laying; female incubates 6–7 eggs for up to 16 days.
Feeding: forages on the ground and about the bases of trees for beetles, wood borers and other invertebrates.
Voice: male's song is a tumbling warble of quick notes, often lasting more than 8 seconds.
Similar Species: *House Wren* (p. 289): less conspicuous barring on the flanks; paler underparts. *Bewick's Wren* (p. 288): long tail; long, bold, white eyebrow. *Marsh Wren* (p. 291): heavy, white streaking on a black back; bold, white eyebrow.

MARSH WREN

Cistothorus palustris

The energetic and reclusive Marsh Wren is associated with cattail and tule marshes and dense, wet meadows. Although it prefers to keep a low profile by staying hidden in the deep vegetation, its distinctive song is one of the characteristic voices of our freshwater and brackish coastal wetlands. Patient observers might be rewarded with a brief glimpse of a this bird perching atop a cattail as it briefly evaluates its territory. • Marsh Wrens occasionally destroy the nests and eggs of other Marsh Wrens and other marsh-nesting songbirds. It is believed that this behavior reduces competition over limited food resources when it comes time to feed their young. Its wetland neighbor, the Red-winged Blackbird, has long regarded the Marsh Wren as a potential enemy, and it occasionally launches its own counter-offensive attacks.

ID: white chin; light brown upper-parts; black triangle on the upper back is streaked with white; long, thin, downcurved bill; white eyebrow; unstreaked brown crown.
Size: *L* 5 in.
Status: local, generally common year-round resident; very uncommon to fairly common migrant; common breeder from mid-April to late October; rare to fairly common winter visitor outside breeding areas.
Habitat: *Breeding:* freshwater or brackish marshes dominated by cattails or tules; also uses flooded willow thickets; non-breeding wanderers may move to 10,000 ft. *Winter* and *In migration:* coastal saltmarshes and dry, brushy thickets and riparian tangles.
Nesting: globe-like nest is woven near water with cattails, tule, weeds and grass and lined with cattail down; female incubates 4–6 eggs for 12–16 days.
Feeding: gleans vegetation and 'flutter-catches' for adult aquatic invertebrates, especially dragonflies and damselflies; occasionally eats other birds' eggs.
Voice: song is a rapid-fire series of *zig-zig-zig-zig* notes and squeaks like an old sewing machine; may sing at night; call is a scolding *chek.*
Similar Species: *Bewick's Wren* (p. 288): longer tail is joggled side-to-side; lacks the white streaking on the black back. *House Wren* (p. 289) and *Winter Wren* (p. 290): faint buff eyebrow; lack the white streaking on a black back.

AMERICAN DIPPER
Cinclus mexicanus

The American Dipper is among the world's most unusual songbirds: along fast-flowing mountain waters, it stands on an exposed boulder, performing deep knee-bends to the gurgle and roar of the raging torrent. This bird will suddenly plunge into the frigid water, disappearing momentarily below the surface to walk along the streambed of rocks and gravel in search of hidden aquatic insect larvae. Fitted with scaly nose plugs, strong claws, dense plumage, 'eyelids' to protect against water spray and an oil gland to waterproof its feathers, the American Dipper is able to survive a lifetime of ice-cold forays. • Naturalist John Muir wrote of the American Dipper: 'Find a fall, or cascade, or rushing rapid … and there you will find the complementary Ouzel, flitting about in the spray, diving in foaming eddies, whirling like a leaf among beaten foam-bells; ever vigorous and enthusiastic, yet self-contained, and neither seeking nor shunning your company.'

ID: slate gray plumage; head and neck are darker than the body; short tail; pinkish legs; straight, black bill; stout body; flashes whitish eyelids. *Immature:* paler bill; paler underparts.

Size: L 7¹/₂ in.

Status: widespread, variably common resident.

Habitat: swift, clear and cold permanent mountain streams with boulders and waterfalls edged with steep cliffs and ledges for nesting; may also use the margins of clear, cold lakes, ponds and subalpine tarns.

Nesting: built into a rock ledge, overhang, uprooted tree or commonly beneath a bridge; bulky globe nest of moss and grass; nest entrance faces the water; female incubates 4–5 eggs for up to 17 days.

Feeding: wades or flies through the water or plunges below the surface for larval aquatic insects, fish fry and eggs.

Voice: vocal throughout the year; warbled song is clear and melodious; alarm call is a harsh *tzeet*.

Similar Species: none.

GOLDEN-CROWNED KINGLET
Regulus satrapa

Not much larger than a Rufous Hummingbird, the Golden-crowned Kinglet is difficult to see clearly as it flits and hovers among conifer twigs in its hyperactive search for insects. This kinglet is the smallest songbird in North America and has acquired a reputation of friendliness and approachability. Golden-crowned Kinglets have, on occasion, been known to allow themselves to be petted or even picked up by humans. • In winter, these birds are frequently seen or heard among roaming multi-species flocks that often include Ruby-crowned Kinglets, Mountain Chickadees, Red-breasted Nuthatches and Brown Creepers. • Their ever-present, high-pitched calls are faint and often lost in the slightest woodland breeze, but Golden-crowned Kinglets are continually on the move, so once they are heard, they can be spotted easily. • *Regulus* is derived from the Latin *rex*, meaning 'king.'

ID: olive back; darker wings and tail; light underparts; dark cheek; 2 white wing bars; black eye line; white eyebrow; black border to the crown. *Male:* reddish-orange crown. *Female:* yellow crown.

Size: *L* 4 in.

Status: fairly common to abundant year-round resident; fairly common to common breeder from April to September; irregular, rare to sometimes abundant migrant and visitor in lowlands from late September to early April.

Habitat: *Breeding:* dense, mature short-needle coniferous forests (especially coast redwood forests, cool, shady, north-facing interior forests and red fir stands). *Winter* and *In migration:* exotic and native conifer forests and plantations and mixed deciduous, oak and riparian woodlands.

Nesting: usually in the outer limbs of a conifer; semi-hanging nest of moss, lichens, twigs and leaves; female incubates 8–9 eggs for about 15 days.

Feeding: gleans and hovers for insects, insect eggs, berries and occasionally sap among the forest canopy.

Voice: song is a faint, high-pitched, accelerating *I…am…not…a…CHEST-nut-backed CHICK-a-dee*; call is a very high-pitched *tsee tsee tsee*.

Similar Species: *Ruby-crowned Kinglet* (p. 294): bold, broken, white eye ring; lacks the black border to the crown. *Chickadees* (pp. 276–78): all have a black bib.

RUBY-CROWNED KINGLET
Regulus calendula

The loud, long, rollicking song of the Ruby-crowned Kinglet is a familiar tune that bursts from flowering lowland thickets in April and through June in the high mountains. • Engaged in spring courtship, the male holds his small ruby crown erect in an effort to impress prospective mates. Throughout most of the year, however, the crown remains hidden among the dull feather tips on top of the bird's head. • During migration, Ruby-crowned Kinglets are regularly seen flitting about high treetops, intermingled with warblers and vireos. In winter, kinglets commonly move through woodlands as part of mixed species foraging flocks that include chickadees, titmice, nuthatches, creepers and several species of warblers. • A quickly moving Ruby-crowned Kinglet is easily mistaken for an *Empidonax* flycatcher or a resident Hutton's Vireo. Quick distinguishing clues are the kinglet's energetic wing-flicking, thinner bill and pale toes.

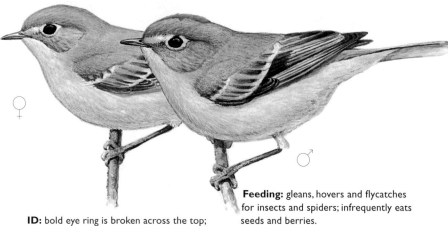

Feeding: gleans, hovers and flycatches for insects and spiders; infrequently eats seeds and berries.

Voice: male's song is an accelerating and rising *tea-tea-tea-tew-tew-tew look-at-Me, look-at-Me, look-at-Me*.

Similar Species: *Golden-crowned Kinglet* (p. 293): dark cheek; black border to the crown; male has an orange crown bordered by yellow; female has a yellow crown. *Orange-crowned Warbler* (p. 311): no eye ring or wing bars. *Empidonax flycatchers* (pp. 242–47): larger; most have a complete eye ring or no eye ring; larger bill; longer tail; lack the red crown. *Hutton's Vireo* (p. 257): thicker bill; larger; slightly longer tail; lacks the red crown and the black patch below the lower wing bar; flicks its wings less persistently; gray-blue toes.

ID: bold eye ring is broken across the top; 2 bold, white wing bars; dark patch below the lower wing bars; olive green upperparts; dark wings and tail; light underparts; short tail; flicks its wings. *Male:* small, red crown (usually not seen). *Female:* lacks the red crown.

Size: L 4 in.

Status: common migrant from late March into early May and from late September to mid-November; surpassingly abundant visitor from mid-September to early May; rare to locally common breeder from mid-May to early October.

Habitat: *Breeding:* subalpine coniferous forests at 4000–10,000 ft. *Winter* and *In migration:* practically all trees and shrubbery.

Nesting: usually in a conifer; semi-hanging nest of moss, lichens, twigs and leaves; female incubates 7–9 eggs for up to 16 days.

BLUE-GRAY GNATCATCHER
Polioptila caerulea

This fidgety inhabitant of woodlands and brushy areas seems to be constantly on the move. With its long tail cocked in the air like a wren, it flits from shrub to shrub, gleaning insects from branches and the surfaces of leaves. As it moves, it issues its banjo-like twang call to announce its energetic presence. • During courtship, a male gnatcatcher accompanies his prospective mate around his territory. Once a bond is established, the pair remains close during nest building and egg laying. The small, cup-shaped nest is usually saddled on the branch of a deciduous tree and is built by both adults. • Although these birds undoubtedly eat gnats, those insects do not represent a substantial portion of their diet. • The scientific name *caerulea* is from the Latin word for 'blue.'

♂

breeding

ID: blue-gray upperparts; long, thin tail; white eye ring; pale gray underparts; no wing bars; black uppertail with white outer tail feathers. *Breeding male:* darker upperparts; black border on the side of the forecrown.
Size: L 4¹/₂ in.
Status: locally rare to fairly common spring migrant and summer breeder from early April to mid-August; uncommon to fairly common fall migrant from August to mid-October; occasional in winter, but regular along coast south of Monterey Bay.
Habitat: *Breeding:* mixed oak and chaparral slopes, mountain mahogany, mixed-oak woodlands and foothills with blue oak to about 6000 ft. *Winter* and *In migration:* various lowland habitats, including riparian woodlands, urban and suburban parks and gardens and brushy areas near water.

Nesting: on a limb or fork in a deciduous tree; lichen-covered cup nest of plant fibers and grass is bound by spider silk; female incubates 3–4 eggs for up to 15 days.
Feeding: gleans vegetation and flycatches for insects, spiders and other invertebrates.
Voice: call is a banjo-like, high-pitched twang: *chee;* male's song is a low warble, often beginning with *zee-u zee-u.*
Similar Species: *Ruby-crowned Kinglet* (p. 294) and *Hutton's Vireo* (p. 257): olive green overall; short tail; wing bars.

WESTERN BLUEBIRD
Sialia mexicana

Like the feathers of all blue birds, Western Bluebird feathers are not actually pigmented blue. The blue color is a result of the feather's microscopic structure: shiny blues that change hue and intensity with the angle of view are produced by iridescence (like soap bubbles); dull blues come from 'Tyndall scatter,' the same process that produces the blue of the sky. • In northern California, Western Bluebirds usually manage to raise two broods of young each year. A second clutch of eggs is often laid just as the first brood has left the nest, even though the first set of young still rely on their parents for food. • In fall and over the winter months, Western Bluebirds often flock together with Yellow-rumped Warblers around good crops of mistletoe berries or berry-producing shrubs.

ID: chestnut red breast; light gray belly and undertail coverts; dark bill and legs; some chestnut on the back. *Male:* deep blue head, back, wings and chin; chestnut red sides and flanks. *Female:* light eye ring; gray-brown head and back; bluish wings and tail.
Size: *L* 7 in.
Status: uncommon to common year-round resident (high-elevation and northern breeders may move to milder areas for winter).
Habitat: *Breeding:* broken oak and oak-conifer woodlands, oak savannahs, riparian woodlands and open pine forests from near sea level to about 7000 ft (may breed up to more than 10,000 ft). *Winter* and *In migration:* lowland valleys, agricultural lands interspersed by woodlands and tree groves, and northwest coastal lowlands.
Nesting: in an abandoned woodpecker cavity, natural cavity or nest box; nest is built of stems, conifer needles and twigs; female incubates 4–6 eggs for up to 17 days.
Feeding: swoops from a perch to pursue flying insects; also forages on the ground for invertebrates; highly reliant on ground foraging or on mistletoe berries in winter.
Voice: song is a harsh *cheer cheerful charmer;* call is a soft *few* or a harsh *chuck.*
Similar Species: *Mountain Bluebird* (p. 297): lacks the chestnut underparts; female is more brown overall. *Lazuli Bunting* (p. 346): smaller overall; thicker, conical bill; white wing bars; white sides and flanks. *Townsend's Solitaire* (p. 298): never has a reddish breast; peach-colored patches in the wings and tail.

MOUNTAIN BLUEBIRD

Sialia currucoides

The destruction of habitat that supported cavity-riddled, standing dead trees, and increased competition with aggressive European Starlings for remaining cavities, have forced many bluebirds to seek nesting habitat in artificial nest boxes. Fortunately for the Mountain Bluebird, starlings shun the high meadows and forest glades sought out by this bird upon its spring arrival in the back country. • During migration and over winter, it is not uncommon to discover flocks of 100 or more Mountain Bluebirds traveling and foraging together. • Mountain Bluebirds breed in Alaska, farther north than any other North American bluebird.

ID: black eyes, bill and legs. *Male:* sky blue body; upperparts are darker than the underparts. *Female:* sky blue wings, tail and rump; blue-gray back and head; gray underparts.

Size: *L* 7 in.

Status: fairly common to common migrant and breeder from April to October; erratic, fairly common to common visitor from mid-October to mid-April.

Habitat: *Breeding:* open and broken subalpine forests at 4000–12,000 ft. *Winter* and *In migration:* lowland grasslands and savannahs, arid grassy valleys and agricultural fields.

Nesting: in an abandoned woodpecker cavity, natural cavity or nest box; cavity is lined with plant stems, grass, conifer needles, twigs and feathers; female incubates 5–6 pale blue eggs for 13 days.

Feeding: swoops from a perch for flying and terrestrial insects; also forages on the ground for a variety of invertebrates, such as beetles, ants and bugs.

Voice: call is a low *turr turr*; male's song is a short warble of churs.

Similar Species: *Western Bluebird* (p. 296): male has a chestnut red breast. *Pinyon Jay* (p. 262): much larger; longer bill. *Blue Grosbeak* (p. 345): thick, conical bill; rusty-brown wing bars; black tail. *Lazuli Bunting* (p. 346): thick, conical bill; male has a cinnamon breast and white wing bars. *Western Scrub-Jay* (p. 261): gray underparts and back. *Townsend's Solitaire* (p. 298): peach-colored patches in the wings and tail; white outer tail feathers. *Steller's Jay* (p. 260): much larger; prominent crest.

TOWNSEND'S SOLITAIRE
Myadestes townsendi

Few birds characterize the mountain forests of the West better than the Townsend's Solitaire. Slim and graceful, this bird makes up for its plain plumage with remarkable bursts of sustained song. • Solitaires nest in open or broken pine and fir forests within the zone of winter snows, where undergrowth is sparse and the ground lies exposed. They are inconspicuous birds, perching for minutes at a time at the tip-top of a tall tree or snag, or on the upturned roots of a fallen tree. Their habit of dropping to the ground to snatch food items suggests the familar foraging strategies of bluebirds. • During the colder months, Townsend's Solitaires move southward and to lower elevations, defending feeding territories among junipers and mistletoe-bearing trees. • Audubon named this western bird in honor of John Kirk Townsend, one of North America's great early ornithologists.

ID: gray overall; darker wings and tail; peach-colored wing patches (a buffy stripe in flight); white eye ring; white outer feathers on the long, thin, square-ended tail. *Juvenile:* brown body is heavily spotted with buff tippings to most feathers; pale eye ring.
Size: *L* 8¹/₂ in.
Status: fairly common migrant and summer breeder locally from 5000–10,000 ft; scattered breeders occur widely below 5000 ft; very sparse migrant along the coast and in lowlands west of the Cascade-Sierra divide; winters in foothills.
Habitat: *Breeding:* montane and subalpine forests with rock outcrops, talus slopes, fell-fields, cutbanks or up-ended trees at 6000–10,000 ft; nests to 2000 ft near the coast. *Winter* and *In migration:* variably lightly wooded habitats at lower elevations; favors trees with berries.
Nesting: on the ground, in a bank or among upturned tree roots; cup nest is built with twigs and grasses and is well-lined with conifer needles; incubates 4 eggs for up to 13 days; eggs are pale blue, patterned with brown.
Feeding: flycatches by sallying from an exposed perch, drops from a perch to the ground for invertebrates and berries; plucks berries from trees.
Voice: song is a lovely shrill that often rises and falls abruptly, lasting 10–30 seconds; call-note is a single, piping *heep*.
Similar Species: *Northern Mockingbird* (p. 304): larger; paler underparts; more white in the sides and tail; bold white patches in wings; found in lowlands. *Bluebirds* (pp. 296–97): similar shape, but both sexes lack the white sides to the tail and the peachy wing patches.

SWAINSON'S THRUSH

Catharus ustulatus

The upward spiral of this bird's song lifts one's spirits with each rising note. The inspiring song can be heard late on spring evenings because the Swainson's Thrush is routinely among the last of the forest songsters to be silenced by nightfall. • The Swainson's Thrush is most often seen on its breeding grounds, perched high in a treetop, cast in silhouette against the colorful sky at dusk. In migration, it skulks about the ground under low shrubs and tangles, occasionally finding itself in backyards and neighborhood parks. This wary bird does not usually allow for easy viewing opportunities—it often gives a sharp warning call well before danger approaches. • The Swainson's Thrush, along with the Swainson's Hawk, was named after William Swainson, an English zoologist and illustrator.

ID: olive brown to reddish-brown upperparts; bold white eye ring; buffy cheek; moderately spotted throat and breast; white belly and undertail coverts; brownish-gray flanks.

Size: *L* 7 in.

Status: fairly common to common migrant from late April to early June and from late August to September; locally rare to common breeder from early May to mid-August.

Habitat: dense, shady shrubs. *Breeding:* riparian thickets and tangles at 4500–8000 ft in the northeast; moist, well-shaded canyons and humid, dense forest understories to 7000 ft in the west.

Nesting: usually in a shrub or small tree; small cup nest is built with grass, moss,

leaves, roots and lichens; female incubates 3–4 eggs for 12–13 days.

Feeding: gleans vegetation and forages on the ground for invertebrates; also eats berries.

Voice: song is a slow, rolling, rising spiral: *cor, cor, corDEElia, DEElia, DEElia;* call is a mellow, rising *wit;* migrants call at night.

Similar Species: *Hermit Thrush* (p. 300): grayish-brown face, head and back; rusty rump and tail; heavily spotted breast. *American Robin* (p. 301): larger; immature has a darker head and orange underparts with heavy black spotting.

HERMIT THRUSH

Catharus guttatus

Beauty in forest birds is often gauged by sound and not appearance. By this criterion the Hermit Thrush is certainly one of the most beautiful birds in northern California. The exquisite song of the Hermit Thrush has inspired many writers, including naturalist John Burroughs: 'Listening to this strain on the lone mountain, with the full moon just rounded on the horizon, the pomp of your cities and the pride of your civilization seemed trivial and cheap.' • Two of the Hermit Thrush's features can be remembered by association with its name: its memorable song always begins with a single, lone (hermit) note; its rump and tail are red, like a lonely old hermit wearing nothing but a pair of red long johns.

ID: rust-colored tail and rump; gray-brown face, head, back and upperwings; pale eye ring; black-spotted breast; light undertail coverts; brownish-gray flanks.

Size: L 7 in.

Status: fairly common migrant from March to mid-May and from September to early November; uncommon to abundant breeder from mid-April to mid-September; locally rare to very common visitor from late September to early April; all populations are migratory, so different birds are present in summer and winter.

Habitat: *Breeding:* well-shaded coniferous and higher evergreen oak forests, often on ridges on upper hillsides; montane riparia from near sea level to 10,000 ft; open forests of mountain mahogany, pinyon pine, limber pine and aspen at 7000–10,000 ft east of the Sierra-Cascade. *Winter* and *In migration:* varied, dense, low vegetation and adjacent edge.

Nesting: in a small tree or shrub; occasionally on the ground; cup nest is built with grass, twigs and mud; female incubates 4 eggs for up to 13 days.

Feeding: forages on the ground and gleans vegetation for insects and other invertebrates; also eats berries.

Voice: male's song is a series of flute-like phrases at varying pitches, with each spiral preceded by a lone, thin note; call is a whining *twee,* a low *chuck,* or a loud *teer.*

Similar Species: *Swainson's Thrush* (p. 299): buffy cheek; olive- or rusty-brown back, rump and tail. *Fox Sparrow* (p. 336): stockier build; conical bill; brown or reddish triangle-shaped breast spots. *American Robin* (p. 301): larger; immature has a darker head and orange underparts with heavy black spotting.

AMERICAN ROBIN

Turdus migratorius

A familiar bird to most North Americans, the ubiquitous American Robin flourishes among suburban lawns, gardens and parks. Even though this bird is commonly associated with urban environments, it is also widespread and common throughout many of northern California's natural habitats. • Although it might look as though robins listen for worms beneath a lawn, they are actually searching visually for movements in the soil—they tilt their heads to the side because their eyes are placed on the sides of their head. • During fall and winter, an influx of robins migrating south from northern states and Canadian provinces may result in gatherings of tens of thousands of birds. • The American Robin was named by English colonists after the robin found in their native land. Somewhat resembling each other, they are only distantly related.

ID: gray-brown back; darker head; white throat streaked with black; white undertail coverts; broken, white eye ring; yellow, black-tipped bill. *Male:* black head; deeper, brick red breast. *Juvenile:* heavily spotted breast. *Female:* dark gray-brown head; light red-orange breast.
Size: *L* 10 in.
Status: locally uncommon to common year-round resident; fairly common to common breeder from mid-February to late September; uncommon to abundant fall migrant and winter visitor; found in varying numbers throughout northern California; withdraws from higher mountains in winter.
Habitat: riparian woodlands, forests with open meadows, forest edges, roadsides, backyards, parks, cities, orchards, pastures and agricultural windbreaks to over 10,000 ft.

Nesting: in a coniferous or deciduous tree or shrub; cup nest of grass, moss and loose bark is cemented with mud; female incubates 4 light blue eggs for 11–16 days.
Feeding: forages on the ground and among vegetation for larval and adult insects, worms, other invertebrates and berries; hundreds may forage together from October to March.
Voice: song is an evenly spaced warble: *cheerily cheer-up cheerio;* call is a rapid *tut-tut-tut.*

Similar Species: *Varied Thrush* (p. 302): 2 orange wing bars; adult has a black breast band; juvenile has a white belly. *Other thrushes:* smaller; immatures lack orange on the breast.

VARIED THRUSH
Ixoreus naevius

The haunting courtship song of the Varied Thrush is unlike any other. The shrill tones of its long, drawn-out whistle penetrate well through the dense vegetation and drifting mist enshrouding this bird's forest habitat. Few listeners can remain stolidly unaffected by this thrush's stirring performance. • Early spring usually proves to be the hardest time of year for birds because food supplies and fat reserves are at a minimum. During heavy, cold, spring storms, many Varied Thrushes (as well as other songbirds) perish—often only days or hours before the re-emergence of warm spring weather and new food abundance. • Non-breeding birds have been reported at elevations as high as 10,000 ft during the summer months. In winter, northern California traditionally welcomes a variable influx of Varied Thrushes from points farther north.

ID: dark upperparts; orange eyebrow; orange throat and belly; 2 orange wing bars. *Male:* black breast band; deep blue-black upperparts. *Female:* like the male but muted; brown upperparts; fainter breast band.
Size: L 9¹/₂ in.
Status: uncommon year-round resident; locally or irregularly rare to abundant migrant and visitor from late September to late March.
Habitat: cool, humid and shady coniferous forests with a dense understory; also uses interior oak woodlands, tall chaparral and riparian woodlands in shady canyons, ravines, gullies and dense coniferous forests; frequently appears in residential areas.

Nesting: often against the trunk of a conifer; bulky cup nest of twigs, leaves, moss and grass; female incubates 3–4 eggs for 14 days.
Feeding: forages on the ground and among vegetation for insects, seeds and berries.
Voice: male's song is a series of sustained, single notes ('trills-on-buzzes') delivered at different pitches, with a lengthy pause between each note; call is a rich, underbreath *chuck*.
Similar Species: *American Robin* (p. 301): lacks the black breast band and the orange eyebrow, throat and wing bars.

WRENTIT
Chamaea fasciata

Unlike most songbirds, Wrentits do not migrate and they mate for life. They are secretive birds, preferring to remain concealed within dense tangles of brush and scrub, rarely crossing open areas where predators could interrupt their feeble flights without warning. A pair of Wrentits may spend an entire lifetime together in an area no larger than a few acres. • This bird's bouncing, trilling voice is heard much more than the bird is actually seen. Wrentits scold human intruders in pairs—though shy, they usually approach within several feet before flitting away.

ID: grayish-brown plumage; small, dark bill; yellowish eyes; buff throat; long, rounded tail (often cocked up); fine chest streaks.
Size: L 6–6¹/₂ in.
Status: locally uncommon to abundant year-round resident.
Habitat: hilly brushland, including lowland and montane chaparral, coastal sage scrub, northern coastal scrub and shrubby tangles along the edges of streams and suburban gardens; readily colonizes regenerating logged sites.
Nesting: pair builds a compact, open cup of bark strips and spider webs; nest is lined with soft plant fibers and hair; outer surface is often coated with lichen; pair incubates 4 pale greenish-blue eggs for about 16 days; both adults feed the young.

Feeding: actively gleans from low branches, twigs and foliage; occasionally hovers or hangs upside down on foliage; insects taken in spring and summer; many berries taken in fall and winter; will take sugarwater and softer items from bird feeders.
Voice: male's song is a short series of accelerating whistled notes ending in a trill; female's song lacks the trill; purring rattle call often betrays this bird's presence.
Similar Species: *Bushtit* (p. 281): smaller; unstreaked, pale gray plumage; brown crown. *Bewick's Wren* (p. 288): white eyebrow; light underparts. *Winter Wren* (p. 290): much shorter tail.

303

NORTHERN MOCKINGBIRD
Mimus polyglottos

The Northern Mockingbird has an amazing vocal repertoire. Known to sing over 400 different song types, this bird imitates other birds, barking dogs and even musical instruments. It can imitate other sounds so perfectly that computer analysis of sonagrams is often unable to detect differences between the original source and the mockingbird. • During winter, mockingbirds establish and defend territories in berry-rich areas, including suburban parks and gardens. Generous offerings of suet and raisins can go a long way in attracting mockingbirds and other feathered friends. • To flush insects and scare off predators, mockingbirds frequently raise their wings and tails. • Mockingbirds have colonized much of northern California only during the 20th century. • The scientific name *polyglottos* is Greek for 'many tongues,' and refers to the bird's varied vocal repertoire.

ID: gray upperparts; dark wings and long tail; 2 white wing bars; white outer tail feathers; light gray underparts. *In flight:* large white patch at the base of the black primaries. *Juvenile:* paler overall; spotted breast.
Size: *L* 10 in.
Status: locally rare to common year-round resident at lower elevations; rare east of the Cascade-Sierra; wanderers routinely appear outside breeding areas, most frequently in fall and winter.
Habitat: orchards, agricultural areas, canyons, valleys and parks and gardens in cities, towns and suburbs with an abundance of berry-producing trees and shrubs to 3500 ft.
Nesting: often in a small shrub or small tree; cup nest is built with twigs, grass, fur and leaves; female incubates 3–5 eggs for 12–13 days.

Feeding: gleans vegetation and forages on the ground for beetles, ants, wasps and grasshoppers; also eats berries; visits feeders for suet and raisins.
Voice: song is a variable musical medley, with the phrases often repeated 3 times or more; call is a harsh *chair* or *chuck*; habitually imitates other songs and noises; often silent and reclusive.
Similar Species: *Northern Shrike* (p. 255) and *Loggerhead Shrike* (p. 254): thicker, hooked bill; black mask; juveniles are stockier and have fine barring on the underparts. *Townsend's Solitaire* (p. 298): prominent eye ring; peach rather than white in the wings. *Sage Thrasher* (p. 305): heavily streaked underparts; faded white wing bars. *Clark's Nutcracker* (p. 263): much larger; much larger bill; darker underparts; white wing patch on the trailing edge of the secondary feathers; more white in the tail.

SAGE THRASHER

Oreoscoptes montanus

The Sage Thrasher is intricately linked to open flats of sagebrush east of the Cascades and Sierra Nevada. These thrashers are regularly seen perched on the tops of sage and other shrubs, belting out long, warbling phrases. • This bird was formerly known as the Mountain Mockingbird or Sage Mockingbird because of its mockingbird-like mannerisms: while perched, the Sage Thrasher slowly raises and lowers its tail, and while running along the ground, it holds its tail high. • 'Thrasher' is derived from 'thrush'—thrashers belong to the family Mimidae, the mimic thrushes. *Oreoscoptes* is Greek for 'mimic of the mountains'—really a misconception because most of their range lies outside the Cascades and Sierra Nevada, largely in the intermountain Great Basin.

ID: gray-brown upperparts; heavily streaked underparts; yellow eyes; short, slim, straight bill. *In flight:* white tail corners; 2 white wing bars (often faded).

Size: *L* 8¹/₂ in.

Status: fairly common migrant from mid-February to early May; uncommon to abundant breeder from mid-March to late September; very rare or local migrant from mid-August to mid-November.

Habitat: *Breeding:* sagebrush and greasewood flats and shrublands dominated by tall sagebrush. *In migration:* sagebrush flats, open brushland and coastal sage scrub.

Nesting: usually in a larger sagebrush; bulky cup nest is made of grass, twigs and leaves and lined with fine vegetation; pair incubates 3–5 eggs for up to 17 days.

Feeding: forages on the ground extensively among vegetation for invertebrates and larvae; also eats berries.

Voice: male's complex, warbled song is sustained, lasting up to 2 minutes, with the phrases usually repeated without a pause; calls include a high *churr* and *chuck;* a notable night singer.

Similar Species: *Northern Mockingbird* (p. 304): juvenile has less heavily streaked underparts; large, white wing patches; white outer tail feathers. *Swainson's Thrush* (p. 299) and *Hermit Thrush* (p. 300): stockier overall; lack the streaking on the belly; dark eyes; pinkish legs; avoid sagebrush flats.

CALIFORNIA THRASHER
Toxostoma redivivum

Concealed by dense chaparral or riparian thickets, the vigorous scratching and digging of the California Thrasher is usually detected by ear rather than by eye. Using its extra-long, downcurved bill, this thrasher digs noisily in the dirt and tosses leaves aside in a determined search for seeds, ants, grubs, beetles and other food. • More often than not, a peek into the dense bushes will reveal little more than the flash of the thrasher's long tail or a short glimpse of its peachy underparts as it retreats. A well-performed squeaking and pishing session, however, is probably enough to cause a California Thrasher to emerge curiously from a secret hiding spot.

ID: dark upperparts; long, downcurved bill; peachy undertail coverts and belly; light tan eyebrow.
Size: L 11–13 in.
Status: fairly common to common year-round resident.
Habitat: dense thickets and brushland in chaparral, riparian woodlands and coastal sage scrub.
Nesting: in a dense shrub or thicket near the ground; pair builds a bulky cup of twigs and sticks lined with soft vegetation and strips of bark; pair incubates 3–4 brown-spotted, pale blue eggs for 12–14 days; both adults feed the young.

Feeding: eats mostly insects, berries and small fruit; also takes seeds, nuts and other plant material; uses its bill to dig in the ground and flip over debris.
Voice: song is a loud series of rambling, squeaky phrases, each phrase repeated once or twice; call is a low *chuck*.
Similar Species: *California Towhee* (p. 325): much smaller; lacks the long, downcurved bill. *Sage Thrasher* (p. 305): dark streaking on the white undersides; shorter, straight bill. *Northern Mockingbird* (p. 304): lacks the long, downcurved bill; pale gray and whitish body plumage.

EUROPEAN STARLING

Sturnus vulgaris

The European Starling is one of the most abundant urban birds in North America. Starlings were introduced to this continent in 1890 and 1891, when about 200 were released into New York's Central Park as part of the local Shakespearean society's plan to introduce to the city all the birds mentioned in the author's works. Starlings spread to almost every corner of the continent often at the expense of many native birds unable to compete for nest sites. Only parts of Alaska, the Arctic and the highest mountain regions are left unconquered by this bird. • Starlings have found tremendous success by associating themselves with urban areas—buildings and other structures provide these birds with plenty of suitable nesting habitat. Despite many concerted efforts to control or even eradicate this species, European Starlings have continued to assert their claim to home in the Americas.

breeding

ID: short, squared tail; dark eyes. *Breeding:* blackish, iridescent plumage; yellow bill. *Fall adult:* brown plumage overall; white spotting on the underparts; dark bill. *In flight:* short, pointed, triangular wings. *Juvenile:* gray-brown plumage; brown bill. **Size:** L 8¹/₂ in.

Status: introduced; uncommon to abundant year-round resident; common to surpassingly abundant visitor from November to late March; withdraws from middle elevations in winter.

Habitat: open areas, including towns, cities, agricultural fields, landfills, roadside ditches, broken woodlands and riparian woodlands to 7000 ft.

Nesting: in an abandoned woodpecker cavity, natural cavity, nest box or almost any other cavity; nest is made of grass, twigs and straw; female incubates 4–6 bluish eggs for 12–14 days.

Feeding: diversely omnivorous, including invertebrates, berries, seeds and garbage; aerially flycatches for termites and flying ants in late summer.

Voice: rambling whistles, squeaks and gurgles; imitates other birds throughout the year; dependent juveniles fill spring with insistent churring cries.

Similar Species: *Brewer's Blackbird* (p. 351): longer tail; black bill; lacks the light spotting; male has yellow eyes. *Brown-headed Cowbird* (p. 352): male has a longer tail and a shorter, conical, dark bill; lacks the light spotting; juvenile has streaked underparts, a stout bill and a longer tail.

AMERICAN PIPIT
Anthus rubescens

American Pipits are birds of open, treeless environments. In northern California, they spend summer in the alpine meadows that carpet the slopes of the highest Sierra Nevada peaks, extending from Tower Peak in Mono County to the Rocky Basin Lakes and Franklin Lakes of Tulare County. This resilient bird breeds only on alpine or arctic tundra. • Many American Pipits arriving on their breeding territories are already paired up—courtship and pair formation often occur at lower elevations, which saves valuable time during a brief nesting season. • During the winter months, this bird is commonly seen among shortgrass patches, barren fields, lawns and beaches of the lowlands. Its plain wardrobe and continuous habit of bobbing its short tail readily distinguishes it from other birds.

non-breeding

ID: faintly streaked, gray-brown upperparts; lightly streaked 'necklace' on the upper breast; streaked breast and flanks; black legs; black tail with white outer feathers; buff-colored underparts; slim body; bobs its tail constantly. *Breeding:* more richly colored about the head and breast.
Size: L 6–7 in.
Status: uncommon to very common migrant from April to mid-May and from early September to late November; uncommon to very common visitor from early September to April; rare and local breeder from mid-May to late September.
Habitat: *Breeding:* alpine tundra and wet meadows above 10,000 ft, often near tarns with exposed gravel shores. *Winter and In migration:* open areas of very short grass or barren ground, including agricultural areas, plowed fields, lawns, sod farms, sea beaches and the margins of lakes, rivers and streams.

Nesting: in a shallow depression; small cup nest is made with coarse grass and sedges and is sometimes lined with fur; frequently has an overhanging canopy; female incubates 4–5 eggs for 13–15 days.
Feeding: walks, does not hop; gleans the ground and vegetation for terrestrial and freshwater invertebrates and seeds.
Voice: familiar flushing and flight call is a reedy *jeet* or *jee-jeet*; male delivers a shrill series of *chwee* notes during his exuberant aerial display on breeding grounds.
Similar Species: *Horned Lark* (p. 268): black 'horns' and facial markings; less white in the tail. *Brewer's Sparrow* (p. 328): unstreaked breast; conical bill; stout body; lacks the white outer tail feathers.

CEDAR WAXWING
Bombycilla cedrorum

A backyard crammed with berry-laden trees and shrubs is a magnet for huge flocks of wandering Cedar Waxings. In fall and winter, waxwings gorge themselves on fruit left hanging on trees and shrub branches. If the fruits have fermented, the waxwings are occasionally rendered flightless from intoxication. • A varying availability of food resources produces irregular incursions outside the breeding areas. Cedar Waxwings remain close to their northern breeding grounds during warm winters if local berry crops are productive. In other years, birds are forced to roam far to survive. • Waxwings were named for the red, wax-like droplets on the tips of their secondary flight feathers. Practiced observers learn to recognize the presence of these lovely, polished birds by their wheezy, quavering trills overhead.

ID: cinnamon crest; brown upperparts; black mask; yellow wash on the belly; gray rump; yellow, terminal tail band; white undertail coverts; red spots on the wings. *Juvenile:* no mask; streaked underparts; gray-brown body.
Size: *L* 7 in.
Status: fairly common breeder from May to late September; local and irregularly common to very common migrant and visitor in foothills and lowlands from mid-September to late May.
Habitat: *Breeding:* riparian groves and mixed forest edge to about 3000 ft. *Winter* and *In migration:* most natural habitats and urban areas with an abundance of food, especially berries and fruits, to 10,000 ft;

concentrations occur in juniper stands and native and exotic fruiting trees and shrubs.
Nesting: in a coniferous or deciduous tree or shrub; cup nest is made with twigs, grass, moss and lichens and is often lined with fine grass and plant down; female incubates 3–5 eggs for 12–16 days; among our later-nesting songbirds.
Feeding: gleans vegetation; also eats buds, flowers, berries and fruit, especially during fall and winter; flycatches extensively in summer and fall.
Voice: faint, high-pitched trilling whistle: *tseee-tseee-tseee.*
Similar Species: *Bohemian Waxwing:* larger; grayer; rusty undertail coverts; yellow and white wing patches.

309

PHAINOPEPLA
Phainopepla nitens

Striking in its glossy plumage and saucy in character, the Phainopepla leads a mysterious existence. This bird varies somewhat in distribution and abundance within northern California. • Much of this bird's life revolves around mistletoe, which provides nesting habitat and a source of food. Once eaten, the pulpy, sticky-coated seeds slip through the bird's digestive system to be deposited on a new host tree or shrub branch, helping the parasitic plant colonize new territory. The mistletoe's tangled growth, sprouting in bushy tangles from elevated tree and shrub branches, also provides a concealing foundation for the Phainopepla's nest. This close, mutually beneficial relationship between plant and bird is known as 'mutualism.' • The name Phainopepla is derived from Greek words meaning 'shining robe,' referring to the male's elegant plumage.

ID: raised crest; red eyes. *Male:* all-black plumage; white wing patch is seen in flight. *Female* and *Immature:* dark wings and tail on an otherwise gray body; pale wing patch is seen in flight.
Size: *L* 7³/₄ in.
Status: highly variable abundance; distribution is not well understood; generally uncommon to locally fairly common breeder from late March to early November; rare visitor from November to March; permanent resident some years throughout range, but absent other years.
Habitat: broken mixed, oak and riparian woodlands containing mistletoe and other berry-producing plants; non-breeders may

wander to 8000 ft; occasionally attracted to exotic shrub plantings.
Nesting: placed in a mistletoe tangle or in the fork of a shrub or tree; male builds most of the shallow, cup-shaped nest with twigs, vegetation, animal hair and spider webs; pair incubates the eggs (male often takes over during daylight) and raises the young.
Feeding: eats mostly seasonally available berries and insects; insects are taken by hawking or while flying or hovering.
Voice: seldom-heard song is a short warble; call-note is a low, liquid *wurp?* with an upslurred effect.
Similar Species: *Cedar Waxwing* (p. 309): immature has streaked underparts, a flattened, swept-back crest and a yellow-tipped tail.

ORANGE-CROWNED WARBLER

Vermivora celata

D on't be disappointed if you are unable to see the Orange-crowned Warbler's tell-tale orange crown, because few birders can say they have actually seen this hidden feature. This bird's most distinguishing characteristic is its lack of obvious marks: wing bars, eye rings and color patches are noticeably absent. Its plain appearance also makes it frustratingly similar to females of other warbler species. • Wood-warblers are strictly confined to the New World. All 109 warbler species (56 occurring north of Mexico) are thought to have originated in South America, which boasts the greatest diversity of warblers. • *Vermivora* is Latin for 'worm eating,' and *celata* is derived from the Latin word for 'hidden,' a reference to this bird's inconspicuous crown.

ID: olive-greenish to grayish-olive body; bright yellow undertail coverts; thin, dark eye line; thin, pale eye-arcs; faintly streaked underparts; thin bill; faint orange crown patch.

Size: *L* 5 in.

Status: fairly common year-round resident; fairly common to abundant migrant from mid-February to early May and from July to early October; uncommon to abundant breeder from early April to late August; variably common winter visitor throughout lowlands.

Habitat: *Breeding:* riparian woodlands, chaparral, the understory of broken deciduous or mixed forests and shrubby slopes to 9500 ft. *In migration:* occurs in a great variety of shrubby trees.

Nesting: on the ground; well-hidden, small cup nest is made of coarse grass; incubates 4–5 eggs for 12–14 days.

Feeding: gleans foliage for invertebrates, berries, nectar and sap; 'gapes open' dead, curled leaves.

Voice: male's song is a colorless, flat trill that loses speed and pitch near the end; call is a bright, thin *tsip*, which is easily overlooked.

Similar Species: *Ruby-crowned Kinglet* (p. 294): tiny and plump; broken eye ring; white wing bars. *Wilson's Warbler* (p. 320): female's face is as bright as her underparts; no breast streaks. *Yellow Warbler* (p. 313): brighter head and underparts; thin, complete eye ring; breeding female has faint, reddish breast streaks. *Common Yellowthroat* (p. 319): female has a darker face and upperparts; no breast streaks; seldom seen well up in trees.

NASHVILLE WARBLER

Vermivora ruficapilla

The Nashville Warbler is a regular summer nester in northern California, but it is seen only in fair numbers during migration. It is most noticeable in spring, when males sing their courtship song from the trees and shrubs of open oak woodlands and dry mountain brushfields. • These warblers have an unusual, disjunct distribution. Most warblers are found either east or west of the Rockies, or across the entirety of North America. The Nashville Warbler is one of the few birds found on both sides of the divide but with a broad gap dividing the eastern and western populations. • Nashville Warblers were first described in Tennessee, even though they do not breed there—they merely migrate through. This misrepresentation is not an isolated incident: the Tennessee, Cape May and Connecticut warblers of the East all bear names that reflect their distribution during migration but do not represent their breeding or wintering grounds.

ID: yellow-green upperparts; bold, white eye ring; small, hidden, red crown; yellow underparts (white between the legs); bobs its tail. *Male:* blue-gray head. *Female* and *Immature:* olive-yellow nape and hindcrown; gray face.
Size: L 4³/₄ in.
Status: uncommon migrant from early April to mid-May and from early August to late September; fairly common breeder from mid-April to late August; rare but regular in coastal lowlands in winter.
Habitat: *Breeding:* open oak and conifer forests and brushfields at 2000–8000 ft. *In migration:* riparian, mixed oak and oak-conifer woodlands, orchards and suburban parks and gardens; post-breeding birds may move to 11,000 ft.

Nesting: on the ground; female constructs a cup nest of grass, bark strips, moss, conifer needles and fur; female incubates 4–5 eggs for 11–12 days.
Feeding: gleans foliage for insects, such as caterpillars, flies and aphids; sometimes flycatches.
Voice: male's song is 2-parted: 4 accented couplets followed by a chattering trill; call is a quick, bright *peetz.*
Similar Species: *Virginia's Warbler:* white throat; whiter breast, belly and sides; grayer upperparts. *MacGillivray's Warbler* (p. 318): male has a slate gray head, chin and throat; broken eye-arcs. *Common Yellowthroat* (p. 319): female lacks the gray head.

YELLOW WARBLER
Dendroica petechia

Yellow Warblers are typically active and inquisitive. As they flit from branch to branch in search of juicy caterpillars, aphids and beetles, their lively courtship songs and golden plumage light up the northern California landscape. • These birds are partial to lowland riparian woodlands while breeding, but they occur in a variety of habitats, including desert oases, mixed woodlands, urban gardens and farm-yard orchards, in migration. • Yellow Warblers are among the most frequent victims of cowbird parasitism. Unlike many bird species of the forest interior, however, Yellow Warblers can recognize the foreign eggs, and they will either abandon their nest or build another nest on top of the old eggs. Despite this vigilance, the Yellow Warbler population has still declined, in part because of cowbirds. • The scientific name *petechia* is Latin for 'red spots on the skin.'

♀

♂

breeding

ID: generally yellowish body; black bill; black eyes; dark yellow-olive tail; bright yellow highlights in the wings. *Breeding male:* red breast streaks. *Breeding female:* faint red breast streaks. *Juvenile:* lacks obvious breast streaks; can be quite drab.
Size: *L* 5 in.
Status: fairly common to abundant migrant from mid-April to late May and from late July to early October; uncommon to locally common breeder from late April to late August; a very few birds linger into winter in protected lowlands.
Habitat: *Breeding:* lowland riparian wood-lands, isolated willow stands, dry montane chaparral with scattered trees and montane coniferous forests with a brushy under-story up to about 9000 ft. *In migration:* occurs widely; partial to shade trees.
Nesting: in the fork of a deciduous tree or a small shrub branch; female builds a compact cup nest of grass, plant down,

lichens and spider silk; female incubates 4–5 eggs for 11–12 days.
Feeding: gleans foliage and vegetation for invertebrates, especially caterpillars, inch-worms, beetles, aphids and cankerworms.
Voice: male's song is a fast, frequently repeated *sweet-sweet-sweet I'm so-so sweet;* call is a loud, sweet *chip.*
Similar Species: *Orange-crowned Warbler* (p. 311): lacks the reddish breast streaks; darker plumage overall. *American Goldfinch* (p. 364): black wings and tail; male often has a black forehead. *Wilson's Warbler* (p. 320): male has a black cap; female has a darker crown and upper-parts; shorter, darker tail. *Common Yellowthroat* (p. 319): female lacks the bright yellow wing edgings; darker face and upperparts; seldom seen high in trees.

YELLOW-RUMPED WARBLER

Dendroica coronata

The Yellow-rumped Warbler is the most abundant and widespread wood-warbler in North America. Even though it is a common sight for most birdwatchers, it is still appreciated for its energetic behavior and attractiveness. • This species comes in two forms: the common, yellow-throated 'Audubon's Warbler' of the West and the white-throated 'Myrtle Warbler' breeding in the North and east of the Rocky Mountains. Although 'Myrtles' do not breed in northern California, they are commonly seen along the Pacific coast in migration and during winter. The two forms of the Yellow-rumped Warbler were once considered separate species, but because of their partially overlapping ranges, and close genetic similarities, they are now considered a single species.

♀

'Audubon's Warbler'

♂   *breeding*

ID: both forms flash white tail corners. *Breeding male:* blue-gray to blackish head and back; black streaks on the back; blackish breast and sides. *Breeding female:* gray-brown upperparts; whitish underparts with faint brown breast streaks; fainter yellow patches. *'Audubon's Warbler':* yellow crown, chin and throat, side patches and rump; white belly, undertail coverts and undertail patch; white wing highlights. *'Myrtle Warbler':* white rather than yellow chin and throat; darker cheek; thin, white eye line; strong streaking beneath.
Size: L 5¹/₂ in.
Status: abundant migrant from early April to mid-May; locally uncommon to abundant breeder from early April to late August; common to abundant migrant and visitor from early September to mid-April; 'Myrtle' race is a very uncommon migrant inland and a common migrant

and visitor from mid-September to early May along coast.
Habitat: *Breeding:* broken coniferous forests from sea level (locally) to 11,000 ft. *Winter* and *In migration:* variety of well-vegetated, lowland habitats.
Nesting: in a crotch or on a horizontal limb in a conifer; female constructs a compact cup nest with grass, bark strips, moss, lichens and spider silk; female incubates 4–5 eggs for up to 13 days.
Feeding: hawks, hovers or gleans vegetation for insects; sometimes eats berries; feeds on the ground, on fencelines, building eaves, etc.
Voice: male's song is a brief, bubbling warble, rising or falling at the end; much variation between races and individuals; call is a sharp *chip* or *chet*.
Similar Species: *Townsend's Warbler* (p. 316): yellow face and breast have black streaking; lacks the yellow rump.

BLACK-THROATED GRAY WARBLER
Dendroica nigrescens

The Black-throated Gray Warbler's shrill *weezy-weezy-weezy-wee-zee* song is very similar to the songs of its close relatives, the Townsend's and Hermit warblers, but those two species are easily distinguished from the Black-throated Gray visually by their conspicuous yellow features. Male and female Black-throated Grays have very similar plumage, but the male is distinct because of his darker black markings. • This warbler is highly migratory, and its winter months are spent in Mexico and South America. • The Black-throated Gray Warbler is characteristic of the blend zone between lower oak woodlands and higher conifer forests west of the mountains and juniper and pinyon pine eastward.

breeding

ID: deep gray upperparts with black back streaks; black crown; white eyebrow and broad 'mustache' stripe; yellow lore; sides streaked with black; white belly and undertail; black legs; 2 white wing bars. *Male:* black chin and bib. *Female:* dark gray head; dark streaking on the chin, throat and breast.

Size: *L* 5 in.

Status: fairly common migrant from late March to early May and from early August to October; fairly common to common breeder from mid-April to August; very rare but regular winter visitor.

Habitat: *Breeding:* west of the Cascade-Sierra in oak woodlands, mixed oak-conifer forests and tall brushfields; east of the Cascade-Sierra in juniper and pinyon stands and mountain mahogany. *In migration:* variety of lowland woodlands, chaparral, farmyard and ranchland tree groves and windbreaks, and suburban parks and gardens.

Nesting: usually in a conifer, on a horizontal branch; small cup nest is made of grass, moss, lichens, feathers and fur; female (primarily) incubates the eggs.

Voice: lazy, oscillating *weezy-weezy-weezy-wee-zee*, often rising or falling at the end.

Similar Species: *Black-capped Chickadee* (p. 276) and *Mountain Chickadee* (p. 277): white breast; unstreaked sides; lighter, unstreaked upperparts. *Female 'Myrtle Warbler'* (p. 314): yellow on the crown, sides and rump; thin, white eye line.

TOWNSEND'S WARBLER
Dendroica townsendi

The Townsend's Warbler seems to have found 'greener pastures' in which to nest, but this colorful black-and-yellow bird still graces California during migration and throughout the winter months—a time when most warblers are enjoying the warm climes of tropical America. • Conifer crowns are preferred foraging sites for many wood-warblers, making warbler watching a neck-straining experience. Because they feed largely in tall trees during winter, Townsend's Warblers are often 'under-looked.' Sharp eyes, good birding instincts and a bit of luck will go a long way in helping you meet the striking Townsend's Warbler. • This bird occasionally hybridizes with the closely related Hermit Warbler. • This western bird bears the name of one of the West's pioneer ornithologists, John Kirk Townsend.

breeding

ID: yellow breast and sides are streaked with black; white lower belly and undertail coverts; black ear patch encompasses the eye; olive-greenish upperparts; 2 white wing bars. *Male:* black chin, throat and crown. *Female:* yellow chin and throat; white upper belly; dusky crown and ear patch.
Size: *L* 5 in.
Status: fairly common to very common migrant from late March to late May and from mid-August to late October throughout most of northern California; uncommon to locally very common visitor from October to mid-April.
Habitat: lowland riparian and oak woodlands, mixed oak-coniferous forests, conifer and exotic tree groves and suburban parks and gardens; partial to semi-open, full-crowned lowland conifers in winter.
Nesting: from the mountains of Oregon and northern Idaho to Alaska.
Feeding: gleans vegetation and flycatches for beetles, flies, wasps and caterpillars.
Voice: male's song, heard in April and early May, is wheezy, ascending and variable; call is an incisive, electronic *tzp*.
Similar Species: *Hermit Warbler* (p. 317): gray back; white breast, belly and undertail; all-yellow face lacks the dark ear patch.

HERMIT WARBLER

Dendroica occidentalis

Upon arriving on their favored nesting grounds, male Hermit Warblers will quickly patrol the crowns of the tall coniferous trees that mark the boundaries of their territorial claim. Each treetop affords a defending male a superb singing perch and vantage point from which he will thwart the intrusion of another male, or welcome the arrival of a potential mate. • 'Hermit' is a poor name for this woodwarbler, as it is often seen traveling and foraging in mixed-species flocks during migration. • Along the northernmost limits of its range, the Hermit Warbler occasionally interbreeds with the Townsend's Warbler. Hybrids reveal the yellow head of the Hermit and the darkly streaked, yellow underparts of the Townsend's. • This species is among the most abundant summer birds of closed-canopy conifer forests within its range. Where stands open into park-like settings at higher elevations or on windswept ridges, Hermits give way to 'Audubon's Warblers.'

breeding

ID: bright yellow forehead and face; 2 bold, white wing bars; black-streaked, gray back; white underparts. *Breeding male:* black chin, throat, crown and nape. *Female:* yellow chin; black throat patch; gray crown and nape. *Immature:* white chin; black throat patch; olive crown and back; dingy cheek patch; pale eye ring.
Size: L 4¹/₂–5 in.
Status: uncommon to fairly common migrant from early April to late May and from late July to October; uncommon to abundant breeder from late April to early August; rare, regular winter visitor.
Habitat: extensive conifer forests with minimal hardwoods and high canopy closure from near sea level (locally) to near timberline.
Nesting: female builds a deep, compact open cup of plant fibers, twigs, conifer needles, lichens, moss and spider webs lined with feathers, hair and other soft materials; placed well away from the trunk on a high conifer branch; 4–5 eggs are incubated for about 12 days.

Feeding: forages on branches; gleans, hawks and swings from branch tips; males will sometimes forage higher than females; eats insects, larvae and spiders taken from the high tree canopy; migrating birds often forage in mixed-species flocks.
Voice: song is a highly variable, high-pitched series of shrill, accented notes; call is a sharp, thin *tsik*.
Similar Species: *Townsend's Warbler* (p. 316): dark ear patch; long, dark streaking on the sides of the yellow breast; overwinters, but does not breed, in northern California.

MacGILLIVRAY'S WARBLER

Oporornis tolmiei

Keeping to dense, impenetrable thickets at higher elevations, the MacGillivray's Warbler is a difficult bird to get a clear view of—birders often have difficulty spotting this understory skulker, whose presence is often ascertained only by its loud, rich *chip* call. • Different species of wood-warblers are able to coexist through a partitioning of foraging 'niches' and feeding strategies. Through this intricate partitioning, competition for food sources is reduced and the exhaustion of particular resources is avoided. Some warblers inhabit high treetops, a few feed and nest along outer tree branches, some at high levels and some at lower levels, and others restrict themselves to inner branches and tree-trunks. MacGillivray's Warblers have found their niche among dense understory shrubbery and brushy tangles. • The best time of year to observe this mountain specialty is in spring, when males sit boldly atop taller shrubs to belt out their courtship serenades. • Audubon named this warbler in honor of William MacGillivray, who edited and reworked the manuscript of Audubon's classic work.

breeding

ID: yellow underparts; olive-green upperparts; bold, broken, white eye ring; pinkish legs. *Male:* dark slate gray hood; blackish bib. *Female* and *Immature:* light gray-brown hood and bib; white chin.
Size: L 5–5³/₄ in.
Status: uncommon to fairly common migrant throughout from early April to late May and from mid-August to early October; fairly common breeder from mid-April to late August.
Habitat: *Breeding:* moist, well-shaded, soft chaparral, riparian thickets and dense understory of coniferous forests close to water, to 10,000 ft. *In migration:* moist, shady riparian thickets and other similar habitats.
Nesting: in low trees or shrubs between vertical stems; small cup nest is made with weeds and grasses; female incubates 4 eggs for up to 13 days.
Feeding: gleans low vegetation and the ground for beetles, bees, leafhoppers,

insect larvae and other invertebrates; does not ordinarily ascend high into tall trees.
Voice: clear, rolling *sweeter sweeter sweeter sugar sugar*; call is a low, rich *chip*.
Similar Species: *Nashville Warbler* (p. 312): yellow chin; complete eye ring; white between the legs; bobs its tail. *Common Yellowthroat* (p. 319): female lacks the incomplete eye ring and the grayish bib.

COMMON YELLOWTHROAT

Geothlypis trichas

With so much diversity within the North American wood-warbler clan, it is no surprise that one species has taken to inhabiting wetlands. The Common Yellowthroat shuns the forests favored by most of its kin; instead, it chooses to twitch and buzz in a world of cattails and tules. • Yellowthroats will stubbornly refuse to reveal themselves to a waiting pair of binoculars, but their loud songs are heard with very little effort. • Unfortunately, many wetland species have been displaced because much of northern California's landscape, especially within the Central Valley, has been converted into urban areas and agricultural lands. • The saltmarshes of the greater San Francisco Bay area are the exclusive breeding home of *G. trichas sinuosa*, one of the 11 recognized subspecies of the Common Yellowthroat in North America.

ID: yellow throat; olive-green upperparts; orange legs. *Breeding male:* vivid black mask with a pale upper border. *Female:* no mask.
Size: L 4¹/₂–5¹/₂ in.
Status: fairly common to common year-round resident in the San Francisco Bay area; elsewhere fairly common to common migrant local breeder from late March to mid-October; rare to uncommon winter visitor in lowlands.
Habitat: freshwater and brackish saltwater marshes or meadows with dense stands of cattails and rushes; also found in dense riparian thickets and shrubbery and in terrestrial habitats with unbroken stands of nettle, dock, mustard or fennel.
Nesting: low to the ground, usually in a small shrub or among reeds, cattails, bulrushes or other emergent vegetation; large, compact nest is made of weeds, grass and dead leaves; female incubates 3–5 eggs for 12 days.

Feeding: gleans vegetation and hovers for adult and larval insects, including dragonflies, spiders and beetles; occasionally eats seeds.
Voice: song is a clear, oscillating *witchety witchety witchety-witch* or *REEsitta, REEsitta, REES*; call is a double-toned, reedy *tchep*.
Similar Species: male is distinctive. *Yellow Warbler* (p. 313): chubbier; brighter yellow overall; bright yellow wing-edge highlights. *Wilson's Warbler* (p. 320): face is as bright as the underparts; dark cap; tail and wings are generally darker than the back. *Orange-crowned Warbler* (p. 311): yellowish-green overall; faint breast streaks. *Nashville Warbler* (p. 312): bold, complete white eye ring contrasts against the head or face; not found in marshes; bobs its tail.

WILSON'S WARBLER
Wilsonia pusilla

Even a casual birder's glance into a streamside thicket is sure to spot the energetic flash of a Wilson's Warbler flitting busily around its impenetrable home. Fueled by energy-rich insects, this golden bird flickers through tangles of leaves and branches as if a motionless moment would break some unwritten law of warblerdom. Birders might feel exhausted after scurrying about in hopes of observing this little gem, but the Wilson's Warbler never tires during its lightning-fast performance. • Shrubs still laden with heavy spring snow often greet Wilson's Warblers arriving in their high Sierra breeding grounds during the last few weeks of April. • This bird is most deserving of its name: the Wilson's epitomizes the energetic devotion that pioneer ornithologist Alexander Wilson exhibited in his studies of North American birds.

ID: yellow underparts; yellow-green upperparts; beady, black eyes; thin, black bill; frail, orange legs. *Breeding male:* black cap. *Female:* cap is faint, partial or absent.
Size: L 4¹/₂–5 in.
Status: abundant migrant from mid-March to late May and from early August to early October; uncommon to locally abundant breeder from mid-March to late August; very few may remain into December.
Habitat: cool, moist, riparian habitats with dense deciduous shrub cover, especially streamside thickets of willow, alder and dogwood; also uses wet mountain meadows and the edges of small lakes and springs to 10,000 ft; most numerous in the northwestern fog belt.
Nesting: on the ground, sunken into soft substrate, or in a low shrub or thicket; neat cup nest of moss, grass and leaves is occasionally lined with fine grass; female incubates 4–6 eggs for 10–13 days.

Feeding: gleans vegetation, hovers and catches insects on the wing; eats mostly adult and larval invertebrates.
Voice: song is a loud, stacatto chatter that accelerates toward the end: *chi chi chi chi chi chi chet chet!*; call is a soft, brittle *chet*, similar to the note of the Winter Wren.
Similar Species: male's black cap is distinctive. *Yellow Warbler* (p. 313): crown and back are as bright as the underparts; bright yellow wing edgings; male has red breast streaks. *Common Yellowthroat* (p. 319): female has a dark face and a broken, white eye ring; lacks the bright yellow belly and sides. *Orange-crowned Warbler* (p. 311): faint breast streaks; darker face; not as intensely yellow below.

YELLOW-BREASTED CHAT

Icteria virens

At a length of nearly 8 in, the Yellow-breasted Chat is quite literally a 'warbler and a half.' In some ways, this bird deserves its place as an official member of the wood-warbler clan: its bright yellow coloration and intense curiosity are all typical traits of the warblers. However, the chat's large size, curious vocalizations and noisy thrashing behavior suggest a closer relationship to the mimic thrushes, such as the Gray Catbird and Northern Mockingbird. • Unfortunately, the conversion of valuable riparian habitat to agricultural, industrial and residential land has left chat refugees with fewer secure places to live. Efforts to protect and create natural riparian buffer zones between sources of water and human developments will certainly help ensure the future of this enigmatic bird in northern California.

ID: white 'spectacles'; white 'jaw' line; heavy, black bill; yellow breast; white under-tail coverts; olive-green upperparts; long tail; gray-black legs. *Male:* black lore. *Female:* gray lore.
Size: L 7¹/₂ in.
Status: rare to uncommon migrant from early April to mid-May; rare to very uncommon migrant from late August to early October; locally rare to uncommon breeder from early April to early September.
Habitat: dense riparian thickets bordering streams, small ponds and swampy ground dominated by vine tangles, willows and lush, low shrubbery interspersed by taller trees; sometimes breeds in extensive hillside bramble patches.

Nesting: low in a shrub or small tree; well-concealed, bulky nest is made of leaves, straw and weeds, with a tight inner cup woven with bark and plant fibers; female incubates 3–4 eggs for about 11 days.
Feeding: gleans low vegetation for insects.
Voice: slurred, piping whistles, *kuks*, harsh rattles and 'laughs,' linked together or issued alone in no obvious order; well known for persistent night singing in May and June.
Similar Species: none.

321

WESTERN TANAGER
Piranga ludoviciana

Few birds can match the tropical splendor of the male Western Tanager. His golden body, accentuated by black wings, a black tail and an orange-red face, expresses the true character of this bird. • Western Tanagers are indeed tropical for most of the year, and they only inhabit northern climes during the short summer breeding season. During spring migration, small flocks of Western Tanagers pass over the blossoming woodlands of northern California, occasionally stopping in suburban parks and backyard gardens to complete scheduled, but brief, refueling exercises. In fall, Western Tanagers retreat to Central and South American wintering grounds, where they regroup with even more colorful tanager relatives. • The song of the male tanager can be difficult to learn, because it closely parallels the phrases of the robin's song. The tanager's phrases tend to be hoarser, however, as if the bird has a sore throat. Fortunately, the tanager's hiccup-like *pit-a-tik* call, which signals the end of each song, is quite distinctive.

breeding

ID: *Breeding male:* yellow underparts and rump; 1 yellow and 1 white wing bar; black back, wings and tail; often has red on the forehead or the entire head (variable); pale bill. *Breeding female:* olive-green overall; lighter underparts; darker upperparts; faint wing bars.

Size: *L* 7 in.

Status: fairly common to abundant migrant from mid-April to late May and from August to late September; uncommon to abundant breeder from early May to mid-August; rare winter visitor.

Habitat: *Breeding:* great variety of foothill and mountain forests and woodlands, generally tall conifers with or without a hardwood component, from near sea level to 9000 ft. *In migration:* may appear in almost any stand of trees, no matter how small or isolated.

Nesting: in a fork or on a horizontal branch of a conifer, placed well out from the trunk; cup nest is loosely built of twigs, grass and other plant materials and lined with fine vegetation; female incubates 4 eggs for 13–14 days.

Feeding: gleans vegetation and catches flying insects on the wing; eats wasps, beetles and other insects; also eats fruit; drinks from the ground.

Voice: song is a hoarse, rapid series of dry 2- or 3-note phrases; call is a unique, crisp *pritik* or *priterik*.

Similar Species: male is distinctive. *Bullock's Oriole* (p. 354): female has a thinner, sharper bill and lacks the all-yellow underparts. *Summer Tanager:* female lacks the white wing bars.

GREEN-TAILED TOWHEE

Pipilo chlorurus

In classic towhee style, this bird repeatedly jumps back and forth in the dappled shadows of the forest floor scratching away loose leaf litter and shrubby debris with both feet in its search for insects and hidden seeds. • The Green-tailed Towhee spends most of its life concealed in the dense, low understory of forest openings, but if a threat is presented, it will unwillingly flush or run from cover, giving an annoyed mewing call. The male Green-tailed Towhee will usually only emerge during spring, when he sings clear, whistled notes and raspy trills from an exposed woody perch. • Green-tailed Towhees may be routine summer birds of mountain slopes while remaining entirely unknown in the valleys below. They often join up with White-crowned Sparrows during the fall migration to their Mexican wintering grounds.

ID: orange-rufous crown; green upperparts, most intense on the tail; white throat is bordered by dark and white stripes; sooty-gray face and breast; gray legs; conical, gray bill. *Immature:* brownish overall; streaked upperparts and underparts; pale throat is bordered by dark and white stripes.

Size: L 6¹/₂–7 in.

Status: uncommon to locally common breeder from late April to early September; not often detected in migration.

Habitat: dense, low montane chaparral and open pine forests dominated by bitterbrush, manzanita, currant and sagebrush.

Nesting: on the ground or very low in a bush; deep, bulky, thick-walled cup nest of twigs, grass and bark shreds is lined with fine materials; female incubates 3–4 eggs

for 11 days; female will run from the nest in advance of human intrusion.

Feeding: scratches the ground for insects, seeds and berries; drinks morning dew from leaves; occasionally visits feeding stations.

Voice: song is clear, whistled notes followed by 'squeally,' raspy trills: *swee-too weet chur cheee-churr*; call is a distinctive, nasal *mew*.

Similar Species: *Chipping Sparrow* (p. 327): smaller; white eyebrow; black eye line; mottled brown back. *California Towhee* (p. 325): brown throughout; buffy throat. *Rufous-crowned Sparrow* (p. 326): reddish eye line; lacks the green back.

SPOTTED TOWHEE
Pipilo maculatus

Where dried leaves form a crunchy carpet beneath thickets and patches of shrubs, you just might encounter a Spotted Towhee. Like the Green-tailed Towhee, this large sparrow is a noisy forager that scratches at loose leaf litter by kicking with both feet. Sometimes these birds are so noisy that you might expect an animal of sasquatch-sized proportions to be the source of the ruckus. • Spotted Towhees rarely leave their sub-arboreal world, except to perform their simple courtship song or to furtively eye a threat to their territory. These shy birds can often be enticed into view by 'squeaking' or 'pishing,' noises that alert curious birds to an intrusion. Discerning birders, however, would rather not disturb these busy birds, and instead prefer to enjoy the sound of the towhee's clamorous exploits. • Until recently, the Spotted Towhee was grouped together with the Eastern Towhee (a 'spotless' eastern bird) as a single species, known as Rufous-sided Towhee.

ID: *Male:* black hood, back, wings and tail; rufous flanks; dark, conical bill; bold, white spotting on the wings; white tips on the outer tail feathers; white belly and undertail. *Female:* somewhat drabber and paler overall.
Size: L 7–8¹/₂ in.
Status: fairly common to common year-round resident; summer breeders in northeast and higher Sierran areas move to milder areas in winter; local breeder in valley bottoms and sagebrush plains.
Habitat: riparian thickets, chaparral, brushy ravines, scrubby patches among open forests and woodlands; shady canyons and thick undergrowth in suburban parks and gardens to 8000 ft (rarely to 11,000 ft).

Nesting: low in a bush, on the ground under cover or in a brushy pile; cup nest of leaves, grass and bark shreds is lined with fine materials; female (primarily) incubates 3–4 eggs for 12–13 days.
Feeding: scratches the ground vigorously for seeds and insects; will visit feeding stations periodically; seldom feeds in trees.
Voice: song is a simple, querulous trilling: *here here here PLEASE;* call is a raspy or whining *chee* or *chwaay.*
Similar Species: *Black-headed Grosbeak* (p. 344): stockier; much heavier bill; dark brown eyes; rufous is restricted on the sides. *Dark-eyed Junco* (p. 342): smaller; 'Oregon' race has pale rufous on the back and sides.

CALIFORNIA TOWHEE

Pipilio crissalis

The California Towhee's sharp, metallic *chink* notes burst from bushes and shrubs in a proclamation of this bird's territory. California Towhees are highly territorial, and in the dense vegetation of backyards, city parks and coastal scrub, males establish and aggressively defend their territories. Some males have even been observed attacking their own reflections in low-mounted windows and shiny hubcaps. • California Towhees are very accepting of their human neighbors. This common, year-round resident is regularly seen foraging under picnic tables, on patios, under parked cars or at the foot of a patient admirer. • If a pair becomes separated while foraging, they re-establish contact by squealing atop a bush. Once reunited, they bob rhythmically to reaffirm their bond. • Until recently, the California Towhee and the Canyon Towhee were grouped together as the Brown Towhee, but recent studies have shown that these two birds are distinct from one another and their ranges do not overlap.

ID: brown upperparts; light brown under-parts; rusty undertail coverts; brown crown; buffy throat with a broken, black 'necklace'; short, stout, conical bill; long tail. *Juvenile:* streaked underparts.
Size: L 8¹/₂–10 in.
Status: uncommon to abundant year-round resident.
Habitat: broken chaparral and shrubby tangles, thickets and hedgerows near streams, gardens, cemeteries, parks, wood-land edges, brushfields and farmyards.
Nesting: bulky, open cup of grass, twigs, weeds and strips of bark is lined with hair, fine grasses and rootlets; female incubates 3–4 darkly marked, pale bluish-white eggs for about 11 days; both adults feed the young; pairs may mate for life.
Feeding: forages on the ground, often scratching at litter or soil; often feeds under the shade of large objects; eats mostly seeds and insects; also takes some berries and small fruits.
Voice: song is a series of loud, sharp, accel-erating *chink* notes; call is a single, metallic *chink*; often sings from elevated perches.
Similar Species: *Brewer's Blackbird* (p. 351): female lacks the rusty undertail coverts and the conical bill. *Brown-headed Cowbird* (p. 352): female lacks the rusty undertail coverts. *California Thrasher* (p. 306): larger; long, curved bill; white throat; light eyebrow.

325

RUFOUS-CROWNED SPARROW
Aimophila ruficeps

The Rufous-crowned Sparrow usually avoids the dense chaparral and oak-dominated woodlands that many sparrows prefer. Instead, it remains devoted to the arid, grassy slopes and shrub-strewn, rocky outcroppings that carpet many of interior northern California's canyons and foothills. • During the winter months, Rufous-crowned Sparrows are seen hopping about in search of seeds from sun-dried grasses and herbaceous plants. • When alarmed or disturbed, this sparrow will readily issue a nasal *deer-deer-deer*. • William Swainson first gave the name *Aimophila*, meaning 'blood-loving,' to the Bachman's Sparrow of the eastern U.S. The five other American members of this genus, including the Rufous-crowned variety are western birds.

ID: rufous crown; gray eyebrow and cheek; rufous line behind the eye; white eye ring; black and white whisker stripes; whitish throat; unstreaked, buffy-gray breast. *Juvenile:* buffier overall with a streaked breast and crown.
Size: L 5–6 in.
Status: locally uncommon to fairly common year-round resident.
Habitat: arid, sunny and grassy foothill slopes and canyons with rock outcroppings interspersed with low shrubs; at elevations to 3500 ft.
Nesting: placed on the ground under a shrub or grass clump; open cup of twigs, grass and plant fibers is often lined with

animal hair; 3–4 pale bluish-white eggs; both adults feed the young.
Feeding: forages for seasonally available insects and seeds while walking or hopping on the ground; may feed among shrubs and weeds.
Voice: song is a series of rapid, bubbling warbles and *chip* notes; call is a sharp *deer*, usually given in a series of 2 or 3.
Similar Species: *Chipping Sparrow* (p. 327): black eye line; white eyebrow; lacks the black and white whisker stripes. *American Tree Sparrow*: lacks the black and white whisker stripes; central breast spot.

CHIPPING SPARROW

Spizella passerina

The Chipping Sparrow and the Dark-eyed Junco do not share the same tailor, but they must have attended the same voice classes. The differences between these two birds' songs are downright difficult to learn. The rapid trill of the Chipping Sparrow is slightly faster, drier and more mechanical, but even practiced birders can have difficulty identifying the singer and must often resort to tracking down the source for visual confirmation. • Chipping Sparrows are found from the forest floor to the topmost spires of conifers. They commonly nest at eye level, so you can easily have the good fortune to watch their breeding and nest-building rituals close-up. • 'Chipping' refers to this bird's call. *Passerina* is Latin for 'little sparrow.'

breeding

ID: prominent rufous cap; white eyebrow; black eye line; light gray, unstreaked underparts; mottled brown upperparts; all-dark bill; 2 faint wing bars; pale legs.
Size: *L* 5–6 in.
Status: uncommon to fairly common migrant from late March through April and from late August to late October; uncommon to common breeder from mid-April to August; locally rare to very uncommon winter visitor.
Habitat: *Breeding:* open or semi-open woodlands with a grassy understory, including oak woodlands and orchards, mixed deciduous-coniferous forests, open pinyon-juniper woodlands and pure coniferous forests through the subalpine meadows to 10,500 ft. *In migration:* sagebrush scrub, chaparral, open grassy woodlands, lawns and weedy or brushy fields; most common in the interior.

Nesting: usually low to mid-level in a coniferous tree or oak; compact cup nest is woven with grass, rootlets and fine weeds and lined with fur (often using black horse-hair if available); female incubates 3–4 eggs for 11–14 days.
Feeding: hops along the ground and outer branches gleaning seeds, especially from grasses, dandelions and clovers; also eats adult and larval invertebrates; occasionally visits feeders.
Voice: simple, even, long-sustained trill; call is a light, high-pitched *tsit*.
Similar Species: *Rufous-crowned Sparrow* (p. 326): red eye line; gray eyebrow; black whisker mark. *Green-tailed Towhee* (p. 323): green back; black whisker mark; lacks the black eye line. *American Tree Sparrow:* central breast spot; lacks the bold, white eyebrow and the black eye line.

327

BREWER'S SPARROW
Spizella breweri

Usually lasting more than 10 seconds, the song of this bird is a remarkable outburst of rapid, buzzy trills that constantly change in speed, pitch and quality. • Brewer's Sparrows are among the most abundant western summer songbirds. They are constantly within sight or earshot throughout the treeless sagebrush plains. They range above timberline locally in the Sierra Nevada, particularly as mid-summer, post-breeding dispersants. West of the divide they are scarce, unknown in most areas at any time. • Dr. Thomas Mayo Brewer made significant contributions to the understanding of the breeding behavior of North American birds. Unfortunately, he is most notorious for leading the 'winning side' of the House Sparrow war, which resulted in the introduction of that species to North America.

breeding

ID: light brown, unstreaked underparts; brown cheek patch; faint eye ring; finely streaked, brown upperparts; pale bill; light throat; pale eyebrow and jaw stripe; light-colored legs. *Juvenile:* buffier overall; light streaking on the breast and sides.
Size: L 5–5¹/₂ in.
Status: common migrant from early April to late May and from mid-August to late October; abundant breeder from early May to early August.
Habitat: sagebrush flats, slopes and valleys dominated by tall sagebrush at 3500–10,300 ft; also uses black greasewood and rabbitbrush on alkaline soils surrounding lake beds.
Nesting: in a low, dense shrub (usually sagebrush); small, compact cup nest is woven with grass and roots and lined with fine materials and fur; pair incubates 3–5 eggs for 11–13 days.

Feeding: forages on the ground and gleans low vegetation for adult and larval invertebrates and seeds.
Voice: song is long and extremely variable; buzzes and trills, characterized by frequent changes in speed and pitch; call is a thin *tsit*.
Similar Species: *Other similar sparrows:* juveniles have streaked breasts. *Song* (p. 337), *Savannah* (p. 334), *Lincoln's* (p. 338) and *Vesper* (p. 330) *sparrows:* adults all have streaked breasts. *Grasshopper Sparrow* (p. 335): dark crown with a bright median stripe; lacks the dark jaw stripes; larger bill; seldom in sagebrush.

BLACK-CHINNED SPARROW

Spizella atrogularis

The brushy lower slopes of the Sierra Nevada and Coast Ranges are prime breeding habitat for the tiny, reclusive Black-chinned Sparrow. With the exception of bold, singing spring males, most individuals of this mountain-dwelling species prefer to remain concealed by dense shrubs and tangling thickets. • Found locally through much of the arid southwest, Black-chinned Sparrows are a 'birdwatcher's bird,' known to few but those who seek them out. Their often-impenetrable habitat and ground-foraging behavior causes them to be heard more than they are seen. • Only breeding males display the black chin for which this species is named.

♀

♂

breeding

ID: *Female* and *Fall male:* gray head and underparts; reddish-brown wings and tail; black streaks on a reddish-brown back; pale bill. *Breeding male:* black chin, throat and lores.

Size: *L* 5–5¹/₂ in.

Status: irregular to rare from April to August; almost never seen in migration; reaches northern limits in northern California.

Habitat: steep slopes thoroughly grown to tall, dense 'hard' chaparral, sometimes dotted with small conifers.

Nesting: close to the ground in a low shrub; shallow cup nest of grass, plant stems and fibers is lined with softer materials; 2–4 pale blue eggs (occasionally spotted with brown) are incubated for about 13 days; both adults feed the young.

Feeding: forages on the ground, feeding on seeds and insects; may forage in low shrubs.

Voice: unique song begins with *sweet sweet sweet* notes, accelerating into an extremely rapid trill; call may be a subtle *tsip* or a high, thin *seep*.

Similar Species: *Dark-eyed Junco* (p. 342): plainly dark-hooded; white outer tail feathers; lacks the dark back streaks.

329

VESPER SPARROW

Pooecetes gramineus

For birders who live on the flat grasslands and shrublands that swarm with confusing little brown sparrows, the Vesper Sparrow offers welcome relief: its white outer tail feathers and deeply undulating flight are reliable distinguishing features. The Vesper is also known for its bold and easily distinguished song, which begins with two sets of unforgettable double notes: *here-here! there-there!* • When the business of nesting begins, Vesper Sparrows prospect for a site that provides safety from foraging predators and shelter from inclement weather. The chosen site is usually nestled into a grassy hollow at the base of a low shrub. This set-up provides camouflage, functions as a windbreak and acts like an umbrella. • 'Vesper' is from the Latin for 'evening,' a time when this bird often sings.

ID: chestnut shoulder patch; white outer tail feathers; pale yellow lore; weak flank streaking; white eye ring; dark upper mandible; lighter lower mandible; dark border to rear of the eye patch.

Size: L 5¹/₂–6¹/₂ in.

Status: very uncommon migrant from late March to early May and from late August to mid-November; uncommon breeder from early April to late October; uncommon to fairly common visitor from mid-October to late March.

Habitat: *Breeding:* grassy, rolling hills and shallow valleys interspersed with low shrubs, especially sagebrush, at 4000–10,500 ft. *Winter:* arid grasslands, semi-open shrublands, agricultural areas bordered with brush and newly germinating croplands.

Nesting: in a scrape on the ground; usually under a low shrub or clump of grass; small cup nest is woven with grass and lined with finer materials; female (primarily) incubates 4–5 eggs for 11–13 days.

Feeding: walks and runs along the ground, picking up grasshoppers, beetles, cutworms and seeds.

Voice: 4 characteristic, preliminary notes followed by a descending series of trills: *here-here there-there, everybody-down-the-hill.*

Similar Species: *Savannah* (p. 334), *Sage* (p. 333) and *Song* (p. 337) *sparrows:* lack the white outer tail feathers and the chestnut shoulder patch. *Lincoln's Sparrow* (p. 338): buffy wash on the breast; lacks the white outer tail feathers. *Brewer's Sparrow* (p. 328) and *Grasshopper Sparrow* (p. 335): lack the streaking on the breast, the white outer tail feathers and the chestnut shoulder patch. *American Pipit* (p. 308): thinner bill; grayer upperparts; lacks the brown streaking and the chestnut shoulder patch. *Lapland Longspur* (p. 343): broad, buff eyebrow; reddish edgings on the wing feathers; dark patch on the upper breast.

LARK SPARROW
Chondestes grammacus

Prime habitat for Lark Sparrows in western California is easy to spot: grasses and low shrubs dominate the arid, sun-baked landscape and the full-crowned forms of scattered oaks stand widely separated against the sky. In such rural haunts, male Lark Sparrows sing atop small bushes or low rock outcrops, proclaiming themselves to the world. Their beautiful arias reminded early naturalists of the famed Sky Lark of Europe. • Although these birds are typically seen in open shrubby areas and 'edge' habitat, they occasionally venture into meadows, grassy forest openings and densely wooded areas. In winter and during migration, small flocks of Lark Sparrows are regularly sighted foraging alongside juncos, sparrows and towhees in suburban parks and gardens.

ID: distinctive 'helmet' created by a white throat, eyebrow and crown stripe and a few black lines breaking up an otherwise chestnut-red head; unstreaked, pale breast with a central spot; rounded, black tail with flashy white corners; soft brown, mottled back and wings; pale legs.

Size: L 6 in.

Status: uncommon to common resident; fairly common to locally common migrant (rare along the northwest coast) and generally common breeder from early April to September; rare to locally very common winter visitor.

Habitat: *Breeding:* grassland edges bordered by trees and shrubs, open grassy oak woodlands and savannahs; meadows interspersed with shrubs, semi-open shrublands, agricultural areas and orchard edges to 6000 ft. *Winter:* arid grasslands, borders of pastures and agricultural fields, brushy fields, lawns, parks and gardens, weedy roadsides.

Nesting: on the ground or in a low bush; bulky cup nest of grass and twigs is lined with finer material; occasionally reuses abandoned thrasher or mockingbird nests; female incubates 4–5 eggs for 11–12 days.

Feeding: walks or hops on the ground, gleaning for seeds; also eats grasshoppers and other invertebrates.

Voice: melodious and variable song that consists of short trills, buzzes, pauses and clear notes; song may incorporate the notes of other species common in the area.

Similar Species: no other sparrow has the distinctive head and tail patterns.

BLACK-THROATED SPARROW
Amphispiza bilineata

The Black-throated Sparrow and the Sage Sparrow both prefer the arid, sagebrush-dominated habitat of northeastern California's Great Basin country. The close bond between these two species is further reflected in their shared preference for seeds and insects and in the similar appearance of the juvenile Black-throated Sparrow and the adult Sage Sparrow. • Because of its hot, dry habitat, the Black-throated Sparrow is ordinarily without any source of standing or flowing water. To survive without drinking water, it has evolved a super-efficient physiology that allows it to extract and recycle moisture obtained from its food. • There is danger in building a nest near the ground: Black-throated Sparrow nestlings and eggs are a welcome food item for a number of lizards, snakes, ground squirrels and other animals.

ID: black tail with white edges to the outer feathers; gray cheek and cap; prominent, white eyebrow. *Adult:* black chin, throat and bib; broad, white 'jaw' line; unstreaked, light underparts; dark bill. *Juvenile:* white chin and throat; dark streaking on the upper breast; light lower mandible.
Size: L 4^{1}/$_{2}$–5^{1}/$_{2}$ in.
Status: rare to locally uncommon breeder from mid-April to September; sporadic, does not occur at northern sites every year but occasionally nests on the west slope of Sierra Nevada in 'invasion' years.
Habitat: rocky hills and flatlands covered with sagebrush, greasewood, saltbrush and rabbitbrush; also found on lower mountain slopes with pinyon-juniper woodlands and an understory of open sagebrush.
Nesting: on the ground under the shelter of tall weeds, in a rocky cliff crevice, in a shrub or low in a tree; open cup of twigs,

grass and weeds is lined with hair, fine grasses and rootlets; female incubates 4–5 darkly spotted, creamy to grayish-white eggs over 11–12 days; both adults feed the young.
Feeding: many seeds are taken from the ground in winter; eats mostly insects in summer; forages on the open ground by walking, often in small, loose flocks; may also forage in low shrubs and trees.
Voice: simple but variable song often opens with a few clear notes, followed by a light trill; call is a series of faint, tinkling, chattery notes.

Similar Species: *Sage Sparrow* (p. 333): shorter, thinner, white eyebrow; distinct dark streaking on the sides; fine streaking on the head and back; runs on the ground with its tail held high.

SAGE SPARROW

Amphispiza belli

The paler race of the Sage Sparrow, which occurs in the Great Basin, is commonly found foraging and nesting in areas interspersed with extensive stands of either tall or short sagebrush. A darker subspecies is typically found in chamise-dominated chaparral west of the Sierra. • Each year, males return to the same breeding site, which they defend by singing from exposed perches. Breeding pairs commonly raise two broods a year, usually producing three to four, occasionally two to five, young per brood. • The Sage Sparrow is often distinguished among other sparrows by its habit of wagging and twitching its tail when perched, or by holding its tail upward during running spurts. • Rapid human encroachment in the Coast Ranges might result in local declines in coastal Sage Sparrow populations. • John Cassin, the early, prominent ornithologist and taxonomist from the Philadelphia Academy of Natural Sciences, named this species in honor of John Graham Bell, the taxidermist who first collected a specimen of this bird.

'Bell's Sparrow'

ID: white lore and eye ring contrast with the brownish-gray head; black whisker stripe; white, unstreaked throat, breast and belly; dark, central breast spot; dark streaking on the sides; dark tail has white outer margins; 'Bell's Sparrow' of western California is noticeably darker than interior birds. *Immature:* duller brown overall; heavily streaked.
Size: L 5–6 in.
Status: uncommon to locally fairly common year-round resident; fairly common breeder from early April to early October; a few may remain over winter.
Habitat: Great Basin populations prefer arid brushlands of sagebrush and its associates; western populations use chaparral dominated by dense stands of chamise.
Nesting: close to the ground in a shrub; bulky cup of sticks and twigs is lined with fine grasses, plant matter and occasionally hair; 3–4 darkly spotted or blotched, pale blue eggs are incubated for 13–16 days.

Feeding: seasonally available seeds and insects are taken from the ground or low shrubs; gleans and scratches the ground; forages in small flocks outside the breeding season.
Voice: rhythmic series of 4–6 clear, high-pitched notes with a higher, accentuated 3rd note; high, thin *tink* call is often repeated in a rapid twitter.
Similar Species: *Immature Black-throated Sparrow* (p. 332): bold, long and broad eyebrow; lacks the well-defined streaking on the sides and the complete white eye ring.

SAVANNAH SPARROW
Passerculus sandwichensis

The Savannah Sparrow is a common bird of open, grassy country. Its streaky, dull brown, buff-and-white plumage conceals it perfectly in the long grasses of its preferred habitat. Like most sparrows, the Savannah Sparrow generally prefers to stay out of sight, although small flocks and individuals are sometimes seen darting across roads, highways, open fields and beaches. Fleeing Savannah Sparrows resort to flight only as a last alternative. They prefer to run swiftly and inconspicuously through the long grass like feathered voles. • The common and scientific names of this bird reflect its broad distribution: 'Savannah' refers to the city in Georgia; *sandwichensis* is derived from Sandwich Bay in the Aleutians off Alaska. • Seven subspecies of Savannah Sparrow inhabit or move through California during various seasons.

'Belding's Sparrow'

ID: finely streaked breast; pale, streaked underparts; mottled brown upperparts; yellow lore; light jaw line; pale legs and bill.
Size: L 5–6½ in.
Status: fairly common to common year-round resident; fairly common to abundant migrant and visitor from September to mid-May; common breeder from May to September.
Habitat: *Breeding:* coastal grasslands, estuary meadows, salt marshes, grassy interior valleys, grassy borders of mountain streams, agricultural fields, alkali lakeshores and hay meadows. *Winter:* fields, grasslands, seashore.
Nesting: on the ground, in a scrape sheltered by a canopy of grass or a small bush;

cup nest is woven with grass and lined with fine materials; pair incubates 3–4 eggs for 12–13 days.
Feeding: scratches the ground for seeds and insects.
Voice: dreamy, lisping *tea tea tea teeeeea Today!*
Similar Species: *Vesper Sparrow* (p. 330): white outer tail feathers; chestnut shoulder patches; undulating flight. *Lincoln's Sparrow* (p. 338): buff wash across the breast; buff jaw line; grayer face. *Song Sparrow* (p. 337): browner; heavy breast streaking; gray face; lacks the yellow lore. *Brewer's Sparrow* (p. 328) and *Grasshopper Sparrow* (p. 335): unstreaked breast.

GRASSHOPPER SPARROW

Ammodramus savannarum

If you consistently find yourself in prime Grasshopper Sparrow habitat, odds are you are either a birdwatcher or a rancher—or your vehicle has a habit of breaking down every time you make a trip to your cabin in the Sierra Nevada. Regrettably, few people stop to enjoy California's endangered native savannahs, and as a result these areas and their exceptional birdlife remain largely underappreciated. • The Grasshopper Sparrow is an open-country bird named not for its diet, but for one of its buzzy, insect-like songs. Each male sings two completely different, squeaky courtship songs: one short and the other more sustained. During the courtship flight, the male chases the female through the air, buzzing at a frequency that is inaudible to our ears. • Rather than flying from her nest when flushed, a female Grasshopper Sparrow will run quietly away through the grass to remove herself from danger. • *Ammodramus* is Greek for 'sand runner,' and *savannarum* is Latin for 'of the savannah,' the typical habitat of this species.

ID: buffy, unstreaked breast and sides; buffy cheek; flattened head profile; pale legs; mottled brown upperparts; beady, black eyes; 'sharp' tail; dark crown with a prominent, pale median stripe.
Size: L 4¹/₂–5¹/₄ in.
Status: not completely known; rare to locally fairly common migrant from mid-August to early November; very uncommon to locally common breeder from mid-March to mid-September; seldom detected in winter.
Habitat: grasslands and savannahs in rolling hills and lower mountain hillsides from sea level to 4900 ft.
Nesting: occasionally semi-colonial; in a shallow depression on the ground, usually under a dome of bent grass; small cup nest is woven with grass and lined with plant fibers, fur and small roots; female incubates 4–5 eggs for 12–13 days.
Feeding: gleans the ground and low plants, pecking and scurrying through the grass; eats invertebrates and seeds.
Voice: song is an insect-like buzz: *pit-tuck zee-ee-e-e-e-e-e-e.*
Similar Species: *Brewer's Sparrow* (p. 328): dark jaw stripes; lacks the prominent, pale median crown stripe. *Savannah* (p. 334), *Vesper* (p. 330), *Song* (p. 337) and *Lincoln's* (p. 338) *sparrows:* all have streaked breasts and sides.

335

FOX SPARROW
Passerella iliaca

Despite this large sparrow's shrub-loving tendencies, it is commonly seen scurrying across hiking trails and animal paths in northern California's mountain country. Like neighboring Green-tailed Towhees, Fox Sparrows spend most of their time on the ground, scratching away leaf litter and duff to expose seeds and insects. • The 15 or so subspecies of Fox Sparrows known to occur in California exhibit an array of color variations. *P. iliaca stephensi* and other subspecies that nest in the Sierra Nevada (but winter elsewhere) are distinguished by a gray head and back contrasting with rusty wings, rump and tail. Birds with mostly rusty upperparts tend to be visitors from central or eastern Canada, and Fox Sparrows with uniformly brown upperparts are winter visitors from Canada and Alaska.

ID: breast streaking converges to a central spot; most subspecies have rusty coloration in the rump, tail and wings; some subspecies have all-brown upperparts; head and back may be gray, brown or reddish; thick, light gray bill; pale legs.

Size: L 6½–7½ in.

Status: complex intrastate distribution; generally fairly common to often abundant migrant and visitor in lowlands from mid-September to April; variably common breeder from April to mid-September.

Habitat: *Breeding:* mountain slopes at 3000–9600 ft; montane chaparral and riparia, often interspersed with taller trees and shrubs; also uses aspen stands and open pine forests. *Winter* and *In migration:* brushy lowland thickets, parks, gardens and suburban backyards.

Nesting: on the ground or low in a shrub or small tree; cup nest is woven with twigs, grass, moss and bark shreds and often lined with the hair of large mammals; female incubates 3–4 eggs for 12–14 days.

Feeding: scratches the ground to uncover seeds, berries and invertebrates; visits backyard feeders in winter and migration.

Voice: variable; brilliant warbling slurs, *All I have is what's here dear, won't you won't you take it?*

Similar Species: *Song Sparrow* (p. 337) and *Lincoln's Sparrow* (p. 338): smaller; pale face; dark eye line; dark crown stripes; lighter, differently patterned breast streaking. *Hermit Thrush* (p. 300): spotted breast; thin bill; pale eye ring; lifts its tail. *Swainson's Thrush* (p. 299): olive tail; light breast spots; prominent, buffy eye ring. *Dark-eyed Junco* (p. 342): hooded look; lacks the streaked underparts.

SONG SPARROW
Melospiza melodia

Without a doubt, this well-named sparrow stands among the great California songsters for the complexity, rhythm and sweetness of its springtime rhapsodies. • Song Sparrows (and many other songbirds) learn to sing by listening to their fathers or to rival males. By the time a young male is a few months old, he will have the basis for his own courtship tune. • At least 17 subspecies of Song Sparrows occur in California at various times. This large number suggests that the Song Sparrow is readily adapting to subregional environmental variables, such as climate, substrate coloration and prey selection. Given time, these subspecies may one day become reproductively isolated and hence behave as distinct species.

ID: heavy breast streaking often converges into a central spot; gray face; dark eye line; white jaw line (as if milk has dribbled from the bill); red-brown crown with a gray stripe; dimly streaked back; white throat; rounded tail; plumage and size are variable throughout its range.

Size: *L* 5¹/₂–7 in.

Status: complex; generally a common year-round resident at middle and higher elevations; locally rare to common summer visitor in the mountains; abundant winter visitor.

Habitat: low, dense cover in weedy and brushy thickets; soft chaparral, brush piles, and stands of willows and nettles at 200–5000 ft; some may wander as high as 10,300 ft; some subspecies inhabit marshes.

Nesting: usually on the ground; occasionally in a shrub or small tree; cup nest is woven with grass, leaves and bark shreds and lined with fine materials; female incubates 3–5 eggs for 12–14 days.

Feeding: gleans the ground, shrubs and trees for cutworms, grasshoppers, ants, various other insects and seeds; also eats fruit and visits feeders.

Voice: 1–3 distinctive introductory notes, followed by a pleasant melody: *Hip Hip Hip Hurray Boys, the spring is here again!* or *Maids Maids Maids, hang up your tea kettle kettle kettle*; call is a querulous, anxious *chimp*, often repeated.

Similar Species: *Fox Sparrow* (p. 336): larger; heavier breast streaking; lacks the striping in the face and crown. *Lincoln's Sparrow* (p. 338): smaller; lightly streaked breast with a buffy wash; broader, gray or buff eyebrow. *Savannah Sparrow* (p. 334): yellow lore; lacks the gray face; shorter, notched tail. *Brewer's Sparrow* (p. 328) and *Grasshopper Sparrow* (p. 335): lack the breast streaking.

337

LINCOLN'S SPARROW
Melospiza lincolnii

There is a certain beauty in the plumage of a Lincoln's Sparrow that is greater than the sum of its feathers. Sightings of this bird, linked with the sounds and smells of its natural habitat, can bring an indescribable joy and peace to the hearts of birdwatchers. • Most of the Lincoln's Sparrows breeding in northern California summer in the mosaic of subalpine lake basins, where nesting territories are occasionally flooded by melted snow and swollen streams in spring and early summer. In August and September, most of these birds move to lower elevations, their numbers augmented by migrants from Canada and Alaska. • This sparrow generally prefers to skulk among tall grasses and dense, brushy growth, but it sings its bubbly, wren-like song from a perch.

ID: lightly streaked breast with a buff wash; buff jaw bordered by dark lines; dark brown cap and facial lines with a broad, gray eyebrow and gray median crown line; very faint, white eye ring; white belly; gray collar; brown-gray, mottled upperparts.
Size: L 5³/₄ in.
Status: complex; generally uncommon to fairly common migrant from mid-March to mid-May and from late August to mid-November; uncommon breeder from mid-April to September; uncommon to locally very common visitor from mid-September to mid-April.
Habitat: *Breeding:* boggy lakeshores and mountain meadows at 4000–10,000 ft. *Winter* and *In migration:* moist lowland areas with dense cover, including riparian woodland understory, weedy fields and the brushy borders of ponds, streams and ditches.

Nesting: on the ground, often sunken into soft moss or concealed beneath shrubs; well-hidden cup nest is woven with dry grass and lined with fine materials; female incubates 4–5 eggs for 11–14 days.
Feeding: scratches at the ground, exposing invertebrates and seeds; visits feeders adjacent to appropriate habitat.
Voice: song is a bubbly, *kee kee kee, see see seedle seedle seedle see-see-see-see*; seldom sings in migration; 2 calls: a dreamy *eentz* and a *chk*.
Similar Species: *Song Sparrow* (p. 337): larger; darkly streaked breast lacks the buff wash; white rather than buff jaw line. *Savannah Sparrow* (p. 334): yellow lore; paler, streakier; lacks the distinct buff wash across the breast. *Fox Sparrow* (p. 336): larger; lacks the gray and reddish head stripes; denser breast streaking consists of small triangular spots. *Brewer's Sparrow* (p. 328) and *Grasshopper Sparrow* (p. 335): unstreaked breasts and sides.

WHITE-THROATED SPARROW
Zonotrichia albicollis

Mixed sparingly among the legions of White-crowned and Golden-crowned sparrows in the lowlands from October to April are scattered White-throated Sparrows. These birds typically appear singly or in twos or threes at birdfeeders and at naturally occurring seed sources. White-throats are less prone to venture out into open lawns and crop fields than are White-crowns. They usually remain close to dense shrubbery or thickets, but 'spishing' may draw them into view at the tops of bushes. They are often the first 'rare birds' to come to the attention of novice northern Californian birders—these handsome sparrows are responsible for sparking much initial interest in birds. • White-throated Sparrows summer in the cool northern forests east of the Continental Divide, wintering chiefly in the southern and eastern U.S. The main influx of fall migrants or winter visitors to California takes place in October. Most have departed for their breeding grounds by mid-April, with a few stragglers lingering into May.

ID: black-and-white (or brown-and-tan) striped crown; conspicuous white throat; gray cheek; variably apparent yellow spot between the eyes and bill; black eye line; gray, unstreaked or blurrily streaked underparts; mottled rusty-brown upperparts.
Size: L 6½–7¼ in.
Status: rare to uncommon or locally fairly common migrant and visitor from late September to early May; most numerous in near-coastal lowlands and interior valleys.
Habitat: mix of shrub or tree cover and more open ground is preferred; most often in mixed flocks in residential areas, parks, gardens and unplowed crop fields with adjoining cover; occasional birds may turn up almost anywhere.
Nesting: in Canada and across the northern tier of the eastern U.S.
Feeding: scratches the ground to expose invertebrates and seeds; routinely visits seed feeders where individuals become familiar, typically remaining for weeks or months.
Voice: infrequently heard in northern California; evenly phrased succession of thin, clear whistles: *dear sweet Canada Canada Canada*; call is a hard, metallic *chink*, similar to the note of the White-crowned Sparrow; sometimes single, but usually given in a slow series of many notes from near the top of dense shrubbery.
Similar Species: *White-crowned Sparrow* (p. 340): lacks the white throat and the yellow loral spot; hindcrown is often visibly peaked.

WHITE-CROWNED SPARROW
Zonotrichia leucophrys

Large, bold and smartly patterned, the White-crowned Sparrow brightens brushy expanses and suburban parks and gardens with its cheeky song throughout much of the year. Lowland residents with well-stocked feeders should be familiar with this bird in all of its forms. No fewer than four subspecies inhabit the northern half of the state: *pugetensis* is a locally common partial resident breeder in Del Norte and Humboldt counties and a widespread winter visitor and migrant across California; *nuttalli* is a common, sedentary coastal resident; dark-lored *oriantha* is a breeder in the interior mountains; *gambelii* is an abundant and widespread winter visitor. • The White-crowned Sparrow is North America's most studied sparrow, having given science intriguing insight into avian philopatry and geographic variations in song dialects.

ssp. *gambelii*

ID: bold, black and white head stripes; orange-pink bill; gray face; unstreaked, gray underparts; streaked brown back. *Immature:* brown and tan head stripes. *Juvenile:* heavily pin-streaked, pale breast.
Size: L 5½–7 in.
Status: complex; generally locally fairly common to abundant year-round resident; locally fairly common to very abundant migrant and visitor from mid-September to mid-May; common breeder from April to September.
Habitat: *Breeding:* coastal 'soft' chaparral, coastal and near-coastal suburban parks and gardens, riparian thickets of willow, aspen, sagebrush or sapling trees, shrubby meadows and along the margins of montane ponds and lakes; to 3000 ft along the coast; 6000–11,000 ft in the mountains. *Winter* and *In migration:* lowland suburban parks and gardens, weedy fields, riparian thickets, shrublands, and agricultural areas.

Nesting: often on the ground; occasionally in a shrub or small coniferous tree; neat cup nest is woven with twigs, grass, leaves and bark shreds and lined with fine materials; female incubates 3–5 eggs for 11–14 days.
Feeding: scratches the ground to expose insects and seeds; also eats berries, buds and moss caps; visits birdfeeders.
Voice: song is a highly variable mix of bright whistles, slurs and churring trills (many regional dialects are recognized by ornithologists); call is a hard *pink*.
Similar Species: *White-throated Sparrow* (p. 339): clearly defined white throat; darker bill; yellow lore. *Golden-crowned Sparrow* (p. 341): lacks the white eyebrow; bright golden-yellow forecrown; dark bill.

GOLDEN-CROWNED SPARROW
Zonotrichia atricapilla

The first song heard from returning Golden-crowned Sparrows each September marks a pendulum-swing in the fall migration of birds. Before their arrival, the southward movement is dominated by the exodus of summer-nesting songbirds and by the passage of arctic-nesting shorebirds. By the time these sparrows have staked out winter quarters in roadside hedgerows and in residential parks and neighborhoods, summer is only a memory. Unlike many wintering birds, Golden-crowns sing frequently throughout the colder months. Backyard seed feeders, open ground within quick flight distance to dense shrubs, and dense brush are favored haunts of wintering Golden-crowned Sparrows. • Golden-crowned Sparrows nest in the weather-beaten subalpine meadow-edge and tundra of the western Canadian mountains and Alaska; despite their great abundance in winter, only a few ever linger well into summer in northern California. Shortly prior to their spring departure, the bold black eyebrow and bright golden crown of their breeding plumage begins to appear. • While foraging for seeds and invertebrates, these sparrows often keep company with other ground-feeding birds, such as White-crowned Sparrows and Dark-eyed Juncos.

non-breeding

ID: *Breeding:* broad, black eyebrows converge on the nape; white forecrown; yellow crown stripe; gray hindcrown; gray face; dark bill; unstreaked, gray-brown underparts; streaked upperparts; dotted-looking, thin, white white wing bars. *Non-breeding:* duller overall; eyebrows and crown show varying amounts of black and yellow.
Size: *L* 6–7 in.
Status: uncommon to locally abundant visitor from mid-September to early May; much more numerous west of the Cascade-Sierra.
Habitat: edges of dense, brushy tangles, riparian thickets, broken chaparral close to water and suburban parks and gardens.
Nesting: from British Columbia and western Alberta to Alaska.
Feeding: gleans the ground for invertebrates, buds, seeds and occasionally fruit.

Voice: song is a thin, downslurred, dreamy whistle of 3 notes; call-note is a penetrating *seek*, given most noticeably by flocks assembling in roosting shrubs at dusk.
Similar Species: *White-crowned Sparrow* (p. 340) and *White-throated Sparrow* (p. 339): lack the golden-yellow crown. *Golden-crowned Kinglet* (p. 293): much smaller; thin, needle-like bill; white eyebrow; flits restlessly through foliage, seldom alighting on the ground.

DARK-EYED JUNCO

Junco hyemalis

Juncos are birds of the forest floor in summer, occurring in pairs wherever stands of conifers grow throughout the foothills and mountains of northern California. Juncos arriving at higher-elevation breeding grounds in spring will nest to the lower edges of the winter snowpack, and then follow the retreating cover upslope during later-season efforts. • Of the many races of Dark-eyed Juncos known to occur in northern California, the 'Oregon Junco' is by far the most numerous, remaining abundant throughout the year. • Juncos are nervous and flighty. The scissor-like flash of their white outer tail feathers is a familiar sight along rural roadsides and mountain trails. They are gregarious when not nesting, flocking in shrubby openings that offer open ground on which to search for seeds. These birds are among the most routine visitors to backyard feeders, where they typically form the center of large mixed-species sparrow flocks.

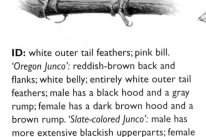

'Oregon Junco'

ID: white outer tail feathers; pink bill. *'Oregon Junco':* reddish-brown back and flanks; white belly; entirely white outer tail feathers; male has a black hood and a gray rump; female has a dark brown hood and a brown rump. *'Slate-colored Junco':* male has more extensive blackish upperparts; female is deep brownish-gray; both have a contrasting white belly.
Size: L 5–6³/₄ in.
Status: *'Oregon Junco':* very common breeder throughout most of forested northern California; retreats from high mountains in winter; remains common in migration and winter. *'Slate-colored Junco':* uncommon migrant and winter visitor throughout lowlands.
Habitat: *Breeding:* forests and other tree stands dominated by conifers and brushy undergrowth. *Migration* and *In winter:* widespread; tends to concentrate in flocks in the vicinity of dependable sources of small seeds.
Nesting: usually on the ground, or low in a shrub or tree; deep cup nest is woven with grass, bark strips and roots and lined with fine materials such as fur; female incubates 3–5 eggs for 12–13 days.
Feeding: scratches the ground for invertebrates; also eats berries and seeds; commonly visits suburban birdfeeders; individuals may return in successive years.
Voice: male's song is a brief, light, dry trill; common call is a quick, kissy *smack* note, uttered almost continuously when bird is anxious; exclamatory series of staccato *tee-tee-tee!* notes at feeders.

Similar Species: *Spotted Towhee* (p. 324): distinctly larger; bold, white spots in the tail corners; rich rufous flanks; white dotting across the wings.

LAPLAND LONGSPUR

Calcarius lapponicus

Longspurs are small songbirds of mostly treeless country, breeding on extensive plains or tundra and wintering in southern grasslands. Of the four North American species, only the Lapland Longspur occurs in any numbers in northern California. Few people—other than birders—living south of this bird's arctic nesting grounds ever become familiar with it. • Lapland Longspurs are ground-dwelling birds regardless of the season, occasionally perching on boulders, logs, posts or along fencelines. In northern California they are very uncommon fall migrants, appearing singly or in small flocks in areas of short and sparse vegetation. Because these habitats are found only locally, and the birds themselves are difficult to see, longspurs are scarce or even unknown in many parts of northern California. • Lapland Longspurs can be searched for by inspecting flocks of Horned Larks and American Pipits. They share with those species a habit of remaining undetected until closely approached, whereupon they flush high into the sky, eventually reassembling on the ground nearby.

non-breeding

ID: *Non-breeding:* partly white outer tail feathers; dark triangle enclosing a buffy ear patch; buffy eyebrow; reddish greater coverts; thin streaking on the sides; variable dark smudging on the mid-breast. *Breeding male:* boldly patterned; bright chestnut nape; black crown and breast; white stripe from behind the eye down the side of the breast. *Breeding female:* closely resembles nonbreeding plumages.

Size: *L* 6¼ in.

Status: local, rare to uncommon fall migrant and rare winter visitor from early October to early May; scarce or unknown in many areas.

Habitat: varied shortgrass or exposed earth habitats, such as plowed fields, shores and mudflats; may flock along plowed roadsides in snowy country.

Nesting: in the Arctic.

Feeding: gleans the ground for seeds and invertebrates.

Voice: male's song is not heard in northern California; frequently heard call-notes are a short, rapid, dry rattle and a descending *tchew*, each call given most often in flight.

Similar Species: *Vesper Sparrow* (p. 330): entirely white outer tail feathers; lacks the broad, buff eyebrow; reddish edgings on the wing feathers; smudgy marking on the breast. *Other longspurs:* all are rare in northern California and are generally seen in nondescript plumages.

BLACK-HEADED GROSBEAK
Pheucticus melanocephalus

Anyone beginning to look at birds in northern California in spring or summer quickly makes acquaintance with Black-headed Grosbeaks. These birds are marvelous singers, advertising territories from late April into early July with extended bouts of complex, accented carolling. Males sing from slightly sheltered perches near the top of a tree, while females forage and conduct nesting chores within the cover of interior foliage, betraying their presence with frequent call-notes. • Black-headed Grosbeaks are most characteristic of riparian thickets, rich oak woodlands and broken conifer forests with a strong hardwood component. They will pay furtive visits to backyard feeders adjacent to dense woodlots. • Black-headed Grosbeaks are sometimes found scavenging alongside Steller's Jays in campgrounds and picnic sites. • The scientific name *Pheucticus* is thought to be derived from the Greek *phycticos*, meaning 'painted with cosmetics'; *melanocephalus* is Greek for 'black-headed.'

ID: chunky, finch-like bird; large, dark, conical bill. *Male:* burnt-orange underparts and rump; black head, back, wings and tail; white wing bars and undertail coverts; yellow underwing linings. *Female:* dark brown upperparts; buffy underparts; lightly streaked flanks; pale eyebrow and crown stripe produce a bold head pattern.
Size: L 7–8 1/2 in.
Status: common migrant from early April to late May and from mid-August to late September; common breeder from late April to mid-August.
Habitat: *Breeding:* varied forests and forest-edge situations and farmyards, parks and suburban tree groves. *In migration:* may appear in almost any stand of trees or tall brush.
Nesting: in a tall shrub or deciduous tree, often near water; cup nest is loosely woven of twigs and lined with fine grass; female builds the nest in 3–4 days; pair incubates 3–5 eggs for 12–14 days.
Feeding: forages the upper canopy for invertebrates and plant foods; occasionally visits birdfeeders; feeds on the ground only occasionally.
Voice: song is a loud, ecstatic carolling, known for its exceptionally rich quality and many accented notes; call is a high-pitched, penetrating *eek*.
Similar Species: male is distinctive. *Rose-breasted Grosbeak:* female has a pale bill and a whiter, pin-streaked breast. *Purple Finch* (p. 357): female is much smaller and has heavily streaked underparts. *Spotted Towhee* (p. 324): black hood and bib; black upperparts with neat white spots on the back; red eyes; white tail corners.

BLUE GROSBEAK
Guiraca caerulea

Blue Grosbeaks share with the Yellow-billed Cuckoo and Bell's Vireo a more generally eastern and central North American affinity. Like those species, they inhabit the Central Valley and outlying interior riparian areas. However, this species, unlike the cuckoo and the vireo, has fared somewhat better. Blue Grosbeaks are not as strictly obligated to dense expanses of 'river jungle,' but prefer the edges of riparian tangles where smaller moist-site shrubs, rank grass and herbaceous annuals provide song perches, foraging areas and cover for nesting. • Blue Grosbeaks were once common throughout the Central Valley, but their numbers have declined, owing to habitat alteration through water management for human use, loss of riparian vegetation and development. • Male Blue Grosbeaks owe their spectacular spring plumage not to a fresh molt but, oddly enough, to feather wear. While they are wintering in Mexico and Central America, their brown feather tips slowly wear away, leaving the vivid, deep-blue plumage that is seen as they arrive on their breeding grounds. The lovely blue color of the plumage is produced by tiny particles in the feathers that reflect only short wavelengths in the light spectrum.

ID: *Male:* royal blue plumage overall; rusty wing bars; stout, dark bill with black around the base. *Female:* soft brown plumage overall; whitish throat; rusty wing bars; rump and shoulder can have hints of blue. *Both sexes:* habitally flick their tails; flight is undulating.

Size: L 6–7¹/₂ in.

Status: rare to locally fairly common migrant and breeder from late April to early September; only infrequently encountered away from general breeding range.

Habitat: thick lowland brush, riparian thickets, margins of wooded riversides, unmanaged weedy fields near water and around sewage ponds.

Nesting: in a shrub or low tree; cup nest is woven with twigs, roots and grass and lined with finer materials, including paper and occasionally shed reptile skins; female incubates 2–5 eggs for 11–12 days.

Feeding: gleans the ground by hopping around, taking insects and occasionally seeds; periodically gleans vegetation; rarely visits feeding stations.

Voice: sweet, warbling song with phrases that rise and fall; call-note is *chink*.

Similar Species: *Lazuli Bunting* (p. 346): smaller; much smaller bill; white belly and undertail coverts; male has a bold, chestnut breast band; female lacks the rusty wing bars and blue on the shoulder. *Indigo Bunting:* smaller; much smaller bill; male lacks the wing bars; female has breast streaking.

345

LAZULI BUNTING
Passerina amoena

A selection of song perches, a bit of low, shrubby cover and some low grass or exposed earth in which to hunt for insects meets the demands of Lazuli Buntings. They are among the most numerous summer birds in many kinds of brushy habitats across northern California. They breed from coastal meadow-edges inland to arid sagebrush slopes and extend through the oak woodlands and chaparral mosaic into openings in high mountain forests. Small flocks are a routine sight at the height of the spring influx in late April and early May, particularly along riparian corridors and in isolated stands of trees near water. • In May, June and July, the male's crisp and varied songs punctuate the 'siesta hours' during which only a handful of other species persistently vocalize. Intensity of singing diminishes as broods are fledged in July, and by late August buntings appear to have largely departed. Before leaving northern California, Lazuli Buntings undergo a partial molt, completing their change of plumage at their wintering grounds.

ID: stout, conical bill. *Male:* turquoise blue hood and rump; chestnut upper breast; white belly; dark wings and tail; 2 bold, white wing bars. *Female:* soft brown overall; hints of blue on the rump.
Size: *L* 5–6 in.
Status: uncommon to abundant migrant and breeder from early April to about mid-September.
Habitat: *Breeding:* expanses of low shrubs with elevated song perches, sagebrush, chaparral, forest edge and streamsides to 9000 ft. *In migration:* lowland areas, including coastal chaparral and foothill canyons.
Nesting: in an upright crotch low in a shrubby tangle; small cup nest is woven with grass and lined with finer grass and hair; female incubates 3–5 eggs for 12 days.

Feeding: gleans the ground and low shrubs for grasshoppers, beetles, other insects and native seeds; visits birdfeeders in some areas.
Voice: male's song is a brief complex of whispering notes: *swip-swip-swip zu zu ee, see see sip see see.*
Similar Species: *Blue Grosbeak* (p. 345): larger body and bill; male is all-blue; both sexes have rusty wing bars, blue on the shoulder, and white bellies and undertail coverts. *Western Bluebird* (p. 296): male is larger; slimmer bill; more extensive chestnut on the breast; no wing bars. *Indigo Bunting:* no wing bars; male lacks the chestnut breast.

RED-WINGED BLACKBIRD

Agelaius phoeniceus

Nearly every cattail marsh worthy of description in California plays host to Red-winged Blackbirds for at least part of the year. 'Red-wings' are year-round residents in northern California, and few Californians have been denied a meeting with this abundant and widespread bird. • The nesting population is vast, but it increases in fall as migrants and prospective winterers arrive from the north to join in clamorous flocks. • Like nearly all of our songbirds, Red-winged Blackbirds take a great many insects in the breeding season, feeding their young a nearly 100 percent protein diet that ensures rapid growth. Following nesting, they swarm into agricultural areas and wetlands, spreading across the ground and picking, probing and inspecting in much the manner of shorebirds. The male's bright red shoulder patches and short, raspy song are his most important tools in the often intricate strategy employed to defend his territory. A richly voiced male who has established a quality territory can attract several mates to his cattail kingdom.

ID: thick-based, pointed, dark bill. *Male:* all-black, except for the large red shoulder patch edged in yellow or buff (occasionally concealed). *Female:* heavily streaked underparts; mottled brown upperparts; faint red shoulder patch; light eyebrow.
Size: *L* 7¹/₂–9¹/₂ in.
Status: common to abundant migrant and year-round resident; winter numbers are increased by migrants from further north.
Habitat: *Breeding:* freshwater cattail marshes, brackish marshes, and the edges of waterbodies overgrown with emergent vegetation. *Winter* and *In migration:* varied agricultural fields, shores, farmyards and suburban parks.
Nesting: colonial and polygynous; in cattails or shoreline weeds and bushes; nest of dried cattail leaves and grass is lined with grass and soft materials; female incubates 3–4 eggs for 10–12 days.
Feeding: gleans the ground for seeds, waste grain and invertebrates; also gleans vegetation, catches insects in flight and eats berries; occasionally visits feeding stations during migration.
Voice: distinctive for its volume and harshness; male's familiar song is an ascending *konk-a-ree!* or a repetition of its genus name: *aj-uh-LAY-us!*
Similar Species: *Tricolored Blackbird* (p. 348): male's shoulder patch is deeper scarlet red, edged in white; female is generally darker, especially on the belly, and seldom shows red on the shoulder. *Brewer's Blackbird* (p. 351) and *Brown-headed Cowbird* (p. 352): females lack the streaked underparts. *Yellow-headed Blackbird* (p. 350): female has a yellow throat and breast.

TRICOLORED BLACKBIRD

Agelaius tricolor

With the exception of small, scattered populations of Tricolored Blackbirds in southern Oregon, Washington and Baja California, this bird's distribution is restricted to California. • Tricolored Blackbirds would appear to be only slightly different from their near look-alikes, Red-winged Blackbirds, but they exhibit a strikingly different breeding strategy. Rather than defending territories, Tricoloreds mass in densely packed nesting concentrations that may run into thousands per acre. The draining of productive marshlands is thought to have played a significant role in the decline or disappearance of larger colonies in recent decades, and breeding birds have been forced to find smaller parcels of habitat. • After the breeding season, males and females often separate into nomadic, gender-specific flocks. These flocks often go on to join large mixed-species flocks that include Red-winged and Brewer's blackbirds, Brown-headed Cowbirds and European Starlings.

ID: *Male:* all-black except for the dark red epaulette bordered below by white. *Female:* blackish-brown upperparts and belly; heavy, dark brown streaking on the breast; whitish to buffy eyebrow. *Immature male:* like the adult female, but darker; orangy shoulder patch with a white lower border.

Size: L 7–9¹/₂ in.

Status: very locally common year-round resident; many become nomadic transients in fall and winter.

Habitat: fields, wetlands and pastures. *Nesting:* freshwater cattail and tule marshes.

Nesting: colonial; female builds a bulky, open cup of marsh vegetation and grasses; sometimes in willows at a marsh edge or tall vegetation in dry fields; female incubates 4 pale greenish-blue eggs with dark markings for about 11 days.

Feeding: tends to forage in flocks on the ground; may forage among trees and shrubs; eats seasonally available insects, seeds and waste grain; often associated with other blackbird flocks outside the breeding season; often feeds with its tail held nearly straight up.

Voice: harsh song is like the Red-winged Blackbird's, but more raspy, nasal and drawn-out; call is a soft *chuk* or a nasal *cap.*

Similar Species: *Red-winged Blackbird* (p. 347): male's red shoulder patch is lighter, more orange-red, and is bordered below by yellow; female has lighter brown upperparts and dark brown streaking on much lighter, buffy undersides. *Brown-headed Cowbird* (p. 352): shorter, more conical bill; male lacks the red shoulder patch; female lacks the streaked chest and light eyebrow. *Brewer's Blackbird* (p. 351): male has yellow eyes and lacks the epaulette; female lacks the streaked chest and the light eyebrow.

WESTERN MEADOWLARK
Sturnella neglecta

The grasslands of northern Calfornia would lose a good measure of their appeal were it not for the evocative songs of the Western Meadowlark. It is a dismaying consequence of human land-use pressure that meadowlarks have indeed declined wherever monoculture, over-grazing or asphalt have replaced large expanses of grass. Western Meadowlarks remain numerous across the intermountain basin regions east of the Cascade-Sierra divide and locally throughout much of the rest of unforested northern California. • The male Western Meadowlark's bright yellow underparts, V-shaped, black 'necklace,' and white outer tail feathers help to attract mates during bouts of courtship singing and flying. • When a predator approaches a nest too closely, the incubating female rushes from the grass in a burst of flashing color. Most predators cannot resist chasing the moving yellow, brown and white target. Once the female has led the predator away from the nest, she folds away her white tail flags, exposes her camouflaged back and walks back to the nest undetected. • This bird was overlooked by the Lewis and Clark expedition because it was con-fused with the Eastern Meadowlark. This oversight is acknowledged in its species name, *neglecta*.

breeding

ID: yellow underparts; broad, black bib; dark-and-light streaked upperparts; short tail with conspicuous white sides; long, pinkish legs; yellow lore; brown crown stripes and eye line; black spotting on the white flanks; slender bill.
Size: L 8–10 in.
Status: common year-round resident; common migrant and winter visitor in small flocks.
Habitat: *Breeding:* grasslands, savannahs, meadows and pastures with medium-height grasses to 8000 ft (to 14,000 ft in the Sierra Nevada); also uses arid, grassy areas dominated by low shrubs. *Winter* and *In migration:* lowland grasslands, meadows, pastures, agricultural areas, grassy roadside ditches, dunelands and farmyards.
Nesting: in a dry depression or scrape on the ground; grass-domed nest with a side entrance is woven into the surrounding vegetation with grass and plant stems; female incubates 3–7 eggs for 13–15 days.

Feeding: walks or runs along the ground, gleaning grasshoppers, crickets and spiders; also eats seeds and probes the soil with its bill for hidden grubs, worms and insects.
Voice: song is a boisterous, rich, liquidy series of flute-like warbles, often beginning with several deliberate notes, accelerating toward the end; call is a sharp *chuck* or *chupp;* also issues a downslurred whistle and a short anxiety chatter.
Similar Species: none.

YELLOW-HEADED BLACKBIRD

Xanthocephalus xanthocephalus

The raw, rasping song of the Yellow-headed Blackbird is a sound characteristic of large western marshes. Often, where there's one 'mustard head,' there are many, which is especially true during spring and summer when these birds assemble in semi-colonial concentrations. Yellow-headed Blackbirds are most abundant in the Central Valley, in the Klamath Basin and in the alkaline Great Basin wetlands. Small colonies are widely known elsewhere. • From their nesting sites, pairs forage as far as a mile or more into croplands and pastures. These birds routinely nest in close association with Red-winged Blackbirds, which arrive earlier in spring only to find their hard-won territories usurped by the later-arriving but aggressive Yellow-heads. • This species probes more deeply than other blackbirds, allowing it to find prey items farther beneath the soil surface.

ID: *Male:* orange-yellow head and breast; all-blackish body; white wing patches; black lore; stout, sharply pointed, black bill; long tail. *Female:* dusky brown overall; dingy yellow breast, throat and eyebrow; hints of yellow in the face. **Size:** *L* 8–11 in.
Status: locally fairly common to common year-round resident; locally rare (on the coast) to common migrant from April to mid-May and from late July to mid-September; locally fairly common breeder from late March to mid-October (early May to late August at higher elevations).
Habitat: *Nesting:* permanent freshwater marshes. *Feeding:* meadows, agricultural fields, shorelines and muddy fields close to nesting sites. *Winter* and *In migration:* agricultural fields, farmyards, meadows and cattle-feed lots; often roosts in freshwater marshes.
Nesting: loosely colonial; in cattail marshes and shoreline shrubs; bulky, deep basket nest of wet vegetation is usually woven into emergent vegetation; female incubates 3–5 eggs for 11–13 days.
Feeding: gleans and probes the ground for seeds, cutworms, beetles, snails, waterbugs and dragonflies; also probes into cattail heads for larval invertebrates.
Voice: male's song is 2 agonized seconds of strained, raspy grating: *ong-hee-RAAANGH!*; flight call is a baritone *kruk* or *kruttuk*; with practice, birders can distinguish Yellow-heads by voice from among mixed-species blackbird swarms.

Similar Species: male is distinctive. *Red-winged* (p. 347), *Tricolored* (p. 348), and *Brewer's* (p. 351) *black-birds* and *Brown-headed Cowbird* (p. 352): females lack the yellow throat and face.

BREWER'S BLACKBIRD

Euphagus cyanocephalus

With most of us well-attuned to wildlife of the 'urban wilderness,' few people even fleetingly aware of birds fail to recognize Brewer's Blackbirds. The development of our landscape has been beneficial to these birds, with agriculture and ranching providing foraging sites and landscaped trees and tall shrubs affording sheltered nest locations. Open or grassy ground upon which to feed, dense nesting cover and song and lookout perches are habitat requirements met nearly throughout unforested northern California. • California's immense network of highways and arterials has offered the Brewer's Blackbird a bounty of vehicle-struck insects. This species exploits the 'roadkill resource' niche more than any other songbird. • Brewer's Blackbirds nest in aggregations of several pairs or in single, widely dispersed pairs. Following nesting, adults and juveniles flock, soon mixing with other blackbirds, Brown-headed Cowbirds and European Starlings in roving mobs that frequent lowland fields and wetlands throughout winter.

ID: *Male:* glossy black plumage; dark metallic blue on the head; subtle green body iridescence; pale yellow eyes. *Female:* flat brown plumage; ordinarily dark eyes.

Size: *L* 8–10 in.

Status: common to abundant year-round resident; mountain breeders withdraw southward or to valleys in winter.

Habitat: wet meadows, grasslands, shores, roadsides, landfills, golf courses, urban and suburban parks and gardens, ranches, farmyards, pastures and freshwater marshes; from sea level to nearly 9000 ft.

Nesting: loosely colonial; on the ground or in a shrub or tree; well-built cup nest is woven with twigs, grass, mud, roots and fur; female incubates 4–6 eggs for 12–14 days.

Feeding: walks with a slow, steady, upright strut, nodding with each step; picks, gleans, and chases on foot after food items, including seeds and a wide variety of terrestrial invertebrates.

Voice: song is an alternation of creaking, 2-noted phrases: *k'shleee…k'SHLAY*; call-note is a toneless, matter-of-fact *check*; adults clatter anxiously at nest intruders.

Similar Species: *Brown-headed Cowbird* (p. 352): smaller; shorter, blunter bill. *Great-tailed Grackle*: much larger; long, thick-based bill; much longer tail. *European Starling* (p. 307): chunkier; shorter-tailed; yellow bill in breeding season; abundant white speckling in fall and winter; broad-based, triangular-looking wings.

BROWN-HEADED COWBIRD
Molothrus ater

The male Brown-headed Cowbird's song, a bubbling, liquidy *glug-ahl-whee*, might well be interpreted by other bird species as 'here comes trouble!' Brown-headed Cowbirds once followed bison herds across the Great Plains (now they follow cattle) and their nomadic lifestyle made it impractical to construct and tend to nests. Their successful alternative was the adoption of the deceptive art of 'nest parasitism': laying eggs in the nests of other songbirds. Over the ages, this strategy has proven to be effective for cowbirds, because many of the parasitized adult songbirds will incubate the cowbird eggs and raise the cowbird chicks without distinguishing them from their own. Hatching in as little as 10 days, nestling cowbirds outcompete their foster siblings. Fledging at nearly adult size, a juvenile cowbird continues to beg after leaving the nest, often dwarfing a Wrentit or Common Yellowthroat that is popping goodies into its gaping mouth. • The expansion of ranching, the fragmentation of forests and the increase of transportation corridors has significantly increased the cowbird's range. The cowbird now parasitizes more than 150 bird species in North America.

ID: *Male:* glossy black plumage; dark brown head; somewhat blunt, conical bill; short, 'double-rounded' tail; dark eyes. *Female:* gray-brown plumage overall; slight blurry streaking on the underparts; dark eyes. *Juvenile:* dull, old-straw color throughout; heavily streaked and scaled.
Size: L 6–8 in.
Status: fairly common to abundant year-round resident.
Habitat: *Brood parasitism:* virtually all unforested terrestrial habitats from sea level to 10,000 ft. *Foraging:* weedy fields, pastures, savannahs, feedlots, livestock corrals, farmyards, ranches, open parks and gardens.
Nesting: no nest is built; female lays as many as 40 eggs a year in the nests of other birds; usually 1 egg per nest, but sometimes up to 8 (probably deposited by several different cowbirds); eggs hatch after 10–13 days.

Feeding: gleans the ground for seeds, waste grain and invertebrates, especially grasshoppers, beetles and true bugs; gleans tree foliage in the breeding season.
Voice: call is a squeaky, high-pitched *wee-tse-tse*; song is a high, liquidy *glug-ahl-whee!* or *phenylphthalien!*
Similar Species: *Brewer's Blackbird* (p. 351): slightly larger; lacks the contrasting brown head and darker body; slimmer bill; longer tail; male has yellow eyes. *Red-winged Blackbird* (p. 347) and *Tricolored Blackbird* (p. 348): females have heavily streaked underparts; males show red on the shoulder. *Yellow-headed Blackbird* (p. 350): twice as large; female has a yellow throat and breast.

HOODED ORIOLE
Icterus cucullatus

The settlement and urbanization of northern California has come at the expense of many birds, but the Hooded Oriole has benefited from human development. Once largely restricted to breeding in the desert oases of the southwestern U.S., Hooded Orioles now nest in many suburban areas throughout the lowlands of northern California. Hooded Orioles are very strongly associated with ornamental palms, weaving their semi-hanging nests in the fronds of many palm species. The planting of fan palms and other suitable nesting plants in residential areas, towns, parks and gardens has allowed this bird to colonize the Central Valley and the larger coastal cities north to Arcata. • Contributing to the expansion of the Hooded Oriole is their fondess for sugarwater. Historically, these slender-billed orioles were content with the natural offerings of desert blooms, but Hooded Orioles can now satisfy their nectarivous cravings at humming-bird feeders.

breeding

ID: slender, slightly downcurved bill; rounded tail. *Male:* orange body with a black throat, upper back, wings and tail; 2 white wing bars. *Female:* greenish; quite nondescript; 2 light wing bars.
Size: *L* 7–8 in.
Status: locally very uncommon to fairly common breeder from late March to late August.
Habitat: tree groves, riparian woodlands, open lowland woods and suburban parks and gardens; rare or absent away from urban and residential areas, but migrants may appear anywhere in lowlands; nests in or near palms.
Nesting: nest is suspended from a palm frond or a deciduous tree branch; female weaves a pouch of plant fibers and grass with materials provided by the male; nest is lined with feathers, hair and plant down; female incubates 4 eggs for about 12–14 days; both adults feed the young.

Feeding: gleans slowly and deliberately within tree or shrub foliage; also probes flowers and hummingbird feeders; omnivorous diet includes insects, berries, small fruits, flower nectar and sugarwater.
Voice: song is a rapid, variable series of throaty whistles, rattles and trills, sometimes incorporating the notes of other species; call is a loud, rising, whistled *weeet*.
Similar Species: *Bullock's Oriole* (p. 354): shorter, straighter bill; male has a black crown, a more square-ended tail with orange outer feathers and a large white wing patch; female has a very light belly. *Black-headed Grosbeak* (p. 344): very stout, conical bill; male is a more subdued burnt-orange and has a black head. *Scott's Oriole:* male is black and yellow, with an all-black head; female is a dusky greenish-yellow, with dark streaking on the throat and head.

BULLOCK'S ORIOLE
Icterus bullockii

The Bullock's Oriole is the common oriole of western North America. It was once thought to interbreed freely with the Baltimore Oriole of eastern North America, and in 1973 the two birds were lumped together by the American Ornithologists' Union as one species, the Northern Oriole. Just as the birding community had adjusted to the change, new studies concluded that interbreeding was sufficiently restricted that they should once again be considered two distinct species. • Although Bullock's Orioles are common and widespread nearly throughout the lowlands and in the mountain riparia of northern California, many people remain unaware of their presence. The glowing orange, black and white plumage of the adult male blends remarkably well with the pronounced sunlit-and-shadowed summer foliage in which orioles spend most of their time. The comparatively drab olive, gray, and white worn by the female ensures the greatest protection from predators in the vicinity of the nest.

ID: *Male:* bright orange eyebrow, cheek, underparts, rump and outer tail feathers; black throat, eye line, cap, back and central tail feathers; square-ended tail; large, white wing patch. *Female:* dusky yellow face, throat and upper breast; gray underparts; olive-gray upperparts and tail; thin, white wing bars.
Size: L 7–8 1/2 in.
Status: uncommon to common migrant from late March to mid-May and from late July to early September; uncommon to locally quite common breeder from mid-April to mid-August.
Habitat: riparian woodlands, oak canyons and woodlands, suburban parks and gardens, isolated tree groves and shelter-belts to 8000 ft.
Nesting: high in a deciduous tree, suspended from near the end of a branch; pouch nest is woven with fine plant fibers, hair and string and lined with plant down, fur and moss; female incubates 4–5 eggs for 12–14 days.

Feeding: gleans canopy vegetation and shrubs for caterpillars, beetles, wasps and other invertebrates; also eats fruit and nectar; occasionally visits feeding stations.
Voice: song is an accented, piping series of 6–8 whistled, rich and guttural notes: *peas-n-tea, Drink-'em, Drink-'em!*
Similar Species: *Hooded Oriole* (p. 353): orange crown; black lore, chin, throat and upper breast; rounded tail; slightly decurved bill; lacks the large white wing patch. *Scott's Oriole:* yellow overall; male has a black hood; female has a blackish throat. *Black-headed Grosbeak* (p. 344): chunkier; heavy, conical bill; black cheek; all-black tail; lacks the large white wing patch. *Summer Tanager* and *Western Tanager* (p. 322): females have thicker, shorter bills and all-yellow underparts.

GRAY-CROWNED ROSY-FINCH

Leucosticte tephrocotis

Rosy-finches are remarkable birds, spending the summer and fall about the summits and higher slopes of mountains that support permanent snowfields or glaciers. Family groups assemble into larger flocks, which remain in and around the alpine zone until driven into the lowlands east of the Sierran crest by the first big storms of winter. • During the nesting season, rosy-finches rely to a great extent on chilled or weakened insects. They walk with shuffling steps across snow patches, inspecting the ever-changing frontier between ice and sky for flying ants, termites, moths, spiders and similar invertebrates. • The Gray-crowned is the most widely distributed of North America's three rosy-finches. Until recently, Gray-crowned, Brown-capped and Black rosy-finches were classified as a single species, simply called the 'Rosy-Finch.' Through geographic separation, and hence reproductive isolation, differences evolved between them that have served to create three unique forms, each worthy of species status.

breeding

ID: yellow, conical bill (dark during the breeding season); black forehead and forecrown; conspicuous gray hindcrown; rosy shoulder, rump and belly; brown cheek, back, chin, throat and breast; short black legs; dark tail and flight feathers.
Size: L 5½–6½ in.
Status: locally uncommon to fairly common year-round resident; locally uncommon to common winter visitor.
Habitat: *Breeding:* generally in close proximity to snowfields, frequenting alpine tundra, rock crevices in talus slopes, glacial cirques and the edges of alpine streams and tarns above timberline (9500–14,000 ft). *Winter:* shrubby lower-elevation slopes, arid valleys, roadsides and townsites; known to roost at night in caves, tunnels, abandoned buildings, mine shafts and locally in disused Cliff Swallow nests.
Nesting: on the ground, among rocks or in a rock crevice; bulky nest is made of moss, grass, fur and feathers; female incubates 4–5 eggs for 12–14 days.
Feeding: walks and hops on the ground, on snow or at the edge of snow or water, gleaning small seeds and insects; occasionally visits feeding stations in winter east of the Sierra; may scavenge crumbs from climbers' lunches.
Voice: calls are high chirping notes and constant chattering; song is a long, goldfinch-like warble.
Similar Species: *Red Crossbill* (p. 360) and *Pine Grosbeak* (p. 356): males are brighter red overall; black bill; lacks the gray-and-black crown. *Cassin's* (p. 358), *House* (p. 359) and *Purple* (p. 357) *finches:* lack the gray-and-black crown; reddish throat and breast; none forages on or flies about summits or alpine snows.

PINE GROSBEAK
Pinicola enucleator

Boreal forests across the Northern Hemisphere are home to Pine Grosbeaks. The distribution of this northern species in California reflects a general biological rule that habitats and their associated plants and animals become more 'northerly' not only with increasing latitude, but with increasing altitude. Just as sunlight falling at a lower angle in the north effects diminished heating of the earth, so too will thinner mountain air at temperate latitudes fail to capture and retain the sun's heat. • Having settled in the red fir forests of central California—perhaps during an age of northern glacial advance—Pine Grosbeaks are now quite isolated there, 'stranded' on this great island of disjunct boreal habitat.

ID: stout, conical, dark bill; white wing bars; black wings and tail. *Male:* rosy red head, underparts and back. *Female* and *Immature:* rusty crown, face and rump; ashy-gray back and underparts.
Size: *L* 8–10 in.
Status: uncommon year-round resident.
Habitat: closed or broken subalpine coniferous forests at 6000–10,000 ft on the western Sierra slope and 8000–10,000 ft on the eastern slope; favors stands of red fir.
Nesting: in a conifer or tall shrub; bulky cup nest is loosely made of twigs, moss, grass, lichens and fur; female incubates 4 eggs for 13–15 days.
Feeding: gleans buds, berries and seeds from trees; also forages on the ground; regularly eats insects in summer; may visit seed feeders in winter.
Voice: song is a short, musical warble; flight call is a loud, distinctive, descending *tew tew tew*.
Similar Species: *Red Crossbill* (p. 360): much smaller; lacks the white wing bars; crossed mandible tips. *Evening Grosbeak* (p. 365): smaller; shorter-tailed; female has a stout, pale bill, a dark whisker stripe and broad, white wing patches.

PURPLE FINCH
Carpodacus purpureus

Purple Finches are routine birds of forested foothills and lower mountain slopes. Partial to a mixture of conifers and deciduous hardwoods, they are regular summer visitors in stands of oak, alder, bigleaf maple, Oregon ash and 'short-needle' conifer associations of many kinds. • Males deliver their songs from highly exposed perches, typically at the tip-top of a live tree. • Unlike the similar-looking House Finch, the Purple Fich shows no affinity for highly developed urban and residential areas. It occasionally visits city backyard feeders in migration, but for much of the year it is found in rural areas. • Purple (*purpureus*) is an overstated description of the adult male's delicate color. Roger Tory Peterson said 'old rose is more like it,' and also likened the appearance to that of a sparrow dipped in raspberry juice.

ID: *Male:* light bill; raspberry red head, throat, breast and nape; dimly brown-and-red streaked back and flanks; reddish-brown cheek; reddish rump; short, notched tail; pale, unstreaked belly; unstreaked or finely streaked undertail coverts. *Female:* dark brown crown, cheek and jaw line; dingy-whitish eyebrow and lower cheek stripe; heavily streaked underparts; unstreaked or very lightly streaked undertail coverts.
Size: L 5¹/₄–6 in.
Status: fairly common year-round resident; spring influx and inconspicuous fall departure or winter appearance in some areas.
Habitat: oak and mixed oak-coniferous woodlands, riparian woodlands, coniferous regrowth and (in winter) lowland trees and brush offering abundant seeds; a frequent visitor to feeders.
Nesting: on a horizontal branch far from the trunk; tight cup nest is woven with twigs, grass, moss, lichens and fur; female incubates 4–5 eggs for 13 days.

Feeding: inconspicuously gleans the ground and vegetation for seeds, buds, berries and insects; readily visits seed feeders.
Voice: song is a bubbly, continuous warble; call is a single, flat *pik*.
Similar Species: *House Finch* (p. 359): rounder head; lankier tail; male lacks the reddish cap; female lacks the distinct cheek patch. *Cassin's Finch* (p. 358): male has a plush-looking, well-defined red crown and a brown nape; larger, conical bill; female lacks the distinct cheek patch; streaked undertail coverts; both sexes have narrow white eye rings. *Gray-crowned Rosy-Finch* (p. 355): brownish overall; gray-and-black crown. *Pine Siskin* (p. 361): slightly smaller; thinner bill; yellow in the wings and tail; densely streaked throughout.

CASSIN'S FINCH
Carpodacus cassinii

The three species of *Carpodacus* finches in North America resemble each other sufficiently to confuse even experienced birders on occasion. In general, House Finches are bottomland birds seldom encountered in forested mountains; Purple Finches range from the lower foothills well upslope through the middle elevations; and Cassin's Finches live in the highest forests within the zone of heavy winter snowpack. • Cassin's Finches are western birds, with an overall range similar to that of ponderosa pine. They spend much time in the crowns of tall pines and firs, remaining inconspicuous until they fly overhead uttering their characteristic calls. • As with Purple Finches, immature male Cassin's Finches require more than a year to change from their drab, streaky, female-like plumage to their reddish adult plumage.

ID: narrow, white eye ring. *Male:* red, plush-looking crown, throat and rump; brown nape; white underparts; streaked undertail coverts and flanks; deeply notched tail; dark-streaked, light brown upperparts. *Female:* indistinct facial patterning; streaked undertail coverts; white underparts, crisply streaked with fine dark lines.
Size: L 5³/₄–6¹/₄ in.
Status: fairly common year-round resident; summer visitor of highest elevations.
Habitat: *Breeding:* montane and subalpine coniferous forests at 4500–10,000 ft, favoring stands of mature red fir, ponderosa or lodgepole pine; uses cottonwoods and other large trees at lower elevations. *Winter* and *In migration:* pinyon-juniper woodlands, mountain or high desert riparia, pine forests and woodlots.
Nesting: on an outer limb in a conifer; cup nest is woven with grass, moss, bark shreds, fur and small roots; female incubates 4–5 eggs for 12–14 days.

Feeding: eats mostly seeds, but also insects and buds in spring and berries in winter; often visits birdfeeders.
Voice: song is a loud, brilliant warble, often incorporating quick snatches of songs of other species; call is a 2- or 3-note *kee-up* or *tiddly-nip.*
Similar Species: *Purple Finch* (p. 357): lacks the eye ring and obvious streaking on the undertail coverts; male has a reddish nape and flanks; dull brownish-red back; female has a distinct cheek patch and denser, less contrasting streaking on the underparts. *House Finch* (p. 359): squared tail; male has a brown cap; female has a smaller, stubbier bill and heavily streaked underparts. *Gray-crowned Rosy-Finch* (p. 355): brownish overall; gray-and-black crown. *Pine Siskin* (p. 361): smaller; thinner bill; densely streaked throughout; yellow in the wings and tail.

HOUSE FINCH
Carpodacus mexicanus

Originally birds of the arid Southwest, House Finches have spread well north and east of their ancestral haunts during the past century. This expansion has been abetted by the introduction and subsequent establishment of birds in the Northeast, so that all states and southern Canadian provinces now host populations of this bird. • House Finches are familiar birds throughout the settled portions of northern California. They occur commonly throughout towns and cities, where they are among the few species to nest within the urban core. Rural country dominated by agriculture or ranching is also to their liking. • The pleasing spring song of the male, given in extended bouts from a powerline or rooftop antenna, is as much a routine afternoon sound of suburban neighborhoods as the shouts of children or the noise of a lawnmower down the street. • Following nesting, family groups coalesce into larger flocks that roam the lowland roadsides, feeding on berries, the seeds of grasses and forbs and agricultural leftovers.

ID: streaked undertail coverts; square tail. *Male:* brown cap; red eyebrow, forecrown, throat and breast; heavily streaked flanks. *Female:* indistinct facial patterning; heavily streaked underparts.
Size: L 5–6 in.
Status: common to abundant year-round resident.
Habitat: almost all unforested habitats with access to water from sea level to 8000 ft; strongly associated with urban areas and agricultural edge habitats.
Nesting: in a cavity, building, dense foliage or an abandoned bird nest; typically in ornamental shrubbery adjacent to buildings; cup nest is woven with grass, twigs, leaves, fur and string; female incubates 4–5 eggs for 12–14 days.
Feeding: gleans low vegetation and the ground for seeds; among the most frequent visitors to suburban feeders; also eats fruits and berries.

Voice: song is a light, lilting warble lasting about 3 seconds, with the last note usually scratchy and rising; flight call, given excitedly when flushed, is a 2-noted *f-LEEP!*; similar, single-note call is uttered while perched.
Similar Species: *Cassin's Finch* (p. 358): slightly chunkier; notched tail; male has a well-defined reddish cap and finely streaked flanks; female has finely streaked underparts. *Purple Finch* (p. 357): more angular forecrown; notched tail; male has a brownish-red upper back and flanks; female has a distinct cheek patch. *Gray-crowned Rosy-Finch* (p. 355): brownish overall; gray-and-black crown. *Pine Siskin* (p. 361): slightly smaller; densely streaked throughout; thinner bill; yellow in the wings and tail.

RED CROSSBILL

Loxia curvirostra

Crossbills are uniquely adapted to a diet of conifer seeds, which they extract from ripening cones with their crossed bill tips and nimble tongue. Owing to the patchy distribution of appropriate cone crops, these birds are nomadic, becoming numerous or even abundant in one area, while remaining scarce or absent in another.

They scour mountain forests for pine cones, and if they discover a bumper crop, they might breed regardless of the season—it is not unusual to hear them singing or to see them nesting in mid-winter. • Studies suggest that the Red Crossbill actually comprises as many as eight 'sibling species,' each form distinguished by vocalizations, bill size and preference for conifer species. The reclassification and development of identification characteristics remains unfinished, however.
• Red Crossbills are often found in tight flocks in forest treetops. Listen for their loud calls wherever the boughs of conifers are heavily burdened with ripe or ripening cones.

ID: black bill with crossed tips. *Male:* dull orange-red to brick red plumage; dark wings and tail. *Female:* olive-gray to dusky-yellow plumage; plain, dark wings. *Immature:* streaked underparts; otherwise resembles the female.
Size: L 5¹/₂–6¹/₂ in.
Status: generally uncommon resident; presence and abundance in a given area is erratic.
Habitat: coniferous forests and woodlots from sea level to timberline; appears infrequently in hardwoods and at birdfeeders.
Nesting: on an outer branch in a conifer; cup nest is loosely woven with twigs, grass, moss, fur and bark strips; female incubates 3–4 eggs for 12–18 days; breeds at any time of the year.
Feeding: extracts conifer seeds from cones with specially adapted crossed mandibles; also eats buds, deciduous tree seeds and occasionally insects; often licks salt, ash or minerals from soil and roadsides; visits feeders infrequently for sunflower seeds or suet.
Voice: song is a clipped, telegraphic succession of scratchy, piping notes interspersed with series of *jip* calls; distinctive call-note is a dry, stacatto *jip*, usually uttered 2–4 times in series; birds of different races sound slightly different from one another.
Similar Species: *Pine Grosbeak* (p. 356): much larger; stubby, conical bill; white wing bars. *Pine Siskin* (p. 361): similar to the immature Red Crossbill, but is smaller, lacks the crossed bill and is streaky throughout. *Gray-crowned Rosy-Finch* (p. 355): brownish overall; gray-and-black crown; does not feed in treetops.

PINE SISKIN

Carduelis pinus

When it rains siskins, it pours. Pine Siskins fluctuate in abundance both seasonally and in accordance with the availability of favored food sources, so you can spend months or even years waiting to see one. Pine Siskins are most numerous during invasive appearances into the lowlands, which take place chiefly in fall, winter and spring. They consume sunflower and niger seeds in great quantities, and a few dozen birds lingering at a dependable feeding station can necessitate daily restocking of feeders. It is important to maintain dry seed—rain-soaked seed can rot, causing salmonellosis outbreaks that may incapacitate or kill siskins and associated feeder-dependent birds. • Tight flocks of these gregarious birds are frequently heard before they are seen. Once you recognize their distinctive chattering, you can confirm the presence of these finches by looking for a flurry of activity in the treetops that reveal occasional flashes of yellow. Look for Pine Siskins dangling and fluttering in the outer twigs of trees.

ID: heavily streaked, more so on the underparts; subdued yellow at the base of the tail feathers and in the wings (easily seen in flight); dull whitish wing bars; slightly forked tail with a constricted base; indistinct facial pattern. *Immature:* dull white in the wings and tail.
Size: L 4¹/₂–5¹/₄ in.
Status: fairly common to locally abundant resident; erratic and at times irruptive; winter populations increase with an influx of migrants from the north or from higher elevations.
Habitat: *Breeding:* coniferous and mixed coniferous-hardwood forests, including exotic plantations. *Winter* and *In migration:* may appear in nearly any habitat.
Nesting: occasionally loosely communal; often on an outer branch in a conifer; nest is woven with grass and small roots and lined with fur and feathers; female incubates 3–4 eggs for 13 days.
Feeding: gleans the ground and vegetation for seeds, buds, thistle seeds and some insects; attracted to road salts, mineral licks and ashes; regularly visits birdfeeders.
Voice: song is an outburst of combined calls of several kinds; flight call is an exuberant *shree!*; members of feeding flocks give a rising, extended *shhrreee* interspersed with hectic *chut-chut-chut* chatter notes.
Similar Species: *Purple* (p. 357), *Cassin's* (p. 358) and *House* (p. 359) *finches:* slightly larger; longer tail; stouter bill; females have no yellow in the wings or tail. *Sparrows* (pp. 326–41) and *longspurs* (p. 343): generally thicker, stubbier bills; lack yellow in the wings and tail. *Goldfinches:* (pp. 362–64): females have more conical bills and their unstreaked underparts are washed with varying amounts of yellow.

LESSER GOLDFINCH
Carduelis psaltria

Lesser Goldfinches are tiny, yellow-and-green birds found most often in pairs or small flocks. Their preference for dry, weedy expanses and proximity to fresh water of any description animates the often dramatic contrast between a northern California watercourse and its arid surroundings. • Despite similar appearances, the Lesser Goldfinch differs from the American Goldfinch by nesting in spring and early summer, showing no great dependence on late-setting weeds and forbs, and occurring in moderate density across the lowlands and foothills rather than in riparian corridors and willow thickets. • In early spring, Lesser Goldfinch pairs begin nesting in woodlands, savannahs, forest edges and commonly in towns and cities. Family groups coalesce somewhat in fall and winter, concentrating in weedy thickets, untilled gardens, meadows, and hillside seeps. They flock to a limited extent with other goldfinches and Pine Siskins.

ID: lemon-yellow underparts and undertail coverts; black wings and tail; small, white wing and tail patches; small, stubby, black bill. *Male:* extensive black cap contrasts moderately with the greenish back. *Female:* greenish upperparts.
Size: L 4–4¹/₂ in.
Status: uncommon to very common year-round resident; most numerous in valleys and foothills below the mountain forest zone; some withdraw from colder areas in winter.
Habitat: various semi-open habitats that provide nest cover, seeds and insects and water for drinking; most numerous in oak woodlands, chaparral and suburban and rural edges.
Nesting: saddled on the outer portion of a limb in a small tree or shrub; cup nest is woven with grass, plant fibers, bark strips, moss and a few feathers; female incubates 4–5 eggs for 12 days.
Feeding: gleans low-growing annuals for seeds and takes insects from tree and shrub foliage; attracted to salt-rich soil, seeps and mineral licks; visits bird-baths and garden hoses for water; readily visits feeders stocked with niger seed.
Voice: distinctive; song is a breezy, closely knit exclamation involving call-notes, chattering and snatches of songs and calls from other species; well-spaced alternation of upslurred and downslurred notes, *teeoo…tooee*; low-pitched *chet-chet-chet* is given at intervals, most often by perched birds; 3rd-greatest mimic among North American birds.
Similar Species: *American Goldfinch* (p. 364): white undertail coverts and rump; male in summer has a black cap on a bright yellow body. *Lawrence's Goldfinch* (p. 363): white undertail coverts; yellow wing patches; male has a black face on a grayish-brown head. *Pine Siskin* (p. 361): grayish-olive; heavily streaked; yellow flashes in the wings and tail.

LAWRENCE'S GOLDFINCH
Carduelis lawrencei

This little gray bird splashed with yellow and black remains somewhat of an enigma in northern California. Considerable numbers of Lawrence's Goldfinches often breed in localized areas for a year or two, then become absent sometimes for years without a trace. Throughout much of its range, the erratic distributional pattern of this species also extends to its migrating and overwintering patterns, making it difficult for birders to predict the location and abundance of this bird from year to year. • As creeks and streams subside or dry up in late summer, Lawrence's Goldfinches are often drawn to dripping faucets, springs, wells and exposed water tanks for drinking and bathing water. • The Lawrence's Goldfinch is, after the Northern Mockingbird, the most accomplished mimic among North American birds.

breeding

ID: grayish overall; short, conical bill; deeply notched tail. *Summer male:* striking; black chin and forehead; yellow breast; yellow on the wings. *Winter male:* lacks the yellow breast. *Female:* yellow wash on the breast and in the wings; lacks the black chin and forehead.

Size: L 4–4³/₄ in.

Status: locally rare to fairly common breeder from early March to early September; irregular beyond its normal range to the far north and northwest counties; scarce migrant or vagrant to the coast.

Habitat: breeds in arid habitats close to water, including oak-pine woodlands, pinyon-juniper woodlands, chaparral, brushy fields, meadows and parks.

Nesting: may nest in loose colonies; female builds an open cup of grass, flower heads, plant down, feathers and hair; placed in a shrub or tree well above the ground; female incubates 4–5 pale bluish-white eggs for 12–13 days; male feeds the female on the nest.

Feeding: eats mostly seeds and some seasonally available insects; forages on flower heads and stalks and in trees and shrubs; occasionally forages on the ground, sometimes in the company of Lesser Goldfinches.

Voice: song is an extended, bubbly twitter, incorporating songs and calls of many different species; flight call is a bell-like *tink-ool*; may give a harsh *key-yerr* when perched; often heard before it is seen.

Similar Species: *American Goldfinch* (p. 364) and *Lesser Goldfinch* (p. 362): males lack the black chin; both sexes lack yellow in the wing; more yellow overall. *Pine Siskin* (p. 361): more slender bill; streaky brownish- or grayish-olive throughout.

363

AMERICAN GOLDFINCH

Carduelis tristis

The social and exuberant American Goldfinch is commonly seen along rural roads, on streamsides and in weedy fields and residential plantings. During late spring and the summer nesting season, pairs concentrate in willow and cottonwood thickets. Following the fledging of juveniles, family flocks gather in larger assemblages and roam the lowlands and foothills in search of weed seeds and other foods. • Even above the sound of traffic in highly developed suburban settings, it is hard to miss the American Goldfinch's distinctive *po-ta-to-chip* call as it swings over parks and gardens in bounding, deeply undulating flight. Unlike Lesser and Lawrence's goldfinches, American Goldfinches seldom knit recognizable songs and calls of other species into their songs.

breeding

ID: *Breeding male:* black forehead, wings and tail; variably bright yellow body; white wing bars, undertail coverts and tail base; orange bill and legs. *Non-breeding male:* dark bill; olive brown back; yellow-tinged head; gray underparts. *Female:* yellow-green upperparts and belly; yellow throat and breast.
Size: L 4¹/₂–5¹/₂ in.

Status: uncommon to very common year-round; transient visitor from mid-October to April; may be most abundant in coastal lowlands.

Habitat: *Breeding:* lowland riparian habitats of willow and other deciduous trees, orchards, open oak woodlands and suburban parks and gardens. *Winter* and *In migration:* also occurs in chaparral, sagebrush, road-sides, and fields; post-breeding movement may take birds high into the mountains.

Nesting: in a fork in a shrub or dense bush; cup nest is tightly woven with plant fibers, grass and spider silk and lined with fur or plant down; female incubates 4–6 eggs for 10–12 days.

Feeding: gleans vegetation for thistle, seeds, insects and berries; commonly visits birdfeeders stocked with niger or sunflower seed.

Voice: song is varied and long, with trills, twitters and exclamatory notes; calls constantly in flight; calls are *po-ta-to-chip* (often delivered in flight) and *dear-me, see-me.*

Similar Species: *Evening Grosbeak* (p. 365): much larger; massive bill. *Wilson's Warbler* (p. 320): greenish back and wings without wing bars; thin bill. *Lesser Goldfinch* (p. 362): yellow undertail coverts; dark legs and bill; male has a broader black cap contrasting moderately with a dark green back. *Lawrence's Goldfinch* (p. 363): yellow wing bars; female has a brownish head and throat; male has a black face on a grayish-brown head. *Pine Siskin* (p. 361): more slender bill; heavily streaked; yellow in the wings and tail.

EVENING GROSBEAK

Coccothraustes vespertinus

Few visitors to birdfeeders inspire as much simple wonder and enjoyment as do Evening Grosbeaks. Their habit of appearing suddenly in numbers in backyards and in flowering trees on city streets has sparked an interest in birds for many people. • These grosbeaks scatter in pairs throughout expanses of conifer forest in summer. Following nesting, they assemble in flocks much like other finch-like birds, moving about the wooded countryside in a manner little understood by even the most experienced birders. Though their incursions into lowland towns and rural settings are unpredictable, they do show a tendency to target the tender young buds of deciduous broadleaf trees.

ID: massive, pale, conical bill; black wings and tail; broad, white wing patches. *Male:* black crown; bright yellow eyebrow and forebrow; dark brown head gradually fades into the golden-yellow belly and lower back. *Female:* gray head and upper back; yellow-tinged underparts; white undertail coverts.

Size: *L* 7–8¹/₂ in.

Status: erratic and irruptive; locally uncommon to common year-round resident; transient from October to early May.

Habitat: *Breeding:* dense higher-elevation coniferous forests; also lower-elevation mixed oak-conifer forests. *Winter and In migration:* mountain and lowland riparian woodlands, oak woodlands and rural and suburban yards, parks and gardens; may wander to 10,000 ft; spectacular incursions occasionally develop in wooded residential areas.

Nesting: on an outer limb in a conifer; flimsy cup nest is loosely woven with twigs, small roots, plant fibers and grass; female incubates 3–4 eggs for 11–14 days.

Feeding: gleans the ground and vegetation for seeds, buds and berries; also eats insects and licks mineral-rich soil; visits birdfeeders for sunflower seeds.

Voice: call is a loud, sharp *clee-ip* with a buzzy undertone.

Similar Species: *American Goldfinch* (p. 364): much smaller body and bill; smaller wing bars; lacks the male's bright yellow eyebrow and forebrow. *Pine Grosbeak* (p. 356): female has a black bill, smaller wing bars and lacks the dark gray head; never seen in lowlands. *Black-headed Grosbeak* (p. 344): female has a broad, buff eyebrow and is browner overall.

HOUSE SPARROW

Passer domesticus

House Sparrows are not 'sparrows' in the same sense as native North American species; they are a members of the Old World family of weaver-finches. House Sparrows were introduced into the United States in the 1850s, ostensibly as part of a plan to control insect crop pests. Rather than alleviating human woes, they immediately began to exploit urban environments, a niche unoccupied by any native bird. Upon their establishment, these charmless birds spread steadily in every direction taken by settlement. Although nonmigratory, they exhibit an uncanny knack for discovering and colonizing highly isolated human venues, ranging from the most far-flung ranch houses—even ghost towns—throughout the rural countryside and into the deepest concrete canyons of the urban core. House Sparrows appear to know little fear, and in a largely predator-free environment, their brazen foraging techniques and aggressive competitiveness serve them well.

Unfortunately, their aggressive behavior has helped them succeed in usurping territory from many native bird species. House Sparrows will nest in any bird box within practical flight distance from foraging sites, which often proves detrimental to populations of such cavity-nesting species as bluebirds and swallows.

breeding

ID: *Breeding male:* gray crown; black bib; stubby bill; chestnut nape; pale gray cheek; white wing bar; brown upperparts streaked with buff; pale gray underparts. *Non-breeding male:* smaller black bib; pale bill. *Female:* plain gray-brown overall; buffy eyebrow; lacks the male's head pattern.
Size: L 5¹/₂–6¹/₂ in.
Status: uncommon to abundant year-round resident.
Habitat: rural, suburban and urban human developments from sea level well into the mountains.
Nesting: often communal, but not colonial; in a nest box, natural cavity, building eave or other artificial cavity; nest is a sprawling, untidy mass of loosely woven grass, cellophane and other human-made materials; female incubates 4–6 eggs for 10–13 days.

Feeding: gleans the ground, livestock manure, vehicle bumpers and low vegetation for seeds, insects, fruit and human food scraps; frequently visits birdfeeders.
Voice: familiar, matter-of-fact, monotone *chirp* or *chep-chep*, often repeated tiresomely; song is a complex alternation of *chirps* and *chep-cheps*.
Similar Species: *Black-throated Sparrow* (p. 332): male has a bold white eyebrow and unstreaked, brown-tinged, gray upperparts. *Black-chinned Sparrow* (p. 329): smaller; male has a pinkish bill and a gray head, rump and underparts.

CHECKLIST OF BIRDS OF NORTHERN CALIFORNIA

Compiled by Don Roberson (September 1999)

The taxonomic order is that of the A.O.U. *Check-list of North American Birds* (7th ed.). This checklist contains 567 species, including 8 established introductions ('I' on the list), 2 extirpated species ('E') and 2 species that the California Bird Records Committee (CBRC) places on a 'supplemental' list (Crested Caracara, Oriental Goldfinch), but which are 'countable' by American Birding Association (ABA) rules. All species that are reviewed by the CBRC (* on the list) have at least one northern California record accepted by the CBRC, or, for recent claims, a record is under review that the compiler considers acceptable (** on the list). The CBRC 'Field List of California Birds' (September 1998) and *North American Birds* files (Middle Pacific Coast Region) were the primary sources of much of this information.

Loons (Gaviidae)
- ❏ Red-throated Loon
- ❏ Arctic Loon*
- ❏ Pacific Loon
- ❏ Common Loon
- ❏ Yellow-billed Loon*

Grebes (Podicipedidae)
- ❏ Pied-billed Grebe
- ❏ Horned Grebe
- ❏ Red-necked Grebe
- ❏ Eared Grebe
- ❏ Western Grebe
- ❏ Clark's Grebe

Albatrosses (Diomedeidae)
- ❏ Shy Albatross**
- ❏ Light-mantled Albatross*
- ❏ Wandering Albatross*
- ❏ Laysan Albatross
- ❏ Black-footed Albatross
- ❏ Short-tailed Albatross*

Shearwaters, Petrels & Fulmars (Procellariidae)
- ❏ Northern Fulmar
- ❏ Great-winged Petrel*
- ❏ Murphy's Petrel
- ❏ Mottled Petrel*
- ❏ Dark-rumped Petrel*
- ❏ Cook's Petrel
- ❏ Stejneger's Petrel*
- ❏ Bulwer's Petrel*
- ❏ Streaked Shearwater*
- ❏ Pink-footed Shearwater

- ❏ Flesh-footed Shearwater
- ❏ Greater Shearwater*
- ❏ Wedge-tailed Shearwater *
- ❏ Buller's Shearwater
- ❏ Sooty Shearwater
- ❏ Short-tailed Shearwater
- ❏ Manx Shearwater *
- ❏ Black-vented Shearwater

Storm-Petrels (Hydrobatidae)
- ❏ Wilson's Storm-Petrel
- ❏ Fork-tailed Storm-Petrel
- ❏ Leach's Storm-Petrel
- ❏ Ashy Storm-Petrel
- ❏ Wedge-rumped Storm-Petrel *
- ❏ Black Storm-Petrel
- ❏ Least Storm-Petrel

Tropicbirds (Phaethontidae)
- ❏ Red-billed Tropicbird
- ❏ Red-tailed Tropicbird *

Boobies (Sulidae)
- ❏ Masked Booby *
- ❏ Blue-footed Booby *
- ❏ Brown Booby *
- ❏ Red-footed Booby *

Pelicans (Pelecanidae)
- ❏ American White Pelican
- ❏ Brown Pelican

Cormorants (Phalacrocoracidae)
- ❏ Brandt's Cormorant
- ❏ Double-crested Cormorant
- ❏ Pelagic Cormorant

Darters (Anhingidae)
- ❏ Anhinga *

Frigatebirds (Fregatidae)
- ❏ Magnificent Frigatebird
- ❏ Great Frigatebird *

Herons (Ardeidae)
- ❏ American Bittern
- ❏ Least Bittern
- ❏ Great Blue Heron
- ❏ Great Egret
- ❏ Snowy Egret
- ❏ Little Blue Heron
- ❏ Tricolored Heron *
- ❏ Reddish Egret *
- ❏ Cattle Egret
- ❏ Green Heron
- ❏ Black-crowned Night-Heron
- ❏ Yellow-crowned Night-Heron *

Ibises & Spoonbills (Threskiornithidae)
- ❏ White-faced Ibis
- ❏ Roseate Spoonbill *

Storks (Ciconiidae)
- [ ] Wood Stork

Vultures (Cathartidae)
- [ ] Black Vulture *
- [ ] Turkey Vulture
- [ ] California Condor (E)

Waterfowl (Anatidae)
- [ ] Fulvous Whistling-Duck
- [ ] Greater White-fronted Goose
- [ ] Emperor Goose *
- [ ] Snow Goose
- [ ] Ross's Goose
- [ ] Canada Goose
- [ ] Brant
- [ ] Trumpeter Swan *
- [ ] Tundra Swan
- [ ] Whooper Swan *
- [ ] Wood Duck
- [ ] Gadwall
- [ ] Eurasian Wigeon
- [ ] American Wigeon
- [ ] American Black Duck *
- [ ] Mallard
- [ ] Blue-winged Teal
- [ ] Cinnamon Teal
- [ ] Northern Shoveler
- [ ] Northern Pintail
- [ ] Garganey *
- [ ] Baikal Teal *
- [ ] Green-winged Teal
- [ ] Canvasback
- [ ] Redhead
- [ ] Ring-necked Duck
- [ ] Tufted Duck
- [ ] Greater Scaup
- [ ] Lesser Scaup
- [ ] Steller's Eider *
- [ ] King Eider *
- [ ] Harlequin Duck
- [ ] Surf Scoter
- [ ] White-winged Scoter
- [ ] Black Scoter
- [ ] Oldsquaw
- [ ] Bufflehead
- [ ] Common Goldeneye
- [ ] Barrow's Goldeneye
- [ ] Smew *
- [ ] Hooded Merganser
- [ ] Common Merganser
- [ ] Red-breasted Merganser
- [ ] Ruddy Duck

Kites, Hawks & Eagles (Accipitridae)
- [ ] Osprey
- [ ] White-tailed Kite
- [ ] Mississippi Kite *
- [ ] Bald Eagle
- [ ] Northern Harrier
- [ ] Sharp-shinned Hawk
- [ ] Cooper's Hawk
- [ ] Northern Goshawk
- [ ] Red-shouldered Hawk
- [ ] Broad-winged Hawk
- [ ] Swainson's Hawk
- [ ] Red-tailed Hawk
- [ ] Ferruginous Hawk
- [ ] Rough-legged Hawk
- [ ] Golden Eagle

Falcons (Falconidae)
- [ ] Crested Caracara *
- [ ] American Kestrel
- [ ] Merlin
- [ ] Gyrfalcon *
- [ ] Peregrine Falcon
- [ ] Prairie Falcon

Grouse & Allies (Phasianidae)
- [ ] Chuckar (I)
- [ ] Ring-necked Pheasant (I)
- [ ] Ruffed Grouse
- [ ] Sage Grouse
- [ ] White-tailed Ptarmigan (I)
- [ ] Blue Grouse
- [ ] Sharp-tailed Grouse (E)
- [ ] Wild Turkey (I)

Quails (Odontophoridae)
- [ ] Mountain Quail
- [ ] California Quail

Rails & Coots (Rallidae)
- [ ] Yellow Rail *
- [ ] Black Rail
- [ ] Clapper Rail
- [ ] Virginia Rail
- [ ] Sora
- [ ] Purple Gallinule *
- [ ] Common Moorhen
- [ ] American Coot

Cranes (Gruidae)
- [ ] Sandhill Crane

Plovers (Charadriidae)
- [ ] Black-bellied Plover
- [ ] American Golden-Plover
- [ ] Pacific Golden-Plover
- [ ] Mongolian Plover *
- [ ] Snowy Plover
- [ ] Wilson's Plover *
- [ ] Semipalmated Plover
- [ ] Killdeer
- [ ] Mountain Plover
- [ ] Eurasian Dotterel *

Oystercatchers (Haematopodidae)
- [ ] Black Oystercatcher

Stilts & Avocets (Recurvirostridae)
- [ ] Black-necked Stilt
- [ ] American Avocet

Sandpipers & Allies (Scolopacidae)
- [ ] Greater Yellowlegs
- [ ] Lesser Yellowlegs
- [ ] Spotted Redshank *
- [ ] Solitary Sandpiper
- [ ] Willet
- [ ] Wandering Tattler
- [ ] Gray-tailed Tattler **
- [ ] Spotted Sandpiper
- [ ] Terek Sandpiper *
- [ ] Upland Sandpiper *
- [ ] Little Curlew *
- [ ] Whimbrel
- [ ] Bristle-thighed Curlew *
- [ ] Long-billed Curlew
- [ ] Hudsonian Godwit *
- [ ] Bar-tailed Godwit *
- [ ] Marbled Godwit
- [ ] Ruddy Turnstone
- [ ] Black Turnstone
- [ ] Surfbird
- [ ] Red Knot
- [ ] Sanderling
- [ ] Semipalmated Sandpiper
- [ ] Western Sandpiper
- [ ] Red-necked Stint *
- [ ] Little Stint *
- [ ] Long-toed Stint *

- ❏ Least Sandpiper
- ❏ White-rumped Sandpiper *
- ❏ Baird's Sandpiper
- ❏ Pectoral Sandpiper
- ❏ Sharp-tailed Sandpiper
- ❏ Rock Sandpiper
- ❏ Dunlin
- ❏ Curlew Sandpiper *
- ❏ Stilt Sandpiper
- ❏ Buff-breasted Sandpiper
- ❏ Ruff
- ❏ Short-billed Dowitcher
- ❏ Long-billed Dowitcher
- ❏ Jack Snipe *
- ❏ Common Snipe
- ❏ Wilson's Phalarope
- ❏ Red-necked Phalarope
- ❏ Red Phalarope

Gulls & Allies (Laridae)

- ❏ South Polar Skua
- ❏ Pomarine Jaeger
- ❏ Parasitic Jaeger
- ❏ Long-tailed Jaeger
- ❏ Laughing Gull
- ❏ Franklin's Gull
- ❏ Little Gull *
- ❏ Black-headed Gull *
- ❏ Bonaparte's Gull
- ❏ Heermann's Gull
- ❏ Mew Gull
- ❏ Ring-billed Gull
- ❏ California Gull
- ❏ Herring Gull
- ❏ Thayer's Gull
- ❏ Iceland Gull **
- ❏ Lesser Black-backed Gull *
- ❏ Western Gull
- ❏ Glaucous-winged Gull
- ❏ Glaucous Gull
- ❏ Black-legged Kittiwake
- ❏ Sabine's Gull
- ❏ Swallow-tailed Gull *
- ❏ Caspian Tern
- ❏ Royal Tern
- ❏ Elegant Tern
- ❏ Common Tern
- ❏ Arctic Tern
- ❏ Forster's Tern
- ❏ Least Tern
- ❏ White-winged Tern *
- ❏ Black Tern
- ❏ Black Skimmer

Alcids (Alcidae)

- ❏ Common Murre
- ❏ Thick-billed Mure *
- ❏ Pigeon Guillemot
- ❏ Long-billed Murrelet *
- ❏ Marbled Murrelet
- ❏ Xantus's Murrelet
- ❏ Craveri's Murrelet
- ❏ Ancient Murrelet
- ❏ Cassin's Auklet
- ❏ Parakeet Auklet *
- ❏ Least Auklet *
- ❏ Crested Auklet *
- ❏ Rhinoceros Auklet
- ❏ Tufted Puffin
- ❏ Horned Puffin

Doves (Columbidae)

- ❏ Rock Dove (I)
- ❏ Band-tailed Pigeon
- ❏ Spotted Dove (I)
- ❏ White-winged Dove
- ❏ Mourning Dove
- ❏ Common Ground-Dove

Cuckoos & Roadrunners (Cuculidae)

- ❏ Black-billed Cuckoo *
- ❏ Yellow-billed Cuckoo
- ❏ Greater Roadrunner

Barn Owls (Tytonidae)

- ❏ Barn Owl

Owls (Strigidae)

- ❏ Flammulated Owl
- ❏ Western Screech-Owl
- ❏ Great Horned Owl
- ❏ Snowy Owl *
- ❏ Northern Pygmy-Owl
- ❏ Burrowing Owl
- ❏ Spotted Owl
- ❏ Barred Owl
- ❏ Great Gray Owl
- ❏ Long-eared Owl
- ❏ Short-eared Owl
- ❏ Northern Saw-whet Owl

Nightjars (Caprimulgidae)

- ❏ Lesser Nighthawk
- ❏ Common Nighthawk
- ❏ Common Poorwill

- ❏ Chuck-will's-widow *
- ❏ Whip-poor-will

Swifts (Apodidae)

- ❏ Black Swift
- ❏ White-collared Swift *
- ❏ Chimney Swift
- ❏ Vaux's Swift
- ❏ White-throated Swift

Hummingbirds (Trochilidae)

- ❏ Broad-billed Hummingbird *
- ❏ Violet-crowned Hummingbird *
- ❏ Blue-throated Hummingbird *
- ❏ Ruby-throated Hummingbird *
- ❏ Black-chinned Hummingbird
- ❏ Anna's Hummingbird
- ❏ Costa's Hummingbird
- ❏ Calliope Hummingbird
- ❏ Broad-tailed Hummingbird
- ❏ Rufous Hummingbird
- ❏ Allen's Hummingbird

Kingfishers (Alcedinidae)

- ❏ Belted Kingfisher

Woodpeckers (Picidae)

- ❏ Lewis's Woodpecker
- ❏ Red-headed Woodpecker*
- ❏ Acorn Woodpecker
- ❏ Gila Woodpecker
- ❏ Williamson's Sapsucker
- ❏ Yellow-bellied Sapsucker
- ❏ Red-naped Sapsucker
- ❏ Red-breasted Sapsucker
- ❏ Nuttall's Woodpecker
- ❏ Downy Woodpecker
- ❏ Hairy Woodpecker
- ❏ White-headed Woodpecker
- ❏ Three-toed Woodpecker *
- ❏ Black-backed Woodpecker
- ❏ Northern Flicker
- ❏ Pileated Woodpecker

Flycatchers (Tyrannidae)
- ❏ Olive-sided Flycatcher
- ❏ Greater Pewee *
- ❏ Western Wood-Pewee
- ❏ Eastern Wood-Pewee *
- ❏ Yellow-bellied Flycatcher *
- ❏ Alder Flycatcher **
- ❏ Willow Flycatcher
- ❏ Least Flycatcher
- ❏ Hammond's Flycatcher
- ❏ Gray Flycatcher
- ❏ Dusky Flycatcher
- ❏ Pacific-slope Flycatcher
- ❏ Cordilleran Flycatcher
- ❏ Black Phoebe
- ❏ Eastern Phoebe
- ❏ Say's Phoebe
- ❏ Vermilion Flycatcher
- ❏ Dusky-capped Flycatcher *
- ❏ Ash-throated Flycatcher
- ❏ Great Crested Flycatcher *
- ❏ Brown-crested Flycatcher
- ❏ Sulphur-bellied Flycatcher *
- ❏ Tropical Kingbird
- ❏ Cassin's Kingbird
- ❏ Thick-billed Kingbird *
- ❏ Western Kingbird
- ❏ Eastern Kingbird
- ❏ Scissor-tailed Flycatcher
- ❏ Fork-tailed Flycatcher *

Shrikes (Laniidae)
- ❏ Brown Shrike *
- ❏ Loggerhead Shrike
- ❏ Northern Shrike

Vireos (Vireonidae)
- ❏ White-eyed Vireo *
- ❏ Bell's Vireo
- ❏ Yellow-throated Vireo *
- ❏ Plumbeous Vireo
- ❏ Cassin's Vireo
- ❏ Blue-headed Vireo *
- ❏ Hutton's Vireo
- ❏ Warbling Vireo
- ❏ Philadelphia Vireo
- ❏ Red-eyed Vireo
- ❏ Yellow-green Vireo *

Jays & Crows (Corvidae)
- ❏ Gray Jay
- ❏ Steller's Jay
- ❏ Blue Jay *

- ❏ Western Scrub-Jay
- ❏ Pinyon Jay
- ❏ Clark's Nutcracker
- ❏ Black-billed Magpie
- ❏ Yellow-billed Magpie
- ❏ American Crow
- ❏ Common Raven

Larks (Alaudidae)
- ❏ Sky Lark *
- ❏ Horned Lark

Swallows (Hirundinidae)
- ❏ Purple Martin
- ❏ Tree Swallow
- ❏ Violet-green Swallow
- ❏ Northern Rough-winged Swallow
- ❏ Bank Swallow
- ❏ Cliff Swallow
- ❏ Barn Swallow

Chickadees (Paridae)
- ❏ Black-capped Chickadee
- ❏ Mountain Chickadee
- ❏ Chestnut-backed Chickadee
- ❏ Oak Titmouse
- ❏ Juniper Titmouse

Bushtits (Aegithalidae)
- ❏ Bushtit

Nuthatches (Sittidae)
- ❏ Red-breasted Nuthatch
- ❏ White-breasted Nuthatch
- ❏ Pygmy Nuthatch

Creepers (Certhiidae)
- ❏ Brown Creeper

Wrens (Troglodytidae)
- ❏ Cactus Wren
- ❏ Rock Wren
- ❏ Canyon Wren
- ❏ Bewick's Wren
- ❏ House Wren
- ❏ Winter Wren
- ❏ Sedge Wren *
- ❏ Marsh Wren

Dippers (Cinclidae)
- ❏ American Dipper

Kinglets (Regulidae)
- ❏ Golden-crowned Kinglet
- ❏ Ruby-crowned Kinglet

Old World Warblers & Allies (Sylviidae)
- ❏ Lanceolated Warbler *
- ❏ Dusky Warbler *
- ❏ Arctic Warbler *
- ❏ Blue-gray Gnatcatcher

Thrushes (Turdidae)
- ❏ Red-flanked Bluetail *
- ❏ Northern Wheatear *
- ❏ Western Bluebird
- ❏ Mountain Bluebird
- ❏ Townsend's Solitaire
- ❏ Veery *
- ❏ Gray-cheeked Thrush *
- ❏ Swainson's Thrush
- ❏ Hermit Thrush
- ❏ Wood Thrush *
- ❏ American Robin
- ❏ Varied Thrush

Babblers (Timaliidae)
- ❏ Wrentit

Mimids & Thrashers (Mimidae)
- ❏ Gray Catbird *
- ❏ Northern Mockingbird
- ❏ Sage Thrasher
- ❏ Brown Thrasher
- ❏ Bendire's Thrasher
- ❏ California Thrasher
- ❏ Le Conte's Thrasher

Starlings (Sturnidae)
- ❏ European Starling (I)

Pipits & Wagtails (Motacillidae)
- ❏ Yellow Wagtail *
- ❏ Gray Wagtail *
- ❏ White Wagtail *
- ❏ Black-backed Wagtail *
- ❏ Red-throated Pipit
- ❏ American Pipit
- ❏ Sprague's Pipit *

Waxwings
(Bombycillidae)
❏ Bohemian Waxwing
❏ Cedar Waxwing

Silky-flycatchers
(Ptilogonatidae)
❏ Phainopepla

New World Warblers
(Parulidae)
❏ Blue-winged Warbler *
❏ Golden-winged Warbler *
❏ Tennessee Warbler
❏ Orange-crowned Warbler
❏ Nashville Warbler
❏ Virginia's Warbler
❏ Lucy's Warbler
❏ Northern Parula
❏ Yellow Warbler
❏ Chestnut-sided Warbler
❏ Magnolia Warbler
❏ Cape May Warbler
❏ Black-throated Blue
   Warbler
❏ Yellow-rumped Warbler
❏ Black-throated Gray
   Warbler
❏ Golden-cheeked Warbler *
❏ Black-throated Green
   Warbler
❏ Townsend's Warbler
❏ Hermit Warbler
❏ Blackburnian Warbler
❏ Yellow-throated Warbler *
❏ Grace's Warbler *
❏ Pine Warbler *
❏ Prairie Warbler
❏ Palm Warbler
❏ Bay-breasted Warbler
❏ Blackpoll Warbler
❏ Cerulean Warbler *
❏ Black-and-white Warbler
❏ American Redstart
❏ Prothonotary Warbler
❏ Worm-eating Warbler *
❏ Ovenbird
❏ Northern Waterthrush
❏ Louisiana Waterthrush *
❏ Kentucky Warbler
❏ Connecticut Warbler *
❏ Mourning Warbler *
❏ MacGillivray's Warbler

❏ Common Yellowthroat
❏ Hooded Warbler
❏ Wilson's Warbler
❏ Canada Warbler
❏ Red-faced Warbler *
❏ Painted Redstart
❏ Yellow-breasted Chat

Tanagers (Thraupidae)
❏ Hepatic Tanager
❏ Summer Tanager
❏ Scarlet Tanager *
❏ Western Tanager

Sparrows & Allies
(Emberizidae)
❏ Green-tailed Towhee
❏ Spotted Towhee
❏ California Towhee
❏ Cassin's Sparrow *
❏ Rufous-crowned Sparrow
❏ American Tree Sparrow
❏ Chipping Sparrow
❏ Clay-colored Sparrow
❏ Brewer's Sparrow
❏ Field Sparrow *
❏ Black-chinned Sparrow
❏ Vesper Sparrow
❏ Lark Sparrow
❏ Black-throated Sparrow
❏ Sage Sparrow
❏ Lark Bunting
❏ Savannah Sparrow
❏ Grasshopper Sparrow
❏ Baird's Sparrow *
❏ Le Conte's Sparrow *
❏ Nelson's Sharp-tailed
   Sparrow
❏ Fox Sparrow
❏ Song Sparrow
❏ Lincoln's Sparrow
❏ Swamp Sparrow
❏ White-throated Sparrow
❏ Harris's Sparrow
❏ White-crowned Sparrow
❏ Golden-crowned
   Sparrow
❏ Dark-eyed Junco
❏ McCown's Longspur
❏ Lapland Longspur
❏ Smith's Longspur *
❏ Chestnut-collared
   Longspur

❏ Rustic Bunting *
❏ Snow Bunting *

Grosbeaks & Buntings
(Cardinalidae)
❏ Rose-breasted Grosbeak
❏ Black-headed Grosbeak
❏ Blue Grosbeak
❏ Lazuli Bunting
❏ Indigo Bunting
❏ Painted Bunting *
❏ Dickcissel

Blackbirds & Allies
(Icteridae)
❏ Bobolink
❏ Red-winged Blackbird
❏ Tricolored Blackbird
❏ Western Meadowlark
❏ Yellow-headed Blackbird
❏ Rusty Blackbird
❏ Brewer's Blackbird
❏ Great-tailed Grackle
❏ Common Grackle *
❏ Brown-headed Cowbird
❏ Orchard Oriole
❏ Hooded Oriole
❏ Baltimore Oriole
❏ Bullock's Oriole
❏ Scott's Oriole

Finches (Fringillidae)
❏ Brambling *
❏ Gray-crowned
   Rosy-Finch
❏ Black Rosy-Finch *
❏ Pine Grosbeak
❏ Purple Finch
❏ Cassin's Finch
❏ House Finch
❏ Red Crossbill
❏ White-winged Crossbill *
❏ Common Redpoll *
❏ Pine Siskin
❏ Lesser Goldfinch
❏ Lawrence's Goldfinch
❏ American Goldfinch
❏ Oriental Greenfinch *
❏ Evening Grosbeak

Old World Sparrows
(Passeridae)
❏ House Sparrow (I)

GLOSSARY

accipiter: a forest hawk (genus *Accipiter*); characterized by a long tail and short, rounded wings; feeds on birds.

altricial: young birds generally helpless for a while after hatching.

arboreal: inhabiting the canopy of trees.

axillars: the feathers of the inner underwing, of the 'wingpit.'

brood: *n.* a family of young from one hatching; *v.* sit on eggs so as to hatch them.

conifer: a cone-producing tree, usually a softwood evergreen (e.g., spruce, pine, fir).

corvid: a member of the crow family (Corvidae); includes crows, jays, magpies and ravens.

coverts: usually refers to upper secondary coverts, short feathers covering base of the secondaries.

covey: a brood or flock of partridges, quails or grouse.

crepuscular: active chiefly during twilight before dawn and after dusk.

crop: an enlargement of the esophagus; serves as a storage structure and (in pigeons) has glands that produce secretions.

dabbling: a foraging technique used by ducks, where the head and neck are submerged but the body and tail remain on the water's surface; dabbling ducks can usually walk easily on land, can take off without running and have brightly colored speculums.

deciduous tree: a tree that loses its leaves annually (e.g., oak, maple, aspen, birch).

dimorphism: the existence of two distinct forms of a species, such as between the sexes.

diurnal: active chiefly during daylight.

drake: time-honored English term referring to the male duck.

eclipse: the dull, female-like plumage that male ducks briefly acquire after molting from their breeding plumage.

elbow patch: a dark spot at the bend of the outstretched wing, seen from below.

flycatching: a feeding behavior where the bird leaves a perch, snatches an insect in mid-air and returns to the same perch; also known as 'hawking' or 'sallying.'

fledgling: a young bird that has left the nest but is dependent upon its parents.

flushing: a behavior where frightened birds explode into flight in response to a disturbance.

gape: the size of the mouth opening.

gular fluttering: a tremulous, rapid flapping of the throat that increases ventilation of the skin, and hence regulates the temperature of a bird otherwise at risk of overheating.

hawking: attempting to capture insects through aerial pursuit.

irruption: a sporadic mass migration of birds into a non-breeding area.

kleptoparasitism: parasitic behavior characterized by the theft of food items procured by another.

larva: a development stage of an animal (usually an invertebrate) that has a different body form from the adult (e.g., caterpillar, maggot).

leading edge: the front edge of the wing as viewed from below.

litter: fallen plant material, such as twigs, leaves and needles, that forms a distinct layer above the soil, especially in forests.

lore: the small patch between the eye and the bill.

molting: the periodic replacement of worn out feathers (often twice a year).

morphology: the science of form and shape.

nape: the back of the neck.

neotropical migrant: a bird that nests in North America but overwinters in the New World tropics.

niche: an ecological role filled by a species.

open country: a landscape that is primarily not forested.

parasitism: a relationship between two species where one benefits at the expense of the other.

phylogenetics: a method of classifying animals that puts the oldest ancestral groups before those that have arisen more recently.

pishing: a repeated sibilant sound made expressly to attract birds.

polygynous: having a mating strategy where one male breeds with several females.

polyandrous: having a mating strategy where one female breeds with several males.

plucking post: a perch habitually used by raptors to remove feathers or fur from prey.

precocial: young birds generally capable of adult behaviors, and so able to promptly abandon the site of hatching and move about with adults.

primaries: the outermost flight feathers.

pygmy-owling: imitating the calls of the Northern Pygmy-Owl to attract birds.

raptor: a carnivorous (meat-eating) bird; includes eagles, hawks, falcons and owls.

riparia: riverine forest, thickets and other stands of woody wetland vegetation; the term is ordinarily used to describe taller streamside cover such as willows, cottonwoods, etc.

rufous: rusty red in color.

sallying: repeated aerial pursuit of insects performed by flying from a perch.

scapulars: feathers of the shoulder, seeming to join the wing and back.

species: a group of reproductively compatible individuals.

speculum: the patterned or colorful secondaries of ducks.

squeaking: making a sound to attract birds by loudly kissing the back of the hand, or by using a specially designed squeaky bird call.

supercilium: a narrow, pale line, generally slightly arched, appearing above the eye.

surf zone: nearshore ocean from shore seaward to where the swell begins to break.

talons: the claws of birds of prey.

tertials: the group of flight feathers closest to the body.

torpor: a state of lowered metabolism enabling a creature to endure conditions during which it cannot find sufficient food to sustain normal activity.

understorey: the shrub or thicket layer beneath a canopy of trees.

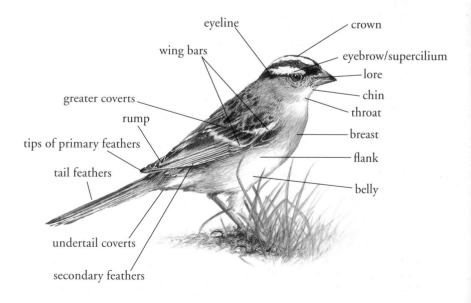

eyeline · crown · wing bars · eyebrow/supercilium · lore · chin · throat · greater coverts · rump · breast · tips of primary feathers · flank · tail feathers · belly · undertail coverts · secondary feathers

BIBLIOGRAPHY

American Ornithologists' Union. 1998. *Check-list of North American Birds.* 7th ed. American Ornithologists' Union, Washington, D.C.

Beedy, E.C., and S.L. Granholm. 1985. *Discovering Sierra Birds: Western Slope.* Yosemite Natural History Association and Sequoia Natural History Association.

Burridge, B. 1995. *Sonoma County Breeding Bird Atlas.* Madrone Audubon Society, Santa Rosa, Calif.

Choate, E.A. 1985. *The Dictionary of American Bird Names.* Rev. ed. Harvard Common Press, Cambridge, Mass.

Clarke, H. 1995. *An Introduction to Northern California Birds.* Mountain Press Publishing Co., Missoula, Mont.

Cogswell, H.L. 1977. *Water Birds of California.* University of California Press, Berkeley.

Cunningham, R.L. 1990. *50 Common Birds of the Southwest.* Southwest Parks and Monuments Association, Tucson.

Dunn, J., and K. Garrett. 1997. *A Field Guide to Warblers of North America.* Houghton Mifflin Co., Boston.

Ehrlich, P.R., D.S. Dobkin and D. Wheye. 1988. *The Birder's Handbook.* Fireside, New York.

Farrand, J., ed. 1983. *The Audubon Society Master Guide to Birding.* Vols. 1–3. Alfred A. Knopf, New York.

Gaines, D. 1988. *Birds of Yosemite and the East Slope.* Humboldt State University Press, Arcata, Calif.

Griggs, J.L. 1997. *All the Birds of North America: American Bird Conservancy's Field Guide.* Harper Collins Publishers, New York.

Harris, S.W. 1996. *Northwestern California Birds.* Humboldt State Univeristy Press, Arcata, Calif.

Hoffmann, R. 1927. *Birds of the Pacific States.* Houghton Mifflin Co., Boston.

Kaufman, K. 1990. *A Field Guide to Advanced Birding.* Houghton Mifflin Co., Boston.

————. 1996. *Lives of North American Birds.* Houghton Mifflin Co., Boston.

Kemper, J. 1999. *Birding Northern California.* Falcon Publishing, Helena, Mont.

McCaskie, G., P. De Benedictis, R. Erickson and J. Morlan. 1988. *Birds of Northern California: An Annotated Field List.* 2nd ed. Golden Gate Audubon Society, Berkeley.

Paulson, D. 1993. *Shorebirds of the Pacific Northwest.* University of British Columbia Press, Vancouver.

Richmond, J. 1985. *Birding Northern California.* Mt. Diablo Audubon Society, Walnut Creek, Calif.

Roberson, D., and C. Tenney. 1993. *Atlas of the Breeding Birds of Monterey County, California.* Monterey Peninsula Audubon Society, Carmel.

Ryser, Jr., F.A. 1985. *Birds of the Great Basin: A Natural History.* University of Nevada Press, Reno.

Scott, S.S. 1987. *Field Guide to the Birds of North America.* National Geographic Society, Washington, D.C.

Shuford, W.D. 1993. *The Marin County Breeding Bird Atlas.* Bushtit Books, Bolinas, Calif.

Small, A. 1994. *California Birds: Their Status and Distribution.* Ibis Publishing Co., Vista, Calif.

Stallcup, R. 1990. *Ocean Birds of the Nearshore Pacific.* Point Reyes Bird Observatory, Stinson Beach, Calif.

Stokes, D.W., and L.Q. Stokes. 1996. *Stokes Field Guide to Birds: Western Region.* Little, Brown and Co., Toronto.

Terres, J.K. 1995. *The Audubon Society Encyclopedia of North American Birds.* Wings Books, New York.

Westrich, L., and J. Westrich. 1991. *Birder's Guide to Northern California.* Gulf Publishing Co., Houston.

Wyatt, B., A. Stoye and C. Harris. 1990. *Birding at the Bottom of the Bay.* 2nd ed. Santa Clara Valley Audubon Society.

INDEX OF COMMON NAMES

Page numbers in boldface type refer to the primary, illustrated species accounts.

INDEX OF SCIENTIFIC NAMES

This index references only the primary species accounts.

ABOUT THE AUTHORS

David Fix first learned his birds in the Pacific Northwest. From his sandbox, at age four or five, he recalls hearing Song Sparrows, but it wasn't until his teens that he began looking seriously at birds. Jobs as a timber cruiser and tree planter in the Oregon and Washington Cascades gave him much early experience with forest birds. More recently, he has complemented his work in wildlife biology with extensive writing. For 20 years, David has been a subregional editor for the quarterly journal, *North American Birds*, and he contributes frequent essays, poetry and artwork to the *Sandpiper*, the newsletter of the Redwood Region Audubon Society. With his partner, Jude Claire Power, and others, David is working to publish the results of a five-year Humboldt County Breeding Bird Atlas project. David and Jude make their home in Bayside, California.

Inspired by wild creatures and wild places, Andy Bezener has developed a keen interest in the study and conservation of birds. Field work with the Canadian Wildlife Service and studies in conservation biology have given Andy joyful insight into the lives of many North American birds. Through photography, writing, public speaking and travel, Andy continues to search for a deeper understanding and greater appreciation of nature. Andy is co-author of Lone Pine's *Rocky Mountain Nature Guide*, *Birds of Boston* and *Birds of New York City, Western Long Island and Northeastern New Jersey*.